WOMEN
and the
POLITICS of CULTURE

WOMEN
and the
POLITICS of CULTURE

Studies
in the
Sexual Economy

Michele Wender Zak
Patricia A. Moots

Longman
New York & London

WOMEN AND THE POLITICS OF CULTURE

Longman Inc., 1560 Broadway, New York, N.Y. 10036
Associated companies, branches, and representatives
throughout the world.

Developmental Editor: Nicole Benevento
Editorial and Design Supervisor: Frances Althaus
Production Supervisor: Ferne Kawahara
Manufacturing Supervisor: Marion Hess
Interior Design: Angela Foote

Library of Congress Cataloging in Publication Data

Zak, Michele Wender.
  Women and the politics of culture.

  Bibliography: p.
  Includes index.
  1. Feminism—History—Addresses, essays, lectures. 2. Sex
discrimination against women—History—Addresses, essays,
lectures. 3. Sex role—History—Addresses, essays, lectures.
4. Women in politics—History—Addresses, essays, lectures. I.
Moots, Patricia A. II. Title.
HQ1121.Z34   305.4'2   82–7776
ISBN 0–582–28391–4   AACR2
Printing: 9 8 7 6 5 4 3 2 1   Year: 91 90 89 88 87 86 85 84 83

Manufactured in the United States of America

Contents

4. Women and the Marketplace   167

5. The Personal as Political   239

PART III The Sexual Economy: Resistance and Struggle   297

6. The Ideas and Origins of Feminism   298

7. Feminism: The Second Wave   366

Acknowledgments

The authors would like to thank the following publishers and writers for their kind permission to reprint from the following:

from *Against Our Will: Men, Women and Rape* by Susan Brownmiller. Copyright © 1975 by Susan Brownmiller. Reprinted by permission of Simon and Schuster, a Division of Gulf & Western Corporation.

from "Black Women and the Pursuit of Inequality" by Elizabeth M. Almquist in *Women: A Feminist Perspective*, edited by Jo Freeman (1979, 2nd ed.), Mayfield Publishing Co., Palo Alto, CA. Reprinted by permission of the author.

from *The Book of Abigail and John: Selected Letters of the Adams Family, 1762–1784*, edited by L. H. Butterfield, Marc Friedlaender, and Mary-Jo Kline. Copyright © 1975 by Harvard University Press. Reprinted by permission of the publisher.

from *The Dialectic of Sex* by Shulamith Firestone. Copyright © 1970 by Shulamith Firestone. Reprinted by permission of William Morrow & Company.

from *Emile* by Jean-Jacques Rousseau. Translated by Barbara Foxley for the Everyman's Library edition. Copyright © 1974 by J. M. Dent & Sons Ltd. Reprinted by permission of the publisher.

from *The Feminine Mystique* by Betty Friedan, by permission of W. W. Norton & Company, Inc. Copyright © 1973, 1963 by Betty Friedan.

Reprinted by permission of Farrar, Straus and Giroux, Inc. Selection, "Flatbush Feminists," adapted and abridged from *The Possible She* by Susan Jacoby. Copyright © 1973, 1979 by Susan Jacoby.

from "Lesbian-Feminist Theory" by Charlotte Bunch in *Our Right to Love* by Virginia Vida and the National Gay Task Force. Copyright © 1978 by Virginia Vida. Reprinted with permission of Prentice-Hall, Inc., Englewood Cliffs, NJ.

from *The Longest War: Sex Differences in Perspective* by Carol Travis and Carole Offir, © 1977 by Harcourt Brace Jovanovich, Inc. Reprinted by permission of the publisher.

from "Miserable" in *A Bintel Brief*, translation and introduction by Isaac Metzker. Copyright © 1971 by Isaac Metzker. Reprinted by permission of Doubleday & Company, Inc.

Selection is reprinted from *New Introductory Lectures on Psychoanalysis* by Sigmund Freud, translated and edited by James Strachey, by permission of W. W. Norton & Company, Inc. Copyright © 1965, 1964 by James Strachey.

from *The Origin of the Family, Private Property, and the State* by Frederick Engels. Copyright © 1942 by International Publishers. Reprinted by permission of the publisher.

from "Politics" translated by Benjamin Jowett, from *The Oxford Translation of Aristotle* edited by W. D. Ross, vol. 10 (1921). Reprinted by permission of Oxford University Press.

from *The Politics of Women's Liberation* by Jo Freeman. Copyright © 1975 by Jo Freeman. Reprinted by permission of the author and Longman Inc.

from *The Psychology of Sex Differences* by Eleanor Emmons Maccoby and Carol Nagy Jacklin with the permission of the publishers, Stanford University Press. Copyright © 1974 by the Board of Trustees of the Leland Stanford Junior University.

from *A Room of One's Own* by Virginia Woolf, copyright © 1929 by Harcourt Brace Jovanovich, Inc.; renewed 1957 by Leonard Woolf. Reprinted by permission of the publisher.

from *The Second Sex* by Simone de Beauvoir, translated by H. M. Parshley. Copyright © 1952 by Alfred A. Knopf, Inc. Reprinted by permission of Alfred A. Knopf, Inc.

from *The Sorrow Dance* by Denise Levertov. Copyright © 1966 by Denise Levertov Goodman. Reprinted by permission of New Directions Publishing Corporation.

from *The Southern Lady: From Pedestal to Politics, 1830–1930* by Anne Firor Scott. Copyright © 1970 by University of Chicago Press. Reprinted by permission of the author and publisher.

Introduction

This book was born out of more than a decade of attempts to shape a satisfactory interdisciplinary survey course in women's studies. The proliferation of such courses across the country attests to a widespread conviction among women's studies teachers and scholars that the study of women is by nature interdisciplinary and that students require an introduction both to the methods of interdisciplinary study and to the content of the study of women as they will encounter it in the various disciplines.

It is the purpose of this book to meet those needs. Thus, we have provided a continuing narrative that includes historical background and advances major themes and issues in the study of women. In addition, the narrative introduces the readings, which were selected according to one or more of the following criteria: the reading contributes to a comprehensive overview of places occupied and functions served by women in Western civilization through the centuries; it offers a coherent and persuasive analysis of the reason(s) women have occupied a given place or served a specific function; it reflects a prevailing mode of thought about women at a particular time that has contributed to the shaping of women's lives; it is a key or exemplary work of scholarship within the discipline it represents. Collectively, the selections were made and organized to illuminate one another in the spirit of interdisciplinary inquiry, to point out major controversies among various disciplines, and to call attention to significant distortions or gaps in our knowledge. The lists of suggested readings provided at the end of the book reflect the major themes of the book, suggest further possibilities for research, and expand the possibilities for interdisciplinary use of the book. Obviously, we have been able to include among the readings only a small and arbitrary selection of those that would be appropriate and useful. We particularly regret that space constraints have prevented inclusion of literary pieces. As partial redemption for that omission, we have referred to poems, plays, and fictional works in the narrative and have included a number of them in the bibliography.

The text is grounded in the premise that the oppressive sexual arrangements endured by women now and in the past are neither

1

accidental nor unrelated. While gaps in knowledge about biology and sex behavior inhibit speculation in that area, we believe patterns emerge both in the process of sexual oppression and in the end product. We have called pattern and product the *sexual economy*. The term "economy," ordinarily used to refer to the exchange of goods and services, is employed here in its larger sense to refer to the functional arrangement of elements within a structure or system. While some risk of confusion may exist because of this usage, we believe it is offset by the usefulness of the term to describe the series of relationships and interactions we call *sexism*.

Women differ, of course, by race, class, and nationality or ethnic identification. Whatever those differences, and they often have been sufficient to obscure from women their commonalities, there is an astonishing similarity in the structures regulating women's lives in otherwise disparate cultures, structures grown out of assumptions about women shared by countless generations of men through time and across space. The sexual economy partakes of, transcends, and sometimes encompasses other categories by which people are organized and oppressed, such as race, class, or sexual preference. Thus, the nature of the oppression suffered by the minority woman because of her race, by a lesbian because of her sexual preference, and by the underclass woman because of her poverty and powerlessness is given shape, detail, and additional dimension by her sexual category. Similarly, the denial to privileged women of the power of self-determination indigenous to male members of the higher classes has been perceived only occasionally by women, who are taught class and race identification first. Such perceptions have sometimes occurred at moments in history when religions, political ideologies, and economic and social systems have undergone change without commensurately affecting the nature of women's lives. Attitudes toward women and the material circumstances of their lives demonstrate a tenacious consistency through time and across cultures.

To understand the sexual economy and recognize its components, it is necessary to identify its sources, trace its development, and analyze its effects. Hence the historical perspective that is a major organizing principle of this book. Hence, also, the materialist perspective that informs our interpretations of the dynamics of the sexual economy. While the importance of myth, human psychology, and religious ideas emerges clearly in this survey of the situation of women, it is equally clear that the sexual economy is most firmly rooted in the historical struggle for the world's wealth and the exercise of power usually contingent upon possession of wealth. Women have most frequently been victims of that struggle, at times mere bystanders, and at times its cheerleaders. There have been, as well, times when women have bravely confronted and challenged the struggle either because of their exclusion from its spoils or because of the suffering it has caused. We have tried to represent the full range of those responses and to give reason to their occurrence at various times and places.

The wide range of historical periods and disciplinary perspectives represented in the book is lent coherence by two recurrent themes that emerge in the sexual economy. The first is a duality in the way men have historically regarded women. Simone de Beauvoir refers to women's "otherness" and to "secondness." We have borrowed those terms as a point of departure for a continuing exploration of women's duality in the eyes of men—as angel and devil, as occupant of the "pit" or the "pedestal" between which women have been shunted through the ages. The second theme draws upon the concept called in the nineteenth century *woman's sphere*. Not unrelated to the alternate deification and disdain of woman through which the first theme is revealed, woman's proper sphere has been defined within virtually all the structures of society around which human lives have been organized and maintained. With its probable roots in woman's reproductive role and its life's blood in domestic activity, the notion of her sphere has varied in its power to oppress from time to time and from class to class. As we shall see, it is a notion exercised by men according to expedience, and one that gained force in the century following the industrial revolution and with the growing power of the middle class. It becomes a key element in the operation of the sexual economy of nineteenth- and twentieth-century Anglo-America upon which this book largely focuses.

That focus itself requires a word of explanation. While the evidence is that a sexual economy in fundamentally similar form circumscribes the lives of women everywhere and has done so through most of time, cultural differences demand their due. We have therefore reluctantly limited ourselves to the history and operation of the Anglo-American experience. Comparative studies are beginning to appear; in the meantime, we make no claims to have decoded a universal sexual economy, but to have illuminated its power in the world occupied by our readers.

The structural organization of the book serves both the historical perspective and the major themes. With seven chapters divided into three parts, the book moves from theories about and descriptions of the roots of women's oppression in Part I, "The Sexual Economy: Its Origins," to Part II documentation of the continuation of that oppression in "The Sexual Economy: Its Operation," and concludes in Part III, The Sexual Economy: Resistance and Struggle," with a focus on the ways women have confronted their oppression, including their attempts to liberate themselves in the major women's movements of the nineteenth and twentieth centuries and individual efforts to shape successful lives within the restrictions of the sexual economy. The historical, theoretical, and descriptive selections in each chapter were made within the context of the book's essential interdisciplinary focus. The result, we believe, is an exposure of the elements of the sexual economy for the reader or student whose need is the wholeness of vision that is the best of all "introductions" to women's studies.

PART I

The Sexual Economy:

Its Origins

Feminist scholars in many disciplines have observed painfully that the secondary status of women has been through time and across space a nearly universal fact of human culture. Indeed, the written history of women emerges as a record of oppression so systematic in its arrangements, so undeviating in its progression, that it constitutes an economy—a sexual economy. The sexual economy is an arrangement of social structures, relationships, and attitudes through the centuries and across cultures that define and limit the functions and offices of individual women and women in communities. Most of the chapters of this book seek to explore the various functions and offices that have fallen to women, beginning in this first chapter with speculation

The Origins of the Patriarchy

about and descriptions of the earliest social structures created by humans and their relationship to basic assumptions about the female.

What were the origins of the sexual economy as we know it? Do explanations lie in the symbiotic relationships between myth-based patterns of thought and empirical realities, as suggested by Simone de Beauvoir, or are there exclusively material cause-and-effect relationships, as proposed by Frederick Engels? Do the "causes" of the oppression of women lie in the political and economic relations that govern people at any given time, or are those oppressive systems themselves simply manifestations of the most deep-seated and persevering assumptions about woman's place? For clues to these mysteries, it is necessary to look to a largely speculative distant past and to some writers and thinkers who have persuasively reconstructed that past.

Among the early students of the origins of the sexual economy were nineteenth-century pioneers in the new science of anthropology. They questioned patriarchal organization and culture as a universal normative standard and fueled a controversy that was reignited in the 1970s by feminist writers and thinkers. Was there a time in some dim, prehistoric past when women were esteemed and held relative or absolute power, or has power always been in the hands of men? The anthropologist and cultural historian Johann Jakob Bachofen was one of the first to challenge the assumption that men and women emerged directly from savagery into a patriarchal society. In his 1861 work, *Das Mutterecht* ("Mother Right"), Bachofen delineated three stages of social evolution: an initial stage of "hetaerism," or sexual promiscuity, from which developed a state of genuine matriarchy, followed by, in the third stage, the supplanting of the matriarchy by patriarchy. During the second stage, Bachofen claimed, societies were not simply matrilineal but were based on "the religious and civil primacy of womanhood" (1967:87). The work of the anthropologist Lewis Henry Morgan supports Bachofen's theory of a stage of sexual promiscuity, from which developed the primitive communal family based upon maternal kinship (1907).

Drawing upon this early work of Bachofen and, in particular, of Morgan, Frederick Engels moved away from the anthropological romanticism of his predecessors and formulated a materialist theory to explain the position of women relative to men. In *The Origin of the Family, Private Property, and the State* (1884), excerpts from which begin the readings in this chapter, Engels builds upon Morgan's delineation of the major stages of social evolution from savagery through barbarism to civilization and posits a primitive society founded on the female gens, one in which line of descent is matrilineal. Engels does not, however, find evidence to support the notion of a primitive matriarchy, that is, a society in which exclusive power is in the hands of women. Rather, Engels, taking his clue from Morgan, posits an egalitarian, tribal past for humanity, in which property was communal and production collective. Engels argues that the evolution of male-owned property as an organizing principle of human society devalued the work of women and led eventually to their subordination. Engel's is the germinal, if interpretative, theory of the relationship of class—economic and social—to sex.

Early twentieth-century anthropologists moved away from the matriarchal view of Bachofen and Morgan. From observations of primate behavior and "evidence" collected in the field, they judged that the evolution of superior intellect of contemporary humans can be traced to their historic male ancestors' success in hunting adaptation. They assigned lesser value to the tasks of women, rendered domestic by childbearing and childrearing. The male hunter, whose activities took him far from home, proclaimed the anthropologist Ashley Montagu, was "called upon to exercise his ingenuity very much more frequently, and in a more varied manner, than the female" (1972:13). To the activities of the male, the argument continues, can be traced the development of first hunting and then domestic implements, which led ultimately to the evolution of culture and art. Thus did theory about the origins of culture as we know it evolve, driven by a masculine bias. The insistent account of the female role as lesser in the evolution of culture has certainly not been without its effect on the way that role has continued to evolve.

Recent feminist scholarship has questioned the notion of the greater importance of the male hunter-warrior, suggesting that hunting and the invention of hunting weapons represent "simply one of a series of integrated activities in the human cultural inventory" (Watson 1976:182). The most compelling concern of any society is the provision of a stable food supply. We now know that women's contributions to the food supply were at least equal to those of men.

Moreover, it is likely that women, responsible for food gathering, developed the implements to harvest and the means to collect, process, preserve, and store foods. "A gathering adaptation," writes anthropologist Adrienne Zihlman, "may even have been the basis for the emergence of hunting." Because men were assured of a share of the food collected by women, they could engage in "time-consuming behaviors which frequently yield no food, such as hunting or obtaining raw materials from some distance away" (1978:18). While the evidence is by no means conclusive, current anthropological interpretations suggest that women were at least partners with men in the evolution of culture. The cooperative efforts of the male and the female in subsistence activities; the role of the woman in nurturing and socializing the young; the development of cooperative child-care systems enabling the more efficient collection of food; the sharing of food, first between the mother and child, and then expanded to include the male; all insured the continuance of the species and the emergence of civilization (Zihlman 1978). Feminist scholars have thus begun to correct the distortion created by a cultural mind-set predicated on the thesis that the present domination of one sex by the other can be not only explained but justified by looking to a prehistoric past.

Ironically, some modern feminist writers and scholars have looked to a remote past for evidence of women's dominance. Based originally on the pioneering work of the nineteenth-century anthropologists and on the twentieth-century writings of Robert Briffault (1927), the theoretical existence of matriarchal societies has been reinforced by such archeological discoveries as those of James Mellaart at Catal Huyuk. A major city-town before 6000 B.C., Catal Huyuk is one of the earliest examples of the beginnings of civilization as we know it. Of the examples of sculpture found by Mellaart, the female figure is predominant; and the male deity, represented as a child, adolescent, or young consort of the goddess, appears to derive his importance primarily from the female. Mellaart's excavations have led some contemporary feminists to conclude that Neolithic women held positions of social and civic importance. Drawing upon such evidence, the works of twentieth-century writers such as Helen Diner (1973), Elizabeth Gould Davis (1972), and Evelyn Reed (1975) have been embraced by many for whom the alleged existence of primitive matriarchies lends credence to current efforts toward the creation of a new feminist order.

Most contemporary academic anthropologists, however, have not been so enthusiastic. Because Bachofen and other proponents of the existence of past matriarchies based their theories primarily on surviving mythologies, social anthropologists—including feminists—have largely rejected their conclusions as lacking historical evidence. Even before the recent controversy began, Simone de Beauvoir considered and rejected the notion of a lost age of feminine supremacy. She acknowledged the primacy of the goddess in mythology, but maintains that it was only as earth mother and goddess that the power of woman was affirmed:

To say that woman was the *Other* is to say that there did not exist between the sexes a reciprocal relation: Earth, Mother, Goddess—she was no fellow creature in man's eyes; it was *beyond* the human realm that her power was affirmed, and she was therefore *outside of* that realm. Society has always been male; political power has always been in the hands of men. (1952: 64–65)

De Beauvoir, in the selection offered here, asserts that the economic interests of men and also their "ontological and moral pretensions" have caused them to make of women the "other." Woman has been seen by man as part of the ambivalent power of nature and thus to be both feared and revered. Drawing upon myth, legend, and anthropological case studies, de Beauvoir offers as explanation for the historical suppression of woman, marked as it is by recurrent periods of apparent reverence, that "man is on the defensive against woman so far as she represents the vague source of the world and obscure organic development" (1952:140).

De Beauvoir's concept of "otherness" and the male defensiveness she identifies form the basis for a range of theories about the origins of patriarchal oppression. According to a number of disparate theories, the fact of otherness has inspired men to control through force. Susan Brownmiller, in *Against Our Will: Men, Women and Rape* (1976), for example, suggests that men's discovery that they could use their genitalia against women as weapons led to a sexual asymmetry in which men are predators and women their natural prey. That in turn led to a Chinese puzzle of male supremacy including monogamy (because of women's need of a protector against the predatory male), the nuclear family that results from monogamy, and even to lack of bonding among women whose contempt for each other derived from their inability to serve as the needed protectors.

A variation on the theme of force, and a departure from the notion of a defensive male need for control over the female as the basis for the development of patriarchal structure, is provided by the anthropologist Marvin Harris. "Male supremacist institutions," he proposes in *Cannibals and Kings*, "rose as a by-product of warfare, of the male monopoly over weapons and the use of sex for the nurturance of aggressive male personalities" (1978:81). In a persuasive insistence on cultural rather than genetic or psychological origins of patriarchal power, Harris first argues that warfare evolved as a response to reproductive and ecological pressures: "War and female infanticide are part of the price our stone age ancestors had to pay for regulating their populations in order to prevent a lowering of living standards to the bare subsistence level" (1978:62). Just as population was controlled by female infanticide rather than male because of the greater value of males in the required hand-to-hand combat, Harris argues, so did the other familiar trappings of patriarchal power derive from the emphasis on war:

> My argument is that all of these sexually asymmetric institutions originated as a by-product of warfare and the male monopoly over military weaponry. Warfare required the organization of communities around a resident core of fathers, brothers, and their sons. This led to the control over resources by paternal-fraternal interest groups and the exchange of sisters and daughters between such groups (patrilineality, patrilocality, and bride-price), to the allotment of women as a reward for male aggressiveness, and hence to polygyny. The assignment of drudge work to women and their ritual subordination and devaluation follows automatically from the need to reward males at the expense of females and to provide supernatural justifications for the whole male supremacist complex. (1978:85–86)

Whether one accepts the materialist analysis of the origins of the sexual economy advanced by Harris or not, one cannot dismiss the power, endurance, and virtual universality of mythological accounts of woman's secondness. Those who have studied the mythologies of the mother-goddess religions of the primitive and ancient worlds will recognize familiar symbols in the Genesis accounts of the creation and the fall—the serpent, the garden of innocence, the fruit of enlightenment, and the fruit of immortal life. Joseph Campbell (1964:9) has pointed out that the serpent who appears before Eve had been revered for at least seven thousand years before the composition of the book of Genesis. The story of mankind's disobedience to God's command and the expulsion from Eden to a life of toil is dependent upon an ancient myth that told not of one but two magic trees, the tree of life and the tree of knowledge of good and evil (*Interpreter's Bible* I, 1952:501). In the earlier mythologies, however, there is no theme of guilt connected with the trees and no divine wrath to descend upon those who partake of their fruit. The knowledge of life is yielded willingly to any man or woman ready to receive it.

That theme of guilt in the Judeo-Christian tradition became central to the interpretation of the origins of humanity. Feminist scholars such as Mary Daly (1968) and Rosemary Radford Ruether (1975) address the misogynism of Christian authors who have taken the Genesis account of Eve's creation from Adam's rib as evidence of her inferiority. Daly reminds us that many contemporary scriptural scholars reject the notion that the story of the later creation of Eve intends to teach the subordination of woman. What is important is that in her original creation, she was equal to Adam (Daly 1968:78). The implication is that all human relationships were intended by God to be mutual. Because of their disobedience, however, God imposed upon Adam and Eve an unnatural relationship, the subjugation of woman to man. Contemporary biblical exegesis suggests that the Genesis accounts should be read within the context of the society that created them. The men who wrote the Genesis stories, it is claimed, may have been merely interpreting the experience of their world, in which women were subjugated to men, rather than making judgments about that world (*Interpreter's Bible* I, 1952:510).

It is interesting to speculate about the authorship of the Genesis accounts and necessary to understand the context within which they were written. The real importance for us today, however, is in recognizing the ways in which the Bible has been interpreted to confirm and perpetuate the patriarchy. It is in the Bible that we find "evidence" of woman's natural weakness, of her dangerous sensuality. In the Bible we find the purest distillation of the fears and dreams about women described by de Beauvoir. In Genesis, Eve is the friend of man, the joy of Eden, and the source of greatest evil as the embodiment of Satan. This early articulation of the deification and disdain with which women are alternately regarded through the centuries that follow ominously spells out a dehumanized past and future for women.

In the modern world, the metaphor of woman's otherness has found most accessible expression in the story of Eve and of the fall. Perhaps most influential in the engraving of that metaphor on the human consciousness was John Milton's epic poem *Paradise Lost*. Virginia Woolf called Milton the "first of the masculinists" (1954:5–6), and indeed, Milton's misogyny and its possible roots in his own life and unhappy marriage have been much analyzed. But the shaping power on future literature and therefore on life resulting from the formalization of his misogyny in his great and influential work has not until recently been similarly analyzed. *Paradise Lost* created a "culture myth," Sandra Gilbert argues in "Reflections on Milton's Bogey." "The story that Milton . . . most notably tells to women is of course the story of woman's secondness, her otherness, and how that otherness leads inexorably to her demonic anger, her sin, her fall, and her exclusion from that garden of the gods which is also for her, the garden of poetry" (1978:370).

Another aspect of the culture myth was written in stone for centuries to come by a founding father of a prevailing modern epistemology, Aristotle. In *Politics*, the work in which Aristotle defines a proper political economy and the relationship of the family to that economy, he defines as well the qualifications of people in various states of life for the roles they are destined to fill. Drawing the mind/body distinction that has been embellished in a thousand ways by succeeding generations to explain and justify the inferior status of women, Aristotle asserts that the "soul rules the body with a despotical rule, whereas the intellect rules the appetites with a constitutional rule." Going on to equate the body with passion, the mind with rationality, he ends with a further equation that lends additional credence to the theories of de Beauvoir: The woman is associated with the body/passion and the man with the mind/rationality. It is only a step, then, to his assertion that the "male is by nature superior, and the female inferior; and the one rules and the other is ruled."

Many centuries later, another philosopher, John Stuart Mill, having observed the degraded position of women in his society, felt compelled to counter Aristotle's arguments. Mill's essay *The Subjection of Women*, published in 1869, is a landmark document in the literature of the long history of women's struggles against political, economic, social, and philosophical constraints on their equality. In the excerpt offered here, Mill provides a fresh challenge to the myth of innate female inferiority by showing how the subordination of women stands out as "an isolated fact in modern social institutions." The notion of women's natural inferiority, Mill argues, is more deeply rooted than that of any other subject class in all of history by the very nature of the institution of marriage. Men, desiring not a forced slave but a willing one, Mill claims, have used all means in their power to enslave the minds of women. Mill's essay is a rational analysis of the causes of women's oppression, as well as an impassioned appeal for political action to secure women's rights.

It would be for succeeding centuries to examine the rationale for women's secondness in relation to exigencies of time and place as well as states of knowledge about sex differences. But the foundation of the sexual economy was well constructed before Western civilization had found its stride.

Frederick Engels postulates three principal forms of marriage, which correspond broadly to three principal stages of human development: savagery, characterized by group marriage; barbarism, by pairing marriage; and civilization, by monogamy. In group marriage the sexes enjoy common conjugal relations within a family circle, and children belong to all the parents of the family. The paternity of children is irrelevant, and descent can be recognized only through the female line. In pairing marriage, the final reduction to the two-person unit, one man and one women, has taken place. Either person can dissolve the marriage tie, and children belong invariably to the mother alone and inherit through her line.

In the excerpt that follows, Engels describes the primarily economic forces that transformed the pairing marriage into the monogamous family as we know it today. Monogamy, and the concurrent overthrow of "mother right," Engels sees as the "world historical defeat of the female sex" and "the first class opposition that appears in history."

THE FAMILY

Frederick Engels

FROM *The Origin of the Family, Private Property, and the State*

A certain amount of pairing, for a longer or shorter period, already occurred in group marriage or even earlier; the man had a chief wife among his many wives (one can hardly yet speak of a favorite wife), and for her he was the most important among her husbands. This fact has contributed considerably to the confusion of the missionaries, who have regarded group marriage sometimes as promiscuous community of wives, sometimes as unbridled adultery. But these customary pairings were bound to grow more stable as the gens developed and the classes of "brothers" and "sisters" between whom marriage was impossible became more numerous. The impulse given by the gens to the prevention of marriage between blood relatives extended still further. Thus among the Iroquois and most of the other Indians at the lower stage of barbarism, we find that marriage is prohibited between *all* relatives enumerated in their system—which includes several hundred degrees of kinship. The increasing complication of these prohibitions made group marriages more and more impossible; they were displaced by the *pairing family*. In this stage, one man lives with one woman, but the relationship is such that polygamy and occasional infidelity remain the right of the men, even though for economic reasons polygamy is rare, while from the woman the strictest fidelity is generally demanded throughout the time she lives with the man and adultery on her part is cruelly punished. The marriage tie can, however, be easily dissolved by either partner; after separation, the children still belong as before to the mother alone. . . .

Thus the history of the family in primitive times consists in the progressive narrowing of the circle, originally embracing the whole tribe, within which the two sexes have a common conjugal relation. The continuous exclusion, first of nearer, then of more and more remote relatives, and at last even of relatives by marriage, ends by making any kind of group marriage practically impossible. Finally, there remains only the single, still loosely linked pair, the molecule with whose dissolution marriage itself ceases. This in itself shows what a small part individual sex love, in the modern sense of the word, played in the rise of monogamy. Yet stronger proof is afforded by the practice of all peoples at this stage of development. Whereas in the earlier forms of the family, men never lacked women but, on the contrary, had too many rather than too few, women had now become scarce and highly sought after. Hence it is with the pairing marriage that there begins the capture and purchase of women— widespread *symptoms*, but no more than symptoms, of the much deeper change that had occurred. These symptoms, mere methods of procuring wives, the pedantic Scot McLennan has transmogrified into special classes of families under the names of "marriage by capture" and "marriage by purchase." In general, whether among the American Indians or other peoples (at the same stage), the conclusion of a marriage is the affair not of the two parties concerned, who are often not consulted at all, but of their mothers. Two persons entirely unknown to each other are often thus affianced; they only learn that the bargain has been struck when the time for marrying approaches. Before the wedding the bridegroom gives presents to the bride's gentile relatives (to those on the mother's side, therefore, not to the father and his relations) which are regarded as gift payments in return for the girl. The marriage is still terminable at the desire of either partner, but among many tribes, the Iroquois for example, public opinion has gradually developed against such separations. When differences arise between husband and wife, the gens relatives of both partners act as mediators, and only if these efforts prove fruitless does a separation take place, the wife then keeping the children and each partner being free to marry again.

The pairing family, itself too weak and unstable to make an independent household necessary or even desirable, in no wise destroys the communistic household inherited from earlier times. Communistic housekeeping, however, means the supremacy of women in the house; just as the exclusive recognition of the female parent, owing to the impossibility of recognizing the male parent with certainty, means that the women—the mothers—are held in high respect. One of the most absurd notions taken over from 18th century enlightenment is that in the beginning of society woman was the slave of man. Among all savages and all barbarians of the lower and middle stages, and to a certain extent of the upper stage also, the position of women is not only free, but honorable. . . .

The communistic household, in which most or all of the women belong to one and the same gens, while the men come from various gentes, is the material foundation of that supremacy of the women which was general in primitive times, and which it is Bachofen's third great merit to have discovered. The reports of travelers and missionaries, I may add, to the effect that women among savages and barbarians are overburdened with work in no way contradict what has been said. The division of labor between the two sexes is determined by quite other causes than by the position of woman in society. Among peoples where the women have to work far harder than we think suitable, there is often much more real respect for women than among our Europeans. The lady of civilization, surrounded by false homage and estranged from all real work, has an infinitely lower social position than the hard-working woman of barbarism, who was regarded among her people as a real lady (lady, *frowa*, *Frau*— mistress) and who was also a lady in character. . . .

Bachofen is also perfectly right when he consistently maintains that the transition from what he calls "hetaerism" or "*Sumpf-zeugung*" to monogamy was brought about primarily through the women. The more the traditional sexual relations lost the naive primitive character of forest life, owing to the development of economic conditions with consequent undermining of the old communism and growing density of population, the more oppressive and humiliating must the women have felt them to be, and the greater their longing for the right of chastity, of temporary or permanent marriage with one man only, as a way of release. This advance could not in any case have originated with the men if only because it has never occurred to them, even to this day, to renounce the pleasures of actual group marriage. Only when the women had brought about the transition to pairing marriage were the men able to introduce strict monogamy—though indeed only for women.

The first beginnings of the pairing family appear on the dividing line between savagery and barbarism; they are generally to be found already at the upper stage of savagery, but occasionally not until the lower stage of barbarism. The pairing family is the form characteristic of barbarism, as group marriage is characteristic of savagery and monogamy of civilization. To develop it further, to strict monogamy, other causes were required than those we have found active hitherto. In the single pair the group was already reduced to its final unit, its two-atom molecule: one man and one woman. . . .

At first, according to mother right—so long, therefore, as descent was reckoned only in the female line—and according to the original custom of inheritance within the gens, the gentile relatives inherited from a deceased fellow member of their gens. His property had to remain within the gens. His effects being insignificant, they probably always passed in practice to his nearest gentile relations— that is, to his blood relations on the mother's side. The children of the dead man, however, did not belong to his gens, but to that of their mother; it was from her that they inherited, at first conjointly with her other blood-relations, later perhaps with rights of priority; they could not inherit from their father because they did not belong to his gens within which his property had to remain. When the owner of the herds died, therefore, his herds would go first to his brothers and sisters and to his sister's children, or to the issue of his mother's sisters. But his own children were disinherited.

Thus on the one hand, in proportion as wealth increased it made the man's position in the family more important than the woman's, and on the other hand created an impulse to exploit this strengthened position in order to overthrow, in favor of his children, the traditional order of inheritance. This, however, was impossible so long as descent was reckoned according to mother right. Mother right, therefore, had to be overthrown, and overthrown it was. This was by no means so difficult as it looks to us today. For this revolution—one of the most decisive ever experienced by humanity—could take place without disturbing a single one of the living members of a gens. All could remain as they were. A simple decree sufficed that in the future the offspring of the male members should remain within the gens, but that of the female should be excluded by being transferred to the gens of their father. The reckoning of descent in the female line and the matriarchal law of inheritance were thereby overthrown, and the male line of descent and the paternal law of inheritance were substituted for them. As to how and when this revolution took place among civilized peoples, we have no knowledge. It falls entirely within prehistoric times. But that it *did* take place is more than sufficiently proved by the abundant traces of mother right which have been collected, particularly by Bachofen. How easily it is accomplished can be seen in a whole series of American Indian tribes where it has only recently taken place and is still taking place under the influence, partly of increasing wealth and a changed mode of life (transference from forest to prairie), and partly of the moral pressure of civilization and missionaries. Of eight Missouri tribes, six observe the male line of descent and inheritance; two still observe the female. Among the Shawnees, Miamis and Delawares the custom has grown up of giving the children a gentile name of their father's gens in order to transfer them into it, thus enabling them to inherit from him. . . .

The overthrow of mother right was the *world historical defeat of the female sex*. The man took command in the home also; the woman was degraded and reduced to servitude; she became the slave of his lust and a mere instrument for the production of children. This degraded position of the woman, especially conspicuous among the Greeks of the heroic and still more of the classical age, has gradually been palliated and glossed over, and sometimes clothed in a milder form; in no sense has it been abolished.

The establishment of the exclusive supremacy of the man shows its effects first in the patriarchal family, which now emerges as an intermediate form. . . .

Its essential features are the incorporation of unfree persons and paternal power; hence the perfect type of this form of family is the Roman. The original meaning of the word "family" (*familia*) is not that compound of sentimentality and domestic strife which forms the ideal of the present-day philistine; among the Romans it did not at first even refer to the married pair and their children but only to the slaves. *Famulus* means domestic slave, and *familia* is the total number of slaves belonging to one man. As late as the time of Gaius, the *familia, id est patrimonium* (family, that is, the patrimony, the inheritance) was bequeathed by will. The term was invented by the Romans to denote a new social organism whose head ruled over wife and children and a number of slaves, and was invested under Roman paternal power with rights of life and death over them all. . . .

Such a form of family shows the transition of the pairing family to monogamy. In order to make certain of the wife's fidelity and therefore of the paternity of the children, she is delivered over unconditionally into the power of the husband; if he kills her, he is only exercising his rights.

With the patriarchal family, we enter the field of written history. . . .

[The monogamous family] develops out of the pairing family, as previously shown, in the transitional period between the upper and middle stages of barbarism; its decisive victory is one of the signs that civilization is beginning. It is based on the supremacy of the man, the express purpose being to produce children of undisputed paternity; such paternity is demanded because these children are later to come into their father's property as his natural heirs. It is distinguished from pairing marriage by the much greater strength of the marriage tie, which can no longer be dissolved at either partner's wish. As a rule, it is now only the man who can dissolve it and put away his wife. The right of conjugal infidelity also remains secured to him, at any rate by custom (the *Code Napoléon* explicitly accords it to the husband as long as he does not bring his concubine into the house), and as social life develops he exercises his right more and more; should the wife recall the old form of sexual life and attempt to revive it, she is punished more severely than ever. . . .

This is the origin of monogamy as far as we can trace it back among the most civilized and highly developed people of antiquity. It was not in any way the fruit of individual sex love, with which it had nothing whatever to do; marriages remained as before marriages of convenience. It was the first form of the family to be based not on natural but on economic conditions—on the victory of private property over primitive, natural communal property. The Greeks themselves put the matter quite frankly: the sole exclusive aims of monogamous marriage were to make the man supreme in the family and to propagate, as the future heirs to his wealth, children indisputably his own. Otherwise, marriage was a burden, a duty which had to be performed whether one liked it or not to gods, state, and one's ancestors. In Athens the law exacted from the man not only marriage but also the performance of a minimum of so-called conjugal duties.

Thus when monogamous marriage first makes its appearance in history, it is not as the reconciliation of man and woman, still less as the highest form of such a reconciliation. Quite the contrary; monogamous marriage comes on the scene as the subjugation of the one sex by the other; it announces a struggle between the sexes unknown throughout the whole previous prehistoric period. In an old unpublished manuscript written by Marx and myself in 1846,[1] I find the words: "The first division of labor is that between man and woman for the propagation of children." And today I can add: The first class opposition that appears in history coincides with the development of the antagonism between man and woman in monogamous marriage, and the first class oppression coincides with that of the female sex by the male. Monogamous marriage was a great historical step forward; nevertheless, together with slavery and private wealth, it opens the

1. The reference here is to the *Deutsche Ideologie* (*German Ideology*), written by Marx and Engels in Brussels in 1845–46 and first published in 1932 by the Marx-Engels-Lenin Institute in Moscow.

period that has lasted until today in which every step forward is also relatively a step backward, in which prosperity and development for some is won through the misery and frustration of others. It is the cellular form of civilized society in which the nature of the oppositions and contradictions fully active in that society can be already studied.

Simone de Beauvoir, whose The Second Sex (1949) *was a pioneering work in feminist scholarship, insists that concrete powers have always been in the hands of men. The central thesis of her book is that woman has always occupied a position secondary to man. Humanity is male, and woman is defined not as herself but as relative to the male. Otherness, de Beauvoir claims, is a fundamental category of human thought. The expression of a duality, that of the self and that of the Other, is to be found even in the most primitive of societies. In the following selection, de Beauvoir examines the dreams and fears that are inspired in man by woman, the "Other."*

DREAMS, FEARS, IDOLS

Simone de Beauvoir

FROM *The Second Sex*

History has shown us that men have always kept in their hands all concrete powers; since the earliest days of the patriarchate they have thought best to keep woman in a state of dependence; their codes of law have been set up against her; and thus she has been definitely established as the Other. This arrangement suited the economic interests of the males; but it comformed also to their ontological and moral pretensions. Once the subject seeks to assert himself, the Other, who limits and denies him, is none the less a necessity to him: he attains himself only through that reality which he is not, which is something other than himself. That is why man's life is never abundance and quietude; it is dearth and activity, it is struggle. Before him, man encounters Nature; he has some hold upon her, he endeavors to mold her to his desire. But she cannot fill his needs. Either she appears simply as a purely impersonal opposition, she is an obstacle and remains a stranger; or she submits passively to man's will and permits assimilation, so that he takes possession of her only through consuming her—that is, through destroying her. In both cases he remains alone; he is alone when he touches a stone, alone when he devours a fruit. There can be no presence of an other unless the other is also present in and for himself: which is to say that true alterity—otherness—is that of a consciousness separate from mine and substantially identical with mine.

It is the existence of other men that tears each man out of his immanence and enables him to fulfill the truth of his being, to complete himself through transcendence, through escape toward some objective, through enterprise. But this liberty not my own, while assuring mine, also conflicts with it: there is the tragedy of the unfortunate human consciousness; each separate conscious being aspires to set himself up alone as sovereign subject. Each tries to fulfill himself by reducing the other to slavery. But the slave, though he works and fears, senses himself somehow as the essential; and, by a dialectical inversion, it is the master who seems to be the inessential. It is possible to rise above the conflict if each individual freely recognizes the other, each regarding himself and the other simultaneously as object and as subject in a reciprocal manner. But friendship and generosity, which alone permit in actuality this recognition of free beings, are not facile virtues; they are assuredly man's highest achievement, and through that achievement he is to be found in his true nature. But this true nature is that of a struggle unceasingly begun, unceasingly abolished; it requires man to outdo himself at every moment. We might put it in other words and say that man attains an authentically moral attitude when he renounces *mere being* to assume his position as an existent; through this transformation also he renounces all possession, for possession is one way of seeking mere being; but the transformation through which he attains true wisdom is never done, it is necessary to make it without ceasing, it demands a constant tension. And so, quite unable to fulfill himself in solitude, man is incessantly in danger in his relations with his fellows: his life is a difficult enterprise with success never assured.

But he does not like difficulty; he is afraid of danger. He aspires in contradictory fashion both to life and to repose, to existence and to merely being; he knows full well that "trouble of spirit" is the price of development, that his distance from the object is the price of his nearness to himself; but he dreams of quiet in disquiet and of an opaque plenitude that nevertheless would be endowed with consciousness. This dream incarnated is precisely woman; she is the wished-for intermediary between nature, the stranger to man, and the fellow being who is too closely identical.[1] She opposes him with neither the hostile silence of nature nor the hard requirement of a reciprocal relation; through a unique privilege she is a conscious being and yet it seems possible to possess her in the flesh. Thanks to her, there is a means for escaping that implacable dialectic of master and slave which has its source in the reciprocity that exists between free beings.

---

1. "...Woman is not the useless replica of man, but rather the enchanted place where the living alliance between man and nature is brought about. If she should disappear, men would be alone, strangers lacking passports in an icy world. She is the earth itself raised to life's summit, the earth become sensitive and joyous, and without her, for man the earth is mute and dead," writes Michel Carrouges (*"Les Pouvoirs de la femme," Cahiers du Sud*, No. 292).

We have seen that there were not at first women whom the males had enslaved nor were there even castes based on sex. To regard woman simply as a slave is a mistake; there were women among the slaves, to be sure, but there have always been free women—that is, women of religious and social dignity. They accepted man's sovereignty and he did not feel menaced by a revolt that could make of him in turn the object. Woman thus seems to be the inessential who never goes back to being the essential, to be the absolute Other, without reciprocity. This conviction is dear to the male, and every creation myth has expressed it, among others the legend of Genesis, which, through Christianity, has been kept alive in Western civilization. Eve was not fashioned at the same time as the man; she was not fabricated from a different substance, nor of the same clay as was used to model Adam: she was taken from the flank of the first male. Not even her birth was independent; God did not spontaneously choose to create her as an end in herself and in order to be worshipped directly by her in return for it. She was destined by Him for man; it was to rescue Adam from loneliness that He gave her to him, in her mate was her origin and her purpose; she was his complement on the order of the inessential. Thus she appeared in the guise of privileged prey. She was nature elevated to transparency of consciousness; she was a conscious being, but naturally submissive. And therein lies the wondrous hope that man has often put in woman: he hopes to fulfill himself as a being by carnally possessing a being, but at the same time confirming his sense of freedom through the docility of a free person. No man would consent to be a woman, but every man wants women to exist. "Thank God for having created woman." "Nature is good since she has given women to men." In such expressions man once more asserts with naive arrogance that his presence in this world is an ineluctable fact and right, that of woman a mere accident—but a very happy accident. Appearing as the Other, woman appears at the same time as an abundance of being in contrast to that existence the nothingness of which man senses in himself; the Other, being regarded as the object in the eyes of the subject, is regarded as *en soi*; therefore as a being. In woman is incarnated in positive form the lack that the existent carries in his heart, and it is in seeking to be made whole through her that man hopes to attain self-realization. . . .

Man seeks in woman the Other as Nature and as his fellow being. But we know what ambivalent feelings Nature inspires in man. He exploits her, but she crushes him, he is born of her and dies in her; she is the source of his being and the realm that he subjugates to his will; Nature is a vein of gross material in which the soul is imprisoned, and she is the supreme reality; she is contingence and Idea, the finite and the whole; she is what opposes the Spirit, and the Spirit itself. Now ally, now enemy, she appears as the dark chaos from whence life wells up, as this life itself, and as the over-yonder toward which life tends. Woman sums up nature as Mother, Wife, and Idea; these forms now mingle and now conflict, and each of them wears a double visage.

Man has his roots deep in Nature; he has been engendered like the animals and plants; he well knows that he exists only in so·far as he lives. But since the coming of the patriarchate, Life has worn in his eyes a double aspect: it is consciousness, will, transcendence, it is the spirit; and it is matter, passivity, immanence, it is the flesh. Aeschylus, Aristotle, Hippocrates proclaimed that on earth as on Olympus it is the male principle that is truly creative: from it came form, number, movement; grain grows and multiplies through Demeter's care, but the origin of the grain and its verity lie in Zeus; woman's fecundity is regarded as only a passive quality. She is the earth, and man the seed; she is Water and he is Fire. Creation has often been imagined as the marriage of fire and water; it is warmth and moisture that give rise to living things; the Sun is the husband of the Sea; the Sun, fire, are male divinities; and the Sea is one of the most nearly universal of maternal symbols. Passively the waters accept the fertilizing action of the flaming radiations. So also the sod, broken by the plowman's labor, passively receives the seeds within its furrows. But it plays a necessary part: it supports the living germ, protects it and furnishes the substance for its growth. And that is why man continued to worship the goddesses of fecundity, even after the Great Mother was dethroned;[2] he is indebted to Cybele for his crops, his herds, his whole prosperity. He even owes his own life to her. He sings the praises of water no less than fire. . . .

But more often man is in revolt against his carnal state; he sees himself as a fallen god: his curse is to be fallen from a bright and ordered heaven into the chaotic shadows of his mother's womb. This fire, this pure and active exhalation in which he likes to recognize himself, is imprisoned by woman in the mud of the earth. He would be inevitable, like a pure Idea, like the One, the All, the absolute Spirit; and he finds himself shut up in a body of limited powers, in a place and time he never chose, where he was not called for, useless, cumbersome, absurd. The contingency of all flesh is his own to suffer in his abandonment, in his unjustifiable needlessness. She also dooms him to death. This quivering jelly which is elaborated in the womb (the womb, secret and sealed like the tomb) evokes too clearly the soft viscosity of carrion for him not to turn shuddering away.

2. "I sing the earth, firmly founded mother of all, venerable grandmother, supporting on her soil all that lives," says a Homeric hymm. And Aeschylus also glorifies the land which "brings forth all beings, supports them, and then receives in turn their fertile seed."

Wherever life is in the making—germination, fermentation—it arouses disgust because it is made only in being destroyed; the slimy embryo begins the cycle that is completed in the putrefaction of death. Because he is horrified by needlessness and death, man feels horror at having been engendered; he would fain deny his animal ties; through the fact of his birth murderous Nature has a hold upon him.

Among primitive peoples childbirth is surrounded by the most severe taboos; in particular, the placenta must be carefully burned or thrown into the sea, for whoever should get possession of it would hold the fate of the newborn in his hands. That membranous mass by which the fetus grows is the sign of its dependency; when it is destroyed, the individual is enabled to tear himself from the living magma and become an autonomous being. The uncleanness of birth is reflected upon the mother. Leviticus and all the ancient codes impose rites of purification upon one who has given birth; and in many rural districts the ceremony of churching (blessing after childbirth) continues his tradition. We know the spontaneous embarrassment, often disguised under mocking laughter, felt by children, young girls, and men at sight of the pregnant abdomen, the swollen bosom of the woman with child. In museums the curious gaze at waxen embryos and preserved fetuses with the same morbid interest they show in a ravaged tomb. With all the respect thrown around it by society, the function of gestation still inspires a spontaneous feeling of revulsion. And if the little boy remains in early childhood sensually attached to the maternal flesh, when he grows older, becomes socialized, and takes note of his individual existence, this same flesh frightens him; he would ignore it and see in his mother only a moral personage. If he is anxious to believe her pure and chaste, it is less because of amorous jealousy than because of his refusal to see her as a body. The adolescent is discountenanced, he blushes, if while roaming with his companions he happens to meet his mother, his sisters, any of his female relatives: it is because their presence calls him back to those realms of immanence whence he would fly, exposes roots from which he would tear himself loose. The little boy's irritation when his mother kisses and cajoles him has the same significance; he disowns family, mother, maternal bosom. He would like to have sprung into the world, like Athena fully grown, fully armed, invulnerable. To have been conceived and then born an infant is the curse that hangs over his destiny, the impurity that contaminates his being. And, too, it is the announcement of his death. The cult of germination has always been associated with the cult of the dead. The Earth Mother engulfs the bones of her children. They are women—the Parcae, the Moirai—who weave the destiny of mankind; but it is they, also, who cut the threads. In most popular representations Death is a woman, and it is for women to bewail the dead because death is their work.[3]

Thus the Woman-Mother has a face of shadows: she is the chaos whence all have come and whither all must one day return; she is Nothingness. In the Night are confused together the multiple aspects of the world which daylight reveals: night of spirit confined in the generality and opacity of matter, night of sleep and of nothingness. In the deeps of the sea it is night: woman is the *Mare tenebrarum*, dreaded by navigators of old; it is night in the entrails of the earth. Man is frightened of this night, the reverse of fecundity, which threatens to swallow him up. He aspires to the sky, to the light, to the sunny summits, to the pure and crystalline frigidity of the blue sky; and under his feet there is a moist, warm, and darkling gulf ready to draw him down; in many a legend do we see the hero lost forever as he falls back into the maternal shadows—cave, abyss, hell. . . .

In all civilizations and still in our day woman inspires man with horror: it is the horror of his own carnal contingence, which he projects upon her. The little girl, not yet in puberty, carries no menace, she is under no taboo and has no sacred character. In many primitive societies her very sex seems innocent: erotic games are allowed from infancy between boys and girls. But on the day she can reproduce, woman becomes impure; and rigorous taboos surround the menstruating female. Leviticus gives elaborate regulations, and many primitive societies have similar rules regarding isolation and purification. In matriarchal societies the powers attributed to menstruation were ambivalent: the flow could upset social activities and ruin crops; but it was also used in love potions and medicines. Even today certain Indians put in the bow of the boat a mass of fiber soaked in menstrual blood, to combat river demons. But since patriarchal times only evil powers have been attributed to the feminine flow. Pliny said that a menstruating woman ruins crops, destroys gardens, kills bees, and so on; and that if she touches wine, it becomes vinegar; milk is soured, and the like. An ancient English poet put the same notion into rhyme:

> *Oh! Menstruating woman, thou'st a fiend*
> *From whom all nature should be screened!*

Such beliefs have survived with considerable power into recent times. In 1878 it was declared in the *British Medical Journal* that "it

---

3. Demeter typifies the *mater dolorosa*. But other goddesses—Ishtar, Artemis—are cruel. Kali holds in her hand a cranium filled with blood. A Hindu poet addresses her: "The heads of thy newly killed sons hang like a necklace about thy neck. . . . Thy form is beautiful like rain clouds, thy feet are soiled with blood."

is an undoubted fact that meat spoils when touched by menstruating women," and cases were cited from personal observation. And at the beginning of this century a rule forbade women having "the curse" to enter the refineries of northern France, for that would cause the sugar to blacken. These ideas still persist in rural districts, where every cook knows that a mayonnaise will not be successful if a menstruating woman is about; some rustics believe cider will not ferment, others that bacon cannot be salted and will spoil under these circumstances. A few vaguely factual reports may offer some slight support for such beliefs; but it is obvious from their importance and universality that they must have had a superstitious or mystical origin. Certainly there is more here than reaction to blood in general, sacred as it is. But menstrual blood is peculiar, it represents the essence of femininity. Hence it can supposedly bring harm to the woman herself if misused by others. According to C. Lévi-Strauss, among the Chago the girls are warned not to let anyone see any signs of the flow; clothes must be buried, and so on, to avoid danger. Leviticus likens menstruation to gonorrhea, and Vigny associates the notion of uncleanness with that of illness when he writes: "Woman, sick child and twelve times impure."

The periodic hemorrhage of woman is strangely timed with the lunar cycle; and the moon also is thought to have her dangerous caprices.[4] Woman is a part of that fearsome machinery which turns the planets and the sun in their courses, she is the prey of cosmic energies that rule the destiny of the stars and the tides, and of which men must undergo the disturbing radiations. But menstrual blood is supposed to act especially on organic substances, halfway between matter and life: souring cream, spoiling meat, causing fermentation, decomposition; and this less because it is blood than because it issues from the genital organs. Without comprehending its exact function, people have realized that it is bound to the reproduction of life: ignorant of the ovary, the ancients even saw in the menses the complement of the sperm. The blood, indeed, does not make woman impure; it is rather a sign of her impurity. It concerns generation, it flows from the parts where the fetus develops. Through menstrual blood is expressed the horror inspired in man by woman's fecundity.

One of the most rigorous taboos forbids all sexual relations with a woman in a state of menstrual impurity. In various cultures offenders have themselves been considered impure for certain periods, or

4. The moon is a source of fertility; it appears as "master of women"; it is often believed that in the form of man or serpent it couples with women. The serpent is an epiphany of the moon; it sheds its skin and renews itself, it is immortal, it is an influence promoting fecundity and knowledge. It is the serpent that guards the sacred springs, the tree of life, the fountain of youth. But it is also the serpent that took from man his immortality. Persian and rabbinical traditions maintain that menstruation is to be attributed to the relations of the woman with the serpent.

they have been required to undergo severe penance; it has been supposed that masculine energy and vitality would be destroyed because the feminine principle is then at its maximum of force. More vaguely, man finds it repugnant to come upon the dreaded essence of the mother in the woman he possesses; he is determined to dissociate these two aspects of femininity. Hence the universal law prohibiting incest,[5] expressed in the rule of exogamy or in more modern forms; this is why man tends to keep away from woman at the times when she is especially taken up with her reproductive role: during her menses, when she is pregnant, in lactation. The Oedipus complex—which should be redescribed—does not deny this attitude, but on the contrary implies it. Man is on the defensive against woman in so far as she represents the vague source of the world and obscure organic development. . . .

It is Christianity which invests woman anew with frightening prestige: fear of the other sex is one of the forms assumed by the anguish of man's uneasy conscience. The Christian is divided within himself; the separation of body and soul, of life and spirit, is complete; original sin makes of the body the enemy of the soul; all ties of the flesh seem evil.[6] Only as redeemed by Christ and directed toward the kingdom of heaven can man be saved, but originally he is only corruption; his birth dooms him not only to death but to damnation; it is by divine Grace that heaven can be opened to him, but in all the forms of his natural existence there is a curse. Evil is an absolute reality; and the flesh is sin. And of course, since woman remains always the Other, it is not held that reciprocally male and female are both flesh: the flesh that is for the Christian the hostile *Other* is precisely woman. In her the Christian finds incarnated the temptations of the world, the flesh, and the devil. All the Fathers of the Church insist on the idea that she led Adam into sin. We must quote Tertullian again: "Woman! You are the gateway of the devil. You persuaded him whom the devil dared not attack directly. Because of you the Son of God had to die. You should always go dressed in mourning and in rags." All Christian literature strives to enhance the disgust that man can feel for woman. Tertullian defines her as "*templum ædificatum super cloacam*" ["a temple built over a sewer"]. St. Augus-

5. According to the view of a sociologist, G. P. Murdock, in *Social Structure* (Macmillan, 1949), incest prohibition can be fully accounted for only by a complex theory involving factors contributed by psychoanalysis, sociology, cultural anthropology, and behavioristic psychology. No simple explanation, like "instinct," or "familiar association," or "fear of inbreeding," is at all satisfactory.—Tr.

6. Up to the end of the twelfth century the theologians, except St. Anselme, considered that according to the doctrine of St. Augustine original sin is involved in the very law of generation: "Concupiscence is a vice . . . human flesh born through it is sinful flesh," writes St. Augustine. And St. Thomas: "The union of the sexes transmits original sin to the child, being accompanied, since the Fall, by concupiscence."

tine called attention with horror to the obscene commingling of the sexual and excretory organs: "*Inter fæces et urinam nascimur*" ["We are born between feces and urine"]. The aversion of Christianity in the matter of the feminine body is such that while it is willing to doom its God to an ignominious death, it spares Him the defilement of being born: the Council of Ephesus in the Eastern Church and the Lateran Council in the West declare the virgin birth of Christ. The first Fathers of the Church—Origen, Tertullian, and Jerome—thought that Mary had been brought to bed in blood and filth like other women; but the opinion of St. Ambrose and St. Augustine was the one that prevailed. The body of the Virgin remained closed. Since the Middle Ages the fact of having a body has been considered, in woman, an ignominy. Even science was long paralyzed by this disgust. Linnaeus in his treatise on nature avoided as "abominable" the study of woman's sexual organs. The French physician des Laurens asked himself the scandalized questions: "How can this divine animal, full of reason and judgment, which we call man, be attracted by these obscene parts of woman, defiled with juices and located shamefully at the lowest part of the trunk?"

Today many other influences interfere with that of Christian thought; and this has itself a number of aspects. But, in the Puritan world among others, hate of the flesh continues to exist; it is expressed, for example, in Faulkner's *Light in August*; the initial sexual adventures of the hero are terribly traumatic. Throughout literature it is common to show a young man upset to the point of nausea after his first coition; and if in actuality such a reaction is very rare, it is not by chance that it is so often described. Especially in Anglo-Saxon countries, which are steeped in Puritanism, woman arouses in most adolescents and in many men a terror more or less openly admitted. The feeling exists rather strongly in France. Michel Leiris writes in his *Âge d'Homme*: "At present I tend to regard the feminine organ as something unclean or as a wound, not less attractive on that account, but dangerous in itself, like everything bloody, mucous, infected." The idea of venereal disease expresses these fears. Woman causes fright not because she gives diseases; the truth is that the diseases seem abominable because they come from woman: I have been told of young people who imagine that too frequent intercourse is enough to give gonorrhea. It is a common belief also that on account of coition a man loses his muscular strength and his clearheadedness, and that his phosphorus is used up and his sensitivity is dulled. True enough, masturbation implies these same dangers; and society even considers it, for moral reasons, as more injurious than the normal sexual function. Legitimate marriage and the wish to have children are protective against the bad effects of eroticism. But I have already said that in every sexual act the Other is implicated; and the Other most often wears the visage of woman. With her, man senses most definitely the passivity of his own flesh. Woman is vampire, she eats and drinks him; her organ feeds gluttonously upon his. Certain psychoanalysts have attempted to provide scientific support for these fancies, suggesting that all the pleasure woman gets from intercourse might come from the fact that she symbolically castrates him and takes possession of his penis. But it would seem that these theories should themselves be submitted to psychoanalysis, and it is likely that the physicians who invent them are engaged in projecting their own ancestral terrors.

The source of these terrors lies in the fact that in the Other, quite beyond reach, alterity, otherness, abides. In patriarchal societies woman retains many of the disquieting powers she possessed in primitive societies. That is why she is never left to Nature, but is surrounded with taboos, purified by rites, placed in charge of priests; man is adjured never to approach her in her primitive nakedness, but through ceremonials and sacraments, which draw her away from the earth and the flesh and change her into a human creature; whereupon the magic she exercises is canalized, like the lightning since the invention of lightning rods and electrical power plants. It even becomes possible to use her powers in the general interest; and here we see another phase in that oscillation which marks the relation of man to his female. He loves her to the extent that she is his, he fears her in so far as she remains the other; but it is as the fearsome other that he seeks to make her more profoundly his—and this is what will bring him to elevate her to the dignity of being a person and lead him to recognize in her a fellow creature. . . .

It was Christianity, paradoxically, that was to proclaim, on a certain plane, the equality of man and woman. In her, Christianity hates the flesh; if she renounces the flesh, she is God's creature, redeemed by the Saviour, no less than is man: she takes her place beside the men, among the souls assured of the joys of heaven. Men and women are both servants of God, almost as asexual as the angels and together, through grace, resistant to earthly temptations. If she agrees to deny her animality, woman—from the very fact that she is the incarnation of sin—will be also the most radiant incarnation of the triumph of the elect who have conquered sin. Of course, the divine Saviour who effects the redemption of men is male; but mankind must co-operate in its own salvation, and it will be called upon to manifest its submissive good will in its most humiliated and perverse aspect. Christ is God; but it is a woman, the Virgin Mary, who reigns over all humankind. Yet only the marginal sects revive in woman the ancient privileges and powers of the great goddesses—the

Church expresses and serves a patriarchal civilization in which it is meet and proper for woman to remain appended to man. It is through being his docile servant that she will be also a blessed saint. And thus at the heart of the Middle Ages arises the most highly perfected image of woman propitious to man: the countenance of the Mother of Christ is framed in glory. She is the inverse aspect of Eve the sinner; she crushes the serpent underfoot; she is the mediatrix of salvation, as Eve was of damnation.

It was as Mother that woman was fearsome; it is in maternity that she must be transfigured and enslaved. The virginity of Mary has above all a negative value: that through which the flesh has been redeemed is not carnal; it has not been touched or possessed. Similarly the Asiatic Great Mother was not supposed to have a husband: she had engendered the world and reigned over it in solitary state; she could be wanton at her caprice, but her grandeur as Mother was not diminished by any wifely servitude. In the same way Mary knew not the stain of sexuality. Like the warlike Minerva, she is ivory tower, citadel, impregnable donjon. The priestesses of antiquity, like most Christian saints, were also virgin: woman consecrated to the good should be dedicated in the splendor of her intact strength; she should conserve in its unconquered integrity the essence of her femininity. If Mary's status as spouse be denied her, it is for the purpose of exalting the Woman Mother more purely in her. But she will be glorified only in accepting the subordinate role assigned to her. "I am the servant of the Lord." For the first time in human history the mother kneels before her son; she freely accepts her inferiority. This is the supreme masculine victory, consummated in the cult of the Virgin—it is the rehabilitation of woman through the accomplishment of her defeat. Ishtar, Astarte, Cybele were cruel, capricious, lustful; they were powerful. As much the source of death as of life, in giving birth to men they made men their slaves. Under Christianity life and death depend only upon God, and man, once out of the maternal body, has escaped that body forever; the earth now awaits his bones only. For the destiny of his soul is played out in regions where the mother's powers are abolished; the sacrament of baptism makes ridiculous those ceremonies in which the placenta was burned or drowned. There is no longer any place on earth for magic: God alone is king. Nature, originally inimical, is through grace rendered powerless to harm. Maternity as a natural phenomenon confers no power. So there remains for woman, if she wishes to rise above her original fault, only to bow to the will of God, which subordinates her to man. And through this submission she can assume a new role in masculine mythology. Beaten down, trampled upon when she wished to dominate and as long as she had not definitely abdicated, she could be honored as vassal. She loses none of her primitive attributes, but these are reversed in sign; from being of evil omen they become of good omen; black magic turns to white. As servant, woman is entitled to the most splendid deification.

And since woman has been subjected as Mother, she will be cherished and respected first of all as Mother. Of the two ancient aspects of maternity, man today wishes to know only the smiling, attractive face. Limited in time and space, having but one body and one finite life, man is but a lone individual in the midst of a Nature and a History that are both foreign to him. Woman is similarly limited, and like man she is endowed with mind and spirit, but she belongs to Nature, the infinite current of Life flows through her; she appears, therefore, as the mediatrix between the individual and the cosmos. When the mother has become a figure of reassurance and holiness, man naturally turns to her in love. Lost in nature, he seeks to escape; but separated from her he wishes to go back. Established firmly in the family, in society, conforming to the laws and customs, the mother is the very incarnation of the Good: nature, to which she belongs in part, becomes good, no longer an enemy of the spirit; and if she remains mysterious, hers is a smiling mystery, like that of Leonardo da Vinci's madonnas. Man does not wish to be woman, but he dreams of enfolding within him all that exists, including therefore this woman, whom he is not; in his worship of his mother he endeavors to take possession of her strange wealth. To recognize that he is son of his mother is to recognize his mother in himself, it is to become one with femininity in so far as femininity is connection with the earth, with life, and with the past.

*In order to understand the pervasive influence on
contemporary thinking of the Genesis accounts of the
creation, it is important first to distinguish between two
separate documents. It is the earlier creation story, found in
Genesis 2, rather than the account written several centuries
later, found in Genesis 1, that has shaped Christian
thinking about women. The earlier version shows Eve as
having been created from the rib of Adam, to be "an help
meet for him." There is no suggestion in the later account
that woman was created as an appendage to man; rather,
man and woman were created simultaneously in the image
of God, with equal powers and equal responsibilities for
God's gifts. The passages from Genesis 1 and 2 that follow
offer two versions of the creation story; the temptation and
the expulsion from Paradise are described in a passage from
Genesis 3.*

THE CREATION AND THE FALL

FROM *Genesis*

Genesis 1: 24–31

24   And God said, Let the earth bring forth the living creature
after his kind, cattle, and creeping thing, and beast of the earth after
his kind; and it was so.

25   And God made the beast of the earth after his kind, and cattle
after their kind, and every thing that creepeth upon the earth after
his kind; and God saw that *it was* good.

26   And God said, Let us make man in our image, after our like-
ness: and let them have dominion over the fish of the sea, and over
the fowl of the air, and over the cattle, and over all the earth, and
over every creeping thing that creepeth upon the earth.

27   So God created man in his *own* image, in the image of God
created he him; male and female created he them.

28   And God blessed them, and God said unto them, Be fruitful,
and multiply, and replenish the earth, and subdue it: and have
dominion over the fish of the sea, and over the fowl of the air, and
over every living thing that moveth upon the earth.

29   And God said, Behold, I have given you every herb bearing
seed, which *is* upon the face of all the earth, and every tree, in which
is the fruit of a tree yielding seed; to you it shall be for meat.

30   And to every beast of the earth, and to every fowl of the air,
and to every thing that creepeth upon the earth, wherein *there is* life,
I have given every green herb for meat: and it was so.

31   And God saw every thing that he had made, and, behold, *it was* very good. And the evening and the morning were the sixth day.

Genesis 2: 1–25

Thus the heavens and the earth were finished, and all the host of them.

2   And on the seventh day God ended his work which he had made; and he rested on the seventh day from all his work which he had made.

3   And God blessed the seventh day, and sanctified it: because that in it he had rested from all his work which God created and made.

4   These *are* the generations of the heavens and of the earth when they were created, in the day that the LORD God made the earth and the heavens,

5   And every plant of the field before it was in the earth, and every herb of the field before it grew: for the LORD God had not caused it to rain upon the earth, and *there was* not a man to till the ground.

6   But there went up a mist from the earth, and watered the whole face of the ground.

7   And the LORD God formed man of the dust of the ground, and breathed into his nostrils the breath of life; and man became a living soul.

8   And the LORD God planted a garden eastward in Eden; and there he put the man whom he had formed.

9   And out of the ground made the LORD God to grow every tree that is pleasant to the sight, and good for food; the tree of life also in the midst of the garden, and the tree of knowledge of good and evil.

10   And a river went out of Eden to water the garden; and from thence it was parted, and became into four heads.

11   The name of the first is Pison: that is it which compasseth the whole land of Hav´-i-läh, where there is gold;

12   And the gold of that land *is* good: there *is* bdellium and the onyx stone.

13   And the name of the second river *is* Gī-hōn: the same *is* it that compasseth the whole land of Ethiopia.

14   And the name of the third river *is* Hĭd´-de-kēl: that is it which goeth toward the east of Assyria. And the fourth river *is* Eū-phrā-tēs.

15   And the LORD God took the man, and put him into the garden of Eden, to dress it and to keep it.

16   And the LORD God commanded the man, saying, Of every tree of the garden thou mayest freely eat:

17   But of the tree of the knowledge of good and evil, thou shalt not eat of it: for in the day that thou eatest thereof thou shalt surely die.

18   And the LORD God said, *It is* not good that the man should be alone; I will make him an help meet for him.

19   And out of the ground the LORD God formed every beast of the field, and every fowl of the air; and brought *them* unto Adam to see what he would call them: and whatsoever Adam called every living creature, that *was* the name thereof.

20   And Adam gave names to all cattle, and to the fowl of the air, and to every beast of the field; but for Adam there was not found an help meet for him.

21   And the LORD God caused a deep sleep to fall upon Adam, and he slept: and he took one of his ribs, and closed up the flesh instead thereof;

22   And the rib, which the LORD God had taken from man, made he a woman, and brought her unto the man.

23   And Adam said, This *is* now bone of my bones, and flesh of my flesh: she shall be called Woman, because she was taken out of Man.

24   Therefore shall a man leave his father and his mother, and shall cleave unto his wife: and they shall be one flesh.

25   And they were both naked, the man and his wife, and were not ashamed.

Genesis 3: 1–24

Now the serpent was more subtle than any beast of the field which the LORD God had made. And he said unto the woman, Yea, hath God said, Ye shall not eat of every tree of the garden?

2   And the woman said unto the serpent, We may eat of the fruit of the trees of the garden:

3   But of the fruit of the tree which *is* in the midst of the garden, God hath said, Ye shall not eat of it, neither shall ye touch it, lest ye die.

4   And the serpent said unto the woman, Ye shall not surely die:

5   For God doth know that in the day ye eat thereof, then your eyes shall be opened, and ye shall be as gods, knowing good and evil.

6   And when the woman saw that the tree *was* good for food, and that it *was* pleasant to the eyes, and a tree to be desired to make *one* wise, she took of the fruit thereof, and did eat, and gave also unto her husband with her; and he did eat.

7   And the eyes of them both were opened, and they knew that they *were* naked; and they sewed fig leaves together, and made themselves aprons.

8   And they heard the voice of the LORD God walking in the garden in the cool of the day: and Adam and his wife hid themselves from the presence of the LORD God amongst the trees of the garden.

9   And the LORD God called unto Adam, and said unto him, Where *art* thou?

10   And he said, I heard thy voice in the garden, and I was afraid, because I *was* naked; and I hid myself.

11   And he said, Who told thee that thou *wast* naked? Hast thou eaten of the tree, whereof I commanded thee that thou shouldest not eat?

12   And the man said. The woman whom thou gavest *to be* with me, she gave me of the tree, and I did eat.

13   And the LORD God said unto the woman, What *is* this *that* thou hast done? And the woman said. The serpent beguiled me, and I did eat.

14   And the LORD God said unto the serpent, Because thou hast done this, thou art cursed above all cattle, and above every beast of the field; upon thy belly shalt thou go, and dust shalt thou eat all the days of thy life:

15   And I will put enmity between thee and the woman, and between thy seed and her seed; it shall bruise thy head, and thou shalt bruise his heel.

16   Unto the woman he said, I will greatly multiply thy sorrow, and thy conception: in sorrow thou shalt bring forth children; and thy desire *shall be* to thy husband, and he shall rule over thee.

17   And unto Adam he said, Because thou hast hearkened unto the voice of thy wife, and hast eaten of the tree of which I commanded thee, saying, Thou shalt not eat of it: cursed *is* the ground for thy sake; in sorrow shalt thou eat *of* it all the days of thy life:

18   Thorns also and thistles shall it bring forth to thee; and thou shalt eat the herb of the field;

19   In the sweat of thy face shalt thou eat bread, till thou return unto the ground; for out of it wast thou taken; for dust thou *art*, and unto dust shalt thou return.

20   And Adam called his wife's name Eve, because she was the mother of all living.

21   Unto Adam also, and to his wife, did the LORD God make coats of skins, and clothed them.

22   And the LORD God said, Behold, the man is become as one of us, to know good and evil: and now, lest he put forth his hand, and take also of the tree of life, and eat, and live for ever:

23   Therefore the LORD God sent him forth from the garden of Eden to till the ground from whence he was taken.

24   So he drove out the man; and he placed at the east of the garden of Eden, cherubims, and a flaming sword which turned every way, to keep the way of the tree of life.

In these selections from Book I of Politics, Aristotle not only
describes the patriarchal family of classical Athens but
provides the premise for belief in women's "natural"
inferiority and the unequal relationship between men and
women, a belief that was to endure for centuries. Concerned
with the "intentions of nature in things," Aristotle's
conclusions were perhaps based on the obvious relationship
of woman to nature because of her reproductive role, and
therefore her association with the body in his mind/body
duality. The causes and effects of that association are
considered in detail in the next chapter.

POLITICS

Aristotle

FROM *Politics*

Every state is a community of some kind, and every community is
established with a view to some good; for mankind always act in
order to obtain that which they think good. But, if all communities
aim at some good, the state or political community, which is the
highest of all, and which embraces all the rest, aims at good in a
greater degree than any other, and at the highest good.

Some people think that the qualifications of a statesman, king,
householder, and master are the same, and that they differ, not in
kind, but only in the number of their subjects. For example, the ruler
over a few is called a master; over more, the manager of a household; over a still larger number, a statesman or king, as if there were
no difference between a great household and a small state. The distinction which is made between the king and the statesman is as follows: When the government is personal, the ruler is a king; when,
according to the rules of the political science, the citizens rule and
are ruled in turn, then he is called a statesman.

But all this is a mistake; for governments differ in kind, as will
be evident to any one who considers the matter according to the
method[1] which has hitherto guided us. As in other departments of
science, so in politics, the compound should always be resolved into
the simple elements or least parts of the whole. We must therefore
look at the elements of which the state is composed, in order that we
may see in what the different kinds of rule differ from one another,

Translated by Benjamin Jowett.
1. Cp. 1256ᵃ2.

and whether any scientific result can be attained about each one of them.

2   He who thus considers things in their first growth and origin, whether a state or anything else, will obtain the clearest view of them. In the first place there must be a union of those who cannot exist without each other; namely, of male and female, that the race may continue (and this is a union which is formed, not of deliberate purpose, but because, in common with other animals and with plants, mankind have a natural desire to leave behind them an image of themselves), and of natural ruler and subject, that both may be preserved. For that which can foresee by the exercise of mind is by nature intended to be lord and master, and that which can with its body give effect to such foresight is a subject, and by nature a slave; hence master and slave have the same interest. Now nature has distinguished between the female and the slave. For she is not niggardly, like the smith who fashions the Delphian knife for many uses; she makes each thing for a single use, and every instrument is best made when intended for one and not for many uses. But among barbarians no distinction is made between women and slaves, because there is no natural ruler among them: they are a community of slaves, male and female. . . .

Out of these two relationships between man and woman, master and slave, the first thing to arise is the family, and Hesiod is right when he says—

"First house and wife and an ox for the plough,"

for the ox is the poor man's slave. The family is the association established by nature for the supply of men's everyday wants, and the members of it are called by Charondas "companions of the cupboard," and by Epimenides the Cretan, "companions of the manager." But when several families are united, and the association aims at something more than the supply of daily needs, the first society to be formed is the village. And the most natural form of the village appears to be that of a colony from the family, composed of the children and grandchildren, who are said to be "suckled with the same milk." And this is the reason why Hellenic states were originally governed by kings; because the Hellenes were under royal rule before they came together, as the barbarians still are. Every family is ruled by the eldest, and therefore in the colonies of the family the kingly form of government prevailed because they were of the same blood. As Homer says:[2]

"Each one gives law to his children and to his wives."

2. *Od.* ix. 114, quoted by Plato, *Laws*, iii. 680 B, and in *N. Eth.* x. 1180ᵃ 28.

. . . When several villages are united in a single complete community, large enough to be nearly or quite self-sufficing, the state comes into existence, originating in the bare needs of life, and continuing in existence for the sake of a good life. And therefore, if the earlier forms of society are natural, so is the state for it is the end of them, and the nature of a thing is its end. For what each thing is when fully developed, we call its nature, whether we are speaking of a man, a horse, or a family. Besides, the final cause and end of a thing is the best, and to be self-sufficing is the end and the best.

Hence it is evident that the state is a creation of nature, and that man is by nature a political animal. And he who by nature and not by mere accident is without a state, is either a bad man or above humanity; he is like the

> *"Tribeless, lawless, heartless one,"*

whom Homer[3] denounces—the natural outcast is forthwith a lover of war; he may be compared to an isolated piece at draughts.

Now, that man is more of a political animal than bees or any other gregarious animals is evident. Nature, as we often say, makes nothing in vain,[4] and man is the only animal whom she has endowed with the gift of speech.[5] And whereas mere voice is but an indication of pleasure or pain, and is therefore found in other animals (for their nature attains to the perception of pleasure and pain and the intimation of them to one another, and no further), the power of speech is intended to set forth the expedient and inexpedient, and therefore likewise the just and the unjust. And it is a characteristic of man that he alone has any sense of good and evil, of just and unjust, and the like, and the association of living beings who have this sense makes a family and a state.

Further, the state is by nature clearly prior to the family and to the individual, since the whole is of necessity prior to the part; for example, if the whole body be destroyed, there will be no foot or hand, except in an equivocal sense, as we might speak of a stone hand; for when destroyed the hand will be no better than that. But things are defined by their working and power; and we ought not to say that they are the same when they no longer have their proper quality, but only that they have the same name. The proof that the state is a creation of nature and prior to the individual is that the individual, when isolated, is not self-sufficing; and therefore he is like a part in relation to the whole. But he who is unable to live in society, or who has no need because he is sufficient for himself, must be

3. *Il.* ix. 63.
4. Cp. 1256[b] 20.
5. Cp. vii. 1332[b] 5.

either a beast or a god: he is no part of a state. A social instinct is implanted in all men by nature, and yet he who first founded the state was the greatest of benefactors. For man, when perfected, is the best of animals, but, when separated from law and justice, he is the worst of all; since armed injustice is the more dangerous, and he is equipped at birth with arms, meant to be used by intelligence and virtue, which he may use for the worst ends. Wherefore, if he have not virtue, he is the most unholy and the most savage of animals, and the most full of lust and gluttony. But justice is the bond of men in states, for the administration of justice, which is the determination of what is just,[6] is the principle of order in political society.

3   Seeing then that the state is made up of households, before speaking of the state we must speak of the management of the household. The parts of household management correspond to the persons who compose the household, and a complete household consists of slaves and freemen. Now we should begin by examining everything in its fewest possible elements; and the first and fewest possible parts of a family are master and slave, husband and wife, father and children. We have therefore to consider what each of these three relations is and ought to be:—I mean the relation of master and servant, the marriage relation (the conjunction of man and wife has no name of its own), and thirdly, the procreative relation (this also has no proper name). . . .

5   But is there any one thus intended by nature to be a slave, and for whom such a condition is expedient and right, or rather is not all slavery a violation of nature?

There is no difficulty in answering this question, on grounds both of reason and of fact. For that some should rule and others be ruled is a thing not only necessary, but expedient; from the hour of their birth, some are marked out for subjection, others for rule.

And there are many kinds both of rulers and subjects (and that rule is the better which is exercised over better subjects—for example, to rule over men is better than to rule over wild beasts; for the work is better which is executed by better workmen, and where one man rules and another is ruled, they may be said to have a work); for in all things which form a composite whole and which are made up of parts, whether continuous or discrete, a distinction between the ruling and the subject element comes to light. Such a duality exists in living creatures, but not in them only; it originates in the constitution of the universe; even in things which have no life there is a ruling principle, as in a musical mode. But we are wandering from the

6. Cp. *N. Eth.* v. 1134ª 31.

subject. We will therefore restrict ourselves to the living creature, which, in the first place, consists of soul and body: and of these two, the one is by nature the ruler, and the other the subject. But then we must look for the intentions of nature in things which retain their nature, and not in things which are corrupted. And therefore we must study the man who is in the most perfect state both of body and soul, for in him we shall see the true relation of the two; although in bad or corrupted natures the body will often appear to rule over the soul, because they are in an evil and unnatural condition. At all events we may firstly observe in living creatures both a despotical and a constitutional rule; for the soul rules the body with a despotical rule, whereas the intellect rules the appetites with a constitutional and royal rule. And it is clear that the rule of the soul over the body, and of the mind and the rational element over the passionate, is natural and expedient; whereas the equality of the two or the rule of the inferior is always hurtful. The same holds good of animals in relation to men; for tame animals have a better nature than wild, and all tame animals are better off when they are ruled by man; for then they are preserved. Again, the male is by nature superior, and the female inferior; and the one rules, and the other is ruled; this principle, of necessity, extends to all mankind. Where then there is such a difference as that between soul and body, or between men and animals (as in the case of those whose business is to use their body, and who can do nothing better), the lower sort are by nature slaves, and it is better for them as for all inferiors that they should be under the rule of a master. For he who can be, and therefore is, another's, and he who participates in rational principle enough to apprehend, but not to have, such a principle, is a slave by nature. Whereas the lower animals cannot even apprehend a principle; they obey their instincts. And indeed the use made of slaves and of tame animals is not very different; for both with their bodies minister to the needs of life. Nature would like to distinguish between the bodies of freemen and slaves, making the one strong for servile labour, the other upright, and although useless for such services, useful for political life in the arts both of war and peace. But the opposite often happens—that some have the souls and others have the bodies of freemen. And doubtless if men differed from one another in the mere forms of their bodies as much as the statues of the Gods do from men, all would acknowledge that the inferior class should be slaves of the superior. And if this is true of the body, how much more just that a similar distinction should exist in the soul? but the beauty of the body is seen, whereas the beauty of the soul is not seen. It is clear, then, that some men are by nature free, and others slaves, and that for these latter slavery is both expedient and right. . . .

12   Of household management we have seen[7] that there are three parts—one is the rule of a master over slaves, which has been discussed already,[8] another of a father, and the third of a husband. A husband and father, we saw, rules over wife and children, both free, but the rule differs, the rule over his children being a royal, over his wife a constitutional rule. For although there may be exceptions to the order of nature, the male is by nature fitter for command than the female, just as the elder and full-grown is superior to the younger and more immature. But in most constitutional states the citizens rule and are ruled by turns, for the idea of a constitutional state implies that the natures of the citizens are equal, and do not differ at all.[9] Nevertheless, when one rules and the other is ruled we endeavour to create a difference of outward forms and names and titles of respect, which may be illustrated by the saying of Amasis about his foot-pan.[10] The relation of the male to the female is of this kind, but there the inequality is permanent. The rule of a father over his children is royal, for he rules by virtue both of love and of the respect due to age, exercising a kind of royal power. And therefore Homer has appropriately called Zeus "father of Gods and men," because he is the king of them all. For a king is the natural superior of his subjects, but he should be of the same kin or kind with them, and such is the relation of elder and younger, of father and son.

13   Thus it is clear that household management attends more to men than to the acquisition of inanimate things, and to human excellence more than to the excellence of property which we call wealth, and to the virtue of freemen more than to the virtue of slaves. A question may indeed be raised, whether there is any excellence at all in a slave beyond and higher than merely instrumental and ministerial qualities—whether he can have the virtues of temperance, courage, justice, and the like; or whether slaves possess only bodily and ministerial qualities. And, whichever way we answer the question, a difficulty arises; for, if they have virtue, in what will they differ from freemen? On the other hand, since they are men and share in rational principle, it seems absurd to say that they have no virtue. A similar question may be raised about women and children, whether they too have virtues: ought a woman to be temperate and brave and just, and is a child to be called temperate, and intemperate, or not? So in general we may ask about the natural ruler, and the natural subject, whether they have the same or different virtues. For

7. 1253^b 3–11.
8. 1253^b 14–1255^b 39.
9. Cp. ii. 1261^a 39, iii. 1288^a 12.
10. Herod. ii. 172.

if a noble nature is equally required in both, why should one of them always rule, and the other always be ruled? Nor can we say that this is a question of degree, for the difference between ruler and subject is a difference of kind, which the difference of more and less never is. Yet how strange is the supposition that the one ought, and that the other ought not, to have virtue! For if the ruler is intemperate and unjust, how can he rule well? if the subject, how can he obey well? If he be licentious and cowardly, he will certainly not do his duty. It is evident, therefore, that both of them must have a share of virtue, but varying as natural subjects also vary among themselves. Here the very constitution of the soul has shown us the way; in it one part naturally rules, and the other is subject, and the virtue of the ruler we maintain to be different from that of the subject;—the one being the virtue of the rational, and the other of the irrational part. Now, it is obvious that the same principle applies generally, and therefore almost all things rule and are ruled according to nature. But the kind of rule differs;—the freeman rules over the slave after another manner from that in which the male rules over the female or the man over the child; although the parts of the soul are present in all of them, they are present in different degrees. For the slave has no deliberative faculty at all; the woman has, but it is without authority, and the child has, but it is immature. So it must necessarily be supposed to be with the moral virtues also; all should partake of them, but only in such manner and degree as is required by each for the fulfillment of his duty. Hence the ruler ought to have moral virtue in perfection, for his function, taken absolutely, demands a master artificer, and rational principle is such an artificer; the subjects, on the other hand, require only that measure of virtue which is proper to each of them. Clearly, then, moral virtue belongs to all of them; but the temperance of a man and of a woman, or the courage and justice of a man and of a woman, are not, as Socrates maintained,[11] the same; the courage of a man is shown in commanding, of a woman in obeying. And this holds of all other virtues, as will be more clearly seen if we look at them in detail, for those who say generally that virtue consists in a good disposition of the soul, or in doing rightly, or the like, only deceive themselves. Far better than such definitions is their mode of speaking, who, like Gorgias,[12] enumerate the virtues. All classes must be deemed to have their special attributes; as the poet says of women,

> *"Silence is a woman's glory,"*

but this is not equally the glory of man. The child is imperfect, and

11. Plato, *Meno,* 72 A–73 C.
12. *Meno,* 71 E, 72 A.

therefore obviously his virtue is not relative to himself alone, but to the perfect man and to his teacher, and in like manner the virtue of the slave is relative to a master. Now we determined[13] that a slave is useful for the wants of life, and therefore he will obviously require only so much virtue as will prevent him from failing in his duty through cowardice or lack of self-control. Some one will ask whether, if what we are saying is true, virtue will not be required also in the artisans, for they often fail in their work through the lack of self-control? But is there not a great difference in the two cases? For the slave shares in his master's life; the artisan is less closely connected with him, and only attains excellence in proportion as he becomes a slave. The meaner sort of mechanic has a special and separate slavery; and whereas the slave exists by nature, not so the shoemaker or other artisan. It is manifest, then, that the master ought to be the source of such excellence in the slave, and not a mere possessor of the art of mastership which trains the slave in his duties.[14] Wherefore they are mistaken who forbid us to converse with slaves and say that we should employ command only,[15] for slaves stand even more in need of admonition than children.

So much for this subject; the relations of husband and wife, parent and child, their several virtues, what in their intercourse with one another is good, and what is evil, and how we may pursue the good and escape the evil, will have to be discussed when we speak of the different forms of government.[16] For, inasmuch as every family is a part of a state, and these relationships are the parts of a family, and the virtue of the part must have regard to the virtue of the whole, women and children must be trained by education with an eye to the constitution,[17] if the virtues of either of them are supposed to make any difference in the virtues of the state. And they must make a difference: for the children grow up to be citizens, and half the free persons in a state are women.

13. 1254^b 16–39, Cf. 1259^b 25 sq.
14. Cp. 1255^b 23, 31–35.
15. Plato, *Laws*, vi. 777 E.
16. The question is not actually discussed in the *Politics*.
17. Cp. v. 1310^a 12–36, viii. 1337^a 11–18.

*In 1869, in one of the most important documents to be
written in the cause of justice for women, John Stuart Mill
challenged the reasons still offered in the nineteenth century
in support of the continuation of a social organization in
which men stand in authority over women. The source of
that oppressive order of society, Mill insisted, lay in
women's inferior muscular strength and the value men
placed on her, not, as was claimed, in the "natural" condition
of humanity. Recalling Aristotle's argument that there are in
the human race "free natures" and "slave natures," Mill
asked, "Was there ever any domination which did not
appear natural to those who possessed it?" Mill called for a
radical rethinking of our most basic assumptions about the
relationships between the sexes.*

THE SOCIAL RELATIONS BETWEEN THE SEXES

John Stuart Mill

FROM *The Subjection of Women*

The object of this Essay is to explain as clearly as I am able, the
grounds of an opinion which I have held from the very earliest
period when I had formed any opinions at all on social or political
matters, and which, instead of being weakened or modified, has been
constantly growing stronger by the progress of reflection and the experience of life: That the principle which regulates the existing social
relations between the two sexes—the legal subordination of one sex
to the other—is wrong in itself, and now one of the chief hindrances
to human improvement; and that it ought to be replaced by a principle of perfect equality, admitting no power or privilege on the one
side, nor disability on the other.

The very words necessary to express the task I have undertaken,
show how arduous it is. But it would be a mistake to suppose that
the difficulty of the case must lie in the insufficiency or obscurity of
the grounds of reason on which my conviction rests. The difficulty is
that which exists in all cases in which there is a mass of feeling to be
contended against. So long as an opinion is strongly rooted in the
feelings, it gains rather than loses in stability by having a preponder-
ating weight of argument against it. For if it were accepted as a result
of argument, the refutation of the argument might shake the solidity

of the conviction; but when it rests solely on feeling, the worse it fares in argumentative contest, the more persuaded its adherents are that their feeling must have some deeper ground, which the arguments do not reach; and while the feeling remains, it is always throwing up fresh intrenchments of argument to repair any breach made in the old. And there are so many causes tending to make the feelings connected with this subject the most intense and most deeply-rooted of all those which gather round and protect old institutions and customs, that we need not wonder to find them as yet less undermined and loosened than any of the rest by the progress of the great modern spiritual and social transition; nor suppose that the barbarisms to which men cling longest must be less barbarisms than those which they earlier shake off. . . .

The generality of a practice is in some cases a strong presumption that it is, or at all events once was, conducive to laudable ends. This is the case, when the practice was first adopted, or afterwards kept up, as a means to such ends, and was grounded on experience of the mode in which they could be most effectually attained. If the authority of men over women, when first established, had been the result of a conscientious comparison between different modes of constituting the government of society; if, after trying various other modes of social organization—the government of women over men, equality between the two, and such mixed and divided modes of government as might be invented—it had been decided, on the testimony of experience, that the mode in which women are wholly under the rule of men, having no share at all in public concerns, and each in private being under the legal obligation of obedience to the man with whom she has associated her destiny, was the arrangement most conducive to the happiness and well being of both; its general adoption might then be fairly thought to be some evidence that, at the time when it was adopted, it was the best: though even then the considerations which recommended it may, like so many other primeval social facts of the greatest importance, have subsequently, in the course of ages, ceased to exist. But the state of the case is in every respect the reverse of this. In the first place, the opinion in favour of the present system, which entirely subordinates the weaker sex to the stronger, rests upon theory only; for there never has been trial made of any other: so that experience, in the sense in which it is vulgarly opposed to theory, cannot be pretended to have pronounced any verdict. And in the second place, the adoption of this system of inequality never was the result of deliberation, or forethought, or any social ideas, or any notion whatever of what conduced to the benefit of humanity or the good order of society. It arose simply from the fact that from the very earliest twilight of human society, every woman (owing to the value attached to her by men, combined with her inferiority in muscular strength) was found in a state of bondage to some man. Laws and systems of polity always begin by recognising the relations they find already existing between individuals. They convert what was a mere physical fact into a legal right, give it the sanction of society, and principally aim at the substitution of public and organized means of asserting and protecting these rights, instead of the irregular and lawless conflict of physical strength. Those who had already been compelled to obedience became in this manner legally bound to it. Slavery, from being a mere affair of force between the master and the slave, became regularized and a matter of compact among the masters, who, binding themselves to one another for common protection, guaranteed by their collective strength the private possessions of each, including his slaves. In early times, the great majority of the male sex were slaves, as well as the whole of the female. And many ages elapsed, some of them ages of high cultivation, before any thinker was bold enough to question the rightfulness, and the absolute social necessity, either of the one slavery or of the other. . . .

The truth is, that people of the present and the last two or three generations have lost all practical sense of the primitive condition of humanity; and only the few who have studied history accurately, or have much frequented the parts of the world occupied by the living representatives of ages long past, are able to form any mental picture of what society then was. People are not aware how entirely, in former ages, the law of superior strength was the rule of life; how publicly and openly it was avowed, I do not say cynically or shamelessly—for these words imply a feeling that there was something in it to be ashamed of, and no such notion could find a place in the faculties of any person in those ages, except a philosopher or a saint. History gives a cruel experience of human nature, in showing how exactly the regard due to the life, possessions, and entire earthly happiness of any class of persons, was measured by what they had the power of enforcing; how all who made any resistance to authorities that had arms in their hands, however dreadful might be the provocation, had not only the law of force but all other laws, and all the notions of social obligation against them; and in the eyes of those whom they resisted, were not only guilty of crime, but of the worst of all crimes, deserving the most cruel chastisement which human beings could inflict. . . .

If people are mostly so little aware how completely, during the greater part of the duration of our species, the law of force was the avowed rule of general conduct, any other being only a special and exceptional consequence of peculiar ties—and from how very recent a date it is that the affairs of society in general have been even pretended to be regulated according to any moral law; as little do people remember or consider, how institutions and customs which never had any ground but the law of force, last on into ages and states of general opinion which never would have permitted their first establishment. Less than forty years ago, Englishmen might still by law hold human beings in bondage as saleable property: within the present century they might kidnap them and carry them off, and work them literally to death. This absolutely extreme case of the law of force, condemned by those who can tolerate almost every other form of arbitrary power, and which, of all others, presents features the most revolting to the feelings of all who look at it from an impartial position, was the law of civilized and Christian England within the memory of persons now living: and in one half of Anglo-Saxon America three or four years ago, not only did slavery exist, but the slave trade, and the breeding of slaves expressly for it, was a general practice between slave states. Yet not only was there a greater strength of sentiment against it, but, in England at least, a less amount either of feeling or of interest in favour of it, than of any other of the customary abuses of force: for its motive was the love of gain, unmixed and undisguised; and those who profited by it were a very small numerical fraction of the country, while the natural feeling of all who were not personally interested in it, was unmitigated abhorrence. . . . How different are these cases from that of the power of men over women! I am not now prejudging the question of its justifiableness. I am showing how vastly more permanent it could not but be, even if not justifiable, than these other dominations which have nevertheless lasted down to our own time. Whatever gratification of pride there is in the possession of power, and whatever personal interest in its exercise, is in this case not confined to a limited class, but common to the whole male sex. Instead of being, to most of its supporters, a thing desirable chiefly in the abstract, or, like the political ends usually contended for by factions, of little private importance to any but the leaders; it comes home to the person and hearth of every male head of a family, and of every one who looks forward to being so. The clodhopper exercises, or is to exercise, his share of the power equally with the highest nobleman. And the case is that in which the desire of power is the strongest: for every one who desires power, desires it most over those who are nearest to him, with whom his life is passed, with whom he has most concerns in common, and in whom any independence of his authority is oftenest likely to interfere with his individual preferences. If, in the other cases specified, power manifestly grounded only on force, and having so much less to support them, are so slowly and with so much difficulty got rid of, much more must it be so with this, even if it rests on no better foundation than those. We must consider, too, that the possessors of the power have facilities in this case, greater than in any other, to prevent any uprising against it. Every one of the subjects lives under the very eye, and almost, it may be said, in the hands, of one of the masters—in closer intimacy with him than with any of her fellow-subjects; with no means of combining against him, no power of even locally overmastering him, and, on the other hand, with the strongest motives for seeking his favour and avoiding to give him offence. In struggles for political emancipation, everybody knows how often its champions are bought off by bribes, or daunted by terrors. In the case of women, each individual of the subject-class is in a chronic state of bribery and intimidation combined. In setting up the standard of resistance, a large number of the leaders, and still more of the followers, must make an almost complete sacrifice of the pleasures or the alleviations of their own individual lot. If ever any system of privilege and enforced subjection had its yoke tightly riveted on the necks of those who are kept down by it, this has. I have not yet shown that it is a wrong system: but every one who is capable of thinking on the subject must see that even if it is, it was certain to outlast all other forms of unjust authority. And when some of the grossest of the other forms still exist in many civilized countries, and have only recently been got rid of in others, it would be strange if that which is so much the deepest-rooted had yet been perceptibly shaken anywhere. There is more reason to wonder that the protests and testimonies against it should have been so numerous and so weighty as they are.

Some will object, that a comparison cannot fairly be made between the government of the male sex and the forms of unjust power which I have adduced in illustration of it, since these are arbitrary, and the effect of mere usurpation, while it on the contrary is natural. But was there ever any domination which did not appear natural to those who possessed it? There was a time when the division of mankind into two classes, a small one of masters and a numerous one of slaves, appeared, even to the most cultivated minds, to be a natural, and the only natural, condition of the human race. No less an intellect, and one which contributed no less to the progress of human thought, than Aristotle, held this opinion without doubt or misgiving; and rested it on the same premises on which the same assertion in regard to the dominion of men over women is usually based, namely that there are different natures among mankind, free natures, and slave natures; that the Greeks were of a free nature, the barbarian races of Thracians and Asiatics of a slave nature. But why need I go back to Aristotle? Did not the slaveowners of the Southern United

States maintain the same doctrine, with all the fanaticism with which men cling to the theories that justify their passions and legitimate their personal interests? Did they not call heaven and earth to witness that the dominion of the white man over the black is natural, that the black race is by nature incapable of freedom, and marked out for slavery? some even going so far as to say that the freedom of manual labourers is an unnatural order of things anywhere. . . .

But, it will be said, the rule of men over women differs from all these others in not being a rule of force: it is accepted voluntarily; women make no complaint, and are consenting parties to it. In the first place, a great number of women do not accept it. Ever since there have been women able to make their sentiments known by their writings (the only mode of publicity which society permits to them), an increasing number of them have recorded protests against their present social condition: and recently many thousands of them, headed by the most eminent women known to the public, have petitioned Parliament for their admission to the Parliamentary Suffrage. The claim of women to be educated as solidly, and in the same branches of knowledge, as men, is urged with growing intensity, and with a great prospect of success; while the demand for their admission into professions and occupations hitherto closed against them, becomes every year more urgent. . . . It must be remembered, also, that no enslaved class ever asked for complete liberty at once. When Simon de Montfort called the deputies of the commons to sit for the first time in Parliament, did any of them dream of demanding that an assembly, elected by their constituents, should make and destroy ministries, and dictate to the king in affairs of state? No such thought entered into the imagination of the most ambitious of them. The nobility had already these pretensions: the commons pretended to nothing but to be exempt from arbitrary taxation, and from the gross individual oppression of the king's officers. It is a political law of nature that those who are under any power of ancient origin, never begin by complaining of the power itself, but only of its oppressive exercise. There is never any want of women who complain of ill usage by their husbands. There would be infinitely more, if complaint were not the greatest of all provocatives to a repetition and increase of the ill usage. It is this which frustrates all attempts to maintain the power but protect the woman against its abuses. In no other case (except that of a child) is the person who has been proved judicially to have suffered an injury, replaced under the physical power of the culprit who inflicted it. Accordingly wives, even in the most extreme and protracted cases of bodily ill usage, hardly ever dare avail themselves of the laws made for their protection: and if, in a moment of irrepressible indignation, or by the interference of neighbours, they are induced to do so, their whole effort afterwards is to disclose as little as they can, and to beg off their tyrant from his merited chastisement.

All causes, social and natural, combine to make it unlikely that women should be collectively rebellious to the power of men. They are so far in a position different from all other subject classes, that their masters require something more from them than actual service. Men do not want solely the obedience of women, they want their sentiments. All men, except the most brutish, desire to have, in the woman most nearly connected with them, not a forced slave but a willing one, not a slave merely, but a favourite. They have therefore put everything in practice to enslave their minds. The masters of all other slaves rely, for maintaining obedience, on fear; either fear of themselves, or religious fears. The masters of women wanted more than simple obedience and they turned the whole force of education to effect their purpose. All women are brought up from the very earliest years in the belief that their ideal of character is the very opposite to that of men; not self-will, and government by self-control, but submission, and yielding to the control of others. All the moralities tell them that it is the duty of women, and all the current sentimentalities that it is their nature, to live for others; to make complete abnegation of themselves, and to have no life but in their affections. And by their affections are meant the only ones they are allowed to have—those to the men with whom they are connected, or to the children who constitute an additional and indefensible tie between them and a man. When we put together three things—first, the natural attraction between opposite sexes; secondly, the wife's entire dependence on the husband, every privilege or pleasure she has being either his gift, or depending entirely on his will; and lastly, that the principal object of human pursuit, consideration, and all objects of social ambition, can in general be sought or obtained by her only through him, it would be a miracle if the object of being attractive to men had not become the polar star of feminine education and formation of character. And, this great means of influence over the minds of women having been acquired, an instinct of selfishness made men avail themselves of it to the utmost as a means of holding women in subjection, by representing to them meekness, submissiveness, and resignation of all individual will into the hands of a man, as an essential part of sexual attractiveness. Can it be doubted that any of the other yokes which mankind have succeeded in breaking, would have subsisted till now if the same means had existed, and had been as sedulously used, to bow down their minds to it? If it had been made the object of the life of every young plebeian to find personal favour in the eyes of some patrician, of every young serf with some seigneur; if domestication with him, and a share of his personal affections, had been held out as the prize which they all should look out for, the most gifted and aspiring being able to reckon on the most desirable prizes; and if, when this prize had been obtained, they had been shut out by a wall of brass from all interests not centering in him, all feelings and desires but those which he shared or inculcated; would not serfs and seigneurs, plebeians and patricians, have been as broadly distinguished at this day as men and women are? and would not all but a thinker here and there, have believed the distinction to be a fundamental and unalterable fact in human nature? . . .

The social subordination of women thus stands out an isolated fact in modern social institutions; a solitary breach of what has become their fundamental law; a single relic of an old world of thought and practice exploded in everything else, but retained in the one thing of most universal interest; as if a gigantic dolmen, or a vast temple of Jupiter Olympius, occupied the site of St. Paul's and received daily worship, while the surrounding Christian churches were only resorted to on fasts and festivals. This entire discrepancy between one social fact and all those which accompany it, and the radical opposition between its nature and the progressive movement which is the boast of the modern world, and which has successively swept away everything else of an analogous character, surely affords, to a conscientious observer of human tendencies, serious matter for reflection.

Theorists who address themselves to the origins of the sexual economy return repeatedly to the ties of women to reproduction. Theories of economic determinism, for example, as we observed in the preceding chapter, are predicated on the notion of the reduced mobility of women because of childbearing and childrearing. While women were contributing to the gens through the gathering and small animal hunting that could accommodate their frequent confinements with pregnancy and nurturing, men were engaged, according to accepted theories of economic determinism, in the major hunting activities that moved them far from home and into contact with representatives from other gens.[1] Those contacts engendered exchanges

2

The Origins of Sex Differences

of information and introduction to raw materials and skills, which in turn provided the basis for the transformation into a social structure based on private property in which men were the primary property owners. Other theorists, particularly the proponents of the existence of prehistorical matriarchies, rely heavily on myths and artifacts that celebrate the procreative feats of women or goddesses as evidence of the ascendant status of women in past cultures.

It is that procreative function that clearly cannot be ignored as we seek explanations for the origins and continuation of the sexual economy as we know it. But how is the evidence to be interpreted? John Stuart Mill and others have shown us how education and culture, preaching the doctrine of biological determinism, have conspired to make women embrace the notion of their secondary status.

---

1. Marvin Harris argues that it was warfare, not hunting, that engendered these contacts and resulted in control of weapons, tools, and skills by men (1978).

To what extent, then, is the long-accepted dictum "biology is destiny" a result of cultural forces? To what extent is our behavior shaped by genetic or biological determinants? A feminist theory of the development of human culture must be aware of the possibility of bias in the interpretation of biological data. Nonetheless, that data cannot be dismissed as we seek explanations for the origins and continuation of the sexual economy as we know it.

Simone de Beauvoir devotes the opening chapter of her monumental work on women, *The Second Sex*, to the biological mandate. Although the central thesis of her work is that cultural determinants throughout history have relegated women to inferior status, de Beauvoir does not ignore biological considerations in her search for the origins of sexism. As the body is the instrument through which the world is apprehended, biology is one key to an understanding of women's perceptions about and place in that world. As we ascend the animal scale, de Beauvoir finds, the two vital components of life, maintenance and creation, are separated definitively in the sexes. The male, whose body is not required to adapt itself to the maintenance of the species, is permitted external expression or creativity. The species insidiously asserts its claim on the female body, however, leaving the female enslaved and alienated in the conflict between her individual needs and her reproductive functions. De Beauvoir catalogs the complex processes of reproduction, many of them superfluous from the point of view of the individual, and describes their usurpation of the whole female organism. "From puberty to menopause," de Beauvoir writes, "woman is the theater of a play that unfolds within her and in which she is not personally concerned" (1952:24). But biology alone is no more sufficient than the "culture myth" de Beauvoir analyzed in the excerpt from her work included in Chapter 1 to explain woman's universal devaluation, her status as "other."

Sherry B. Ortner, drawing upon the work of de Beauvoir, has examined the problem of the universal second-class status of women. What could there be, common to every culture, Ortner asks, that would lead to the devaluation of women? Biological determinism, Ortner finds, is not sufficient explanation. "Biological facts," she argues, "only take on significance of superior/inferior within the framework of culturally defined value systems" (1975:71). It may be, therefore, that women's biological functions have caused them to be perceived as closer to nature than men, who are identified more closely with culture. Every culture, Ortner claims, distinguishes between the operation of nature and of culture (the means by which human consciousness transcends the demands of physical existence or the purely temporal). Ortner, affirming de Beauvoir's findings, asserts that woman's procreative role, which symbolically associated her with the lower animal order, relegates her to social roles of lower status than those of man. Ortner concludes that while woman is in truth no closer to nature than man, the fact that she seems to be so has contributed to the development of social philosophies and institutions that have placed severe limitations on her.

Ortner carefully separates theoretical construction from the ideology grown out of the declaration that "anatomy is destiny," an ideology that has provided motivation and rationale for many systems of sexual oppression. She nonetheless raises, as does de Beauvoir, the specter of biological determinism that many feminist scholars of the 1960s sought to put to rest. Shulamith Firestone, for example, in *The Dialectic of Sex*, granting that the sexual imbalance of power is biologically based, argues that we can no longer justify the maintenance of a system of sex-based discrimination on the grounds of the biological imperative. Firestone argues that ". . . the 'natural' is not necessarily a 'human' value. Humanity has begun to outgrow nature" (1970:10). Firestone suggests that political action is necessary to force man to free himself from the biological conditions that have created his tyranny over woman. As a prescription for a future liberated from the biological imperative, Firestone suggests:

The reproduction of the species by one sex for the benefit of both would be replaced by (at least the option of) artificial reproduction: children would be born to both sexes equally, or independently of either, however one chooses to look at it; the dependence of the child on the mother (and vice versa) would give way to a greatly shortened dependence on a small group of others in general, and any remaining inferiority to adults in physical strength would be compensated for culturally. The division of labor would be ended by the elimination of labor altogether (cybernation). The tyranny of the biological family would be broken. (1970:11)

And indeed, if the "tyranny of biology" is viewed as the result merely of insufficient technology and, as Firestone suggests, the lack of control of reproduction by women, the elimination of the tyranny wants "only" the new medical technology and the feminist political revolution. Other feminist scholars, perhaps less impassioned than Firestone, nonetheless follow her lead in seeking to bring about sexual egalitarianism by the elimination and diminishing of the importance of differences through changed patterns of socialization.

The sociologist Alice Rossi, in her essay "A Biosocial Perspective on Parenting," does not advocate the dismissal of the importance of sex differences; rather, she endorses new attempts to mount "value-free" studies of the biology of sex differences and to reconsider the origins of those differences as respectfully as we consider culturally determined differences. Alice Rossi is one feminist scholar who has seen in biosocial research the promise of a corrective realism in the examination of sex and gender differences to temper the social sciences' "heavy reliance on an egalitarian ideology that denies any innate sex differences and assumes that a 'unisex' socialization will produce man and women free of the traditional culturally induced sex differences" (1977:1). In her examination of the relationship between sex and gender differences and parenting, Rossi deplores both the total dependence of social scientists on assumptions of cultural determinism and what she perceives as a misunderstanding of the possibilities and premises of biosocial research. Rossi argues that, contrary to the claims of Firestone, there probably are innate sex differences and that these differences are at least in part the result of a bioevolutionary process, a process in early human history of "adaptation and selection . . . [which] contributed to sexual dimorphism and a sexual division of labor" (1977:2). Some differences thus created, according to Rossi, might over a long period of time be diminished through compensatory training. She views attempts at creating fully egalitarian societies that do not confront and allow for fundamental biological differences as not only doomed to failure but to the creation of much individual pain and dislocation. Other feminist scholars have disagreed with the conclusions Rossi reaches in her provocative essay. Nancy Chodorow, for example, in *The Reproduction of Mothering* (1978), takes issue with Rossi's conclusion that maternal responses may be genetically embedded in the species. Chodorow admits that there may be genetic bases to certain forms of social arrangements, but insists that they are of such complexity that no one-to-one correspondence between genes and behavior can be discovered. We cannot safely look to bioevolutionary data, she maintains, for evidence of maternal instinct.

In an attempt to provide a review of the discoveries being made by biologists and geneticists about sex and gender differences, and to explore the context of the "cultural framework" in which the research is occurring, we begin this chapter with an overview of "Biological Influences on Human Sex and Gender" by Susan W.

Baker. We approach this area with caution, as do most students of sex or gender differences. One leading researcher, Robert J. Stoller, warns that a "systematic understanding of [the] biology [of sex] is still beyond us" and that methodologies of psychology and the social sciences are essential to our ultimate understanding in this area. Nonetheless, he suggests that the state of the art "with increasing momentum [is] permitting us to see at least the dim outlines of the answers we shall be finding in the next years" (1974:3). Having issued those caveats, Stoller poses the great questions: "To what extent do biological forces play a part in a piece of sexual behavior? How much of an individual's sexual behavior and preferences is thrust upon him by predetermined biological forces, to what extent are pieces of behavior primarily psychological [that is, culturally determined]?" Baker's essay reviews major research and findings to date that have addressed those questions and evaluates the state of the art.

Baker, like most of her colleagues, is careful to acknowledge the limitations of biological/genetic research to answer the riddles of sex and gender identification. For, shadowing all such efforts are fears about the new emphasis on "biosocial" research, fears confronted by Rossi in the article described above. Various theories of behavior, drawing upon Darwin's theory of natural selection, claim that some adaptive behavior is transmitted through the species genetically. An obvious difficulty is in distinguishing behaviors that are independent of culture. Biosocial research carries the stigma of genetic determinism as it has been used in Western civilization to justify the continuance of the status quo. One has only to recall the numerous historical examples of justification of oppressive public policy, based upon the genetic determinist theory of the relationship of race to intelligence, to understand the necessity of treading cautiously in the area of biosocial research.

Perhaps the work most directly responsible for the generalized antipathy of feminists to any notions that invoke biological determinism is the psychoanalytical theory of Sigmund Freud. Working out of the intensely patriarchal nineteenth-century Austrian medical establishment, Freud proclaimed as doctrine that "anatomy is destiny." In the excerpts from the lecture presented here, "Femininity," Freud seeks an answer to the question of whether psychology can solve the "problem of woman." After offering a summary of what was then the extent of biological knowledge about sex differences, he dismisses as serving "no good purpose" the popular identification of "activity with masculinity and passivity with femininity," for which his disciples are primarily responsible. While Freud must be absolved of the blame that has attended his reputation for the perpetuation of that simplistic equation, he is very much responsible for the complicated theory of development that presumably begins with a girl's discovery of her "castration" and ends with, at best, "normal femininity," or less happily, with a "masculinity complex" or a "sexual inhibition [neurosis]."

In recent years, the work of Freud has come under the both critical and sympathetic examination of such feminist scholars as Juliet Mitchell (1975), Nancy Chodorow (1978), and the French feminist followers of Jacques Lacan. Many of these scholars have sought syntheses of feminist, Marxist and psychoanalytic theory. They embrace the tenets of Freudian psychology, but point out the reinterpretations and refinements required if that body of theory is to offer insights into the continuing study of gender and sex differences.

Even so, while the notion of a passive feminine principle opposed to an active aggressive masculine principle has been so long the bête noir of women who have chafed at the limitations these principles imposed, variations on them continue to be explored from several perspectives. While biologists, psychologists, and other scientists study the possibilities of behavior determination by masculine and feminine hormones, writers puzzle over feminine and masculine "principles." Doris Lessing, in *The Golden Notebook*, laments that "women's emotions are still fitted for a kind of society that no longer exists" (1974:314); and Virginia Woolf demands thoughtful consideration of the nature and validity of masculine and feminine principles, which she sees as at once stunting and comforting. In *To The Lighthouse*, Mrs. Ramsay, the mother who is modeled on Julia Stephen, Woolf's own mother, is "delicious fecundity . . . fountain and spray of life," while her husband is "like a beak of brass, barren and bare" (1927:58).

Although we must thus far conclude that the search for answers to questions of the origins of sex differences has met frequent assertion but rare certainty, the search has acquired new dimensions in the last decade. For most of that period, as indicated earlier, emphasis has been on cultural determinants in the development of sex differences. Moreover, as Carol Tavris and Carole Offir point out in the excerpt reprinted in this chapter from their book, *The Longest War: Sex Differences in Perspective*, social learning theory has been the basis of much of the study of the socialization process. Social learning and cognitive-developmental theory have provided particularly useful methods for assessing the means by which cultural values oppressive to women are transmitted. Ordinarily, a child will adopt patterns of behavior, beliefs, and, ultimately, the sex role which she or he is made to feel is appropriate. As Tavris and Offir observe, however, much of the message of appropriateness conveyed by parents, schools, and other institutions is unconscious and is absorbed in large measure by children by the age of two. No wonder, then, that feminists have met with difficulty, even with their own children, in seeking to reorder sex roles.

An exhaustive review of empirical research on the development of sex differences, specifically from the social learning and cognitive-developmental perspective, has been done by Eleanor Emmons Maccoby and Carol Nagy Jacklin. Their *The Psychology of Sex Differences* (1974) has been the point of departure for many recent studies of sex-role development. The excerpt from that work included here is a summary of findings about sex differences from studies occurring from 1966 through 1974. It provides as complete a picture of the state of the art possible in so dynamic a field.

While the work of Maccoby and Jacklin is concerned primarily with empirical studies, work of note is going forward in other areas of psychological research. Nancy Chodorow, for example, offers a personality development theory about gender identity in her article "Family Structure and Feminine Personality." Rejecting sole dependence on biological explanations as well as theories based on assumptions of deliberate socialization patterns, she suggests that sex differences result largely from the internalized relationship of boys and girls to their mothers. Chodorow draws upon traditional psychoanalytic explanations for the establishment of gender identity. For example, it is apparently true, she says, that gender identity is fixed by the age of three; and that for the boy a rather difficult "generalized" identification with the relatively remote father takes place, whereas for the girl identification with the mother is personal and "continuous with her early childhood identifications and attachments" (1974:51).

Rather than invoke Freudian explanations for the early sex differentiation—penis envy, in particular—Chodorow places the phenomenon squarely in a social and cultural context. It is the cultural devaluation of women that intensifies the boy's desire to dissociate himself from his mother, the representation in his world of the feminine, and that same devaluation that reduces the girl's self-esteem because of her inescapable identification with her mother. Behavioral differences, Chodorow continues, grow out of those unconsciously learned sex roles.

In summary, the search for the origins of sex differences has so far yielded few certain answers. It should be clear, however, that the search is under way with a new energy and in a newly responsive mood. While some feminists remain wary of both motive and methodology in gender research, there is a widening recognition of the truth of Ortner's words: "Biological facts only take on significance of superior/inferior within the framework of culturally defined value systems." As long as researchers into gender identity and differences subject their work to rigorous—and determinedly bias-free—scholarship, new knowledge may lead, as Nancy Chodorow has suggested, to social arrangements that will engender social equality between the sexes.

In the essay that follows, Susan W. Baker reviews the current status of research on biological influences on gender identity, gender-role behavior, and sexual orientation. Without denying the possibilities for biological research in understanding sexual behavior and sex differences, Baker couches her work in caveats: Much more research is needed before we can understand the range of limitations of biological influences on behavior and temperament; no study to date of gender identity formation has been able to eliminate environmental factors; and above all, such research need not compromise the search for equality between women and men.

BIOLOGICAL INFLUENCES ON HUMAN SEX AND GENDER

Susan W. Baker

The central question of this review essay is the degree to which sex dimorphic behaviors are environmentally or biologically determined. Asking such a question need not, nor should it, compromise the search for equality between men and women. The term "sex dimorphic behaviors" needs clarification, for they comprise not one, but three groupings of behavioral or psychic phenomena: (1) gender identity, generally defined as the unified and persistent experience of one's self as male, female, or ambivalent; (2) gender-role behavior, the actions and activities that indicate to the self or others the degree to which one is male, female, or ambivalent; and (3) sexual object choice, usually heterosexual, homosexual, or bisexual. (For reasons of space, this review will take up neither transsexualism nor sex differences in cognition.)[1] Researchers in the field of psychoendocrinology investigate to what extent, and in what ways, biology or rearing influences each of these different phenomena.

Despite the fact that this field of inquiry is relatively new, a certain amount of knowledge is commonly held to be true. First, dimorphic biological development, which differentiates females from males, follows certain patterns in animals and humans. Except for the brain, which has yet to be studied in humans, a striking concordance seems to exist between animal and human development in this area. Next, these unfolding sequences consist of particular stages.

1. Obviously, this review essay cannot cover every aspect of a complex field. Instead, it attempts to outline some central issues and present some important data concerning them.
[Signs: Journal of Women in Culture and Society, 1980, vol. 6, no. 1] © 1980 by The University of Chicago. 0097–9740/81/0601–0010$01.00

They are: (a) The genetic, a female pattern of XX sex chromosomes or a male pattern of XY chromosomes. Later, we will deal with another genetic variant, XO, in Turner's syndrome. (b) Gonadal differentiation, from the primordial gonad in the fetus to ovaries in the female and testes in the male. (c) The prenatal hormonal environment. The male in utero is exposed to a high level of virilizing hormones, androgens, and testosterones, while the female is not. (d) The anatomical. The fetus, which has had the potential for both female (Müllerian) and male (Wolffian) internal reproductive systems, develops one of them. An absence of high levels of androgens leads to the Müllerian system; the presence of them in quantity to the Wolffian. Normally, external genitalia next appear from a structure, with a dimorphic capacity, called the genital tubercle. Again, the absence of androgens results in a development along female lines; a presence of androgens in development along male lines (see fig. 1). However, as we shall see below, in some clinical syndromes the anatomy of the external genitalia is ambiguous. Accordingly, sex anatomy itself becomes one of parameters along which we are usually forced to make the distinction between female and male. (e) The postnatal hormonal environment. The biological importance of this becomes especially clear during adolescence, where elevated levels of specific female and male hormones are responsible for secondary sex characteristics. This is also the time during which the gonads assume their mature reproductive capacity.

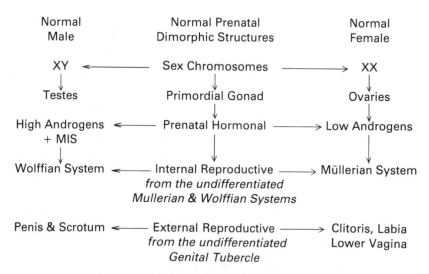

Figure 1. Prenatal sex dimorphic development in normal males and females. The androgen produced by the testes which cause the undifferentiated reproductive systems to differentiate along male lines is testosterone. The testes also make a Müllerian Inhibiting Substance (MIS), which causes regression of the Müllerian system in males.

As the individual, both before and after birth, goes through these five stages, he or she normally has "concordance." That is, the chromosomes, the gonads, the prenatal hormonal environment, the reproductive systems, and the postnatal secondary sex characteristics all line up consistently in female, or male, patterns. However, some individuals are "discordant." That is, at some stages they receive female, at other male, biological influences. The data base for the literature that we will survey has been these discordant individuals. Contemporary psychoendocrinology has focused on those who break, rather than represent, the statistical average. In other words, nature has contrived errors in the usual human development that in some ways mimic the experiments animal researchers have devised in their laboratories.

Six categories of discordancy, or six special human populations, emerge from a study of the literature. Four represent diagnosed, clinical syndromes of some genetic or endogenous that is, internal, disorder of prenatal development: congenital, adrenal hyperplasia (CAH); complete androgen insensitivity, or testicular feminization (TF); partial androgen insensitivity, or Reifenstein's syndrome; and Turner's syndrome, or gonadal dygenesis (see fig. 2). The other two have disorders of the prenatal environment, which may never have been diagnosed and which the exogenous (i.e., external) administration of feminizing or virilizing hormones during the mother's pregnancy has induced. Each population reflects a different interaction between the three sex dimorphic behaviors and the influence of biological or environmental factors upon them. Moreover, each population has contributed data that have allowed various hypotheses to be generated about human sex and gender and about the importance of biological and environmental variables.

Before our presentation of the data and discussion, we wish to note that sex dimorphic behaviors are only those generally found to be more descriptive than not, more often than not for *groups* of normal males and females. The range of individual variation, and the overlap between the behavioral modes, is enormous among those persons with no known "abnormality" of prenatal environment. The "dimorphic" behaviors are those tendencies that differentiate large groups of females and males adequately enough to be labeled.

Psychoendocrinologists have been working with three major hypotheses:

1. Gender identity is *not* determined by chromosomes or by gonadal or prenatal hormonal influence but by rearing. Further, there is a critical period, between eighteen months and two years of life, after which successful sex reassignment will be difficult, if not impossible. However, it is not known if this irreversibility after two

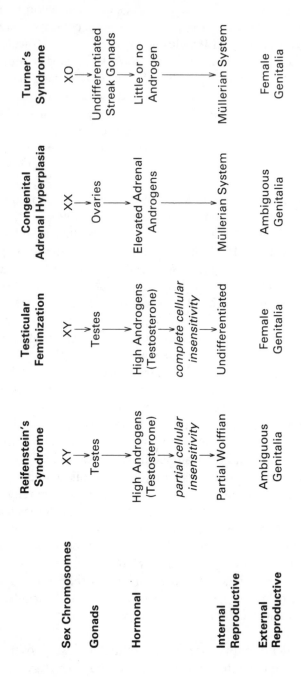

Figure 2. Prenatal sex dimorphic development in four clinical syndromes.

years is determined by the child's experience or by the parents' needs. Gender identity is essentially consolidated by three to four years of age.

2. In contrast, gender-role behavior is influenced by prenatal hormonal environment. This difference in biological influence may be related to the fact that gender identity, unlike gender-role behaviors, requires a psychic state of self-awareness, for which there is no known analogue in the nonhuman animal world and for which there may be no biological etiology.

3. Sexual orientation is generally subsumed under gender role. For our purposes now, it is better considered separately as a dimorphic behavior of sexual object choice that usually appears in adolescence, with obscure relationships to antecedents or influences in earlier behavior.[2] Most researchers in this field think that rearing (i.e., social and environmental factors) determines sexual orientation more than chromosomal, gonadal, or hormonal factors.

Evidence from Clinical Studies

Evidence from the six discordant populations has led to these hypotheses. Let us summarize the evidence from each population in turn.

1. Children and adolescents with a history of elevated prenatal androgens. The only clinical population that has been systematically studied with a history of endogenous prenatal virilization in genetic females is CAH, which is a genetically transmitted condition. The adrenal cortex, unable to produce normal amounts of cortisol from early in fetal life, is therefore overstimulated by the brain to produce elevated amounts of adrenal androgens. The condition occurs in both males and females, but males look normal at birth. In contrast, the elevated levels of adrenal androgens have prenatally acted on the genital tubercle in females, who are then born with ambiguous genitalia. Thus females are usually identified at birth and require early surgical correction of the external genitalia for a normal female appearance. All affected individuals require lifelong management with cortisone replacement to avoid continued postnatal virilization. The internal reproductive system that differentiates (in females) is female, implying that affected girls do not have sufficient androgens during the earlier prenatal critical period for Wolffian reproductive systems to develop.

The relevant evidence from this population for the hypotheses we have outlined follows. Two clinical follow-up studies used semi-

2. F. Whitam, "Child Indicators of Male Homosexuality," *Archives of Sexual Behavior* 6 (1977): 89–96.

structured interviews with mothers and affected female children to assess long-term (current and retrospective) behavior patterns in affected children versus experimental controls.[3] Both studies found that gender identity was female in all cases, and that affected children differed significantly from the controls in various areas of gender-role behaviors, with highly increased incidence of tomboyism, elevated activity level, preference for boys as playmates, little interest in doll play, and generally low interest in infants, etc. Sexual orientation was not examined, because the children were too young; only a few were adolescents in either sample. However, Ehrhardt and Baker reported an adolescent follow-up of the same sample of affected children, now with a mean age of sixteen years.[4] The general pattern of findings was that both interest in and experience with such heterosexual activities as dating, necking, petting and intercourse was delayed. Of the five girls who were not interested, four were the four youngest included in the study. The fifth was a twenty-year-old socially withdrawn girl who avoided close relationships with both men and women. Only one woman reported homosexual fantasies or experiences. She had had both heterosexual and homosexual relationships. It was interesting that while in childhood most of the affected children had reported little interest in their appearance and devoted minimal effort in self-grooming and dressing attractively, this had changed in about half the girls at the time of the follow-up.

Money and Schwartz also reported findings in an adolescent follow-up study of CAH girls.[5] Their findings were quite similar overall, but with a slightly higher incidence of homosexual relationships. However, the incidence remained quite low, and it cannot be concluded that the incidence is significantly greater than would be found in a nonrandom appropriate control sample of equal size. Neither study used a control group, but both demonstrated nonetheless that the affected children's histories of generally tomboyish behavior in no way *determined* a homosexual object choice in adolescence. Most girls were heterosexual in orientation.

The CAH girls in the above studies were all reared as females. What happens to such girls if the syndrome is not accurately diagnosed in early life and they are mistakenly reared as males? The

3. A. Ehrhardt, R. Epstein, and J. Money, "Fetal Androgens and Female Gender Identity in the Early Treated Andrenogenital Syndrome," *Johns Hopkins Medical Journal* 123, no. 3 (1968): 160–67; A. A. Ehrhardt and S. W. Baker, "Fetal Androgens, Human Central Nervous Differentiation, and Behavioral Sex Differences," in *Sex Differences in Behavior*, ed. R. C. Friedman. R M. Richart, and R. L. Vande Wiele (New York: John Wiley & Sons, 1974).

4. A. A. Ehrhardt and S. W. Baker, "Prenatal Androgen Exposure and Future Adolescent Behavior" (paper presented at the International Congress of Sexology, Montreal, 1976).

5. J. Money and M. Schwartz, "Dating, Romantic and Nonromantic Friendships, and Sexuality in 17 Early-treated Adrenogenital Females, Aged 16–25," in *Congenital Adrenal Hyperplasia*, ed. P. A. Lee et al. (Baltimore: University Park Press, 1977), pp. 419–31.

virilization of the external genitalia can be sufficient at times for this to occur. Money and Daley reported findings on a sample of CAH females unambiguously reared as males.[6] They all had a male gender identity, appropriate male gender-role behaviors, and a heterosexual (for gender identity and rearing) sexual object choice.

Thus, from clinical studies on fetally virilized genetic females gender identity was concordant with sex of rearing, gender-role behaviors appeared to be influenced by prenatal environment but were within the range of normal tomboyish girls' behaviors and in no way bizarre, and sexual orientation in most cases was heterosexual to rearing and gender identity.

2. Children and adolescents with a history of androgen insensitivity. Two clinical populations that have been studied fall into this category: the syndrome of complete androgen insensitivity or testicular feminization (TF) and partial androgen insensitivity (Reifenstein's syndrome). Testicular feminization is a quite rare genetically transmitted condition. Individuals with it have (see fig. 2) normal male chromosomes, gonads, and prenatal hormonal levels. However, the cells of their bodies are unable to respond to the elevated gonadal androgens prenatally, and as a result they do not virilize. The testes in normal males make an additional substance called the Müllerian Inhibiting Substance (MIS), produced normally in TF individuals, which is responsible for the lack of differentiation of the Müllerian system. Thus, these individuals in later life do not have reproductive capacity but can have a normal sexual relationship (as the external genitalia are female) and adopt their babies. Masica, Money, and Ehrhardt studied a clinical sample of ten TF girls reared as females.[7] On follow up, gender identity was female in all cases; gender role behaviors were female, that is, not characterized by the "virilized"[8] behavior patterns reported in the CAH-affected individuals. Sexual orientation was heterosexual (by sex of rearing and gender identity) in all cases. Many went on to marry and adopt babies.

---

6. J. Money and J. Daley, "Hyperadrenocortical 46 XX Hermaphroditism with Penile Urethra: Psychological Studies in Seven Cases, Three Reared as Boys, Four as Girls," in Lee et al., pp. 433–46.

7. D. Masica, J. Money, and A. A. Ehrhardt, "Fetal Feminization and Female Gender Identity in the Testicular Feminizing Syndrome of Androgen Insensitivity," *Archives of Sexual Behavior* 1, no. 2 (1971): 131–42.

8. The term "virilization" is generally used in the animal and human literature for those hormonally responsive behaviors that are generally assumed to be most characteristic of males (such as a high degree of rough-and-tumble play in childhood in nonhuman primate males). Defeminization is used to describe a situation where behaviors generally assumed to be more characteristic of females are decreased in frequency by a hormonal manipulation. Most of the human dimorphic behavioral changes we refer to seem to fall most appropriately into the nomenclature of virilization rather than defeminization. An example in humans of defeminization rather than virilization would be if fetally virilized females had loss or severe impairment of menstrual cyclicity.

3. *Reifenstein's syndrome.* These individuals have a genetically transmitted syndrome of partial androgen insensitivity. These individuals, like the CAH females, are identified at birth because of abnormal (ambiguous) genitalia. Genetic and gonadal males who were incompletely virilized prenatally, they have been raised as either males or females. Ideally the decision as to rearing would depend upon the viability of the development of the external genitalia for future sexual functioning. However they have been raised, they generally require some surgical correction of the genitalia. Money and Ogunro interviewed ten subjects with partial androgen insensitivity, eight reared as males and two as females.[9] Nine of the ten subjects' gender identity was concordant with sex of rearing, in spite of severe functional genital difficulties, with four of those raised as males having a "clitoral-sized phallus." One female reported herself as ambivalent about her gender identity. She had three affected siblings who had publicly reannounced their gender identity from female to male in adulthood. The authors speculated that this may have contributed to her ambivalence. Gender-role behaviors were gender appropriate to sex of rearing in all cases. Sexual orientation was exclusively heterosexual in eight of the nine subjects with any sexual experience. Several subjects were married and were parents by adoption. One subject, who had one lesbian experience of brief duration early in her teen years, expressed no interest in having another lesbian experience, but she also had severe doubts about being accepted coitally as a woman.

4. *Turner's syndrome, or gonadal dysgenesis.* This is the last of the clinical populations with a genetic or endogenous disorder that we will discuss. Turner's-syndrome individuals represent something of a special case compared with the other clinical groups; these individuals are missing the second sex chromosome completely, or are genetically mosaic (i.e., some cells are missing the second sex chromosome, some cells may have a normal chromosomal complement, and some have other combinations of normal or abnormal sex chromosomal complements). Individuals with this clinical condition are also not necessarily identified at birth. There is no abnormality of the external genitalia, but there are other associated features which may lead to an early diagnosis and always lead to a diagnosis by early adolescence. The associated features can include kidney and heart abnormalities and other dysmorphic features such as a webbed neck and moderate short stature. The degree to which an affected child displays any or all of these features varies widely. The chromosomal

9. J. Money and B. Ogunro, "Behavioral Sexology: Ten Cases of Genetic Male Intersexuality with Impaired Prenatal and Pubertal Androgenization," *Archives of Sexual Behavior* 3, no. 3 (1974): 181–205.

abnormality leads to undifferentiated or poorly differentiated gonads prenatally. Thus these children do not have reproductive capacity and do not develop secondary sex characteristics or menstruate without hormone replacement. It is for this reason the condition is recognized in early adolescence.

Ehrhardt, Greenberg, and Money evaluated developmental behavior patterns in fifteen Turner's-syndrome girls, using matched controls.[10] All subjects were unambiguously reared as females, and all had a female gender identity. If prenatal hormonal environment plays a predispositional influencing role in later preferred gender-role behaviors (hypothesis 2), one would assume that Turner's girls would be the least "defeminized," as they are the most likely to have the lowest amounts of prenatal gonadal hormones that could have any defeminizing effect on the brain. In this study, gender-role behaviors of affected subjects differed significantly from controls in the areas of an elevated interest in appearance, a lower frequency of active outdoor play, and decreased fighting. The nonsignificant trends in gender-role behaviors were all in the expected direction of a lower frequency of being labeled a tomboy, preferring or content to be a girl, a higher interest in "frilly dresses," extensive preference for girls rather than boys as playmates, play with only dolls versus boys' toys, and a strong, actively expressed interest in infant care. Although the sample was young, among those who were adolescents there were no reports of homosexual fantasies or experiences in either affected children or controls.

5. Children exposed to exogenous feminizing hormones prenatally. In certain animal species, in both males and females, progesterone can antagonize androgen action under certain circumstances.[11] Therefore, it was hypothesized that progesterone might have a similar effect in humans. Yalom, Green, and Fisk, in a double-blind study of the offspring of diabetic mothers treated with diethylbestrol plus progesterone during pregnancy, reported findings that seem to support the hypotheses of an antiandrogenizing effect of progesterone upon some aspects of human gender-role behavior.[12] The twenty hormone-exposed males (aged sixteen to seventeen) were compared with a matched control group. The treated males were reported to be somewhat less assertive and aggressive and had decreased athletic coordination, decreased overall "masculine" interests, and less heterosexual experience compared with controls.

10. A. Ehrhardt, N. Greenberg, and J. Money, "Female Gender Identity and Absence of Fetal Gonadal Hormones: Turner's Syndrome," *Johns Hopkins Medical Journal* 126, no. 5 (1970): 237–48.

11. J. A. Resko, "Fetal Hormones and Their Effect on the Differentiation of the Central Nervous System in Primates," *Federation Proceedings* 34 (1975): 1650–55.

12. I. Yalom, R. Green, and N. Fisk, "Prenatal Exposures to Female Hormones: Effect on Psychosexual Development in Boys," *Archives of General Psychiatry* 28 (1973): 554–61.

There were similar findings in a second study.[13] Here the subjects had been exposed to progesterone prenatally in mothers with pre-eclamptic toxemia. The authors reported findings on both males and females with a matched control group: male subjects had a significantly decreased interest in dating and marriage, females a decreased interest in tomboyish behavior and an increased interest in appearance. The most recent study in this area was reported by Meyer-Bahlburg, Grisanti, and Ehrhardt and Ehrhardt, Grisanti, and Meyer-Bahlburg.[14] The authors looked at males ($N = 13$) and females ($N = 15$) exposed prenatally to medroxy-progesterone acetate (MPA) in a double-blind study with matched controls. Because the subjects were eight to fourteen years of age, data on sexual orientation were not available. As in previous studies, gender identity was not affected, but there were some apparent treatment effects associated with gender-role behaviors in girls. Treated girls showed a lower incidence than the controls of being labeled a tomboy and a greater preference for feminine clothing styles. Hormone-exposed boys did not differ from controls.

6. *Children exposed to erogenous virilizing hormones prenatally.* Ehrhardt and Money reported findings on ten genetic females exposed prenatally to exogenously administered synthetic progestins.[15] The hormones were given to the mothers during pregnancy because of threatened miscarriages. Some of the children evidenced signs of the prenatal virilization at birth, having an enlarged clitoris. Those who required surgery had it within the first year of life. There was no question of postnatal virilization, and these girls did not require medical follow-up or management. Subjects were matched with controls; the age range at follow-up was four to fourteen years. All girls had a female gender identity. The gender-role findings were similar to those in the populations of CAH girls, with a significant tendency in the subject population, as opposed to controls, toward a higher activity level, long-term tomboyish behavior, etc.

This study is important in that it decreases the possibility that postnatal virilization or long-term medical management, with the consequent parental anxiety, is responsible in any way for the gender-role findings in the CAH children. The genital ambiguity at birth was also less severe and more easily correctable with one procedure

13. J. U. Zussman, P. P. Zussman, and K. Dalton, "Post-pubertal Effects of Prenatal Administration of Progesterone" (paper presented at the meeting of the Society for Research in Child Development, Denver, 1975).

14. H. F. L. Meyer-Bahlburg, G. C. Grisanti, and A. A. Ehrhardt, "Prenatal Effects of Sex Hormones on Human Male Behavior: Medroxyprogesterone Acetate (MPA)," *Psychoneuroendocrinology* 2 (1977): 381–90; A. A. Ehrhardt, G. C. Grisanti, and H. F. L. Meyer-Bahlburg, "Prenatal Exposure to Medroxyprogesterone Acetate (MPA) in Girls," ibid., pp. 391–98.

15. A. A. Ehrhardt and J. Money, "Progestin-induced Hermaphroditism: IQ and Psychosexual Identity in a Study of Ten Girls," *Journal of Sexual Research* 3 (1967): 85–100.

in those cases requiring surgery. Thus, the parents were less likely to have long-term lurking fears regarding their daughters as being in any way "at risk" for later problems.

Reinisch and Karow, using the Cattell Personality Inventory, studied twenty-six boys and forty-five girls aged five to seventeen who had been exposed prenatally to various combinations of synthetic progestogens and estrogens.[16] They used untreated siblings as controls. No treated children evidenced any sign of a genital anomaly. Many of the mothers did not recall having taken any drugs during pregnancy. The authors found significant treatment effects: male and female subjects *mainly* exposed to progestogens were more "independent," "sensitive," "self-assured," "individualistic," and "self-sufficient," while male and female subjects exposed primarily to estrogens were more "group oriented" and "group dependent." The authors did not report findings on gender identity or gender-role behaviors. However, the reported findings are of interest in that they indicate a behavioral consequence to prenatal hormone exposure in areas not generally considered sex dimorphic. This study raises the possibility that general temperamental predispositions in human behavior may be influenced by aspects of the prenatal hormonal environment. . . .

Discussion

In general, the studies of clinical populations indicate a rather consistent picture. In females, prenatal exposure to abnormally high levels of androgens or other virilizing hormones results in some behavioral-temperamental consequences, particularly those dimorphic behaviors generally subsumed under the category of gender-role behaviors. In males, androgen insensitivity or prenatal exposure to sufficient levels of hormones that antagonize androgen action results also in behavioral temperamental consequences.

The bulk of the evidence from human studies does *not* support the thesis that prenatal environment is responsible for choice of sex object in adolescence. In fact, with the better controlled, more elaborate studies in nonhuman mammals, where much higher amounts of hormones are given throughout the various critical periods, no one has yet succeeded in producing "homosexual" animals. In those human studies where any subjects in the sample had bisexual or homosexual experiences, no control groups were used, and it is not known, but is unlikely, that the frequency was higher than it would be in other nonrandom appropriate control groups.

16. J. M. Reinisch and W. G. Karow, "Prenatal Exposure to Synthetic Progestins and Estrogens: Effects on Human Development," *Archives of Sexual Behavior* 6 (1977): 89–96.

In the area of gender identity formation, in all systematic studies of human populations except one, gender identity was concordant for sex of rearing regardless of the chromosomal, gonadal, or prenatal hormonal situation. The exception, reporting findings of a gender identity "reversal" in male pseudohermaphrodites and postulating a purely biological explanation, did *not* demonstrate unambivalent rearing in their subjects. In fact, no study to date has been able to exclude confounding environmental factors where there was any visible abnormality at birth. Furthermore, such "proof" would require anthropological and sophisticated prospective studies (which have not been done), and knowledge of the operational environmental variables responsible for formation or imposition upon the infant of a sense of self that is gender-specific. To date we do not know how this information is either communicated by the parents (presumably) or processed by the infant.

There are many difficulties with the human studies, among them the confounding effects of medical condition, frequent use of retrospective interview data, the difficulty of providing adequate controls, and small sample sizes. However, acting within the constraints of ethical human investigation requires many of these limitations. Low subject availability in rare genetic syndromes or other hormonally exposed individuals is also an expectable limitation. In future studies, we hope, a greater range of more sophisticated methodologies may mitigate some of the other limitations in human research.

In spite of the problems, psychoendocrine research has provided a foundation of data that indicates that biological factors, such as hormonal environment before birth, can be a real influence on at least some behavioral and/or temperamental proclivities throughout life. Future research ought to define more clearly the range and limitations of these biological influences. It will probably also investigate the human brain. A wealth of *animal* data indicates differences between male and female brains—in cell nuclear size in specific areas of the brain, and axonal and dendritic growth, both of which are hormonally sensitive during early critical periods and later in life.[17] We also know that the brain has specific receptors for dissimilar hormones, with concentrations of the various receptors in functionally different parts of the brain.[18] It is relatively parsimonious to assume that many of these biologic facts in nonhuman species are probably also true for humans,[19] although to date there are no human data in

17. R. A. Gorski, "Long-Term Hormonal Modulation of Neuronal Structure and Function," in *The Neurosciences: 4th Study Program*, ed. F. O. Schmidt and F. Worden (Cambridge, Mass.: M.I.T. Press, 1979), pp. 969–82.

18. B. McEwen, "Gonadal Steroids and Brain Development," *Biology of Reproduction* 22 (1980): 43–48.

19. R. W. Goy and P. A. Goldfoot, "Neuroendocrinology: Animal Models and Problems of Human Sexuality," *Archives of Sexual Behavior* 4 (1975): 405–20.

any of these areas of research. When we have elucidated some of these issues of dimorphic brain structure in humans, we may then be able to approach the issues of the association between structure and function in humans and the roles of biology and environment in shaping both.

*"What does woman want?" Freud's legendary question to
the women whose biological and psychological character his
theories purported to explain has provided a bemused point
of departure for numerous feminist works. The question
reflects perhaps more than a momentary frustration, for in
his lecture on "femininity" Freud demurs: "That is all I had
to say to you about femininity. It is certainly incomplete and
fragmentary and does not always sound friendly. . . . If you
want to know more about femininity, enquire from your own
experiences of life, or turn to the poets, or wait until science
can give you deeper and more coherent information."
Unfortunately, neither Freud nor, especially, his followers
waited for science or the poets. Rather, Freud's basic
principles of the psychological development of women, about
which he was ordinarily more certain, themselves shaped
much scientific inquiry and provided food for poets for
generations to follow. A number of those essential principles
are included in his lecture "The Psychology of Women"
(1933), from which the following excerpts are taken.*

FEMININITY

Sigmund Freud

FROM *New Lectures in Psychoanalysis*

We are accustomed to employ "masculine" and "feminine" as mental
qualities as well [as biological ones] and have in the same way transferred the notion of bisexuality to mental life. Thus we speak of a person, whether male or female, as behaving in a masculine way in one
connection and in a feminine way in another. But you will soon perceive that this is only giving way to anatomy or to convention. You
cannot give the concepts of "masculine" and "feminine" *any* new
connotation. The distinction is not a psychological one; when you
say "masculine," you usually mean "active," and when you say
"feminine," you usually mean "passive." Now it is true that a relation of the kind exists. The male sex-cell is actively mobile and search-
es out the female one, and the latter, the ovum, is immobile and
waits passively. This behaviour of the elementary sexual organisms is
indeed a model for the conduct of sexual individuals during intercourse. The male pursues the female for the purpose of sexual union,
seizes hold of her and penetrates into her. But by this you have precisely reduced the characteristic of masculinity to the factor of aggressiveness so far as psychology is concerned. You may well doubt

whether you have gained any real advantage from this when you reflect that in some classes of animals the females are the stronger and more aggressive and the male is active only in the single act of sexual union. This is so, for instance, with the spiders. Even the functions of rearing and caring for the young, which strike us as feminine *par excellence*, are not invariably attached to the female sex in animals. In quite high species we find that the sexes share the task of caring for the young between them or even that the male alone devotes himself to it. Even in the sphere of human sexual life you soon see how inadequate it is to make masculine behaviour coincide with activity and feminine with passivity. A mother is active in every sense towards her child; the act of lactation itself may equally be described as the mother suckling the baby or as her being sucked by it. The further you go from the narrow sexual sphere the more obvious will the "error of superimposition"[1] become. Women can display great activity in various directions, men are not able to live in company with their own kind unless they develop a large amount of passive adaptability. If you now tell me that these facts go to prove precisely that both men and women are bisexual in the psychological sense, I shall conclude that you have decided in your own minds to make "active" coincide with "masculine" and "passive" with "feminine." But I advise you against it. It seems to me to serve no useful purpose and adds nothing to our knowledge.[2]

One might consider characterizing femininity psychologically as giving preference to passive aims. This is not, of course, the same thing as passivity; to achieve a passive aim may call for a large amount of activity. It is perhaps the case that in a woman, on the basis of her share in the sexual function, a preference for passive behaviour and passive aims is carried over into her life to a greater or lesser extent, in proportion to the limits, restricted or far-reaching, within which her sexual life thus serves as a model. But we must beware in this of underestimating the influence of social customs, which similarly force women into passive situations. All this is still far from being cleared up. There is one particularly constant relation between femininity and instinctual life which we do not want to overlook. The suppression of women's aggressiveness which is prescribed for them constitutionally and imposed on them socially favours the development of powerful masochistic impulses, which succeed, as we know, in binding erotically the destructive trends which have been

1. I.e., mistaking two different things for a single one. The term was explained in *Introductory Lectures*, XX.
2. The difficulty of finding a psychological meaning for "masculine" and "feminine" was discussed in a long footnote added in 1915 to Section 4 of the third of his *Three Essays*, and again at the beginning of a still longer footnote at the end of Chapter 4 of *Civilization and its Discontents*.

diverted inwards. Thus masochism, as people say, is truly feminine. But if, as happens so often, you meet with masochism in men, what is left to you but to say that these men exhibit very plain feminine traits?

And now you are already prepared to hear that psychology too is unable to solve the riddle of femininity. The explanation must no doubt come from elsewhere, and cannot come till we have learnt how in general the differentiation of living organisms into two sexes came about. We know nothing about it, yet the existence of two sexes is a most striking characteristic of organic life which distinguishes it sharply from inanimate nature. However, we find enough to study in those human individuals who, through the possession of female genitals, are characterized as manifestly or predominantly feminine. In conformity with its peculiar nature, psycho-analysis does not try to describe what a woman is—that would be a task it could scarcely perform—but sets about enquiring how she comes into being, how a woman develops out of a child with a bisexual disposition. In recent times we have begun to learn a little about this, thanks to the circumstance that several of our excellent women colleagues in analysis have begun to work at the question. The discussion of this has gained special attractiveness from the distinction between the sexes. For the ladies, whenever some comparison seemed to turn out unfavourable to their sex, were able to utter a suspicion that we, the male analysts, had been unable to overcome certain deeply-rooted prejudices against what was feminine, and that this was being paid for in the partiality of our researches. We, on the other hand, standing on the ground of bisexuality, had no difficulty in avoiding impoliteness. We had only to say: "This doesn't apply to *you*. You're the exception; on this point you're more masculine than feminine."

We approach the investigation of the sexual development of women with two expectations. The first is that here once more the constitution will not adapt itself to its function without a struggle. The second is that the decisive turning-points will already have been prepared for or completed before puberty. Both expectations are promptly confirmed. Furthermore, a comparison with what happens with boys tells us that the development of a little girl into a normal woman is more difficult and more complicated, since it includes two extra tasks, to which there is nothing corresponding in the development of a man. Let us follow the parallel lines from their beginning. Undoubtedly the material is different to start with in boys and girls: it did not need psycho-analysis to establish that. The difference in the structure of the genitals is accompanied by other bodily differences which are too well known to call for mention. Differences emerge too in the instinctual disposition which give a glimpse of the later nature of women. A little girl is as a rule less aggressive, defiant and self-sufficient; she seems to have a greater need for being shown affection and on that account to be more dependent and pliant. It is probably only as a result of this pliancy that she can be taught more easily and quicker to control her excretions: urine and faeces are the first gifts that children make to those who look after them, and controlling them is the first concession to which the instinctual life of children can be induced. One gets an impression, too, that little girls are more intelligent and livelier than boys of the same age; they go out more to meet the external world and at the same time form stronger object-cathexes. I cannot say whether this lead in development has been confirmed by exact observations, but in any case there is no question that girls cannot be described as intellectually backward. These sexual differences are not, however, of great consequence: they can be outweighed by individual variations. For our immediate purposes they can be disregarded.

Both sexes seem to pass through the early phases of libidinal development in the same manner. It might have been expected that in girls there would already have been some lag in aggressiveness in the sadistic-anal phase, but such is not the case. Analysis of children's play has shown our women analysts that the aggressive impulses of little girls leave nothing to be desired in the way of abundance and violence. With their entry into the phallic phase the differences between the sexes are completely eclipsed by their agreements. We are now obliged to recognize that the little girl is a little man. In boys, as we know, this phase is marked by the fact that they have learnt how to derive pleasurable sensations from their small penis and connect its excited state with their ideas of sexual intercourse. Little girls do the same thing with their still smaller clitoris. It seems that with them all their masturbatory acts are carried out on this penis-equivalent, and that the truly feminine vagina is still undiscovered by both sexes. It is true that there are a few isolated reports of early vaginal sensations as well, but it could not be easy to distinguish these from sensations in the anus or vestibulum; in any case they cannot play a great part. We are entitled to keep to our view that in the phallic phase of girls the clitoris is the leading erotogenic zone. But it is not, of course, going to remain so. With the change to femininity the clitoris should wholly or in part hand over its sensitivity, and at the same time its importance, to the vagina. This would be one of the two tasks which a woman has to perform in the course of her development, whereas the more fortunate man has only to continue at the time of his sexual maturity the activity that he has previously carried out at the period of the early efflorescence of his sexuality.

We shall return to the part played by the clitoris; let us now turn to the second task with which a girl's development is burdened. A boy's mother is the first object of his love, and she remains so too during the formation of his Oedipus complex and, in essence, all through his life. For a girl too her first object must be her mother (and the figures of wet-nurses and foster-mothers that merge into her). The first object-cathexes occur in attachment to the satisfaction of the major and simple vital needs,[3] and the circumstances of the care of children are the same for both sexes. But in the Oedipus situation the girl's father has become her love-object, and we expect that in the normal course of development she will find her way from this paternal object to her final choice of an object. In the course of time, therefore, a girl has to change her erotogenic zone and her object—both of which a boy retains. The question then arises of how this happens: in particular, how does a girl pass from her mother to an attachment to her father? or, in other words, how does she pass from her masculine phase to the feminine one to which she is biologically destined?

It would be a solution of ideal simplicity if we could suppose that from a particular age onwards the elementary influence of the mutual attraction between the sexes makes itself felt and impels the small woman towards men, while the same law allows the boy to continue with his mother. We might suppose in addition that in this the children are following the pointer given them by the sexual preference of their parents. But we are not going to find things so easy; we scarcely know whether we are to believe seriously in the power of which poets talk so much and with such enthusiasm but which cannot be further dissected analytically. We have found an answer of quite another sort by means of laborious investigations, the material for which at least was easy to arrive at. For you must know that the number of women who remain till a late age tenderly dependent on a paternal object, or indeed on their real father, is very great. We have established some surprising facts about these women with an intense attachment of long duration to their father. We knew, of course, that there had been a preliminary stage of attachment to the mother, but we did not know that it could be so rich in content and so long-lasting, and could leave behind so many opportunities for fixations and dispositions. During this time the girl's father is only a troublesome rival; in some cases the attachment to her mother lasts beyond the fourth year of life. Almost everything that we find later in her relation to her father was already present in this earlier attachment and has been transferred subsequently on to her father. In short, we get

3. Cf. *Introductory Lectures*, XXI.

an impression that we cannot understand women unless we appreciate this phase of their pre-Oedipus attachment to their mother.

We shall be glad, then, to know the nature of the girl's libidinal relations to her mother. The answer is that they are of very many different kinds. Since they persist through all three phases of infantile sexuality, they also take on the characteristics of the different phases and express themselves by oral, sadistic-anal and phallic wishes. These wishes represent active as well as passive impulses; if we relate them to the differentiation of the sexes which is to appear later—though we should avoid doing so as far as possible—we may call them masculine and feminine. Besides this, they are completely ambivalent, both affectionate and of a hostile and aggressive nature. The latter often only come to light after being changed into anxiety ideas. It is not always easy to point to a formulation of these early sexual wishes; what is most clearly expressed is a wish to get the mother with child and the corresponding wish to bear her a child— both belonging to the phallic period and sufficiently surprising, but established beyond doubt by analytic observation. The attractiveness of these investigations lies in the surprising detailed findings which they bring us. Thus, for instance, we discover the fear of being murdered or poisoned, which may later form the core of a paranoic illness, already present in this pre-Oedipus period, in relation to the mother. Or another case: you will recall an interesting episode in the history of analytic research which caused me many distressing hours. In the period in which the main interest was directed to discovering infantile sexual traumas, almost all my women patients told me that they had been seduced by their father. I was driven to recognize in the end that these reports were untrue and so came to understand that hysterical symptoms are derived from phantasies and not from real occurrences. It was only later that I was able to recognize in this phantasy of being seduced by the father the expression of the typical Oedipus complex in women. And now we find the phantasy of seduction once more in the pre-Oedipus prehistory of girls; but the seducer is regularly the mother. Here, however, the phantasy touches the ground of reality, for it was really the mother who by her activities over the child's bodily hygiene inevitably stimulated, and perhaps even roused for the first time, pleasurable sensations in her genitals.[4]

I have no doubt you are ready to suspect that this portrayal of the abundance and strength of a little girl's sexual relations with her

4. In his early discussions of the aetiology of hysteria Freud often mentioned seduction by adults as among its commontes causes (see, for instance, Section I of the second paper on the neuro-psychoses of defence and Section II (*b*) of "The Aetiology of Hysteria." But nowhere in these early publications did he specifically inculpate the girl's father.

mother is very much overdrawn. After all, one has opportunities of seeing little girls and notices nothing of the sort. But the objection is not to the point. Enough can be seen in the children if one knows how to look. And besides, you should consider how little of its sexual wishes a child can bring to preconscious expression or communicate at all. Accordingly we are only within our rights if we study the residues and consequences of this emotional world in retrospect, in people in whom these processes of development had attained a specially clear and even excessive degree of expansion. Pathology has always done us the service of making discernible by isolation and exaggeration conditions which would remain concealed in a normal state. And since our investigations have been carried out on people who were by no means seriously abnormal, I think we should regard their outcome as deserving belief. . . .

I believe we have found this specific factor [the ending of the girl's attachment to the mother] and indeed where we expected to find it, even though in a surprising form. Where we expected to find it, I say, for it lies in the castration complex. After all, the anatomical distinction [between the sexes] must express itself in psychical consequences. It was, however, a surprise to learn from analyses that girls hold their mother responsible for their lack of a penis and do not forgive her for their being thus put at a disadvantage.

As you hear, then, we ascribe a castration complex to women as well. And for good reasons, though its content cannot be the same as with boys. In the latter the castration complex arises after they have learnt from the sight of the female genitals that the organ which they value so highly need not necessarily accompany the body. At this the boy recalls to mind the threats he brought on himself by his doings with that organ, he begins to give credence to them and falls under the influence of fear of castration, which will be the most powerful motive force in his subsequent development. The castration complex of girls is also started by the sight of the genitals of the other sex. They at once notice the difference and, it must be admitted, its significance too. They feel seriously wronged, often declare that they want to "have something like it too," and fall a victim to "envy for the penis," which will leave ineradicable traces on their development and the formation of their character and which will not be surmounted in even the most favourable cases without a severe expenditure of psychical energy. The girl's recognition of the fact of her being without a penis does not by any means imply that she submits to the fact easily. On the contrary, she continues to hold on for a long time to the wish to get something like it herself and she believes in that possibility for improbably long years; and analysis can show that, at a period when knowledge of reality has long since rejected the fulfilment of the wish as unattainable, it persists in the unconscious and retains a considerable cathexis of energy. The wish to get the longed-for penis eventually in spite of everything may contribute to the motives that drive a mature woman to analysis, and what she may reasonably expect from analysis—a capacity, for instance, to carry on an intellectual profession—may often be recognized as a sublimated modification of this repressed wish.

One cannot very well doubt the importance of envy for the penis. You may take it as an instance of male injustice if I assert that envy and jealousy play an even greater part in the mental life of women than of men. It is not that I think these characteristics are absent in men or that I think they have no other roots in women than envy for the penis; but I am inclined to attribute their greater amount in women to this latter influence. Some analysts, however, have shown in inclination to depreciate the importance of this first instalment of penis-envy in the phallic phase. They are of opinion that what we find of this attitude in women is in the main a secondary structure which has come about on the occasion of later conflicts by regression to this early infantile impulse. This, however, is a general problem of depth psychology. In many pathological—or even unusual—instinctual attitudes (for instance, in all sexual perversions) the question arises of how much of their strength is to be attributed to early infantile fixations and how much to the influence of later experiences and developments. In such cases it is almost always a matter of complemental series such as we put forward in our discussion of the aetiology of the neuroses.[5] Both factors play a part in varying amounts in the causation; a less on the one side is balanced by a more on the other. The infantile factor sets the pattern in all cases but does not always determine the issue, though it often does. Precisely in the case of penis-envy I should argue decidedly in favour of the preponderance of the infantile factor.

The discovery that she is castrated is a turning-point in a girl's growth. Three possible lines of development start from it: one leads to sexual inhibition or to neurosis, the second to change of character in the sense of a masculinity complex, the third, finally, to normal femininity. We have learnt a fair amount, though not everything, about all three.

The essential content of the first is as follows: the little girl has hitherto lived in a masculine way, has been able to get pleasure by the excitation of her clitoris and has brought this activity into relation with her sexual wishes directed towards her mother, which are often active ones; now, owing to the influence of her penis-envy, she

5. See *Introductory Lectures*, XXII and XXIII.

loses her enjoyment in her phallic sexuality. Her self-love is mortified by the comparison with the boy's far superior equipment and in consequence she renounces her masturbatory satisfaction from her clitoris, repudiates her love for her mother and at the same time not infrequently represses a good part of her sexual trends in general. No doubt her turning away from her mother does not occur all at once, for to begin with the girl regards her castration as an individual misfortune, and only gradually extends it to other females and finally to her mother as well. Her love was directed to her *phallic* mother; with the discovery that her mother is castrated it becomes possible to drop her as an object, so that the motives for hostility, which have long been accumulating, gain the upper hand. This means, therefore, that as a result of the discovery of women's lack of a penis they are debased in value for girls just as they are for boys and later perhaps for men. . . .

Along with the abandonment of clitoridal masturbation a certain amount of activity is renounced. Passivity now has the upper hand, and the girl's turning to her father is accomplished principally with the help of passive instinctual impulses. You can see that a wave of development like this, which clears the phallic activity out of the way, smooths the ground for femininity. If too much is not lost in the course of it through repression, this femininity may turn out to be normal. The wish with which the girl turns to her father is no doubt originally the wish for the penis which her mother has refused her and which she now expects from her father. The feminine situation is only established, however, if the wish for a penis is replaced by one for a baby, if, that is, a baby takes the place of a penis in accordance with an ancient symbolic equivalence. It has not escaped us that the girl has wished for a baby earlier, in the undisturbed phallic phase: that, of course, was the meaning of her playing with dolls. But that play was not in fact an expression of her femininity; it served as an identification with her mother with the intention of substituting activity for passivity. *She* was playing the part of her mother and the doll was herself: now she could do with the baby everything that her mother used to do with her. Not until the emergence of the wish for a penis does the doll-baby become a baby from the girl's father, and thereafter the aim of the most powerful feminine wish. Her happiness is great if later on this wish for a baby finds fulfilment in reality, and quite especially so if the baby is a little boy who brings the longed-for penis with him. Often enough in her combined picture of "a baby from her father" the emphasis is laid on the baby and her father left unstressed. In this way the ancient masculine wish for the possession of a penis is still faintly visible through the femininity now achieved. But perhaps we ought rather to recognize this wish for a penis as being *par excellence* a feminine one.

With the transference of the wish for a penis-baby on to her father, the girl has entered the situation of the Oedipus complex. Her hostility to her mother, which did not need to be freshly created, is now greatly intensified, for she becomes the girl's rival, who receives from her father everything that she desires from him. For a long time the girl's Oedipus complex concealed her pre-Oedipus attachment to her mother from our view, though it is nevertheless so important and leaves such lasting fixations behind it. For girls the Oedipus situation is the outcome of a long and difficult development; it is a kind of preliminary solution, a position of rest which is not soon abandoned, especially as the beginning of the latency period is not far distant. And we are now struck by a difference between the two sexes, which is probably momentous, in regard to the relation of the Oedipus complex to the castration complex. In a boy the Oedipus complex, in which he desires his mother and would like to get rid of his father as being a rival, develops naturally from the phase of his phallic sexuality. The threat of castration compels him, however, to give up that attitude. Under the impression of the danger of losing his penis, the Oedipus complex is abandoned, repressed and, in the most normal cases, entirely destroyed, and a severe super-ego is set up as its heir. What happens with a girl is almost the opposite. The castration complex prepares for the Oedipus complex instead of destroying it; the girl is driven out of her attachment to her mother through the influence of her envy for the penis and she enters the Oedipus situation as though into a haven of refuge. In the absence of fear of castration the chief motive is lacking which leads boys to surmount the Oedipus complex. Girls remain in it for an indeterminate length of time; they demolish it late and, even so, incompletely. In these circumstances the formation of the super-ego must suffer; it cannot attain the strength and independence which give it its cultural significance, and feminists are not pleased when we point out to them the effects of this factor upon the average feminine character.

To go back a little. We mentioned as the second possible reaction to the discovery of female castration the development of a powerful masculinity complex. By this we mean that the girl refuses, as it were, to recognize the unwelcome fact and, defiantly rebellious, even exaggerates her previous masculinity, clings to her clitoridal activity and takes refuge in an identification with her phallic mother or her father. What can it be that decides in favour of this outcome? We can only suppose that it is a constitutional factor, a greater amount of activity, such as is ordinarily characteristic of a male. However that may be, the essence of this process is that at this point in development the wave of passivity is avoided which opens the way to the turn towards femininity. The extreme achievement of such a masculinity complex would appear to be the influencing of the choice of an object in the sense of manifest homosexuality. Analytic experience teaches us, to be sure, that female homosexuality is seldom or never a direct continuation of infantile masculinity. Even for a girl of this kind it seems necessary that she should take her father as an object for some time and enter the Oedipus situation. But afterwards, as a result of her inevitable disappointments from her father, she is driven to regress into her early masculinity complex. The significance of these disappointments must not be exaggerated; a girl who is destined to become feminine is not spared them, though they do not have the same effect. The predominance of the constitutional factor seems indisputable; but the two phases in the development of female homosexuality are well mirrored in the practices of homosexuals, who play the parts of mother and baby with each other as often and as clearly as those of husband and wife. . . .

I have promised to tell you of a few more psychical peculiarities of mature femininity, as we come across them in analytic observation. We do not lay claim to more than an average validity for these assertions; nor is it always easy to distinguish what should be ascribed to the influence of the sexual function and what to social breeding. Thus, we attribute a larger amount of narcissism to femininity, which also affects women's choice of object, so that to be loved is a stronger need for them than to love. The effect of penis-envy has a share, further, in the physical vanity of women, since they are bound to value their charms more highly as a late compensation for their original sexual inferiority.[6] Shame, which is considered to be a feminine characteristic *par excellence* but is far more a matter of convention than might be supposed, has as its purpose, we believe, concealment of genital deficiency. We are not forgetting that at a later time shame takes on other functions. It seems that women have made few contributions to the discoveries and inventions in the history of civilization; there is, however, one technique which they may have invented—that of plaiting and weaving. If that is so, we should be tempted to guess the unconscious motive for the achievement. Nature herself would seem to have given the model which this achievement imitates by causing the growth at maturity of the pubic hair that conceals the genitals. The step that remained to be taken lay in making the threads adhere to one another, while on the body they stick into the skin and are only matted together. If you reject this idea as fantastic and regard my belief in the influence of lack of a penis on the configuration of femininity as an *idée fixe*, I am of course defenceless.

The determinants of women's choice of an object are often made unrecognizable by social conditions. Where the choice is able to

6. Cf. Section II of "On Narcissism"

show itself freely, it is often made in accordance with the narcissistic ideal of the man whom the girl had wished to become. If the girl has remained in her attachment to her father—that is, in the Oedipus complex—her choice is made according to the paternal type. Since, when she turned from her mother to her father, the hostility of her ambivalent relation remained with her mother, a choice of this kind should guarantee a happy marriage. But very often the outcome is of a kind that presents a general threat to such a settlement of the conflict due to ambivalence. The hostility that has been left behind follows in the train of the positive attachment and spreads over on to the new object. The woman's husband, who to begin with inherited from her father, becomes after a time her mother's heir as well. So it may easily happen that the second half of a woman's life may be filled by the struggle against her husband, just as the shorter first half was filled by her rebellion against her mother. When this reaction has been lived through, a second marriage may easily turn out very much more satisfying.[7] Another alteration in a woman's nature, for which lovers are unprepared, may occur in a marriage after the first child is born. Under the influence of a woman's becoming a mother herself, an identification with her own mother may be revived, against which she had striven up till the time of her marriage, and this may attract all the available libido to itself, so that the compulsions to repeat reproduces an unhappy marriage between her parents. The difference in a mother's reaction to the birth of a son or a daughter shows that the old factor of lack of a penis has even now not lost its strength. A mother is only brought unlimited satisfaction by her relation to a son; this is altogether the most perfect, the most free from ambivalence of all human relationships.[8] A mother can transfer to her son the ambition which she has been obliged to suppress in herself, and she can expect from him the satisfaction of all that has been left over in her of her masculinity complex. Even a marriage is not made secure until the wife has succeeded in making her husband her child as well and in acting as a mother to him.

A woman's identification with her mother allows us to distinguish two strata: the pre-Oedipus one which rests on her affectionate attachment to her mother and takes her as a model, and the later one from the Oedipus complex which seeks to get rid of her mother and take her place with her father. We are no doubt justified in saying that much of both of them is left over for the future and that neither of them is adequately surmounted in the course of development. But the phase of the affectionate pre-Oedipus attachment is the decisive

7. This had already been remarked upon earlier, in "The Taboo of Virginity"
8. This point seems to have been made by Freud first in a footnote to Chapter VI of *Group Psychology*. He repeated it in the *Introductory Lectures*, XIII, and in Chapter V of *Civilization and its Discontents*.

one for a woman's future: during it preparations are made for the acquisition of the characteristics with which she will later fulfil her role in the sexual function and perform her invaluable social tasks. It is in this identification too that she acquires her attractiveness to a man, whose Oedipus attachment to his mother it kindles into passion. How often it happens, however, that it is only his son who obtains what he himself aspired to! One gets an impression that a man's love and a woman's are a phase apart psychologically.

The fact that women must be regarded as having little sense of justice is no doubt related to the predominance of envy in their mental life; for the demand for justice is a modification of envy and lays down the condition subject to which one can put envy aside. We also regard women as weaker in their social interests and as having less capacity for sublimating their instincts than men. The former is no doubt derived from the dissocial quality which unquestionably characterizes all sexual relations. Lovers find sufficiency in each other, and families too resist inclusion in more comprehensive associations.[9] The aptitude for sublimation is subject to the greatest individual variations. On the other hand I cannot help mentioning an impression that we are constantly receiving during analytic practice. A man of about thirty strikes us as a youthful, somewhat unformed individual, whom we expect to make powerful use of the possibilities for development opened up to him by analysis. A woman of the same age, however, oftens frightens us by her psychical rigidity and unchangeability. Her libido has taken up final positions and seems incapable of exchanging them for others. There are no paths open to further development; it is as though the whole process had already run its course and remains thenceforward insusceptible to influence—as though, indeed, the difficult development to femininity had exhausted the possibilities of the person concerned. As therapists we lament this state of things, even if we succeed in putting an end to our patient's ailment by doing away with her neurotic conflict.

That is all I had to say to you about femininity. It is certainly incomplete and fragmentary and does not always sound friendly. But do not forget that I have only been describing women in so far as their nature is determined by their sexual function. It is true that that influence extends very far; but we do not overlook the fact that an individual woman may be a human being in other respects as well. If you want to know more about femininity, enquire from your own experiences of life, or turn to the poets, or wait until science can give you deeper and more coherent information.

---

9. Cf. some remarks on this in Chapter XII (D) of *Group Psychology*.

Although research into the possibility of biological predisposition to gender identity is at too early a stage to justify acceptance the astonishing power of the socialization process has been repeatedly demonstrated. As Baker points out, socialization affects gender identity even in cases of psychosexual abnormalities. In the following selection, Tavris and Offir summarize and describe three theoretical models for the learning of differential sex roles: social learning, cognitive-developmental, and identification.

SOCIALIZATION THEORY

Carol Tavris
Carole Offir

FROM *The Longest War: Sex Differences in Perspective*

Social-Learning Theory

The basis of much contemporary research on sex typing is social-learning theory, a product of the behaviorist school of psychology. Behaviorists emphasize observable events and their consequences rather than internal feelings or drives. Years ago they formulated a set of principles to describe simple learning in animals; later they applied these principles to the complex learning skills and social behavior of people (thus the term *social*-learning theory). Behaviorists believe that all learning, including how we learn to be masculine or feminine, can be explained with the same basic rules.

The most important learning principle is that *behavior is controlled by its consequences.* An act that is regularly followed by a reward, or reinforcer, tends to occur again; an act that produces punishment—or is ignored—drops off in frequency. In the animal lab, for example, a hungry rat that gets a tasty morsel when it presses a bar will probably press the bar again. A rat that gets an electric shock when it presses the bar will soon stop pressing. The same principle works with people. If parents reward little girls for playing with dolls ("What a sweet little Mommy you are!"), girls will tend to play with dolls. If adults punish them for playing with baseball bats ("You don't want *that* for Christmas, silly"), girls will not develop much interest in Little League. Whether the rewards and punishments are handed out deliberately or not, the effect is the same.

With human beings, direct on-the-spot reinforcement is often unnecessary because language offers some convenient shortcuts. For instance, parents can tell their daughter that they disapprove of her hitting other children and that they like it when she helps in the kitchen. Anticipated rewards and punishments affect behavior just as real ones do. As psychologist Walter Mischel (1966) says, "A man does not have to be arrested for wearing dresses in public to learn about the consequences of such behavior." In addition, children can learn about the consequences of what they do by observing what happens to other people. Being the intelligent little persons that they are, they participate vicariously in the experiences of others and draw their own conclusions.

Most learning theorists feel that reinforcement alone cannot explain how children learn everything that their sex is expected to do and not to do. Parents would be kept busy twenty-four hours a day rewarding and punishing, rewarding and punishing, for each detail of behavior. Besides, most adults are not aware of the many mannerisms, gestures, and speech habits that are part of their sex roles. Such nuances, say the theorists, must be learned through imitation. Children do a lot of apparently spontaneous imitating; possibly they copy other people because adults have rewarded them for copying in the past, or perhaps they are simply natural mimics.

Most studies of imitation (or *modelling*) have been done in the laboratory rather than in real-life settings, and in the laboratory psychologists can often predict what sorts of models children will choose to imitate. For example, they tend to imitate adults who are friendly, warm, and attentive (Bandura and Huston 1961). They also imitate powerful people, that is, adults who control resources that are important to the child, whether intangibles like the privilege of playing outside or tangibles like cookies and toys (Bandura, Ross, and Ross 1963a; Mischel and Grusec 1966). Because parents are the most nurturant and powerful people in a child's world, they are assumed to be very effective models.

In order to explain how girls become feminine and boys masculine, social-learning theory assumes that children copy people similar to themselves—in particular, the same-sex parent and friends. As Mischel (1970) observes, "Boys do not learn baseball by watching girls and girls do not learn about fashions from observing boys." But research has not confirmed this key assumption. When children in an experiment have a chance to copy adults, they show no consistent tendency to mimic one sex more than the other. Researchers who have tried to correlate more global personality traits of parent and child (rather than concentrating on a particular action) do not find that children resemble the same-sex parent more than the opposite-sex parent (Maccoby and Jacklin 1974).

One plausible explanation for the discrepancy between theory and data is that children observe both sexes, but as they grow older they are most likely to do what they have learned by imitating same-sex models, because that path leads to reward and the other to punishment (Bandura and Walters 1963; Mischel 1970). "Both men and women know how to curse or to fight or use cosmetics or primp in front of mirrors," Mischel comments, but they don't do these things equally often. A three-year-old boy may innocently dress up in his mother's clothes and make-up, but if he does so at age fifteen he'll be in trouble.

Parents may be potent models, but children grow up with many influential people, not all of whom agree on what behavior is appropriate. (One of us recalls a favorite uncle who could be counted on to give her a really good "boy's toy" amidst all the dolls and clothes on her birthday.) For that matter, parents often do not agree on how to treat their children. Children have an entire smorgasbord of models to copy—parents, teachers, friends, siblings—with the result that each of us is a unique composite of many influences. Children must sift through conflicting demands and expectations, often finding, for example, that they cannot please both parents and friends at the same time. They have to figure out why something they did pleased their mother but angered their father, and why they were punished for fighting at one time but not another. And they have to deal with the fact that the behavior a parent displays may not be the one the parent rewards.[1]

Several writers have pointed out that fathers can teach their daughters to be feminine and mothers can teach their sons to be masculine, either by encouraging sex-typed behavior directly or by playing a complementary role (Mussen and Rutherford 1963). A parent may even communicate what's expected of the child by being mildly seductive (Chodorow 1974). Despite his liberated attitudes, a friend reports, "I tend to see little girls as cute, cuddly, and flirtatious—actually sexy—and I have quasi-sexual responses to them. Little boys evoke a completely different reaction in me." This friend is no dirty old man; he is simply perceptive about reactions that appear to be common though not always conscious.

---

1. Parents often punish aggressive children by spanking them. In doing so, they are modeling the very behavior they would like to get rid of: "Hitting is bad" (whack!). To their chagrin, the parents may discover later that their children have learned to express anger by hitting; aggressive children tend to have parents who harshly punish aggressiveness in the home (Bandura 1960; Sears, Maccoby, and Levin 1957). Social-learning research suggests that the best method is to praise the behavior you do want and ignore—rather than punish—the behavior you don't.

Cognitive-Development Theory

Social-learning theory views the child from the outside. It describes how the child is shaped by external events but has much less to say about what goes on in the child's head. Lawrence Kohlberg (1966, 1969) proposes another approach that emphasizes how children think. As learning theorists see it, children (and adults) of all ages learn things in the same ways—through reinforcement and modelling. But cognitive theory, like psychoanalytic theory, says that all children pass through certain *stages of development*, and that the way they learn depends on the stage they have reached. The Swiss psychologist Jean Piaget has shown that children's ability to reason and their understanding of the physical and social world change in predictable ways as they mature. Kohlberg argues that these changes affect the way they assimilate information about the sexes.

Thus, although two-year-olds can apply the labels "boy" and "girl" correctly to themselves and others, their concept of gender is very concrete. Preschool children rely on physical features such as dress and hairstyle to decide who falls in which category. Girls are people with long hair, boys are people who never wear dresses. Many children at this stage believe they can change their own gender at will simply by getting a haircut or a new outfit. They do not yet have the mental machinery to think of gender as adults do. All the reinforcement in the world, Kohlberg believes, won't alter that fact.

At this age, children can be quite rigid in their insistence that the rules they see as appropriate for a certain category of people or objects be obeyed. For example, a preschool girl may become confused or upset if her mother wears a man's suit to a Halloween party or if her father carries the mother's purse at the supermarket. The child seeks a tangible sign to distinguish between male and female and between herself and the opposite sex. A girl may reason, for instance, that since boys wear pants but girls often wear skirts, she'd better stick to skirts. One colleague recalls that she was the despair of her liberated relatives when, at four, she insisted on wearing dresses instead of practical jeans.

By the age of six or seven, children understand that gender is permanent. This is a consequence not of rewards and punishments, in Kohlberg's view, but of a growing ability to grasp that certain basic characteristics of people and objects do not change even though less basic ones may. Just as the amount of water remains the same when it is poured from a short, fat glass into a tall, thin one, a woman remains a woman when she wears pants. Children at this age know that they are and always will be female or male. Now their task is to find out what to do to bring their actions into line with the label. Social-learning theory says that girls learn feminine behavior and boys learn masculine behavior because they are rewarded for doing so. Cognitive-development theory takes a different position: it assumes that children and adults try to maintain a coherent and balanced picture of themselves and the world, in which beliefs, actions, and values are congruent. The knowledge that gender is permanent motivates the child to discover how to be a competent or "proper" girl or boy. As a consequence, she or he finds female or male activities rewarding. Reinforcements and models help show children how well they are doing, but essentially children socialize themselves.

Despite the differences between social-learning and cognitive-developmental theory, it is often hard to choose between them when explaining an observation. For example, one study found that bright children preferred dolls of the same sex as themselves—regarded as a sign of sex-typing—at younger ages than children of average intelligence (Kohlberg and Zigler 1967). The cognitive interpretation is that the bright child matures earlier in mental capacity and therefore understands and assimilates sex-role demands faster than the average child. That is, the bright child goes through the same developmental stages in the same order as other children, but more quickly. The social-learning interpretation is that intelligent children need fewer lessons (fewer reinforcements) before they know what is expected of them (Mischel 1970).

Identification

Many psychologists believe that a third process accounts for sex-role learning: the tendency of children to identify with the same-sex parent. The child wants to be like the parent and copies his or her values, mannerisms, personality, and ambitions, not just specific acts. Because of identification, children develop a stronger emotional commitment to their sex role than to behavior that is not tied to their masculinity or femininity. Freud's theory of psychosexual development is an identification theory *par excellence*, and it was Freud who first introduced the term. Freud believed that children incorporate ("introject") large chunks of the same-sex parent's personality into their own, mainly as a way of reducing the anxiety and conflict caused by Oedipal desires. Today most theories of identification do not give such a central place to sexual motivation. Instead they emphasize the child's desire to be similar to someone of the same sex; to be like someone who is powerful; to enjoy vicariously the position of someone who has status; or to reproduce the feelings experienced when the model gave the child love and attention. In some theories, attachment and dependency cause identification; in others identification leads to attachment and dependency.

One appeal of this approach is that it is more encompassing than, say, the behaviorists' attention to specific acts. Instead of counting reinforcements and situational forces that cause a boy to strike back at the neighborhood bully, identification theories can leapfrog over particular events and concentrate on a global personality trait, the boy's aggressiveness. Most behaviorists do not much like the concept of personality; they prefer to concentrate on events they can see and quantify. Personality theorists think that people acquire certain motivations and traits—ambitiousness, warmth, aggressiveness, dependence, and so on—that lead them to behave consistently across situations. The problem is that personality is hard to measure. Suppose you want to know, as many researchers do, what sorts of parents produce demure little girls and tough little boys. There are more studies in this than summer sunflowers, but they yield a tangle of conclusions. Most studies try to account for some personality trait in the child by looking at the parent's personality, perhaps by relating the child's aggressiveness, dependence, or "femininity" to the parent's warmth, hostility, or child-rearing philosophy (for example, permissive vs. restrictive). These efforts are like trying to photograph bacteria with a Brownie. The method is usually too clumsy for its object.

The general concept of identification is plausible, but in practice it is hard to say when identification has occurred. Often people use the term loosely, as in, "I respected my father, but I identified with my mother." Psychologists define the term differently, depending on who is theorizing. For one it means that a child wants to be like a parent; for another that a child actually behaves like the parent; for a third that a child feels closest to the parent. You can see how hard it is to interpret this concept. If you walk, talk, and bake like your mother, if you have her endearing mannerisms and infuriating habits, but you have the literary tastes of your father and want to be an accountant like him, with which parent have you identified? In addition, in some studies people say they are "most like" one parent but "feel closest to" the other. Clearly the idea that girls learn to be feminine by identifying with their mothers and boys learn to be masculine by identifying with their fathers is too simple.

Identification has been used to explain not only the traditional course of sex-role learning but less traditional outcomes. For example, numerous researchers have been interested in why some girls become career women. They generally find that girls whose mothers worked outside the home or had a career are more likely than girls with homemaking mothers to follow a career and to have unconventional attitudes toward the female role (Frieze, Parsons, and Ruble 1972; Tangri 1972; Almquist and Angrist 1971). But some nontraditional women apparently got that way by identifying with (feeling closer to) their fathers rather than their mothers (Tangri 1972). The conclusion at the moment is that a girl is most likely to grow up non-traditional if she identifies with either her father or her nontraditional mother. (Until very recently, little work was done with nontraditional men, possibly because they are an even rarer species.)

Even when a child does turn out like a parent, "identification" is not necessarily the process responsible. Indeed, the child's behavior may not be based on the parent's at all. Albert Bandura (1969) illustrates this point with a parable about a big-game hunter who came face to face with a hungry lion. "As he prepared to shoot the onrushing beast, the gun jammed. Helpless and terrified, the hunter promptly closed his eyes and began to pray rapidly. Moments passed and, much to his surprise, nothing happened. Puzzled by this unexpected turn of events, the hunter cocked his head and slowly opened his eyes to find the lion also bowed in prayer. The jubilant hunter loudly exclaimed, 'Thank God, you are responding to my prayers!' The lion promptly replied, 'Not at all. I'm saying grace.'"

Despite such problems, identification theories raise some interesting issues. For example, in many ways growing up may be easier for girls than for boys. Most theorists believe that infants of both sexes start out with a stronger attachment to the mother, because she does most of the childcare and provides most of the nurturance. For girls, identification is relatively simple; they just continue the attachment to the mother.[2] For boys, the matter is more complicated. In order to become masculine and enter the world of men, they must break away from their mothers and identify with their fathers, who are around the house less often and are less involved with the children. Girls have many examples around them of what women do, but boys have a much vaguer idea of what men do; they are surrounded by female relatives and teachers in their early years. David Lynn (1966) thinks that "the father as a model for the boy is analogous to a man showing the major outline but lacking most details." A boy knows he should *not* be a sissy but has a harder time figuring out what he *should* be. He may turn to fiction and symbolic models, following a fantasized stereotyped image of the male role instead of identifying with a real person, as girls do.

These three theories give us some good ideas of how sex-typing occurs in general, but it is hard to predict how any given child will turn out. A child does not copy the parents in a mechanical way. The child may follow in the parent's footsteps only if the parent is wearing comfortable shoes—and is satisfied with his or her role (Frieze,

2. Freudians would disagree; see Chapter 5 [of Tavris and Offir].

Parsons, and Ruble 1972). If a mother chronically complains about her fate, her daughter may vow, "I'll never be like her!" Or the mother may seem happy enough, but her daughter may imitate the father for reasons that have nothing to do with gender. Perhaps she just likes him more. Maccoby and Jacklin tell of a little girl who held tenaciously to the belief that only boys could become doctors, even though her own mother was a physician. Apparently she was influenced more by the attitudes and behavior of people outside her family than by the real-life model who was closest to her.

It is easier to play quarterback on Monday morning, and all these theories can trace an individual's adult behavior to childhood antecedents after the fact. A social-learning theorist would look at the person's history of rewards and punishments—all that family attention for good grades and apathy for making the team (or vice versa). An identification theorist would try to see which parent the person resembles most, especially in values and ambitions. A cognitive theorist would point to the child's mental processes and ways of assimilating information.

Although learning, cognitive, and identification theories emphasize different aspects of sex-role learning, many psychologists help themselves to a little of each. For example, social-learning theorists are supposed to stick to observable behavior, but many of them feel comfortable with the idea that identification is more than just imitation and that children adopt not only behaviors but rules and values. Kohlberg's ideas have influenced many researchers who began their work in the social-learning tradition. Eventually the best elements of the three formulations may be combined into one unified approach.

REFERENCES

Almquist, Elizabeth M., and Angrist, Shirley S. 1971. Role model influences on college women's career aspirations. *Merrill-Palmer quarterly* 17:263–79.

Bandura, Albert 1969. Social-learning theory of identificatory processes. In *Handbook of socialization theory and research*, ed. David A. Goslin, pp. 213–62. Chicago: Rand McNally.

———. 1960. Relationship of family patterns to child behavior disorders. Progress report, United States Public Health Research Grant M1734. Stanford University.

Bandura, Albert, and Huston, Aletha C. 1961. Identification as a process of incidental learning. *Journal of abnormal and social psychology* 63:311–18.

Bandura, Albert; Ross, Dorothea; and Ross, Sheila A. 1963a. A comparative test of the status envy, social power, and secondary reinforcement theories of identificatory learning. *Journal of abnormal and social psychology* 67:527–34.

Bandura, Albert, and Walters, Richard H. 1963. *Social learning and personality development*. New York: Holt, Rinehart and Winston.

Chodorow, Nancy. 1974. Family structure and feminine personality. In *Woman, culture, and society*, eds. Michelle Zimbalist Rosaldo and Louise Lamphere, pp. 43–66. Stanford: Stanford University Press.

Frieze, Irene; Parson, Jacque; and Ruble, Diane. 1972. Some determinants of career aspirations in college women. Paper read at UCLA Symposium on Sex Roles and Sex Differences. Los Angeles.

Kohlberg, Lawrence. 1966. A cognitive-developmental analysis of children's sex-role concepts and attitudes. In *The development of sex differences*, ed. Eleanor E. Maccoby, pp. 82–173. Stanford, California: Stanford University Press.

––––––. 1969. Stage and sequence: the cognitive-developmental approach to socialization. In *Handbook of socialization theory and research*, ed. David A. Goslin, pp. 347–480. Chicago: Rand McNally.

Kohlberg, Lawrence, and Zigler, Edward. 1967. The impact of cognitive maturity on the development of sex-role attitudes in the years 4 to 8. *Genetic psychology monographs* 75:89–165.

Lynn, David B. 1966. The process of learning parental and sex-role identification. *Journal of marriage and the family* 28:466–70.

Maccoby, Eleanor Emmons, and Jacklin, Carol Nagy. 1974. *The psychology of sex differences*. Stanford, California: Stanford University Press.

Mischel, Walter. 1966. A social-learning view of sex differences in behavior. In *The development of sex differences*, ed. Eleanor E. Maccoby, pp. 56–81. Stanford, California: Stanford University Press.

––––––. 1970. Sex-typing and socialization. In *Carmichael's manual of child psychology*, vol. 2, ed. Paul H. Mussen, pp. 3–72. New York: Wiley.

Mischel, Walter, and Grusec, Joan. 1966. Determinants of the rehearsal and transmission of neutral and aversive behaviors. *Journal of personality and social psychology* 3:197–205.

Mussen, Paul H., and Rutherford, Eldred. 1963. Parent-child relations and parental personality in relation to young children's sex-role preferences. *Child development* 34:589–607.

Sears, Robert R.; Maccoby, Eleanor E.; and Levin, Harry. 1957. *Patterns of child rearing*. Evanston, Illinois: Row, Peterson.

Tangri, Sandra Schwartz. 1972. Determinants of occupational role innovation among college women. *Journal of social issues* 28(2):177–99.

The classic work from which the selection that follows has been excerpted is based on a comprehensive literature search of texts of social-learning theory from 1966 through 1974. That impressive work provided the catalyst for a great deal of research that has taken place since 1974, research that both confirms and contradicts the findings summarized here. We can look forward to new understandings of sex-role differences from scholars in this active and dynamic research area.

Maccoby's and Jacklin's research is additionally valuable in the context of this chapter because of their concern with the relationship of age to sex-role development. Developmental changes must certainly be considered in any attempt to identify the origins of sex differences.

SUMMARY AND COMMENTARY

Eleanor Emmons Maccoby
Carol Nagy Jacklin

FROM *The Psychology of Sex Differences*

Summary of Our Findings

Unfounded Beliefs About Sex Differences

1. That girls are more "social" than boys. The findings: First, the two sexes are equally interested in social (as compared with nonsocial) stimuli, and are equally proficient at learning through imitation of models. Second, in childhood, girls are no more dependent than boys on their caretakers, and boys are no more willing to remain alone. Furthermore, girls are not more motivated to achieve for social rewards. The two sexes are equally responsive to social reinforcement, and neither sex consistently learns better for this form of reward than for other forms. Third, girls do not spend more time interacting with playmates; in fact, the opposite is true, at least at certain ages. Fourth, the two sexes appear to be equally "empathic," in the sense of understanding the emotional reactions of others; however, the measures of this ability have so far been narrow.

Any differences that exist in the "sociability" of the two sexes are more of kind than of degree. Boys are highly oriented toward a peer group and congregate in larger groups; girls associate in pairs or small groups of age-mates, and may be somewhat more oriented toward adults, although the evidence for this is weak.

2. That girls are more "suggestible" than boys. The findings: First, boys and girls are equally likely to imitate others spontaneously. Second, the two sexes are equally susceptible to persuasive communications, and in face-to-face social-influence situations (Asch-type experiments), sex differences are usually not found. When they are, girls are somewhat more likely to adapt their own judgments to those of the group, although there are studies with reverse findings. Boys, on the other hand, appear to be more likely to accept peer-group values when these conflict with their own.

3. That girls have lower self-esteem. The findings: The sexes are highly similar in their overall self-satisfaction and self-confidence throughout childhood and adolescence; there is little information about adulthood, but what exists does not show a sex difference. However, there are some qualitative differences in the areas of functioning where the two sexes have greatest self-confidence: girls rate themselves higher in the area of social competence; boys more often see themselves as strong, powerful, dominant, "potent."

Through most of the school years, the two sexes are equally likely to believe they can influence their own fates, rather than being the victims of chance or fate. During the college years (but not earlier or later), men have a greater sense of control over their own fate, and greater confidence in their probable performance on a variety of school-related tasks that they undertake. However, this does not imply a generally lower level of self-esteem among women of this age.

4. That girls are better at rote learning and simple repetitive tasks, boys at tasks that require higher-level cognitive processing and the inhibition of previously learned responses. The findings: Neither sex is more susceptible to simple conditioning, or excels in simple paired-associates or other forms of "rote" learning. Boys and girls are equally proficient at discrimination learning, reversal shifts, and probability learning, all of which have been interpreted as calling for some inhibition of "available" responses. Boys are somewhat more impulsive (that is, lacking in inhibition) during the preschool years, but the sexes do not differ thereafter in the ability to wait for a delayed reward, to inhibit early (wrong) responses on the Matching Familiar Figures test (MFF) or on other measures of impulsivity.

5. That boys are more "analytic." The findings: The sexes do not differ on tests of analytic cognitive style. Boys do not excel at tasks that call for "decontextualization," or disembedding, except when the task is visual-spatial; boys' superiority on the latter tasks seems to be accounted for by spatial ability (see below), and no sex differences in analytic ability are implied. Boys and girls are equally likely to respond to task-irrelevant aspects of a situation, so that neither sex excels in analyzing and selecting only those elements needed for the task.

6. That girls are more affected by heredity, boys by environment.
The findings: Male identical twins are more alike than female identical twins, but the two sexes show equivalent amount of resemblance to their parents.

Boys are more susceptible to damage by a variety of noxious environmental agents, both prenatally and postnatally, but this does not imply that they are generally more influenced by environmental factors. The correlations between parental socialization techniques and child behavior are higher for boys in some studies, higher for girls in others. Furthermore, the two sexes learn with equal facility in a wide variety of learning situations; if learning is the primary means whereby environmental effects come about, sex equivalence is indicated.

7. That girls lack achievement motivation. The findings: In the pioneering studies of achievement motivation, girls scored higher than boys in achievement imagery under "neutral" conditions. Boys need to be challenged by appeals to ego or competitive motivation to bring their achievement imagery up to the level of girls'. Boys' achievement motivation does appear to be more responsive to competitive arousal than girls', but this does not imply a generally higher level. In fact, observational studies of achievement strivings either have found no sex difference or have found girls to be superior.

8. That girls are auditory, boys visual. The findings: The majority of studies report no differences in response to sounds by infants of the two sexes. At most ages boys and girls are equally adept at discriminating speech sounds. No sex difference is found in memory for sounds previously heard.

Among newborn infants, no study shows a sex difference in fixation to visual stimuli. During the first year of life, results are variable, but neither sex emerges as more responsive to visual stimuli. From infancy to adulthood, the sexes are highly similar in interest in visual stimuli, ability to discriminate among them, identification of shapes, distance perception, and a variety of other measures of visual perception.

Sex Differences That Are Fairly Well Established

1. That girls have greater verbal ability than boys. It is probably true that girls' verbal abilities mature somewhat more rapidly in early life, although there are a number of recent studies in which no sex difference has been found. During the period from preschool to early adolescence, the sexes are very similar in their verbal abilities. At about age 11, the sexes begin to diverge, with female superiority increasing through high school and possibly beyond. Girls score higher on tasks involving both receptive and productive language, and on "high-level" verbal tasks (analogies, comprehension of difficult written material, creative writing) as well as upon the "lower-level" measures (fluency). The magnitude of the female advantage varies, being most commonly about one-quarter of a standard deviation.

2. That boys excel in visual-spatial ability. Male superiority on visual-spatial tasks is fairly consistently found in adolescence and adulthood, but not in childhood. The male advantage on spatial tests increases through the high school years up to a level of about .40 of a standard deviation. The sex difference is approximately equal on analytic and nonanalytic spatial measures.

3. That boys excel in mathematical ability. The two sexes are similar in their early acquisition of quantitative concepts, and their mastery of arithmetic during the grade-school years. Beginning at about age 12–13, boys' mathematical skills increase faster than girls'. The greater rate of improvement appears to be not entirely a function of the number of math courses taken, although the question has not been extensively studied. The magnitude of the sex differences varies greatly from one population to another, and is probably not so great as the difference in spatial ability. Both visual-spatial and verbal processes are sometimes involved in the solution of mathematical problems; some math problems can probably be solved in either way, while others cannot, a fact that may help to explain the variation in degree of sex difference from one measure to another.

4. That males are more aggressive. The sex difference in aggression has been observed in all cultures in which the relevant behavior has been observed. Boys are more aggressive both physically and verbally. They show the attenuated forms of aggression (mock-fighting, aggressive fantasies) as well as the direct forms more frequently than girls. The sex difference is found as early as social play begins—at age 2 or 2½. Although the aggressiveness of both sexes declines with age, boys and men remain more aggressive through the college years. Little information is available for older adults. The primary victims of male aggression are other males—from early ages, girls are chosen less often as victims.

Open Questions: Too Little Evidence, or Findings Ambiguous

1. Tactile sensitivity. Most studies of tactile sensitivity in infancy, and of the ability to perceive by touch at later ages, do not find sex differences. When differences are found, girls are more sensitive, but such findings are rare enough that we cannot have confidence that the difference is a meaningful one. Additional work is needed with some of the standard psychophysical measurements of tactile sensitivity, over a range of ages. Most of the existing studies in which the data are analyzed by sex have been done with newborns.

2. Fear, timidity, and anxiety. Observational studies of fearful behavior usually do not find sex differences. Teacher ratings and self-reports, however, usually find girls to be more timid or more anxious. In the case of self-reports, the problem is to know whether the results reflect "real" differences or only differences in the willingness to report anxious feelings. Of course, the very willingness to assert that one is afraid may lead to fearful behavior, so the distinction may not turn out to be important. However, it would be desirable to have measures other than self-report (which make up the great bulk of the data from early school age on) as a way of clarifying the meaning of the girls' greater self-attribution of fears and anxiety.

3. Activity level. Sex differences in activity level do not appear in infancy. They begin to be seen when children reach the age of social play. During the preschool years, when sex differences are found they are in the direction of boys' being more active. However, there are many instances in which sex differences have not been found. Some, but not all, of the variance among studies can be accounted for by whether the measurement situation was social. That is, boys appear to be especially stimulated to bursts of high activity by the presence of other boys. But the exact nature of the situational control over activity level remains to be established. Activity level is responsive to a number of motivational states—fear, anger, curiosity—and is therefore not a promising variable for identifying stable individual or group differences. More detailed observations are needed on the vigor and qualitative nature of play.

4. Competitiveness. When sex differences are found, they usually show boys to be more competitive, but there are many studies finding sex similarity. Madsen and his colleagues find sex differences to be considerably weaker than differences between cultures and, in a number of studies, entirely absent. Almost all the research on competition has involved situations in which competition is maladaptive. In the Prisoner's Dilemma game, for example, the sexes are equally cooperative, but this is in a situation in which cooperation is to the long-run advantage of both players and the issue is one of developing mutual trust. It appears probable that in situations in which competitiveness produces increased individual rewards, males would be more competitive, but this is a guess based on commonsense considerations, such as the male interest in competitive sports, not upon research in controlled settings. The age of the subject and the identity of the opponent no doubt make a difference—there is evidence that young women hesitate to compete against their boyfriends.

5. Dominance. Dominance appears to be more of an issue within boys' groups than girls' groups. Boys make more dominance attempts (both successful and unsuccessful) toward one another than do girls. They also more often attempt to dominate adults. The dominance relations between the sexes are complex: in childhood, the sex segregation of play groups means that neither sex frequently attempts to dominate the other. In experimental situations in which the sexes are combined, the evidence is ambiguous on whether either sex is more successful in influencing the behavior of the other. Among adult mixed pairs or groups, formal leadership tends to go to males in the initial phases of interaction, but the direction of influence becomes more sex-equal the longer the relationship lasts, with "division of authority" occurring along lines of individual competencies and division of labor.

6. *Compliance.* In childhood, girls tend to be more compliant to the demands and directions of adults. This compliance does not extend, however, to willingness to accept directions from, or be influenced by, age-mates. Boys are especially concerned with maintaining their status in the peer group, and are probably therefore more vulnerable to pressures and challenges from this group, although this has not been well established. As we have seen in the discussion of dominance, it is not clear that in mixed-sex interactions either sex is consistently more willing to comply with the wishes of the other.

7. *Nurturance and "maternal" behavior.* There is very little evidence concerning the tendencies of boys and girls to be nurturant or helpful toward younger children or animals. Cross-cultural work does indicate that girls between the ages of 6 and 10 are more often seen behaving nurturantly. Within our own society, the rare studies that report nurturant behavior are observational studies of free play among nursery school children; sex differences are not found in these studies, but the setting normally does not include children much younger than the subjects being observed, and it may be that the relevant elicitors are simply not present. Female hormones play a role in maternal behavior in lower animals, and the same may be true in human beings, but there is no direct evidence that this is the case. There is very little information on the responses of adult men to infants and children, so it is not possible to say whether adult women are more disposed to behave maternally than men are to behave paternally. If there is a sex difference in the tendency to behave nurturantly, it does not generalize to a greater female tendency to behave altruistically over varying situations. The studies of people's willingness to help others in distress have sometimes shown men more helpful, sometimes women, depending on the identity of the person needing help and the kind of help that is needed. The overall finding on altruism is one of sex similarity.

In Chapters 5 and 6, we raised the question of whether the female is more passive than the male. The answer is complex, but mainly negative. The two sexes are highly similar in their willingness to explore a novel environment, when they are both given freedom to do so. Both are highly responsive to social situations of all kinds, and although some individuals tend to withdraw from social interaction and simply watch from the sidelines, such persons are no more likely to be female than male. Girls' greater compliance with adult demands is just as likely to take an active as a passive form; running errands and performing services for others are active processes. Young boys seem more likely than girls to put out energy in the form of bursts of strenuous physical activity, but the girls are not sitting idly by while the boys act; they are simply playing more quietly. And their play is fully as organized and planful (possibly more so), and has as much the quality of actively imposing their own design upon their surroundings as does boys' play. It is true that boys and men are more aggressive, but this does not mean that females are the passive victims of aggression—they do not yield or withdraw when aggressed against any more frequently than males do, at least during the phases of childhood for which observations are available. With respect to dominance, we have noted the curious fact that while males are more dominant, females are not especially submissive, at least not to the dominance attempts of boys and girls their own age. In sum, the term "passive" does not accurately describe the most common female personality attributes.

Returning to one of the major conclusions of our survey of sex differences, there are many popular beliefs about the psychological characteristics of the two sexes that have proved to have little or no basis in fact. How is it possible that people continue to believe, for example, that girls are more "social" than boys, when careful observation and measurement in a variety of situations show no sex difference? Of course it is possible that we have not studied those particular situations that contribute most to the popular beliefs. But if this is the problem, it means that the alleged sex difference exists only in a limited range of situations, and the sweeping generalizations embodied in popular beliefs are not warranted.

However, a more likely explanation for the perpetuation of "myths," we believe, is the fact that stereotypes are such powerful things. An ancient truth is worth restating here: if a generalization about a group of people is believed, whenever a member of that group behaves in the expected way the observer notes it and his belief is confirmed and strengthened; when a member of the group behaves in a way that is not consistent with the observer's expectations, the instance is likely to pass unnoticed, and the observer's generalized belief is protected from disconfirmation. We believe that this well-documented process occurs continually in relation to the expected and perceived behavior of males and females, and results in the perpetuation of myths that would otherwise die out under the impact of negative evidence. However, not all unconfirmed beliefs about the two sexes are of this sort. It is necessary to reconsider the nature of the evidence that permits us to conclude what is myth and what is (at least potentially) reality.

PART II

The Sexual Economy:

Its Operation

3

In our search for the roots of woman's oppression, we have looked to the fields of anthropology, sociology, psychology, philosophy, economics, biology, literature, and religion. From those disciplines we have culled some of the most cogent, as well as the most influential and widely accepted, theories of the origins of the sexual economy and sex differences. The catalog includes the rise of the concept of private property and the appropriation by man of the fruits of woman's labor; man's fear of woman's "power" and the consequent employment of his mythologies and religions to define woman as "the other"; and biological differences, real or perceived, that have contributed to her subordination and devaluation.

CHAPTER 3

From Pit to Pedestal

Less problematical than the question of its origins, perhaps, but fully as complicated, is that of the perpetuation of the sexual economy. Because separation of the sexes, rather than their shared humanity, characterizes human history from the earliest writings, theories that seek to account for that separation assume central importance in the study of women. That separation becomes a point of departure for analysis of the oppression of women. De Beauvoir's notion of "otherness" inevitably and invariably becomes "secondness." Moreover, it does so consistently, at times and in places notable for the most progressive as well as the most regressive notions of human possibilities. Although it is certainly true, as Ruth H. Bloch has argued, that the history of sex roles cannot be traced in one continuous line of development but must be seen as proceeding in a "tension between similarity and distinctiveness in men and women" (1978:237), it is nonetheless true that sexual oppression has enjoyed an astonishingly consistent perpetuation through time and space.

Social scientists have taught us in this century to think of much of human behavior as having been "conditioned" or "socialized." And indeed, much of the research in women's studies of the last decade has revealed the importance of those processes in the creation of a complex of institutionalized social values and cultural attitudes about woman that have placed severe limitations on her. Some attention is paid in this chapter to the function of socialization in the continuing oppression of women. We believe, however, that it is important to see that process in the larger historical context in which the vested interest of men—at least of some men—is in maintaining women's secondness. Consequently, this chapter examines a number of "control strategies" that have been exercised, often under the guise of protection, to ensure woman's continued compliance with her inferior status.

As significant, perhaps, for the general understanding of human behavior as for that of sexual oppression is the emergence in this examination of the supporting framework of mythology within which man has for centuries controlled and directed women's lives. The mythology has prescribed an ideal of feminine behavior, which in turn has sporadically and selectively rescued woman from the pit of fear and contempt in which we saw her cast by the patriarchs. Having been rescued, however, she has been placed on a pedestal that has divested her of any of her former remnants of autonomy. The pedestal as a metaphor derives quite clearly from the concepts of otherness and separation with which we are here concerned. And, like the pit, it embodies the dysjunction between the view men choose to have of women at any given time and the realities of women's lives. The casting of sexual oppression into myth and symbol has not only intensified the effects of her separateness but has made resistance to it all the more difficult.

The ideal of feminine behavior that reached its apotheosis in the nineteenth century and has come to be called the "cult of true womanhood" (Welter 1972:245) was shaped over the course of many centuries. It appears that the "paterfamilias" model as described by Aristotle dates from earliest written history and continues with cultural variations to contemporary times. Within that context, however, the extent of limitations placed on women, if not the basic fact of their secondness, seems to have varied with different belief systems and economic structures. Nor did periods of flowering or blight in the general human struggle for freedom and dignity necessarily include or exclude women. Even in the "cradle" of Western democracy, women's lives were, if anything, more cramped than under the more primitive social organizations it replaced. While the men of classical Athens, for example, spent their days in the beautiful public buildings—the marketplace, the gymnasium—women of the upper classes remained in their dark, squalid homes (Pomeroy 1975:79). Valued almost solely in their role as mothers, their lives were so constricted that "it was even possible in some law cases to pretend that they did not exist" (Bullough 1974:66).

Roman women of the upper classes fared generally better. Nevertheless, the fear and distrust of women discussed extensively in the previous chapter is pervasive in extant Roman literature. Like the Homeric period Greeks who blamed Pandora for opening the box containing all the evils and diseases that beset humanity, Romans blamed the alleged meddling of women for a host of their social ills. In spite of legislation that gave the Roman woman some independence in the marriage relationship and some personal autonomy not enjoyed by her Greek sister, it is clear that the notion of woman's otherness, which was to become the foundation for a symbology of sexual oppression, obtained in ancient Rome. A familiar note is struck in the writings of a second-century A.D. Roman, Juvenal, whose convictions about woman's proper sphere are apparently outraged by the intellectual pretensions of a class of women who will be called in later centuries, with comparable contempt, "bluestockings": "I hate a woman," he complains, "who is forever consulting and poring over the 'Grammar of Palaemon,' who observes all the rules and laws of language, who like an antiquary quotes verses that I never heard of, and corrects her unlettered female friends for slips of speech that no man need trouble about; let husbands at least be permitted to make slips in grammar" (quoted in Bullough 1974:93). Juvenal's disdain is reflected in Roman legal theory, supported by the underlying principles of *infirmitas sexus* and *levitas animi*, the "weakness and light-mindedness of the female sex," which mandated all women to be under the custody of males (Pomeroy 1975:150).

More than the slight legal gains Roman women had won were lost during the centuries in which Christianity gained a foothold and became accepted as the dominant religion in the Western world. The contempt for women that informed *infirmitas sexus* and *levitas animi* deepened with the focus of the new religion on asceticism and renunciation of worldly things. Sexual purity became an essential tenet in Christianity, and women were increasingly suspect because of the sexual desire they stirred in men. In her analysis of "Misogynism and Virginal Feminism in the Fathers of the Church," Rosemary Radford Ruether discusses patristic doctrine, which, drawing upon the Aristotelian notion of the mind-body dualism, deemed spirituality to be exclusively male and assigned carnality unequivocally to woman. That "natural" carnality of woman cast her into the pit from which she might emerge only as mother or virgin. The former redemption derived from the necessity of procreation, but it was only a partial redemption. According to the patristic Augustine, totally sinless procreation was not possible, and the marital act was therefore intrinsically debasing both to men and to women. A surer route to redemption under patristic doctrine was offered to women, as well as to men, who chose chastity. As virgin, woman was allowed a share of spirituality and personhood, but only at the expense of crushing out her bodily and her female "nature." The redeemed woman thus becomes "unnatural" in a way contrary to the God-given order. "That woman has a rational mind equivalent to man's is never entirely denied," Ruether writes. "But since she is somehow made peculiarly the symbol of 'body' in relation to the male . . . and is associated with all the sensual and depraved characteristics of mind through this peculiar 'corporeality,' her salvation must be seen not as an affirmation of her nature but a negation of her nature, both physically and mentally, and a transformation into a possibility beyond her natural capacities" (1974:161). Thus was the field prepared for the worship of virginity that culminated in the cult of the Virgin Mary, a variation on an ancient source of sexual oppression.

Scholars do not agree about the effect on the lives of women of the cult of the Virgin or about its sources. It is the case, however, that the attitudes of the Christian fathers toward women were at least temporarily modified by the adoration of Mary. Woman could no longer be viewed merely as the evil temptress, the woman who stood between Adam and God in Paradise. Of even more dubious effect on the ordinary lives of women was the "cult of the lady," a corollary to Mariolatry of the twelfth and thirteenth centuries, in which knights died for the honor of their ladies (as well as their God). The exaltation of the lady was not practiced outside the aristocratic caste, and even within that class, as Barbara Tuchman has pointed out, courtly love was an "artificial, a literary convention, a fantasy (like modern pornography) more for purposes of discussion than for everyday practice" (1978:36). That the adoration of the Virgin and the lady resided primarily in fiction or myth is not at all to minimize the point that is a major theme of this work: fictional accounts of the nature and role of women can be most damaging, especially as compounded by the tension in the lives of women between the fiction and the reality they know. In this case, the examples both of the Virgin Mary and of the lady were raised before women as the nearly impossible, but nonetheless attainable, ideal. The image of carnal woman, however, survived the veneration of Mary and the worship of the lady, and the stage was set for centuries of shunting women between the pit and the pedestal (Power 1975:26–27).

As one traces the progress of women through the centuries, the significance of class emerges strongly. For, as Greek women of the upper classes lived out their lives in dimly lit townhouses and well-to-do Roman women lived in families in which, along with children and slaves, they were valued primarily as property, the lot of most women was of necessity quite different. The effect of class can be seen with clarity during the Middle Ages. Under the feudal system that dominated the medieval economy, the demands of survival ensured women's equal participation in the economy. "A social position," Eileen Power suggests, "is never solely created by theatrical notions; it owes more to the inescapable pressure of facts, the give and take of daily life. And the social position which these facts created in medieval society was neither one of superiority nor of inferiority, but one of rough and ready equality. For in daily life man could not do without woman" (1975:34). Peasant women worked side by side with their husbands, although they generally earned less for the same work. Women were active in the crafts and guilds, and although they were barred from certain trades, they had monopolies of others, usually the food and textile trades. The merchant's wife moved freely in town and country or formed with her husband, children, and servants or apprentices the independent commodity- or services-producing unit that was fundamental to economic life in Western civilization prior to the industrial revolution. The chatelaine or lady of the manor discharged onerous duties in the management of a large household, which was a self-sufficient center of industry, producing within its walls all the necessities for the maintenance of life. She did so often during periods of long absence of her husband, who was occupied by the continual wars of the period. There would come a time, however, when man could do without woman, or believed he could. That time, attendant upon the hegemony of the bourgeoisie in the eighteenth century and the isolation of women from the "give and take of daily life," would see the attempt to create a social position for middle-class women out of theatrical notions, out of a web of fiction and myth.

If the early chapters of this book have placed emphasis upon the function of the church in shaping attitudes about women, it is because for many hundreds of years Christianity was deeply rooted within the basic fabric of Western culture and society. "Christianity was the matrix of medieval life: even cooking instructions called for boiling an egg 'during the length of time wherein you can say a Miserère'" (Tuchman 1978:32). The medieval church had popularized the notion, inherited from Aristotle, of a divinely ordered universe, in which all animate as well as inanimate beings are arranged in a fixed and connected hierarchy. The notion survived into the sixteenth century as the "great chain of being," to which all creatures and substances are assigned a precise position, with man occupying a place between the angels and the beasts. If the Renaissance version of the great chain of being was an expression of a new optimism, of faith in a harmonious, discernible world order, the growth of

Renaissance humanism did not in fact win a decisive victory over the old medieval misanthropy. E. M. W. Tillyard, in his classic study of *The Elizabethan World Picture*, has pointed out the negative implications of such a world view: "If the Elizabethans believed in an ideal order animating earthly order, they were terrified lest it should be upset, and appalled by the visible tokens of disorder that suggested its upsetting" (n.d.:16). As we shall see, successive centuries, drawing upon an inherited medieval-Renaissance fear of disorder and chaos, assigned woman firmly to an inferior position in the hierarchical order and employed a variety of control strategies to ensure that she did not contribute to the "upsetting" of the ideal order.

With the waning of the power of the church, the growth of humanism, and the ultimate appearance of Protestantism in the sixteenth century came the diminution of adoration of the Virgin Mary and of the lady in the context of courtly love. In fact, Bullough tells us, "Protestants in general condemned the courtly lover's worship of women as disgusting effeminacy" (1974:195). Certainly, the distrust of women by the patristic fathers detailed by Ruether had no parallel among the Protestant fathers. But if reformed theology accorded women greater respect in the marriage role, it reinforced patriarchal dominance within family life, based upon the model of the "unmediated power of a thundering patriarchal God" (Bloch 1978:238–39). If anything, the Reformation saw the hardening of notions about women's place, and in general, the good woman was one who accepted her subordinate role and kept her place. In the more "practical" spirit of the age, Martin Luther declared that "woman was created for the benefit (*usum*) of man, that is, for the prudent and sensible training of children. Everyone does best when he does that for which he was created. 'A woman handles a child better with her smallest finger than a man does with both hands (*Fausten*).' Therefore, let everyone stick to that work to which God has called him and for which he was created" (1959:133–34).

It was also during this period that women suffered one of the highest costs in the long history of sexual apartheid. "The great age of witchcraft" extended in Europe from the mid-fifteenth century to the late seventeenth, and during that time many thousands were burned at the stake or otherwise executed, the large majority of whom were women.[1] It is not without irony that the witch craze grew in intensity during a period of Renaissance humanism and reached its peak during the great seventeenth-century Age of Reason, drawing its exponents from among Europe's most enlightened clerics, princes, scholars, and lawyers. But reason is relative, H. R. Trevor-Roper reminds us in his classic work on the subject, *Religion, the Reformation and Social Change*. There are many theories to explain the witchcraft hysteria, including the association of Eve with primordial evil that we traced to the patriarchs and find in the work of the seventeenth-century poet John Milton. In a world fearful of the apocalypse and ravaged by religious war and epidemic, the witch, like the Jew throughout history, was an easy scapegoat for society's ills. Trevor-Roper locates the origins of the witch craze in the mountainous regions of Christian Europe where church and state had never fully penetrated and where the life style of the peasants was antithetical to that of the feudal overlords. It was not the individual old woman casting spells who generated the witch craze, Trevor-Roper tells us, but unassimilable social groups who could not be made to conform to orthodoxies of church and state. But the primary victims of the great social upheavals of the period were

1. It is difficult to determine precisely how many people were executed as witches. One authority suggests that the number may have exceeded 9 million (Hughes 1965). As Trevor-Roper has documented, the female population of some villages was often almost completely destroyed.

women, most of them desperately poor, often old and eccentric (1967).

Their persecution by both Catholic fathers and Protestant reformers was facilitated by the publication in 1486 of the *Malleus Maleficarum* ("Hammer of Witches") by two Dominican fathers and beloved sons of the Pope, Heinrich Kramer and Jacob Sprenger. The *Malleus*, an encyclopedia of demonology and a manual of procedure to be used by the inquisitors in the trial and extermination of witches, explained that witches were more likely to be female than male because women knew no moderation whether in goodness or in vice, that they had defective intelligence, inordinate passions, and weak memories. Woman is more likely, they insisted, to consort with the devil because "she is more carnal than a man, as is clear from her many carnal abominations." Kramer and Sprenger singled out midwives in particular, who "surpassed all others in wickedness" (1928:44). It was, significantly, the autonomous and independent wise woman and healer who was particularly repugnant to the church fathers. The witch is but another manifestation of the fear and distrust inspired in man by woman that was described by de Beauvoir. It was that fear of woman's power that led men, during the most virulent phase of the witch persecutions, to put to death the "good" witch with the "bad."

To secure her conviction, the ordinary rules of evidence were suspended, circumstantial evidence being sufficient to prove witchcraft:

And the circumstantial evidence need not be very cogent: it was sufficient to discover a wart, by which the familiar spirit was suckled; an insensitive spot which did not bleed when pricked; a capacity to float when thrown into water; or an incapacity to shed tears. Recourse could even be had to "lighter *indicia*," such as a tendency to look down when accused, signs of fear, or the mere aspect of a witch, old, ugly or smelly. (Trevor-Roper 1967:120)

Torture no doubt prompted the confessions of most of the accused, "creating witches where none were and multiplying both victims and evidence" (Trevor-Roper 1967:126). But it is difficult to account for the spontaneous and voluntary confessions to heinous crimes of those who were not tortured, confessions that, when uttered by women, seemed to confirm male convictions of the inherent evil of woman, as well as her "lack of moderation." In *Religion and the Decline of Magic* (1971), Keith Thomas places the witchcraft persecutions in England squarely within an economic context. The most isolated and dependent members of the community were women. As early commercial capitalism created agricultural specialization, rising prices, and urban dislocation, the position of women, living under conditions of abject poverty, deteriorated rapidly. Many were reduced to begging. The prevailing Christian ethic directed the more fortunate members of the community to extend charity to such women, but self-interest often led the affluent to deny aid. Perhaps guilt, then, led the more affluent, in the absence of a rational explanation for a sudden affliction, to accuse the denied beggar woman of using the black arts to bring about his misfortunes. In such a world, the solemn pact with the devil, promising the power of revenge, may have become, in the words of Trevor-Roper, "subjective reality" to powerless women (1967:126). It is a pattern that we will come to recognize in the illness, hysteria, and madness of the increasingly isolated middle-class women of the nineteenth century.

For all its intensity and horror, neither the persecutions of witches nor the injunctions of Reformation leaders successfully quelled the continuing struggle of some women to understand and to escape the bonds of sexual apartheid. The seventeenth century, dubbed the Age of Reason, brought into question the old Aristotelian notion of nature as a fixed hierarchy as new quests for knowledge were initiated by Galileo, Copernicus, and Kepler. At the same time, the "salon" movement, which began in France, provided a fresh challenge to accepted notions about women's roles. In the earlier days of that movement especially, the gathering of artists and intellectuals into the drawing rooms or "salons" of often bright, well-educated, and sometimes unconventional women held a promise of sexual equality. The existence of the *salonières*, or "bluestockings" as they were called in Restoration England, was the double-edged sword that promised new possibilities for the lives of women and the provocation for ever more virulent satirical attacks by new generations of poets and dramatists.

The eighteenth century, often grandly dubbed the Age of Enlightenment, was a watershed period in the progress of human rights. The humanism of the Renaissance had mitigated medieval superstition and the sense of helplessness at the hands of a mysterious destiny; the progress of physics and mathematics in the seventeenth century had revolutionized knowledge about the nature of the material world. As a result, the eighteenth century was prepared to believe in an ordered but comprehensible universe and in man's capacity to affect his destiny through the exercise of his powers of reason. But this breakthrough was indeed for "man." The documents that were to change the course of history—the Declaration of the Rights of Man, the Declaration of Independence (in which all "men" were declared to be equal)—and the literary masterpieces that described the new world view—Pope's *Essay on Man*, for example—neither forgot woman nor implied her inclusion under the generic term "man." She was, rather, pointedly excluded as a creature of emotion, incapable of the reason that distinguished her male counterpart from the animals and placed him immediately below the angels in that century's version of the "great chain of being."

While Aristotle's methodology was abandoned as unscientific, his conclusions deemed unverifiable by experimentation or observation, the essential Aristotelian dualism of the passion-driven woman and the reason-directed man achieved new importance in the age of Locke, Jefferson, and Rousseau. Although some of the leading thinkers of the century—the French *philosophes*, for example—professed to be advocates of women's equality, they seemed to concentrate their attention on women's alleged defects. There were a few significant critiques of women's oppression, such as *La Religieuse* ("The Nun"). In that work *philosophe* Denis de Diderot created a semifictional female character whose involuntary induction into a religious order because she had no dowry and thus no marital prospects led to her dishonor and ultimate death. But accounts of woman's vanities, her silliness, her lack of intellectual capacity prevailed. *Infirmitas sexus* and *levitas animi* lived on in characters like Alexander Pope's Belinda who might "stain her honor or her new brocade;/Forget her prayers, or miss a masquerade" (*Rape of the Lock*, III, Canto II, 11. 107–8).

One of the basic precepts of the philosophes was that of "natural law." They believed that human beings were endowed with reason and that through the proper cultivation of that reason, and its exercise, basic laws of nature could be discerned that would lead humanity to a better world. In addition to the all-important role that belief played in the revolutions that marked the eighteenth century and the consequent dismantling of such "unnatural" institutions as monarchy and colonial rule, it was largely responsible for a new attitude toward education. It was, after all, only through education that the powers of reason could be sufficiently developed to allow distinction between what was good and what was evil in nature. Education provided for at least the possibility of human perfectibility, and more significantly, of human equality.

Social philosopher Jean Jacques Rousseau advances in his *Emile* the philosophy that man is by nature good and that it is the corrupting influence of civilization that causes him to depart from his true "nature." He proposes a "negative" system of education according to which natural impulses and sentiments will be allowed to unfold, while artificial, external influences will be prevented. It is that treatise which, as we shall see, so outraged Mary Wollstonecraft, who saw in it an insidious reworking of the commonly held view that women possessed inferior minds and were incapable of developing them. How painful must it have been for her to see that women were not to be included in the new belief in the power of reason. Rather, "natural law" was to be invoked to justify and explain sex differences. "The reason which teaches a woman her duty," Rousseau explains in the excerpt from *Emile* included here, is simple. "The obedience and fidelity which she owes to her husband, the tenderness and care due to her children, are such natural and self-evident consequences of her position that she cannot honestly refuse her consent to the inner voice which is her guide, not fail to discern her duty in her natural inclination."

It is clear that as an increasingly secular world withdrew from the notion of woman as evil temptress and from the veneration of the Virgin, and as the goals of the Enlightenment were assumed by some women to apply to them as well as to men, adjustments in the mystique of "otherness" were necessary if the patriarchal order was to be maintained. The nineteenth century was equal to the challenge. Many excellent studies and critical works are now available on women in the nineteenth century, particularly women in Victorian England. We explore the period in other contexts—work and marriage, for example—in succeeding chapters. Of significance here are the adaptations that were made during that century of sometimes ancient strategies for controlling women according to the exigencies of a secular civilization largely under the control of its middle class. Perhaps most startling is the renaissance in mythic proportions of the medieval cult of the lady by Anglo-American men as anxious to assert their claims to aristocracy as to justify their treatment of women.[2]

Stripped of its religious significance, its derivation from Mariolatry, the nineteenth-century version of the cult demanded a lady whose "sole function was marriage and procreation (the two, needless to say, were considered as one)" (Vicinus 1973:x). And in that capacity, the perfect lady was made the official guardian of her family's and her society's morality. In a world increasingly guided by business interests under new industrial capitalism and by the new concepts of social Darwinism defined most frequently in monetary terms, the role of guardian of the public morality was a lonely one. Moreover, as the notion of the defenseless lady was made to serve social, political, economic and domestic ends, the effect was as devastating as if it had derived from material reality. Increasingly in the postindustrial world, the chasm between the prevailing view of woman and the true nature of her life deepened.

The ideal of feminine behavior and woman's sphere as public philosophy and as control strategy reached its apotheosis in the American Old South. There, the patriarchy we have seen adapted to various cultures and political systems over the centuries incorporated African slavery as well as the subordination of women. Eugene Genovese offers in his study of slavery, *Roll, Jordan, Roll*, a definition of paternalism that is helpful to our attempts to analyze the Byzantine entanglement of class, race, and sex in the Old South. Insisting upon the centrality of class relations in paternalism, Genovese

---

2. For a compelling account of the effect of the application of this myth on women in the nineteenth century, see W. J. Cash, *The Mind of the South*, especially Chap. 3.

traces the origins of southern paternalism to class power in racial form, to an unjust social order in which the available—in this case, black—lower classes were pressed into the service of their "masters." "Southern paternalism," then, "like every other paternalism . . . grew out of the necessity to discipline and morally justify a system of exploitation" (1972:4). In the selection from her study of *The Southern Lady* included here, Anne Firor Scott makes explicit the role of southern paternalism in the sexual economy. "Women, along with children and slaves," she says, "were expected to recognize their proper and subordinate place and to be obedient to the head of the family. Any tendency on the part of any of the members of the system to assert themselves against the master threatened the whole, and therefore slavery itself. It was no accident that the most articulate spokesmen for slavery were also eloquent exponents of the subordinate role of women."

To ensure that women continued to see the appropriateness of that assigned role, girls were trained from earliest childhood to the ideals of perfection and submission. The image of the self-denying, compassionate, pious wife and mother was reinforced by the family, the schools, popular and religious literature, and evangelical theology. While the nineteenth century provides us with histories of women who rejected the notion that they were destined to be subservient to men, middle- and upper-class women generally absorbed the myth of female inferiority and took their place upon the pedestal as guardians of public and private morality. In her study, Scott discusses the reasons why the model of the perfect and submissive wife was accepted so widely, not only in the American South, but among the new leisure class in general.

An illuminating footnote to the persuasive reasons Scott offers is once more provided by Genovese's discussion of paternalism. In exploring the role of paternalism in the perpetuation of slavery, Genovese declares that "wherever paternalism exists, it undermines solidarity among the oppressed by linking them as individuals to their oppressors. A lord (master, padroné, patron, padron, patão) functions as a direct provider and protector to each individual or family, as well as to the community as a whole" (1972:5). While, as Genovese points out, "impressive solidarity and collective resistance to their masters" was displayed by slaves of the Old South, and while, as we shall see, women have struggled against the constraints of the sexual economy, the pervasive effect of paternalism is to diffuse resistance and engender some degree of loyalty toward or identification with the oppressor. In American slavery those effects of paternalism militated against slaves' identification with each other as a class. For women—and here the analogy must be sharply modified, for wife or daughter is but rarely to husband or father as slave is to master—identification with the oppressor has mitigated the possibility of seeing past apparent class distinctions to the commonality of sexual oppression.

At significant historical moments—during the nineteenth-century abolition movement, for example—the paternalistic ethos enveloping the sexual economy has become transparent. At those moments, many women have found it possible to see through their individual relationships with men—relationships of patronage, dependence, loyalty, or affection—to the systemic sexual subordination that made those relationships both more and less than they should have been. Those moments are more fully considered in succeeding pages. For now, it is important chiefly to acknowledge the overriding importance of paternalism as a control strategy in the sexual economy, and to see in the dependence on and identification with the oppressor under paternalism a major source of the class factions and racial antagonisms that have blunted two centuries of feminist attacks on the sexual economy.

Had the identification been less pervasive, or if nineteenth-century women of the middle and upper classes had not, as Scott suggests, feared the social disorganization that might attend serious challenge of the only social order they knew, they might perhaps have sounded the hollowness of the feminine model of defenseless-ness, submissiveness, and purity. Those ideals were maintained at the expense not only of their own vigorous pursuit of life and happiness but of that of the health, happiness, and no doubt years of life of women in slavery. A moving articulation of the bitter selectivity of the feminine ideal was made by ex-slave and feminist Sojourner Truth. In her now famous remarks made before the 1851 women's rights convention in Akron, Ohio, and reprinted here, Sojourner Truth challenged the litany of femininity being rehearsed by a man at that convention. Not for her or her sisters in slavery was the deference to feminine helplessness, to need for protection, to the sanctity of motherhood. Their lot, rather, was unremitting work and powerlessness to protect what they most valued—their families.

Additional evidence that the much-vaunted sanctity of the family was selectively applied because it was valuable chiefly as mortar for the patriarchal structure is manifest in the treatment of the black family after emancipation. In *The Black Family in Slavery and Freedom, 1750–1925*, Herbert G. Gutman argues convincingly that strong black family ties survived the adversities of slavery through a remarkable series of adaptations and that, contrary to the claims of such earlier social scientists and historians as Daniel Moynihan, Kenneth Stampp and Stanley Elkins, no "tangle of pathology" or "deep-seated structural distortions" born in slavery produced the "irregular" family structure and consequent dislocation of mid-twentieth-century black Americans. It was, rather, racism and the postemancipation disenfranchisement of American blacks that isolated them from the mainstream of national culture, Gutman asserts, and led to the widespread unemployment and poverty that created the real "Negro problem" (1976:542). Racial subordination independent of slavery gathered force during the Civil War and continued to gain strength as blacks began the mass migration to the North. Gutman's work traces the progressive unmasking of contempt for the black family and for the black woman as the center of that family. That contempt gave the lie to claims of reverence for the idea of the family, of womanhood, of marriage and motherhood beyond the clear usefulness of those institutions to the maintenance of the patriarchy.

No more for poor immigrant women, arriving in America in increasing numbers as the nineteenth century wore on, than for black women was room made on the pedestal. The hard lot of immigrant women as workers is explored in a later chapter. It is important here to note the universal absence of a protective male arm for women who braved the frontier, the cruel cities, the factory. Of what value was the model of the perfect, submissive wife and mother to the poor young immigrant women who took over hardened and accelerated work from genteel Yankee women in the Lowell, Massachusetts, textile factories? To the "greenhorns" whose naiveté and poverty led them into prostitution in the big cities? To the pioneer women driven slowly mad by the hard work and loneliness of the frontier? To the rural woman whose strength and competence on the land counted for little in her struggle to make a home for her family in industrial cities where families' only value was to feed the industrial machine? We are left few records of the historical experience of these ordinary women. There are diaries kept by pioneer women and surviving letters to friends and family or to advice columns like the

"Bintel Brief" reprinted here from the Yiddish *Daily Forward*. Often, what we know of those real lives lived beyond the curtain of myth we glean from fiction, where we find characters like Willa Cather's Antonia (*My Antonia*); O. E. Rolväag's pioneer woman, Beret (*Giants in the Earth*); or Harriet Arnow's Gertie (*The Dollmaker*), who was thrust from her relatively secure rural home into the inhumane and destructive industrial environment of wartime Detroit.

The madness that seems to have been the fate of so many women in the nineteenth century is the subject of Charlotte Perkins Gilman's classic autobiographical short story, "The Yellow Wallpaper." Her story reveals the destructive effect of the imposition of the model of "true womanhood" on a woman whose membership in the privileged upper middle class spared her the struggle for survival but not the pain of powerlessness. Gilman saw woman's subordinate position not as the result of inferior intelligence or capabilities but as the consequence of man's interference with natural law. While the middle- and upper-class male was trained to take his place in the competitive arena of industrial capitalism, the female, firmly removed from the "give and take of daily life," became a social parasite.[3] Such a woman we see in the narrator of "The Yellow Wallpaper," who longs for "congenial work" but is able to translate her art only into madness. Gilman's story is the account of a woman's discovery of a double trapped within the walls of her bedroom (1973). The woman creeping behind the yellow wallpaper "represents not only the protagonist's own divided self but all women who are imprisoned, bound and inhibited by a society which insists that women are childlike, merely decorative, and incapable of self-actualization" (Rigney 1978:123).

3. See especially Charlotte Perkins Gilman's "Parasitism and Civilized Vice," in *Woman's Coming of Age*, ed. Samuel Schmalhausen and V. F. Calverton (New York, 1931).

The old cult of the lady, having undergone a number of mutations, and in the face of the real circumstances of ordinary women's lives, continues to be used as a control strategy to shape women's behavior in the twentieth century. In her article " 'Nice Girl': Social Control of Women through a Value Construct," the sociologist Greer Litton Fox identifies "normative controls" that offer women protection but severely circumscribe their potential for power and.independence (1977). Such value constructs as "nice girl" and "lady" offer women protection and security but limit severely their freedom of movement in the world. Women are taught from early childhood, for example, to exercise self-control, to avoid expressions of aggression, to be "nicer" than men. Such control, claims Fox, operating through the mechanisms of shared values and normative standards, gives the appearance of nonrestriction and involves both sexes as control agents. Moreover, there is little respite from the strictures of "lady-like" behavior as control is exerted over the entire life cycle of a woman and over a broad range of behavioral contexts. One must continually earn one's status as a "nice girl," Fox claims, and thus continual compliance is ensured. Fox's article documents clearly the costs to women of such control strategies in loss of freedom and self-determination. "But to the extent that such constructs limit the expression of the human and humane qualities of both women and men," she writes, "then no one profits" (1977:817).

It is obviously impossible to enumerate and describe all the control strategies employed in the perpetuation of the sexual economy. We have chosen instead to isolate major concepts within which particular control strategies are contained—religious misogyny, paternalism, the myth of the lady, and the "nice girl" construct, for example. In so doing, we have regretfully omitted exploration of a number of specific control strategies of historical significance, including the use of art, literature, and popular culture to establish standards of beauty for women in the context of an insistence that beauty—and youthful beauty at that—is an essential component of the feminine ideal. The fight against this control strategy has been a major one for twentieth-century feminists, who have struck out at beauty contests, the air-brushed image of feminine beauty promoted by *Playboy* Magazine, and physical attractiveness as a criterion for employment in already sharply curtailed "women's jobs." While this phenomenon has caused pain for many women, its most devastating effect has perhaps been on those women whose inability to meet established standards is intensified by race and ethnic identification. A most poignant depiction of that needless pain can be discovered in Toni Morrison's novel *The Bluest Eye*. The novel focuses on the tragic childhood of "a little black girl who wanted to rise up out of the pit of her blackness and see the world with blue eyes" (1972:137), and is narrated by another little black girl whose early response to the impossible standards of white beauty bewilderingly accepted by the black world around her is to destroy white baby dolls.

One control strategy that demands fuller treatment here is the chillingly effective threat of sexual violence. A recent study by Allan Griswold Johnson, "On the Prevalence of Rape in the United States," employs highly reliable survey data, including reports from the Federal Bureau of Investigation and the U.S. Department of Justice, to estimate that, given current conditions in the United States, 20 to 30 percent of girls now twelve years old will suffer a violent sexual attack at some point during their lives. Because of the lack of reliable data about sexual violence against children under the age of twelve, we must conclude with Johnson that even these figures are conservative. The data indicate clearly that sexual violence cannot be attributed to an aberrant strain located outside the experience of "normal" male society, but must be placed squarely within "the everyday fabric of relations between men and women in patriarchal society" (1980:145).

Such is the conclusion of a number of important studies of violence against women, including Kate Millett's *Sexual Politics* (1970); Andrea Dworkin's *Woman Hating* (1974); Linda Gordon's *Woman's Body, Woman's Right* (1977); and Susan Brownmiller's *Against Our Will: Men, Women and Rape* (1976). In the selections from her historical study of rape included here, Brownmiller maintains that "a sexual assault is an invasion of bodily integrity and a violation of freedom and self-determination." Women's fear of that assault in a male-dominated world has made rape a "woman's problem" rather than "a societal problem resulting from a distorted masculine philosophy of aggression." Reduced mobility, reduced independence, and consequently reduced self-determination for women are products of that fear that in turn contribute significantly to the maintenance of the sexual economy.

Recent years have seen numerous attempts by women to chart the sexual economy, to assess its damage, to recover losses, and to eliminate the destructive controls that limit human possibilities. As we seek to decode the sexual economy, we should, however, guard against viewing women merely as passive victims, a view that places women outside history. Carroll Smith-Rosenberg, in "The New Woman and the New History," reminds us of the limitations of "traditional" history, which accepts a "traditional hierarchy of significance" and "traditional political periodization" (1975:186). Some historians trained in what has been called "old" history have studied the ways in which women have been affected by and responded to politically significant periods or events and have contributed much to what Gerda Lerner, in *The Majority Finds Its Past*, calls "compensatory history" (1979:145). Such studies provide us with a record of the lives of women who have overcome extreme adversity to achieve a position in a corner of the public world, but they tell us very little about the experience of the great mass of women throughout history. Lerner and Smith-Rosenberg note in recent years a broadening of focus among historians of women, who, borrowing concepts from sociology and psychology, have established as central to the historical process a study of the nature of the female experience within the culture shared by men and women. This broadening of focus has taken place within the context of two more general influences, Smith-Rosenberg points out, the current women's movement and the new social history, without which the new women's history could not have been written. The new social history developed techniques making it possible to "turn from a study of the notable and public to the analysis of the domestic world of the inarticulate, the working class, the immigrant, and the black—and even of the women within these groups" (1975:188).[4]

Lerner provides a perspective for our study as she cautions against looking for women in "the empty spaces of traditional history," an approach that considers history in male-centered terms. If

---

4. In a review of Lawrence Stone's *The Past and the Present*, Gertrude Himmelfarb draws upon Stone's distinctions between "old" history and "new" history as follows: "the new history . . . is analytic rather than narrative; it relies on such techniques as quantification, model-building and psychoanalysis; it focuses upon groups more often than individuals, and the masses more often than elites. . . . The 'old history,' by contrast, typically concerns itself with political events, diplomacy, revolutions and wars; its customary method is narrative; and its most prominent characters are kings, politicians and public figures" (*New York Times Book Review*, 10 January 1982, pp. 9, 24–25). It is clear that this change in emphasis among a new school of historians was conducive to the great advances in the study of the history of women over the last decade. It is equally clear that the study of women's history—as well as the work of women historians—has contributed substantially to the advances of "new" history.

women are invisible, Lerner insists, it is because we have failed to ask questions of history that are appropriate to women. Lerner identifies the central question that historians must ask: "What would history be like if it were seen through the eyes of women and ordered by values they define?" (1979:178). What Smith-Rosenberg calls the new women's history places women at the "center of our analytic scheme," allowing us to examine the "complex interplay between the macrocosm of social structure and belief systems, the microcosm of family structure and the existential experience of being female" (1975:189).

Women's history is at a critical transitional stage as questions of methodology, perspective, and focus emerge. Historians of working-class and ethnic women and historians of middle-class women, for example, each must ask different questions about the influences of the industrial revolution, the birth-control movement, or evolving sexual mores; and each must develop different methods to answer those questions (Smith-Rosenberg 1975:189–90). Both groups of historians should have as their goal the examination of the female experience from multiple perspectives. Smith-Rosenberg identifies four important sets of determinants that must be considered by historians: "the economic and demographic structure of society; a variety of cultural belief systems including both the traditional concerns of intellectual history (political, religious and scientific ideologies) and such newer and essentially female areas of concern as gender-role definitions, attitudes toward children and toward sexuality; the internal dynamics of primary institutions such as the family and child rearing agencies; and finally, basic human psychological needs" (1975:198).

The approach suggested here, whether it is called women's history or new history, allows us to place women squarely in the center of our analysis as we turn our attention to women in the public world.

There is much that is worthy of praise in Rousseau's Emile. *Rousseau understood the wrongs suffered by children under an authoritarian system of education and insisted that the child's interests and abilities be respected. Yet the great champion of individual liberty for mankind assigned to woman an inferior role and proposed a system of education for her in accordance with her "natural" limitations. Woman, according to Rousseau, is to be taught to turn the strengths of the other sex to her own advantage, finding a way "to make us desire what she cannot achieve unaided and what she considers necessary or pleasing."*

WOMAN OBSERVES, MAN REASONS

Jean Jacques Rousseau

FROM *Emile*

To what shall we reduce the education of our women if we give them no law but that of conventional prejudice? Let us not degrade so far the sex which rules over us, and which does us honour when we have not made it vile. For all mankind there is a law anterior to that of public opinion. All other laws should bend before the inflexible control of this law; it is the judge of public opinion, and only in so far as the esteem of men is in accordance with this law has it any claim on our obedience.

This law is our individual conscience. I will not repeat what has been said already; it is enough to point out that if those two laws clash, the education of women will always be imperfect. Right feeling without respect for public opinion will not give them that delicacy of soul which lends to right conduct the charm of social approval; while respect for public opinion without right feeling will only make false and wicked women who put appearances in the place of virtue.

It is, therefore, important to cultivate a faculty which serves as judge between the two guides, which does not permit conscience to go astray and corrects the errors of prejudice. That faculty is reason. But what a crowd of questions arise at this word. Are women capable of solid reason; should they cultivate it, can they cultivate it successfully? Is this culture useful in relation to the functions laid upon them? Is it compatible with becoming simplicity?

The different ways of envisaging and answering these questions lead to two extremes; some would have us keep women indoors sewing and spinning with their maids; thus they make them nothing more than the chief servant of their master. Others, not content to secure their rights, lead them to usurp ours; for to make woman our superior in all the qualities proper to her sex, and to make her our equal in all the rest, what is this but to transfer to the woman the superiority which nature has given to her husband?

The reason which teaches a man his duties is not very complex; the reason which teaches a woman hers is even simpler. The obedience and fidelity which she owes to her husband, the tenderness and care due to her children, are such natural and self-evident consequences of her position that she cannot honestly refuse her consent to the inner voice which is her guide, nor fail to discern her duty in her natural inclination.

I would not altogether blame those who would restrict a woman to the labours of her sex and would leave her in profound ignorance of everything else; but that would require a standard of morality at once very simple and very healthy, or a life withdrawn from the world. In great towns, among immoral men, such a woman would be too easily led astray; her virtue would too often be at the mercy of circumstances; in this age of philosophy, virtue must be able to resist temptation; she must know beforehand what she may hear and what she should think of it.

Moreover, in submission to man's judgment she should deserve his esteem; above all she should obtain the esteem of her husband; she should not only make him love her person, she should make him approve her conduct; she should justify his choice before the world, and do honour to her husband through the honour given to the wife. But how can she set about this task if she is ignorant of our institutions, our customs, our notions of propriety, if she knows nothing of the source of man's judgment, nor the passions by which it is swayed? Since she depends both on her own conscience and on public opinion, she must learn to know and reconcile these two laws, and to put her own conscience first only when the two are opposed to each other. She becomes the judge of her own judges, she decides when she should obey and when she should refuse her obedience. She weighs their prejudices before she accepts or rejects them; she learns to trace them to their source, to foresee what they will be, and to turn them in her own favour; she is careful never to give cause for blame if duty allows her to avoid it. This cannot be properly done without cultivating her mind and reason.

I always come back to my first principle and it supplies the solution of all my difficulties. I study what is, I seek its cause, and I discover in the end that what is, is good. I go to houses where the master and mistress do the honours together. They are equally well educated, equally polite, equally well equipped with wit and good taste,

both of them are inspired with the same desire to give their guests a
good reception and to send every one away satisfied. The husband
omits no pains to be attentive to every one; he comes and goes and
sees to every one and takes all sorts of trouble; he is attention itself.
The wife remains in her place; a little circle gathers round her and
apparently conceals the rest of the company from her; yet she sees
everything that goes on, no one goes without a word with her; she
has omitted nothing which might interest anybody, she has said
nothing unpleasant to any one, and without any fuss the least is no
more overlooked than the greatest. Dinner is announced, they take
their places; the man knowing the assembled guests will place them
according to his knowledge; the wife, without previous acquaintance,
never makes a mistake; their looks and bearing have already shown
her what is wanted and every one will find himself where he wishes
to be. I do not assert that the servants forget no one. The master of
the house may have omitted no one, but the mistress perceives what
you like and sees that you get it; while she is talking to her neigh-
bour she has one eye on the other end of the table; she sees who is
not eating because he is not hungry and who is afraid to help himself
because he is clumsy and timid. When the guests leave the table
every one thinks she has had no thought but for him, everybody thinks
she has had no time to eat anything, but she has really eaten more
than anybody.

When the guests are gone, husband and wife talk over the events
of the evening. He relates what was said to him, what was said and
done by those with whom he conversed. If the lady is not always
quite exact in this respect, yet on the other hand she perceived what
was whispered at the other end of the room; she knows what so-and-
so thought, and what was the meaning of this speech or that gesture;
there is scarcely a change of expression for which she has not an explanation in readiness, and she is almost always right.

The same turn of mind which makes a woman of the world such
an excellent hostess, enables a flirt to excel in the art of amusing a
number of suitors. Coquetry, cleverly carried out, demands an even
finer discernment than courtesy; provided a polite lady is civil to
everybody, she has done fairly well in any case; but the flirt would
soon lose her hold by such clumsy uniformity; if she tries to be
pleasant to all her lovers alike, she will disgust them all. In ordinary
social intercourse the manners adopted towards everybody are good
enough for all; no question is asked as to private likes or dislikes provided all are alike well received. But in love, a favour shared with
others is an insult. A man of feeling would rather be singled out for
ill-treatment than be caressed with the crowd, and the worst that
can befall him is to be treated like every one else. So a woman who

wants to keep several lovers at her feet must persuade every one of them that she prefers him, and she must contrive to do this in the sight of all the rest, each of whom is equally convinced that he is her favourite.

If you want to see a man in a quandary, place him between two women with each of whom he has a secret understanding, and see what a fool he looks. But put a woman in similar circumstances between two men, and the results will be even more remarkable; you will be astonished at the skill with which she cheats them both, and makes them laugh at each other. Now if that woman were to show the same confidence in both, if she were to be equally familiar with both, how could they be deceived for a moment? If she treated them alike, would she not show that they both had the same claims upon her? Oh, she is far too clever for that; so far from treating them just alike, she makes a marked difference between them, and she does it so skilfully that the man she flatters thinks it is affection, and the man she ill uses thinks it is spite. So that each of them believes she is thinking of him, when she is thinking of no one but herself.

A general desire to please suggests similar measures; people would be disgusted with a woman's whims if they were not skilfully managed, and when they are artistically distributed her servants are more than ever enslaved.

> "*Usa ogn'arte la donna, onde sia colto*
> *Nella sua rete alcun novello amante;*
> *Nè con tutti, nè sempre un stesso volto*
> *Serba; ma cangia a tempo atto e sembiante.*"
>
> TASSO, *Jerus. Del.*, c. iv., v. 87.

What is the secret of this art? Is it not the result of a delicate and continuous observation which shows her what is taking place in a man's heart, so that she is able to encourage or to check every hidden impulse? Can this art be acquired? No; it is born with women; it is common to them all, and men never show it to the same degree. It is one of the distinctive characters of the sex. Self-possession, penetration, delicate observation, this is a woman's science; the skill to make use of it is her chief accomplishment.

This is what is, and we have seen why it is so. It is said that women are false. They become false. They are really endowed with skill not duplicity; in the genuine inclinations of their sex they are not false even when they tell a lie. Why do you consult their words when it is not their mouths that speak? Consult their eyes, their colour, their breathing, their timid manner, their slight resistance, that is the language nature gave them for your answer. The lips always say "No," and rightly so; but the tone is not always the same, and that cannot lie. Has not a woman the same needs as a man, but without the same right to make them known? Her fate would be too cruel if she had no language in which to express her legitimate desires except the words which she dare not utter. Must her modesty condemn her to misery? Does she not require a means of indicating her inclinations without open expression? What skill is needed to hide from her lover what she would fain reveal! Is it not of vital importance that she should learn to touch his heart without showing that she cares for him? It is a pretty story that tale of Galatea with her apple and her clumsy flight. What more is needed? Will she tell the shepherd who pursues her among the willows that she only flees that he may follow? If she did, it would be a lie; for she would no longer attract him. The more modest a woman is, the more art she needs, even with her husband. Yes, I maintain that coquetry, kept within bounds, becomes modest and true, and out of it springs a law of right conduct.

One of my opponents has very truly asserted that virtue is one; you cannot disintegrate it and choose this and reject the other. If you love virtue, you love it in its entirety, and you close your heart when you can, and you always close your lips to the feelings which you ought not to allow. Moral truth is not only what is, but what is good; what is bad ought not to be, and ought not to be confessed, especially when that confession produces results which might have been avoided. If I were tempted to steal, and in confessing it I tempted another to become my accomplice the very confession of my temptation would amount to a yielding to that temptation. Why do you say that modesty makes women false? Are those who lose their modesty more sincere than the rest? Not so, they are a thousandfold more deceitful. This degree of depravity is due to many vices, none of which is rejected, vices which owe their power to intrigue and falsehood.[1]

On the other hand, those who are not utterly shameless, who take no pride in their faults, who are able to conceal their desires even from those who inspire them, those who confess their passion most reluctantly, those are the truest and most sincere, these are they on whose fidelity you may generally rely.

The only example I know which might be quoted as a recognised exception to these remarks is Mlle. de L'Enclos; and she was

---

1. I know that women who have openly decided on a certain course of conduct profess that their lack of concealment is a virtue in itself, and swear that, with one exception, they are possessed of all the virtues; but I am sure they never persuaded any but fools to believe them. When the natural curb is removed from their sex, what is there left to restrain them? What honour will they prize when they have rejected the honour of their sex? Having once given the rein to passion they have no longer any reason for self-control. "Nec femina, amissa pudicitia, alia abnuerit." No author ever understood more thoroughly the heart of both sexes than Tacitus when he wrote those words.

considered a prodigy. In her scorn for the virtues of women, she practised, so they say, the virtues of a man. She is praised for her frankness and uprightness; she was a trustworthy acquaintance and a faithful friend. To complete the picture of her glory it is said that she became a man. That may be, but in spite of her high reputation I should no more desire that man as my friend than as my mistress.

This is not so irrelevant as it seems. I am aware of the tendencies of our modern philosophy which make a jest of female modesty and its so-called insincerity; I also perceive that the most certain result of this philosophy will be to deprive the women of this century of such shreds of honour as they still possess.

On these grounds I think we may decide in general terms what sort of education is suited to the female mind, and the objects to which we should turn its attention in early youth.

As I have already said, the duties of their sex are more easily recognised than performed. They must learn in the first place to love those duties by considering the advantages to be derived from them—that is the only way to make duty easy. Every age and condition has its own duties. We are quick to see our duty if we love it. Honour your position as a woman, and in whatever station of life to which it shall please heaven to call you, you will be well off. The essential thing is to be what nature has made you; women are only too ready to be what men would have them.

The search for abstract and speculative truths, for principles and axioms in science, for all that tends to wide generalisation, is beyond a woman's grasp; their studies should be thoroughly practical. It is their business to apply the principles discovered by men, it is their place to make the observations which lead men to discover those principles. A woman's thoughts, beyond the range of her immediate duties, should be directed to the study of men, or the acquirement of that agreeable learning whose sole end is the formation of taste; for the works of genius are beyond her reach, and she has neither the accuracy nor the attention for success in the exact sciences; as for the physical sciences, to decide the relations between living creatures and the laws of nature is the task of that sex which is more active and enterprising, which sees more things, that sex which is possessed of greater strength and is more accustomed to the exercise of that strength. Woman, weak as she is and limited in her range of observation, perceives and judges the forces at her disposal to supplement her weakness, and those forces are the passions of man. Her own mechanism is more powerful than ours; she has many levers which may set the human heart in motion. She must find a way to make us desire what she cannot achieve unaided and what she considers necessary or pleasing; therefore she must have a thorough knowledge of man's mind; not an abstract knowledge of the mind of man in general, but the mind of those men who are about her, the mind of those men who have authority over her, either by law or custom. She must learn to divine their feelings from speech and action, look and gesture. By her own speech and action, look and gesture, she must be able to inspire them with the feelings she desires, without seeming to have any such purpose. The men will have a better philosophy of the human heart, but she will read more accurately in the heart of men. Woman should discover, so to speak, an experimental morality, man should reduce it to a system. Woman has more wit, man more genius; woman observes, man reasons; together they provide the clearest light and the profoundest knowledge which is possible to the unaided human mind; in a word, the surest knowledge of self and of others of which the human race is capable. In this way art may constantly tend to the perfection of the instrument which nature has given us.

In her study of The Southern Lady, Anne Firor Scott examines the widely accepted culturally defined image of the lady and its effect upon women's behavior. The idea of the lady, Scott explains, was part of the larger American culture, but in the South, because of more deeply rooted patriarchal values, particular care was taken to ensure that women embraced the notion. Earlier we examined the fear of woman that caused men to relegate her to a position as the "other." That same fear, Scott insists, "lay beneath the surface of the flowery praise of women." In the following pages from her book, Scott describes the lives of antebellum women who made heroic efforts to occupy with grace and dignity the "sphere to which God had appointed them." Their private journals and diaries testify to the enormity of their burden and show that the realities of their lives were often in conflict with the image.

THE IMAGE: QUEEN OF THE HOME

Anne Firor Scott

FROM *The Southern Lady: From Pedestal to Politics
1830–1930*

I f talking could make it so, antebellum southern women of the upper class would have been the most perfect examples of womankind yet seen on earth. If praise could satisfy all of woman's needs, they would also have been the happiest. Literary journals, sermons, novels, commencement addresses—wherever men spoke there was praise of Woman, and exhortation to further perfection.

This marvelous creation was described as a submissive wife whose reason for being was to love, honor, obey, and occasionally amuse her husband, to bring up his children and manage his household. Physically weak, and "formed for the less laborious occupations," she depended upon male protection. To secure this protection she was endowed with the capacity to "create a magic spell" over any man in her vicinity. She was timid and modest, beautiful and graceful, "the most fascinating being in creation . . . the delight and charm of every circle she moves in."

Part of her charm lay in her innocence. The less a woman knew of life, Ellen Glasgow once remarked bitterly, the better she was supposed to be able to deal with it. Her mind was not logical, but in the absence of reasoning capacity her sensibility and intuition were highly developed. It was, indeed, to her advantage that "the play of instincts and of the feelings is not cramped by the controlling influence of logic and reason." She was capable of acute perceptions about human relationships, and was a creature of tact, discernment, sympathy, and compassion. It was her nature to be self-denying, and she was given to suffering in silence, a characteristic said to endear her to men. Less endearing, perhaps, but no less natural, was her piety and her tendency to "restrain man's natural vice and immorality." She was thought to be "most deeply interested in the success of every scheme which curbs the passions and enforces a true morality." She was a natural teacher, and a wise counselor to her husband and children.[1] . . .

From earliest childhood girls were trained to the ideals of perfection and submission. A magazine for children published in Charleston, recording the death of a seven-year-old, spoke of her as "peculiarly amiable and engaging; her behaviour marked with a delicate sense of propriety, happily mingled with an artless innocence." She was praised for being kind and considerate to her servants. The fiction in the same magazine was filled with pious, obedient little girls.[2] Boarding schools for young ladies, to which more and more girls were sent as the century wore on, emphasized correct female behavior more than intellectual development. In at least one school the girls wrote their English compositions on such subjects as modesty, benevolence, and the evils of reading novels.[3]

By the time they arrived at their teens most girls had absorbed the injunctions of the myth. One young woman wrote in her diary that she longed to die because she had not found a husband, adding, "I know I would make a faithful, obedient wife, loving with all my heart, yielding entire trust in my husband."[4]

The image of the submissive woman was reinforced by evangelical theology. Daniel R. Hundley, a young Alabama lawyer who wrote a sociological analysis of the antebellum South, relied on Saint Paul's authority for asserting that women should "content themselves with their humble household duties."[5] Southern pulpits repeated the apostle's injunction that women should keep silent in the churches. One minister argued that women needed "the hope and

1. The quotations and descriptions here are from the *Southern Literary Messenger* 1 (1835), but similar ones are found in the *Southern Ladies Companion*, the *Southern Quarterly Review*, and many speeches, novels, memoirs, and poems.

2. *The Rosebud* 1, no. 13 (24 November 1831): 521 and passim.

3. "A Folder of Student Compositions," 1840, Inverson L. Brooks Papers, Southern Historical Collection, University of North Carolina (hereafter cited as SHC UNC).

4. "Anonymous Diary of a Young Woman Living near Natchez," Manuscript Department, William R. Perkins Library, Duke University (hereafter cited as MS Dept., Duke).

5. *Social Relations in Our Southern States* (New York: H. B. Price, 1860), p. 74.

prospects of religion more . . . than the other sex" to soften the pains of living and help women bear with patience and submission the inevitable trials of life, among which he suggested might be "a husband of acid temper." A North Carolina doctor wrote that "God in his inscrutable wisdom has appointed a place and duty for females *out of which* they can neither accomplish their destiny nor secure their happiness!!"[7] . . .

Women made heroic efforts to live up to what was expected of them. One, who could hardly bear the sound of her husband tuning his violin, bit her lip and said nothing, murmuring about self-abnegation.[8] There was no rest for the conscience. "We owe it to our husbands, children and friends," wrote a Louisiana housewife, "to represent as nearly as possible the ideal which they hold so dear."[9] "'Tis man's to act, 'tis woman's to endure," reflected an Alabama novelist in the midst of trials with a husband she did not much respect, and financial problems beyond her power to solve.[10] Women were made, indeed, the long-suffering wife of the violinist concluded, "to suffer and be strong."[11] "Give me a double portion of the grace of thy Spirit that I may learn meekness," wrote the self-flagellating wife of a minister.[12] . . .

Many women assumed that if they were unhappy or discontented in the "sphere to which God had appointed them" it must be their own fault and that by renewed effort they could do better. "My besetting sins are a roving mind and an impetuous spirit," wrote one woman whose diary is filled with admonitions to herself to be systematic, diligent, prudent, economical, and patient with her servants.[13] Josephine Clay Habersham was a gentle and gifted woman who presided with skill and dignity over a large plantation in eastern Georgia. A devoted mother who could write, "I wish always to have a sweet babe to mind, care for and love," she still felt it necessary to make a constant effort to cultivate a cheerful spirit, to ask God for help with her "dull and wayward heart," and to ask forgiveness for not being a more faithful servant.[14] A girl of eighteen prayed to be useful and bemoaned the "vain desires that every now

6. D. A. Clark, "Beauties of Female Piety," quoted in Guion G. Johnson *Ante-Bellum North Carolina* (Chapel Hill: University of North Carolina Press, 1937), pp. 228–29.

7. Dr. James A. Norcum to Mary B. Harvey 25 May 1848, Norcum Papers, N.C. Department of Archives and History, Raleigh.

8. Ella Gertrude Clanton Thomas Diary, 30 November 1858, MS Dept., Duke.

9. Caroline Merrick to "my dear friend," 23 May 1857, Department of Archives and Manuscripts, Louisiana State University, Baton Rouge (hereafter cited as Dept. of Archives, LSU).

10. Caroline Lee Hentz Diary, 5 March 1836, SHC UNC.

11. E. G. C. Thomas Diary, New Year's Day 1858, MS Dept., Duke.

12. Lucilla McCorkle Diary, 12 July 1846, SHC UNC.

13. Lucilla McCorkle Diary, 1 December 1850, SHC UNC.

14. *Ebb Tide*, ed. Spencer B. King (Athens, Ga: University of Georgia Press, 1958), pp. 77, 103–4.

and then trouble this prevailing one [to love God] and my flesh is so weak, I am always failing."[15] . . .

There is little doubt that religious faith served an important function at a time when many children and adults died for no apparent reason. A firm belief that death was a manifestation of God's will made it easier to bear what otherwise would have been an intolerable burden. It is also clear that the requirements for salvation dovetailed neatly with the secular image of women. Religious women were persuaded that the very qualities which made any human being a rich, interesting, assertive personality—a roving mind, spirit, ambition—were propensities to be curbed. No matter what secret thoughts a woman might have about her own abilities, religion confirmed what society told her—namely, that she was inferior to men.

The language of piety and the desire for salvation, the belief in an eternal life, were not, of course, confined to women. The same phrases abound in the letters, diaries, and sermons of many men. The significant difference was that for men submission to God's will in spiritual matters was considered to be perfectly compatible with aggressive behavior and a commanding position in life. Men expected to be obeyed by women, children, and slaves, to be the decision makers and the ultimate source of secular authority.

Daniel Hundley's myth of the southern gentleman complements the image of the southern lady. The gentleman, Hundley insisted, in addition to being finely formed and highly educated, was firm, commanding, and a perfect patriarch. "The natural dignity of manner peculiar to the southern gentleman is doubtless owing to his habitual use of authority from his earliest years." The weakness and dependence of women was thrown into bold relief by his virility and mastery of his environment.[16] Husbands were frequently referred to in the words used for God: Lord and Master.

The rigid definition of the proper role and behavior of southern women requires explanation. It is not that the constellation of ideas which constituted the image of the southern lady was peculiar to the American South; men in Victorian England conjured up a similar myth in poems like Coventry Patmore's "The Angel in the House."[17] Harriet Martineau was speaking of all American women, not just those of the South, when she described them as lying down at night "full of self-reproach for the want of piety which they do not

15. Sarah Wadley Journal, 20 August 1863, SHC UNC.
16. *Social Relations*, pp. 56–61.
17. Walter Houghton, *The Victorian Frame of Mind* (New Haven: Yale University Press, 1957), pp. 341–430.

know how to attain."[18] But, as William R. Taylor has noted, southern plantation novelists were "fanatical" in idolizing and idealizing southern women. The evidence adduced in this chapter bears out his observation with respect to southern men in general.[19]

Such men continued an old tradition in Western history. The myth of the lady was associated with medieval chivalry. Books of advice on proper behavior for both men and women dated back to the invention of printing. Castiglione's *The Courtier*, a sixteenth-century book of etiquette, set the style for such books, and by the eighteenth century books specifically directed to women were widely read in England and in America. Usually written by men, they emphasized the softness, purity, and spirituality of women while denying them intellectual capacity. Women were instructed to please their husbands, attend to their physical needs, cover up their indiscretions, and give them no cause for worry. All such descriptions and injunctions were included in the southern creed.[20]

But the fact that such ideas had been around for a long time does not explain why they were so enthusiastically embraced by antebellum southerners. Other models were available for a sparsely settled rural society. The good woman of Proverbs, for example, who worked willingly with her hands, got up early and set all in her household to work, bought and sold land, and didn't worry about her appearance might have been an excellent ideal.[21] Why was she not chosen?

We know very little about the relationship of ideology to social structures and understand very little about the social consequences of unconscious needs. Even so, it is possible to speculate that, as with so much else in the antebellum South, slavery had a good deal to do with the ideal of the southern lady. Because they owned slaves and thus maintained a traditional landowning aristocracy, southerners tenaciously held on to the patriarchal family structure. The patriarchy had been the norm in seventeenth-century England. Transported to Virginia and adopted as a social pattern by the planters there, it

18. *Society in America*, abridged version (New York: Doubleday, Anchor, 1962), p. 337.
19. *Cavalier and Yankee* (New York: Braziller, 1963), pp. 123–55.
20. See Chilton Latham Powell, *English Domestic Relations, 1487–1653* (New York: Columbia University Press, 1917), for a description of early English advice books. Janet Wilson James, "Changing Ideas about Women in the United States, 1776–1825," 1954 Ph.D. dissertation in the Schlesinger Library, Radcliffe College, is an excellent study of the advice books which were widely read in America. A collection of these books may also be found in the Schlesinger Library. Eileen Power, *Medieval People* (London: Methuen, 1924), chapter 4, provides a charming exposition of one such book, which, on the wife's duty to the husband, offered a direct forecast of the southern image: "She is to be loving, humble, obedient, careful and thoughtful for his person, silent regarding his secrets, and patient if he is foolish and allows his heart to stray toward other women."
21. Prov. 31.

lived on into the nineteenth century in the whole South.[22] A future officer of the Confederacy explained the theory of the family common among his contemporaries, and related it directly to the institution of slavery:

The Slave Institution of the South increases the tendency to dignify the family. Each planter is in fact a Patriarch—his position compels him to be a ruler in his household. From early youth, his children and servants look up to him as the head, and obedience and subordination become important elements of education.... Domestic relations become those which are most prized.[23]

Women, along with children and slaves, were expected to recognize their proper and subordinate place and to be obedient to the head of the family. Any tendency on the part of any of the members of the system to assert themselves against the master threatened the whole, and therefore slavery itself. It was no accident that the most articulate spokesmen for slavery were also eloquent exponents of the subordinate role of women. George Fitzhugh, perhaps the most noted and certainly among the most able of these spokesmen, wrote, for example:

So long as she is nervous, fickle, capricious, delicate, diffident and dependent, man will worship and adore her. Her weakness is her strength, and her true art is to cultivate and improve that weakness. Woman naturally shrinks from public gaze, and from the struggle and competition of life.... In truth, woman, like children, has but one right and that is the right to protection. The right to protection involves the obligation to obey. A husband, a lord and master, whom she should love, honor and obey, nature designed for every women.... If she be obedient she stands little danger of maltreatment.[24]

If the need to maintain the slave system contributed to the insistence upon perfect, though submissive, women, so did the simple fact that a male-dominated society was good for men. Some of the characteristics demanded of the southern lady were also expected of women in other parts of the United States and require no more complex explanation than that any ruling group can find a theory to

22. William Byrd to Charles, Earl of Orkney, 5 July 1726, describing his life as a patriarch, in the *Virginia Magazine of History and Biography* 32 (January 1924): 27. See also Peter Laslett, introduction to Robert Filmer, *Patriarchal:* "It is worth pointing out...that the descendants of the Virginia planters, who became the slaveholders of the Southern States, were the heads of a classic type of patriarchal household, so that it survived until the middle of the nineteenth century even in so rationalistic and equalitarian a society as the U.S.A." (Oxford: B. Blackwell, 1949), p. 26.

23. Christopher C. G. Memminger, Lecture before the Young Men's Library Association of Augusta, Georgia, 1851, quoted in W. S. Jenkins, *Pro-Slavery Thought in the Old South* (Chapel Hill: University of North Carolina Press, 1935), p. 210.

24. *Sociology for the South* (Richmond: Morris, 1854), pp. 214–15.

justify its position. Like aristocrats, Communists, and bourgeois businessmen, southern men had no trouble finding theoretical support for a way of life that was decidedly to their advantage. Obedient, faithful, submissive women strengthened the image of men who thought themselves vigorous, intelligent, commanding leaders.

Such women also contributed considerably to manly creature comforts. Ellen Glasgow put it this way in one of her novels:

The cares she met with such serenity had been too heavy for her strength; they had driven the bloom from her cheeks and the lustre from her eyes; and, though she had not faltered at her task, she had drooped daily and grown older than her years. The master might live with lavish disregard of the morrow, not the master's wife. For him were the open house, the shining table, the well-stocked wine cellar and the morning rides over the dewey fields; for her the care of her home and children, and of the souls and bodies of the black people that had been given into her hands.[25]

Despite the vigor of their statements, there is some evidence that southern men did not feel altogether secure in their self-proclaimed position of lord and master of the whole patriarchy. Fear lay beneath the surface of the flowery praise of woman and the insistence that God had made her the way men wanted her to be. Otherwise it is hard to see why men spent so much time and energy stating their position. One of Beverly Tucker's leading characters discussed the way he proposed to educate his daughter. She must be raised, he said, to take for granted her husband's superiority, to rely on his wisdom, to take pride in his distinction. "Even should her faculties be superior to his, he cannot raise her so high but that she will still feel herself a creature of his hands."[26]

What were they afraid of, these would-be patriarchs who threatened to withdraw their love from women who disagreed with them or aspired to any forbidden activity? Partly, perhaps, that the women to whom they had granted the custody of conscience and morality might apply that conscience to male behavior—to sharp trading in the market place, to inordinate addiction to alcohol, to nocturnal visits to the slave quarters. Men were aware, too, that the woman who had been so firmly put in her place, the home, often showed unusual power within that restricted domain. She raised the children; she set the standards for behavior. In 1802 a visiting Englishman commented that in North Carolina "the legislative and executive powers of the house belong to the mistress, the master has nothing to do with administration; he is a monument of uxoriousness

---

25. *The Battle Ground* (New York: Doubleday & Page, 1902), p. 48.
26. *George Balcombe* (New York, 1836), 2:52.

and passive endurance."[27] Two decades later a North Carolinian wrote to a friend contemplating matrimony that he must be "prepared to have his nose occasionally ground . . . and that he must not drink or play cards."[28] If women could exert so much power even in their restricted position who could tell what they might do with more freedom?

The omens were there to see. Southern men often identified the work of the hated abolitionists with the work of "strong-minded" northern women. A Virginian wrote to a friend in 1853:

You have doubtless seen in the newspapers the struggle we have with the strong-minded women as they call themselves in the World Temperance Convention. If you have seen a true account of the matter you will see that we gained a perfect triumph, and I believe have given a rebuke to this most impudent clique of unsexed females and rampant abolitionists which must put down the petticoats—at least as far as their claim to take the platforms of public debate and enter into all the rough and tumble of the war of words.

His college professor correspondent replied: "I most heartily rejoice with you in the defeat of those shameless amazons."[29] It was a paradox that men who asserted that God made woman as they wished her to be, or that the feminine qualities they admired were given by nature, were afraid that women would break out of the God-given and natural mode of behavior.

If these speculations ring true, one pressing question still remains. Since the ideal of perfection placed a great strain upon women, why did they tolerate their role? One reason is suggested by the early indoctrination already mentioned: the institutions and mores of the society all pointed in the same direction. Churches, schools, parents, books, magazines, all promulgated the same message: be a lady and you will be loved and respected and supported. If you defy the pattern and behave in ways considered unladylike you will be unsexed, rejected, unloved, and you will probably starve.

The persistence of the complementary images of the soft, submissive, perfect woman and of the strong, commanding, intelligent, and dominant man in the face of an exigent reality that often called for quite different qualities suggests that these images had deep

27. John Davis, *Personal Adventures and Travels of Four and a Half Years in the United States of America,* quoted in Katherine Jones, *Plantation South* (Indianapolis: Bobbs-Merrill, 1957), p. 85.

28. Quoted in Johnson, *Ante-Bellum North Carolina,* p. 243.

29. John Hartwell Cocke is the writer of the first letter. He is discussed in Clement Eaton's *The Mind of the Old South* (Baton Rouge: Louisiana State University Press, 1964) as "the liberal mind in a southern context" (pp. 11–12). Obviously his liberalism did not extend to women who chose to be "strong-minded"! George Fitzhugh was the recipient of the letter.

significance for the men and women who believed in them. A society increasingly threatened from the outside had every reason to try to diminish internal threats to its stability. George Fitzhugh made this quite explicit when he equated any change in the role of women *or* in the institution of slavery with the downfall of the family and the consequent demise of society. If the distance between the myth and reality became so great that it could not be overlooked, then the situation might be threatening indeed.

Though many southern women were worried about slavery, few had any vision of a society different from the one they knew. Perhaps, they, too, sensed a threat of social disorganization inherent in any challenge to male dominance. For whatever reasons, most of them tried to live up to the Sisyphean task expected of them.

*This famous short speech by the ex-slave and suffragist
Sojourner Truth was delivered impromptu at a meeting
presided over by Mrs. Frances D. Gage, who recorded the
speech. Born a slave in New York in the late eighteenth
century, Sojourner Truth was sold away from both her
parents in childhood and later was to have some of her own
children sold away from her. When she stripped away the
hypocrisy of the "defenseless woman" argument in this
speech, she spoke out of the bitterest of personal experience.*

AIN'T I A WOMAN?

Sojourner Truth

Well, children, where there is so much racket there must be something out of kilter. I think that 'twixt the niggers of the South and the women of the North, all talking about rights, the white men will be in a fix pretty soon. But what's all this here talking about?

That man over there says women need to be helped into carriages, and lifted over ditches, and to have the best place everywhere. Nobody ever helps me into carriages, or over mud-puddles, or gives me any best place! . . . And ain't I a woman? Look at me! Look at my arm! I have ploughed, and planted, and gathered into barns, and no man could head me! And ain't I a woman? I could work as much and eat as much as a man—when I could get it—and bear the lash as well! And ain't I a woman? I have borne thirteen children, and seen them most all sold off to slavery, and when I cried out with my mother's grief, none but Jesus heard me! And ain't I a woman?

Then they talk about this thing in the head; what's this they call it? ["Intellect," whispered someone near.] That's it, honey. What's that got to do with women's rights or niggers' rights? If my cup won't hold but a pint, and yours holds a quart, wouldn't you be mean not to let me have my little half-measure full?

Then that little man in black there, he says women can't have as much rights as men, because Christ wasn't a woman! Where did your Christ come from? Where did your Christ come from? From God and a woman! Man had nothing to do with Him. . . .

If the first woman God ever made was strong enough to turn the world upside down all alone, these women together ought to be able to turn it back, and get it right side up again! And now they are asking to do it, the men better let them.

It seems that women, denied many forums for the resolution of their problems, particularly in the public world, have turned often to advice columns in newspapers and magazines. So it was in the "Bintel Brief," an advice column that appeared in the Forward, *a daily Yiddish newspaper that has been published for more than eighty years. The* Forward *was an indispensable feature of life for the Eastern European Jewish immigrants who flooded the Lower East Side of New York between 1880 and 1925. Not only did it chronicle the often disaster-scarred lives of its readers and their world, but it sometimes took an active role in those lives. For example, when men who left their wives and children numbered so many at one time and women pleaded for their return in letters to the "Bintel Brief," the* Forward *printed a special column to trace them. In the 1909 letter reprinted here, another familiar misery of immigrant women is documented. Many young immigrant girls, without protection either of decent work or wages or of the pedestal of their middle-class sisters, were lured into brothels and onto the streets.*

A LETTER FROM "MISERABLE"

FROM *A Bintel Brief*

Dear Editor,

Please print my letter and give me an answer. You might possibly save my life with it. I have no peace, neither day nor night, and I am afraid I will go mad because of my dreams.

I came to America three years ago from a small town in Lithuania, and I was twenty years old at that time. Besides me, my parents had five more unmarried daughters. My father was a Hebrew teacher. We used to help out by plucking chickens, making cigarettes, washing clothes for people, and we lived in poverty. The house was like a Gehenna. There was always yelling, cursing, and even beating of each other. It was bitter for me till a cousin of mine took pity on me. He sent a steamship ticket and money. He wrote that I should come to America and he would marry me.

I didn't know him, because he was a little boy when he left our town, but my delight knew no bounds. When I came to him, I found he was a sick man, and a few weeks later he died.

Then I began to work on ladies' waists. The "pleasant" life of a girl in the dreary shop must certainly be familiar to you. I toiled, and like all shopgirls, I hoped and waited for deliverance through a good match.

Landsleit and matchmakers were busy. I met plenty of prospective bridegrooms, but though I was attractive and well built, no one grabbed me. Thus a year passed. Then I met a woman who told me she was a matchmaker and had many suitors "in stock." I spilled out all my heartaches to her. First she talked me out of marrying a work-worn operator with whom I would have to live in poverty, then she told me that pretty girls could wallow in pleasure if they made the right friends. She made such a connection for me. But I had not imagined what that meant.

What I lived through afterwards is impossible for me to describe. The woman handed me over to bandits, and when I wanted to run away from them they locked me in a room without windows and beat me savagely.

Time passed and I got used to the horrible life. Later I even had an opportunity to escape, because they used to send me out on the streets, but life had become meaningless for me anyway, and nothing mattered anymore. I lived this way for six months, degraded and dejected, until I got sick and they drove me out of that house.

I appealed for admission into several hospitals, but they didn't want to take me in. I had no money, because the rogues had taken everything from me. I tried to appeal to *landsleit* for help, but since they already knew all about me, they chased me away. I had decided to throw myself into the river, but wandering around on the streets, I met a richly dressed man who was quite drunk. I took over six hundred dollars from him and spent the money on doctors, who cured me.

Then I got a job as a maid for fine people who knew nothing about my past, and I have been working for them for quite a while. I am devoted and diligent, they like me, and everything is fine.

A short time ago the woman of the house died, but I continued to work there. In time, her husband proposed that I marry him. The children, who are not yet grown up, also want me to be their "mother." I know it would be good for them and for me to remain there. The man is honest and good; but my heart won't allow me to deceive him and conceal my past. What shall I do now?

Susan Brownmiller, in her thorough and definitive study of rape from a feminist perspective, identifies rape closely with the very origins of sexual oppression we have discussed here. With the advent of private property and the consequent concern with inheritance rights came, Brownmiller argues, "man's historic desire to maintain sole, total and complete access to woman's vagina." Thus, it evolved that the "criminal act he viewed with horror and punished as rape was not sexual assault per se, but an act of unlawful possession." That notion survives today in the treatment of women as property and in our cultural value system that subscribes to a theory of "aggressive male domination over women as a natural right." Women must fight back, Brownmiller maintains, by establishing rape in our criminal code as criminal violence rather than as an act of "irrational, impulsive, uncontrollable lust."

WOMEN FIGHT BACK

Susan Brownmiller

FROM *Against Our Will: Men, Women and Rape*

To a woman the definition of rape is fairly simple. A sexual invasion of the body by force, an incursion into the private, personal inner space without consent—in short, an internal assault from one of several avenues and by one of several methods—constitutes a deliberate violation of emotional, physical and rational integrity and is a hostile, degrading act of violence that deserves the name of rape.

Yet by tracing man's concept of rape as he defined it in his earliest laws, we now know with certainty that the criminal act he viewed with horror, and the deadly punishments he saw fit to apply, had little to do with an actual act of sexual violence that a woman's body might sustain. True, the law has come some distance since its beginnings when rape meant simply and conclusively the theft of a father's daughter's virginity, a specialized crime that damaged valuable goods before they could reach the matrimonial market, but modern legal perceptions of rape are rooted still in ancient male concepts of property.

From the earliest times, when men of one tribe freely raped women of another tribe to secure new wives, the laws of marriage and the laws of rape have been philosophically entwined, and even today it is largely impossible to separate them out. Man's historic desire to maintain sole, total and complete access to woman's vagina, as codified by his earliest laws of marriage, sprang from his need to be the sole physical instrument governing impregnation, progeny and inheritance rights. As man understood his male reality, it was perfectly lawful to capture and rape some other tribe's women, for what better way for his own tribe to increase? But it was unlawful, he felt, for the insult to be returned. The criminal act he viewed with horror and punished as rape was not sexual assault *per se*, but an act of unlawful possession, a trespass against his tribal right to control vaginal access to all women who belonged to him and his kin.

Since marriage, by law, was consummated in one manner only, by defloration of virginity with attendant ceremonial tokens, the act man came to construe as criminal rape was the illegal destruction of virginity outside a marriage contract of his making. Later, when he came to see his own definition as too narrow for the times, he broadened his criminal concept to cover the ruination of his wife's chastity as well, thus extending the law's concern to nonvirgins too. Although these legal origins have been buried in the morass of forgotten history, as the laws of rape continued to evolve they never shook free of their initial concept—that the violation was first and foremost a violation of *male* rights of possession, based on *male* requirements of virginity, chastity and consent to private access as the female bargain in the marriage contract (the underpinnings, as he enforced them, of man's economic estate).

To our modern way of thinking, these theoretical origins are peculiar and difficult to fully grasp. A huge disparity in thought— male logic versus female logic—affects perception of rape to this very day, confounding the analytic processes of some of the best legal minds. Today's young rapist has no thought of capturing a wife or securing an inheritance or estate. His is an act of impermanent conquest, not a practical approach to ownership and control. The economic advantage of rape is a forgotten concept. What remains is the basic male-female struggle, a hit-and-run attack, a brief expression of physical power, a conscious process of intimidation, a blunt, ugly sexual invasion with possible lasting psychological effects on all women.

When rape is placed where it truly belongs, within the context of modern criminal violence and not within the purview of ancient masculine codes, the crime retains its unique dimensions, falling midway between robbery and assault. It is, in one act, both a blow to the body and a blow to the mind, and a "taking" of sex through the use or threat of force. Yet the differences between rape and an assault or a robbery are as distinctive as the obvious similarities. In a prosecutable case of assault, bodily damage to the victim is clearly evident. In a case of rape, the threat of force does not secure a tangible commodity as we understand the term, although sex traditionally has been viewed by men as "the female treasure"; more precisely, in rape the threat of force obtains a highly valued sexual service through temporary access to the victim's intimate parts, and the intent is not merely to "take," but to humiliate and degrade. . . .

Rape, as the current law defines it, is the forcible perpetration of an act of sexual intercourse on the body of a woman *not one's wife*. The exemption from rape prosecutions granted to husbands who force their wives into acts of sexual union by physical means is as ancient as the original definition of criminal rape, which was synonymous with that quaint phrase of Biblical origin, "unlawful carnal knowledge." To our Biblical forefathers, any carnal knowledge outside the marriage contract was "unlawful." And any carnal knowledge within the marriage contract was, by definition, "lawful." Thus, as the law evolved, the idea that a husband could be prosecuted for raping his wife was unthinkable, for the law was conceived to protect *his* interests, not those of his wife. Sir Matthew Hale explained to his peers in the seventeenth century, "A husband cannot be guilty of rape upon his wife for by their mutual matrimonial consent and contract the wife hath given up herself in this kind to her husband, which she cannot retract." In other words, marriage implies consent to sexual intercourse at all times, and a husband has a lawful right to copulate with his wife against her will and by force according to the terms of their contract.

The most famous marital rape in literature, occurring onstage in the popular television serial but offstage in the novel, is that of Irene by Soames in *The Forsyte Saga*. As Galsworthy presents the Soamesian logic, the logic of Everyhusband, although perhaps not of Galsworthy himself, the denied husband has "at last asserted his rights and acted like a man." In his morning-after solitude while he hears Irene still crying in the bedroom, Soames muses, "The incident was really of no great moment; women made a fuss about it in books; but in the cool judgment of right-thinking men, of men of the world, such as he recollected often received praise in the Divorce Court, he had but done his best to sustain the sanctity of marriage, to prevent her from abandoning her duty. . . . No, he did not regret it."

In the cool judgment of right-thinking women, compulsory sexual intercourse is not a husband's right in marriage, for such a "right" gives the lie to any concept of equality and human dignity. Consent is better arrived at by husband and wife afresh each time, for if women are to be what we believe we are—equal partners—then intercourse must be construed as an act of mutual desire and not as a wifely "duty," enforced by the permissible threat of bodily harm or of economic sanctions.

In cases of rape within a marriage, the law must take a philosophic leap of the greatest magnitude, for which the ancient concept of conjugal rights (female rights as well as male) might continue to have some validity in annulments and contested divorces—civil procedures conducted in courts of law—it must not be used as a shield to cover acts of force perpetrated by husbands on the bodies of their wives. There are those who believe that the current laws governing assault and battery are sufficient to deal with the cases of forcible rape in marriage, and those who take the more liberal stand that a sexual assault law might be applicable only to those men legally separated from their wives who return to "claim" their marital "right," but either of these solutions fails to come to grips with the basic violation.

Since the beginning of written history, criminal rape has been bound up with the common law of consent in marriage, and it is time, once and for all, to make a clean break. A sexual assault is an invasion of bodily integrity and a violation of freedom and self-determination wherever it happens to take place, in or out of the marriage bed. I recognize that it is easier to write these words than to draw up a workable legal provision, and I recognize the difficulties that juries will have in their deliberations when faced with a wife who accuses her husband of forcing her into copulation against her will, but the principle of bodily self-determination must be established without qualification, I think, if it is to become an inviolable principle on any level. And revolutionary as this principle may appear to the traditions of Anglo-American jurisprudence, it is accepted as a matter of course and human dignity in the criminal codes of Sweden and Denmark and in the codes of the U.S.S.R. and other countries in the Communist bloc as well, although how it works out in practice I cannot say. (Certain of these European countries, including Switzerland and Yugoslavia, also equate economic threats, such as the threatened loss of a job, with threats of physical force in cases of rape.)

The concept of consent rears its formidable head in the much debated laws of statutory rape, but here consent is construed in the opposite sense—not as something that cannot be retracted, as in marriage, but as something that cannot be given. Since the thirteenth-century Statutes of Westminster, the law has sought to fix an arbitrary age below which an act of sexual intercourse with a female, with or without the use of force, is deemed a criminal offense that deserves severe punishment because the female is too young to know her own mind. Coexistent with these statutory rape laws, and somewhat contradictory to them, have been the laws governing criminal incest, sexual victimization of a child by a blood relation, where the imposition of legal penalties has been charitably lenient, to say the least—yet another indication of the theoretical concept that the child "belongs" to the father's estate. Under current legislation, which is by no means uniform, a conviction for statutory rape may draw a life sentence in many jurisdictions, yet a conviction for incest rarely carries more than a ten-year sentence, approximately the same maximum penalty that is fixed by law for sodomy offenses.

If protection of the bodily integrity of all children is to be genuinely reflected in the law, and not simply the protection of patriarchal interests, then the current division of offenses (statutory rape for outsiders; incest for members of the victim's family) must be erased. Retaining a fixed age of consent seems a necessary and humane measure for the protection of young girls and young boys alike, although it must be understood that any arbitrary age limit is at best a judicious compromise since sexual maturity and wisdom are not automatically conferred with the passage of time. Feminists who have applied themselves to this difficult question are in agreement that all children below the age of twelve deserve unqualified protection by a statutory age provision of sexual assault legislation, since that age is reasonably linked with the onset of puberty and awareness of sex, its biologic functions and repercussions. In line with the tradition of current statutory rape legislation, offenses committed against children below the age of twelve should carry the maximum penalty, normalized to twenty years. Recognizing that young persons above twelve and below sixteen remain particularly vulnerable to sexual coercion by adults who use a position of authority, rather than physical force, to achieve their aim (within the household or within an institution or a medical facility, to give three all-too-common examples), the law ought to be flexible enough to allow prosecutorial discretion in the handling of these cases under a more limited concept of "statutory sexual assault," with corresponding lesser penalties as the outer age limits are reached.

"Consent" has yet another role to play in a case of sexual assault. In reviewing the act, in seeking to determine whether or not a crime was committed, the concept of consent that is debated in court hinges on whether or not the victim offered sufficient resistance to the attack, whether or not her will was truly overcome by the use of force or the threat of bodily harm. The peculiar nature of sexual crimes of violence, as much as man's peculiar historic perception of their meaning, has always clouded the law's perception of consent.

It is accepted without question that robbery victims need not prove they resisted the robber, and it is never inferred that by handing over their money, they "consented" to the act and therefore the act was no crime. Indeed, police usually advise law-abiding citizens not to resist a robbery, but rather to wait it out patiently, report the offense to the proper authorities, and put the entire matter in the hands of the law. As a matter of fact, successful resistance to a robbery these days is considered heroic.

In certain middle-class neighborhoods in New York City, people who must be out on the streets late at night, coming home from work, taking a trip to the deli, or walking the dog, have taken to carrying a ten-dollar bill as "mugger money" to satisfy the aims and rage of any robber who might accost them. Clearly, the feeling seems to be that the loss of a few bucks is a better bargain than the risk of physical violence. Handing over money at knife point, or dipping into one's wallet to assuage a weaponless but menacing figure on a dark, deserted street, may be financially painful or emotionally distressing, but it hardly compares to the massive insult to one's self-determination that is sustained during a sexual assault.

In a sexual assault physical harm is much more than a threat; it is a reality because violence is an integral part of the act. Body contact and physical intrusion are the purpose of the crime, not appropriation of a physically detached and removable item like money. Yet the nature of the crime as it is practiced does bear robbery a close resemblance, because the sexual goal for the rapist resembles the monetary goal of the robber (often both goals are accomplished during the course of one confrontation if the victim is a woman), and so, in a sex crime, a bargain between offender and victim may also be struck. In this respect, a sexual assault is closer in victim response to a robbery than it is to a simple case of assault, for an assaultive event may not have a specific goal beyond the physical contest, and furthermore, people who find themselves in an assaultive situation usually defend themselves by fighting back.

Under the rules of law, victims of robbery and assault are not required to prove they resisted, or that they didn't consent, or that the act was accomplished with sufficient force, or sufficient threat of force, to overcome their will, because the law presumes it highly unlikely that a person willingly gives away money, except to a charity or to a favorite cause, and the law presumes that no person willingly submits to a brutal beating and the infliction of bodily harm and permanent damage. But victims of rape and other forms of sexual assault do need to prove these evidentiary requirements—that they resisted, that they didn't consent, that their will was overcome by overwhelming force and fear—because the law has never been able to satisfactorily distinguish an act of mutually desired sexual union from an act of forced, criminal sexual aggression. . . .

A new approach to the law and to law enforcement can take us only part of the way. Turning over to women 50 percent of the power to enforce the law and maintain the order will be a major step toward eliminating *machismo*. However, the ideology of rape is aided by more than a system of lenient laws that serve to protect offenders and is abetted by more than the fiat of total male control over the lawful use of power. The ideology of rape is fueled by cultural values that are perpetuated at every level of our society, and nothing less than a frontal attack is needed to repel this cultural assault.

The theory of aggressive male domination over women as a natural right is so deeply embedded in our cultural value system that all recent attempts to expose it—in movies, television commercials or even in children's textbooks—have barely managed to scratch the surface. As I see it, the problem is not that polarized role playing (man as doer; woman as bystander) and exaggerated portrayals of the female body as passive sex object are simply "demeaning" to women's dignity and self-conception, or that such portrayals fail to provide positive role models for young girls, but that cultural sexism is a conscious form of female degradation designed to boost the male ego by offering "proof" of his native superiority (and of female inferiority) everywhere he looks.

Critics of the women's movement, when they are not faulting us for being slovenly, straggly-haired, construction-booted, whiny sore losers who refuse to accept our female responsibilities, often profess to see a certain inexplicable Victorian primness and antisexual prudery in our attitudes and responses. "Come on, gals," they say in essence, "don't you know that your battle for female liberation is part of our larger battle for sexual liberation? Free yourselves from all your old hang-ups! Stop pretending that you are actually offended by those four-letter words and animal noises we grunt in your direction on the street in appreciation of your womanly charms. When we plaster your faceless naked body on the cover of our slick magazines, which sell millions of copies, we do it in sensual obeisance to your timeless beauty—which, by our estimation, ceases to be timeless at age twenty or thereabouts. If we feel the need for a little fun and go out and rent the body of a prostitute for a half hour or so, we are merely engaging in a mutual act between two consenting adults, and what's it got to do with you? When we turn our movie theaters into showcases for pornographic films and convert our bookstores to outlets for mass-produced obscene smut, not only should you marvel at the wonders of our free-enterprise system, but you should applaud us for pushing back the barriers of repressive middle-class morality, and for our strenuous defense of all the civil liberties you hold so dear, because we have made obscenity the new frontier in defense of freedom of speech, that noble liberal tradition. And surely you're not against civil liberties and freedom of speech, now, are you?"

The case against pornography and the case against toleration of prostitution are central to the fight against rape, and if it angers a large part of the liberal population to be so informed, then I would question in turn the political understanding of such liberals and their true concern for the rights of women. Or to put it more gently, a feminist analysis approaches all prior assumptions, including those of the great, unquestioned liberal tradition, with a certain open-minded suspicion, for all prior traditions have worked against the cause of women and no set of values, including that of tolerant liberals, is above review or challenge. After all, the liberal *politik* has had less input from the feminist perspective than from any other modern source; it does not by its own considerable virtue embody a perfection of ideals, it has no special claim on goodness, rather, it is most receptive to those values to which it has been made sensitive by others.

The defense lawyer mentality had such a hold over the liberal tradition that when we in the women's movement first began to politicize rape back in 1971, and found ourselves on the side of the prosecutor's office in demanding that New York State's rape laws be changed to eliminate the requirement by corroborative proof, the liberal establishment as represented by the American Civil Liberties Union was up in arms. Two years later the ACLU had become sensitized to the plight of rape victims under the rules of law, thanks to the lobbying efforts of feminist lawyers, and once this new concern for rape victims was balanced against the ACLU's longstanding and just concern for the rights of all defendants, the civil-liberties organization withdrew its opposition to corroboration repeal. This, I believe, was a philosophic change of significant proportions, and perhaps it heralds major changes to come. In any event, those of us who know our history recall that when the women's liberation movement was birthed by the radical left, the first serious struggle we faced was to free ourselves from the structures, thought processes and priorities of what we came to call the *male* left—and so if we now find ourselves in philosophic disagreement with the thought processes and priorities of what has been no less of a male liberal tradition, we should not find it surprising.

Once we accept as basic truth that rape is not a crime of irrational, impulsive, uncontrollable lust, but is a deliberate, hostile, violent act of degradation and possession on the part of a would-be conqueror, designed to intimidate and inspire fear, we must look toward those elements in our culture that promote and propagandize these attitudes, which offer men, and in particular, impressionable, adolescent males, who form the potential raping population, the ideology and psychologic encouragement to commit their acts of aggression *without awareness, for the most part, that they have committed a punishable crime*, let alone a moral wrong. The myth of the heroic rapist that permeates false notions of masculinity, from the successful seducer to the man who "takes what he wants when he wants it," is inculcated in young boys from the time they first become aware that being a male means access to certain mysterious rites and privileges, including the right to buy a woman's body. When young men learn that females may be bought for a price, and that acts of sex command set prices, then how should they not also conclude that that which may be bought may also be taken without the civility of a monetary exchange?

That there *might* be a connection between prostitution and rape is certainly not a new idea. Operating from the old (and discredited) lust, drive and relief theory, men have occasionally put forward the notion that the way to control criminal rape is to ensure the ready accessibility of female bodies at a reasonable price through the legalization of prostitution, so that the male impulse might be satisfied with ease, efficiency and a minimum of bother. Alas for these androcentric pragmatists, even Dr. Kinsey could unearth "no adequate data to prove the truth or falsity" of such a connection. Twenty years after Kinsey others of a similar mind were still trying, although the evidence still suggested that men who make frequent use of brothels are several years older than men who are usually charged with criminal rape. To my mind the experience of the American military in Vietnam, where brothels for GI's were officially sanctioned, even incorporated into the base-camp recreation areas, should prove conclusively that the availability of sex for a small price is no deterrent to the decision to rape, any more than the availability of a base-camp shooting range is a deterrent to the killing of unarmed civilians and children.

But my horror at the idea of legalized prostitution is not that it doesn't work as a rape deterrent, but that it institutionalizes the concept that it is man's monetary right, if not his divine right, to gain access to the female body, and that sex is a female service that should not be denied the civilized male. Perpetuation of the concept that the "powerful male impulse" must be satisfied with immediacy by a cooperative class of women, set aside and expressly licensed for this purpose, is part and parcel of the mass psychology of rape. Indeed, until the day is reached when prostitution is totally eliminated (a millennium that will not arrive until men, who create the demand, and not women who supply it, are fully prosecuted under the law), the false perception of sexual access as an adjunct of male power and privilege will continue to fuel the rapist mentality. . . .

A law that reflects the female reality and a social system that no longer shuts women out of its enforcement and does not promote a masculine ideology of rape will go a long way toward the elimination of crimes of sexual violence, but the last line of defense shall always be our female bodies and our female minds. In making rape a *speakable* crime, not a matter of shame, the women's movement has already fired the first retaliatory shots in a war as ancient as civilization. When, just a few years ago, we began to hold our speak-outs on rape, our conferences, borrowing a church meeting hall for an afternoon, renting a high-school auditorium and some classrooms for a weekend of workshops and discussion, the world out there, the world outside of radical feminism, thought it was all very funny.

"You're talking about *rape*? Incredible! A *political* crime against women? How is a sex crime political? You're actually having women give testimony about their own rapes and what happened to them afterwards, the police, the hospitals, the courts? Far out!" And then the nervous giggles that betray confusion, fear and shame disappeared and in their place was the dim recognition that in daring to speak the unspoken, women had uncovered yet another part of our oppression, perhaps the central key: historic physical repression, a conscious process of intimidation, guilt and fear.

Within two years the world out there had stopped laughing, and the movement had progressed beyond the organizational forms of speak-outs and conferences, our internal consciousness-raising, to community outreach programs that were imaginative, original and unprecedented: rape crisis centers with a telephone hot line staffed twenty-four hours a day to provide counseling, procedural information and sisterly solidarity to recent rape victims and even to those whose assault had taken place years ago but who never had the chance to talk it out with other women and release their suppressed rage; rape legislation study groups to work up model codes based on a fresh approach to the law and to work with legislators to get new laws adopted; anti-rape projects in conjunction with the emergency ward of a city hospital, in close association with policewomen staffing newly formed sex crime analysis squads and investigative units. With pamphlets, newletters, bumper stickers, "Wanted" posters, combative slogans—"STOP RAPE"; "WAR—WOMEN AGAINST RAPE"; "SMASH SEXISM, DISARM RAPISTS!"—and with classes in self-defense, women turned around and seized the offensive.

The wonder of all this female activity, decentralized grass-roots organizations and programs that sprung up independently in places like Seattle, Indianapolis, Ann Arbor, Toronto, and Boulder, Colorado, is that none of it had been predicted, encouraged, or faintly suggested by men anywhere in their stern rules of caution, their friendly advice, their fatherly solicitude in more than five thousand years of written history. That women should *organize* to combat rape was a women's movement invention. . . .

There can be no private solutions to the problem of rape. A

woman who follows this sort of special cautionary advice to the letter and thinks she is acting in society's interest—or even in her own personal interest—is deluding herself rather sadly. While the risk to one potential victim might be slightly diminished (and I even doubt this, since I have known of nuns who were raped within walled convents), not only does the number of potential rapists on the loose remain constant, but the ultimate effect of rape upon the woman's mental and emotional health has been accomplished *even without the act*. For to accept a special burden of self-protection is to reinforce the concept that women must live and move about in fear and can never expect to achieve the personal freedom, independence and self-assurance of men.

That's what rape is all about, isn't it? And a possible deep-down reason why even the best of our concerned, well-meaning men run to stereotypic warnings when they seek to grapple with the problem of rape deterrence is that they *prefer* to see rape as a woman's problem, rather than as a societal problem resulting from a distorted masculine philosophy of aggression. For when men raise the spectre of the unknown rapist, they refuse to take psychologic responsibility for the nature of his act.

In preceding chapters we have seen emerge a complex of structures created and invoked by men in their oppression of women. Men's most cherished institutions and epistemologies—religion, education, the arts and sciences—have lent substance and form to the notion of woman's "otherness," to the separation from the male-defined normative standards against which women have found it so difficult to struggle. In the light of that complexity, single-cause theories accounting for the oppression of women, however valid they may have been in describing particular experience or historical process, have proved inadequate to decode the sexual economy. Analyses, therefore, like Engels' notion of the derivation of sexual oppression

CHAPTER 4

Women and the Marketplace

from the advent of the institution of private property (Chapter 1, this volume), and the Marxist analysis of women's relationship to the means of production as the source of sexual oppression, while compelling, are insufficient to account for woman's condition. A multitude of attitudes and structures around which human life has been organized must also be considered.

In an argument that we examine in greater detail in the next chapter, Juliet Mitchell (1973) describes woman's condition as a unity of elements that combine in different ways at different times in history. The key elements or structures of woman's condition—production, reproduction, sexuality, and the socialization of children—are historically entangled and form a woman's estate that encompasses both her exploitation in the labor situation and the awarding to her of her own "place"—the universe of the family. Mitchell is undoubtedly correct in her assertion that the "liberation of women can only be achieved if *all four* structures in which they (women) are integrated are transformed." However, we must not lose sight of what de Beauvoir has taught us well—the power of the idea to assume independent life. The *idea* of woman's place, with its capacity to outlive structural changes, we have seen in tracing the historical shunting of women between pit and pedestal; and we have witnessed the staying power of such ideas, particularly as they are incorporated into social mythology. As we turn our attention now to the effects of the sexual economy on women's relationship to the public world, particularly as workers, it will be helpful to be alert to the frequent symbiosis between the idea of woman's place and the structures that have created or that sustain the idea.

Perhaps the most fundamental of symbioses, as we have seen, is that of woman's place and the family. The centrality of woman's role in the family is acknowledged by Elise Boulding in her attempt to trace the historical roots of occupational segregation. Women in Western countries today are largely confined to a limited number of job categories (nearly 80 percent in 1979 were in clerical, sales, service, factory or plant jobs), a confinement that limits pay and status. Boulding, in her essay reprinted here, "Familial Constraints on Women's Work Roles," seeks to establish the source of this familiar segregation and to trace its progress through time. The source, which she defines as women's reproductive life, appears to have established the earliest role in production for women as "home" centered. Women in the earliest known societies were gatherers, hunters of small game, tenders of the camp or homesite, while men ranged far in the hunting of large game and in pursuit of warfare. Although there probably was no lesser value placed on "women's work" at that stage, "women's range of productivity increasingly narrowed as men, during their hunting journeys, began locating sources of flint and other materials valued for tools and for ceremonials." In an argument reminiscent of Engels' notion of private property as the "historical defeat of the female sex," Boulding cites the accumulation of wealth and property as a cause of the emergence of law and the consequent emergence of the concept of the male-headed household. The concept, she claims, made subsidiary household members of the great mass of middle- and working-class women and provided the basis for continued and intensified occupational segregation of women. The male head of household concept became the focal one for social, economic, and familial organization, but "in any period of history for which data is available, one-fifth to one-half of the heads of households were women." The result of the "fiction of male support" has been, through history, low wages and restricted economic opportunities.

The peculiar capacity of men to sustain belief in an official idea of woman's place while violating that idea in the name of expediency is identified by Boulding as an early phenomenon. She cites, for example, the 1563 Elizabethan Statute of Artifices under which ". . . every woman free or bound, under 60, and not carrying on a trade or calling, provided she had no land, and was not in domestic or other service, was liable to be called upon to enter service either in the fields or otherwise, and if she refused, she was imprisoned until she complied." On the one hand, such inconsistency illustrates the close ties between sex and class oppression, for, as the last chapter demonstrated, working-class and poor women have always occupied a more flexible "place" than their middle- and upper-class sisters in the eyes of a male ruling class. But in a more general sense, it is demonstration of the eternally adjustable boundaries of woman's place, which tend to be defined primarily in accordance with prevailing economic need and circumstance, and of that dysjunction identified in the last chapter between the view men choose to have of women at any given time and the realities of women's lives.

The economic exploitation of women documented by Boulding assumed new character in the eighteenth century with the industrial revolution. Until about 1750, the family constituted the primary production unit in the Western world, with women and children shouldering responsibility for the family's survival along with the husband and father. With industrialization, the family's home-based production was displaced by the factory with devastating results for women.

In *Woman's Work: The Housewife, Past and Present*, the historian Ann Oakley defines a cause-and-effect relationship between the development of industrial capitalism in the West and the absolute economic dependence of women on men that she claims was theretofore the exception rather than the rule among the working classes. Oakley points out that a transitional period did occur between the displacement of the family as producer and the total identification of the man as breadwinner which was the normative standard by mid-nineteenth century. At first, women followed their traditional work in textiles (the first industrialized manufacturing process) into the factories, continuing the general class view of the time that women and children should support themselves through their labor. But the separation of home from work with attendant child care problems, compounded by the emergence of the notion that "work outside the home for married women was a misfortune and a disgrace" (1976:50), eventually confirmed the ideal, if not the reality, of economic dependence on men for women of all classes. The danger in this analysis lies in the implication that women in the preindustrial period enjoyed real independence and equality with men. That was patently not the case, as Boulding's history suggests and recent historical work confirms.

While the notion of separate spheres for men and women was to rise to ideology as a result of the separation of home and workplace engendered by the industrial revolution, the rough division of labor predicated on biological differences existed prior to that period, and indeed throughout human history. Preindustrial women often led lives of crushing responsibilities. As Carl Degler observes in *At Odds: Women and the Family in America from the Revolution to the Present*, "their tasks were not only diverse but almost endless. Over the long term of a lifetime they were probably more arduous and demanding than those performed by men." Testament to that arduousness was provided by a traveler in eighteenth-century Carolina who reported that "the ordinary women take care of Cows, Hogs, and other small Cattle, make Butter and Cheese, spin cotton and flax, help to sow and reap corn, wind silk from the worms, gather Fruit, and look after the House (quoted from Julia Cherry Spruill in Degler 1980:363). As Degler continues,

Looking after the house was itself a heavy task, since that included not only cleaning the physical interior but the washing and mending of the family's clothes, preparing meals under the handicaps of an open fireplace and no running water, preserving the various kinds of foods, making all the soap, candles, and most of the medicines used by the family, as well as all the clothes for the family. And then, as the quotation suggests, the woman had to be ready at planting or harvest time to help in the fields. On top of all this, of course, was the bearing and rearing of children. During the colonial years, when families of six children were common, this task was close to a full job in itself. It was this almost unending congeries of jobs that probably gave birth to the well-known tag line that a woman's work is never done. Unlike the work of the husband-farmer, women's work went on after dark and at an undiminished pace throughout the year. (1980:363–64)

For those women, charged with manufacturing virtually all the goods consumed by their families, separation of production from the workplace and increased manufacture of consumable goods by factories could hardly have been much regretted. Nor could the increasing re-location of families to urban areas. The much-chronicled horrors of urban life under nineteenth-century industrial capitalism, however real, did not in fact stand in contrast to an idyllic rural past where men and women shared equally and happily in labors of love.

Whatever the advantages and disadvantages to women of rural versus urban life, the movement from farms to cities that accelerated throughout the nineteenth century served as catalyst to the developing notion of separate spheres discussed at length in Chapter 3. By the latter half of the nineteenth century, ideology defining women's proper place had the social and economic realities of women's lives firmly under heel. Idle wives and daughters served as evidence of success and manhood for prosperous middle-class men and eventually for working-class men, in spite of incomes sorely in need of supplement. At last that idleness and the concomitant economic dependence became a basic political and social tenet of the century. Perhaps the most graphic description of the political significance of women's economic dependence is given us by Thorstein Veblen in *The Theory of the Leisure Class*. Productive labor, he explains, having become "derogatory to respectable women ... special pains should be taken in the construction of women's dress, to impress upon the beholder the fact (often indeed a fiction) that the wearer does not and can not habitually engage in useful work" (1953:126). Veblen judges that the elaborately confining styles of clothing worn by women reveal the servitude of women to men:

To apply this generalization to women's dress, and put the matter in concrete terms: the high heel, the skirt, the impracticable bonnet, the corset, and the general disregard of the wearer's comfort which is an obvious feature of all civilized women's apparel, are so many items of evidence to the effect that in the modern civilized scheme of life the woman is still, in theory, the economic dependent of the man—that perhaps in a highly idealized sense, she still is the man's chattel. The homely reason for all this conspicuous leisure and attire on the part of the woman lies in the fact that they are servants to whom, in the differentiation of economic functions, has been delegated the office of putting in evidence their master's ability to pay. (1953:127)

Further credence was lent to the notion of woman's special place by the new ideology of frail health, according to which woman's unique biology predisposed her to illness and insanity. Physicians warned women to limit their physical activities during puberty and child-bearing years when the demands of the uterus were particularly acute. As one physician warned, it was "as if the Almighty, in creating the female sex, had taken the uterus and built up a woman around it" (quoted in Rothman 1978:23). Simple domestic pursuits, it was suggested, should be preferred to serious study, which threatened to interfere with the central nervous system and the reproductive organs, leading to "brain fever" and sterility. Perhaps, suggests Alice Rossi, the widespread rise of hysteria and mental illness among nineteenth-century women can be attributed to "the conflict inherent in the lack of fit between the cultural ideal of True Womanhood and the social reality of homemaking and maternal roles" (1974:252).

Opportunities for women were thus effectively restricted both by the symbolic function they served in the middle-class ideology and by the myth of "virtuous womanhood" whose sources and ramifications we traced in the preceding chapter. While attractive opportunities for productive and lucrative work were virtually eliminated, the need, often the compulsion, to work still existed for many women. And, not surprisingly, the need for women's labor in the marketplace was not obliterated by the prevailing ideologies of the period. The conflict was handled in different ways, depending on distinctions of class, race, and ethnic origin. In the case of "genteel" women—white and Anglo-Saxon—the answer was to create women's jobs, jobs whose functions and wages were tied to notions of what, when, and how women could "properly" work. In the selection included here from *Woman's Proper Place: A History of Changing Ideals and Practices, 1870 to the Present*, Sheila Rothman observes that "the late nineteenth century began a sex-stereotyping of occupations that would persist through most of the twentieth century. This was the moment when typists, stenographers, department store clerks and school teachers all became prototypically female."

Having explored in preceding chapters the sources of "women's special sphere," including technology, the new consumer society, and the conviction of the male medical establishment that women were physically frail and emotionally unstable, Rothman concludes that "notions of when women could properly work and what they could properly do contributed in critical ways to legitimating distinctions that were frankly discriminatory." Through a series of rationalizations, the crux of which has come down to current generations as training, education, and work for women as "something to fall back on," the way into the work force and into higher education for young, unmarried women was smoothed. The place in the work force, once secured, was circumscribed in a manner familiar to us today. In addition to their confinement to a relatively few categories of work, women were restricted to and have remained at the lower end of the employment ladder. As Rothman points out, women have long occupied the ranks of elementary school teachers, typists and stenographers, clerks and cashiers. Men, by contrast, have had carrers, "rising from clerks to become managers, from teachers to become principals."

In a male-dominated economy, women afforded a less expensive and an expendable labor supply since their work might be regarded as temporary and more tractable than the labor of less educated and less refined men—often immigrants—who would be available to work at comparable wages and with comparable lack of opportunities for advancement. The latter rationale Rothman sees as particularly the reason for the domination of women in teaching and in secretarial work, which was no longer seen, after the invention of the typewriter, as a training ground for business and political leaders. For the poor, black, and immigrant women who comprised most of the female work force at the turn of the century, however, there was no question of "proper" work for women. Even more than in the white-collar or "genteel" jobs described by Rothman, women of the underclass furnished a source of cheap and dispensable unskilled labor in textile mills, tobacco factories, the garment and shoe industries, in food processing and canning, and even, as Barbara Mayer Wertheimer relates, in heavy industries such as foundries and tinplate mills. In *We Were There: The Story of Working Women in America*, Wertheimer describes the exploitation of women in the tenement sweatshops, in steam laundries, and in other occupations involving the most oppressive working conditions with the most meager pay. "By 1910," she observes, "in spite of society's attitude, growing numbers of women worked outside the home and composed 21 percent of the country's work force" (1977:210). Women's jobs in almost all cases were just that—women's jobs—unskilled and dead-end. Women were largely excluded from labor unions, as we shall see later, and thus earned on the average one-third the wages of union men and one-half those of nonunion men. For such meager pay, Wertheimer reports, women suffered from such appalling working conditions as those reported by Helen Campbell in 1893:

Feather-sorters, fur-workers, cotton-sorters, all workers on any material that gives off dust, are subject to lung and bronchial troubles. In soap-factories the girls' hands are eaten by the caustic soda, and by the end of the day the fingers are often raw and bleeding. In making buttons, pins, and other manufactures . . . there is always liability of getting the fingers jammed or caught. For the first three times the wounds are dressed without charge. After that the person injured must pay expenses. . . .

In food preparation girls who clean and pack fish get blistered hands and fingers from the saltpetre. . . . Others in "working stalls" stand in cold water all day. . . .

In match-factories . . . necrosis often attacks the worker, and the jaw is eaten away. . . . (1977:213)

Women's jobs included another dimension unfamiliar to the male worker—what we in modern parlance have named "sexual harassment." Upton Sinclair's famous novel about workers in the meat-packing industry, *The Jungle* (1960), offers a classic description of that particular form of oppression. Sinclair's book makes palpable the hypocrisy of the "cult of womanhood" in a society in which no deference was paid to sex and age among an underclass where value was reduced to their capacity to work. Sex merely lent another dimension to the abuse of their humanity suffered by workers in that inglorious "gilded age." Ona's suffering of sexual abuse at the hands of her boss in *The Jungle* is the underside of the pedestal occupied by her middle- and upper-class sisters. The myth of female spirituality, whatever the considerable cost of that form of dehumanization to middle- and upper-class women, was maintained at even more exacting cost to women of the underclass. Ona's pain, and that of her husband, Jurgis, in the face of his powerlessness to protect her from the man who controlled their economic fate, must serve to remind us again of the inextricable ties of the sexual economy to the class system.

The complexity of those ties is emphasized by the failure of economically exploited men to discern the class implications of the attitudes toward women they shared with their oppressors. That failure can been seen with particular poignancy in Jewish culture. Jewish women, whose Old Country tradition it had been to work and maintain intercourse with the public world more than in most immigrant groups, worked hard in the home when they also worked outside, and when marriage or children made it difficult or impossible for them to go out to work. In the selection from *The Jewish Woman in America* by Charlotte Baum, Paula Hyman, and Sonja Michel, included here, the common situation in immigrant communities of women who take in piecework to contribute to the support of the family is described. The burden borne by those women is rendered significantly heavier by child care responsibilities and the reality of their shared struggle for survival with their men. A double burden was carried by the Jewish mother (familiar to Polish, Italian, and other immigrant women as well) whose efforts to maintain both roles resulted in a continued secondness in the public world to which she was denied claim of membership and from which financial need prevented her escape.

The failure of working men to support working women of their own class in their common struggle against economic oppression is clearly evident in the labor organizing movement. This aspect of the sexual economy is particularly regrettable because of the heroic part played by women in so many labor struggles. The efforts on behalf of working people of individual women organizers such as Mother Mary Jones have earned them the attention of historians. Our attention and admiration must be given, as well, to working women struggling as a group, who adhered to the principles of a movement that had largely ignored their interests. An important event in the history of their struggle occurred in the 1909 strike of shirtwaist makers against the infamous Triangle Waist Company. An essentially unorganized trade, garment workers were dominated by young Russian-Jewish women. Helen Marot's 1910 account of the strike in "A Woman's Strike—An Appreciation of the Shirtwaist Makers of New York" (Baxandall, Gordon, and Reverby 1976:187–93) estimates that of the thirty thousand workers who answered the call "six thousand were Russian men; two thousand Italian women; possibly one thousand American women and about twenty or twenty-one thousand Russian Jewish girls" (1976:189). Eighty percent, then, were women, and women without trade union experience. Yet, with the help of the Women's Trade Union League, the women carried the day, enduring for more than thirteen weeks marked by deprivation, physical exposure, harassment, arrests and imprisonment. When success came, credit was owed to the women who had been largely ignored by labor organizers. And they continued to be ignored in most trades even after this demonstration that, as Marot claims became a trade union truism, " 'women make the best strikers,'. . . Working women have been less ready than men to make the initial sacrifice that trade-union membership calls for, but when they reach the point of striking they give themselves as fully and as instinctively to the cause as they give themselves in their personal relationships" (1976:190).

Women have participated in, contributed to, and led many strikes since 1909, but it has been against a constant background of antagonism or lack of support from male unionists. Often, women have been forced to work through a system of dual unionism, organized into separate locals at a frequently lower pay scale than their male counterparts. So, too, they have formed supportive coalitions like the Women's Trade Union League (WTUL) whose work was partially underwritten by the American Federation of Labour under Samuel Gompers. Dependence on the male-dominated and unsympathetic American Federation of Labor (AFL) created problems for women organizers, however, as in the case of WTUL's effort to support the largely female textile workers in the Lowell, Massachusetts, strike of 1912. The AFL's lack of interest in organizing unskilled workers like the textile workers was in direct conflict with WTUL's desire to support women workers where they were—in the ranks of the unskilled—and on that and subsequent occasions the WTUL was forced to withdraw. Although exclusion of unskilled workers is a thing of the past, and dual unionism occurs rarely, women remain largely unrepresented in the labor movement. The organization of unskilled industrial workers begun by the International Workers of the World (IWW) and carried on by the Congress of Industrial Organizations (CIO), has long since taken place, but the movement appears still disinclined to organize where women are—in clerical jobs, for example. Even the recently organized (1974) Coalition of Labor Union Women (CLUW), successful as it has been in fostering a sense of solidarity among already organized women, has had little measurable effect in persuading male union officers of the importance of women's special problems as workers, and even less of the importance of those of black women.

Added to the complications of class distinctions in the sexual economy's control of women in the public world is the race factor. As the work of Herbert Gutman discussed in the last chapter has demonstrated, the effect of racism after the Civil War was devastating to the black family as institution, as well as to individual members as they struggled to establish themselves in occupations and to survive in a hostile world. Urban unemployment and underemployment were endemic among blacks who had been driven from the land after the war, and have continued at a "disaster level" ever since (Gutman 1977:467). Blacks were largely barred from white-collar and factory jobs, and were directed instead into the unskilled and service jobs that maintained in "freedom" a semblance of their situation in slavery. In 1905, 86 percent of black males in New York City worked as unskilled labor and in service occupations, as compared to 30 percent of Jewish males and 47 percent of Italian males working in comparable occupations. Unemployment, restriction to low-level job categories, and consequently inadequate incomes had all the effects on blacks that might be expected. It is Gutman's thesis, as discussed earlier, that the family disruption, poverty, and crime that have plagued blacks in the century since slavery are clearly derived from the economic facts rehearsed above, not from a "culture of poverty" bred among Afro-Americans through three hundred years of enslavement, as "slavery-specific" theorists like Daniel Moynihan would have it; and certainly not from a matriarchal family structure allegedly created by the dislocation of the African family under slavery. Black women have suffered from the same occupational segregation as have black men, with the addition of sex discrimination. Black women have indeed worked in greater numbers than white women to support children made fatherless, not by slavery, but by social conditions created by racism and poverty, or to provide desperately needed supplement to a husband's income. But their work always was monetarily valued less highly even than that of the exploited black male, and never put them in a position to challenge the economic and family dominance as argued by matriarchal theorists (Ryan 1978:389). Not only was the black woman confined to "women's jobs," but she was limited to a ghetto within even that category. "Where black women did work in mills," for example, "it was at the heavy labor jobs or as janitresses, not at the machines" (Wertheimer 1977:228). The specialized job segregation continued into the twentieth century as black women toiled primarily as domestics as well as in the heavy jobs they were assigned in the nineteenth century.

Perhaps the most painful aspect of the black woman's relationship to the public world, however, has been a variation of the pit and pedestal theme. The notion of the "black matriarchy," originating in the work of students of poverty like Daniel Moynihan, was seized by blacks and whites alike in the mid-1960s to explain the widening economic gap between the two races. Racism had upset the natural order of the sexes, it was claimed, and male dominance must be restored if black children are to be prepared to take their appropriate places in a liberated world. In a not unfamiliar pattern, "the black woman became a scapegoat for institutionalized racism, and the bugbear of black matriarchy distracted attention from the structural inequities of the American economic system" (Ryan 1978:389). Black women, as we have seen white women do on similar occasions, responded with some ambivalence to the new model of femininity imposed on them, and for some time there was indication that it would be embraced as an appropriate "next stage" in the black liberation movement. Thus, the black sociologist Joyce Ladner could predict that "the traditional 'strong' black woman has probably outlived her usefulness because this role has been challenged by the black man, who has demanded that white society acknowledge his manhood and deal directly with him instead of using his woman—considered the weaker sex—as a buffer" (quoted in Ryan 1978:392).

Ambivalence on this issue exacerbated divisions already present in the growing women's movement because of class differences, and because of the manner in which class and race differences among women were emphasized by the roles they were assigned as they emerged gradually into the postindustrial public world. Perceptions of shared oppression in the sexual economy have smoothed over some of those divisions, as an article by Diane Almquist in this chapter reveals. It is important to remind ourselves repeatedly, however, of the roots in real class and race differences of divisions among women that continue to trouble us in the present.

Given the pain, the inequity, and the lack of either job satisfaction or reasonable monetary reward available in the public world to most women in the time periods we have considered here, a woman's most practical alternative often seemed to be marriage, and preferably marriage to a man whose financial prospects offered her a reasonable guarantee of lifelong security. Financial security she might find, if she were lucky, but the marriage contract proferred no promise of economic equality. In fact, as Leo Kanowitz explains in *Women and the Law* (1969:35), a woman sacrificed at marriage a number of legal privileges with economic implications that she held as a single woman. In certain areas of the law, single women in England enjoyed almost equal status with single men. They could, for example, engage in contracts and manage and control their own property. Women who married, however, lost these and other rights.

The legal basis for the loss of rights suffered by the married woman was "the feudal doctrine of coverture." Predicated on the long-standing notion of the male head of household discussed earlier, the doctrine was described by Blackstone in his *Common Law* in the following terms: "By marriage, the husband and wife are one person in law; that is, the very being or legal existence of the woman is suspended during the marriage, or at least is incorporated and consolidated" (quoted in Kanowitz 1969:35). The implications for increased dependence of women on men are manifest in this doctrine. In return for relinquishment of her property, or rights to dispose of that property, and of many legal rights only peripherally related to the question of property, such as the right to sue, the woman was promised continuing economic support from her husband for herself and her children. The compromise in integrity, autonomy, and dignity exacted from the married woman in order to ensure the keeping of that vague promise, or the sufficiency of support, has been recorded in letters, diaries, and other accounts by women themselves over the generations; analyzed by political and economic scholars; and described poignantly by writers of fiction, drama, and poetry. Perhaps the most familiar example of the latter is Henrik Ibsen's play *A Doll's House*. The degrading play-acting of Nora to satisfy her husband's notion of her as childlike, as his "little squirrel," in order to obtain funds from him to meet her legitimate financial obligations, is well known.

At least one nineteenth-century political analyst believed that marriage under such conditions, placing such requirements on women, differed little from prostitution. The nineteenth-century anarchist Emma Goldman wrote "The Traffic in Women" to point out the relationship between women's economic and social inferiority and prostitution. The problem, Goldman insisted, is not one of morality but of economics. Increased urbanization and industrial congestion, she argued, left many young women with only the choice between "industrial slavery" and the street. The problem, however, extends well beyond that of the young woman in the street or in the brothel. Goldman saw the dependent position of all women as prostitution: "Nowhere is woman treated according to the merit of her work, but rather as a sex. It is therefore almost inevitable that she should pay for her right to exist, to keep a position in whatever line, with sex favors. Thus it is merely a question of degree whether she sells herself to one man, in or out of marriage, or to many men" (1972:179). Believing economic exploitation of women under industrial capitalism to be the cause of prostitution, Goldman did not see the institution of marriage as affording women much protection. Citing statistics from the *History of Prostitution* by Dr. William Sanger, revealing a substantial number of prostitutes in the nineteenth century to be married women, Goldman observed ironically that "evidently there was not much of a guaranty for their safety and purity in the sanctity of marriage" (1972:180). Neither vice raids nor hypocritical harangues by political leaders anxious to distract the public from a "great social wrong" (1972:177) will eradicate prostitution, Goldman insisted; only a recognition of prostitution as a product of social conditions will accomplish that.

As we survey the record of women in the marketplace in America, one period emerges as both different from and absolutely congruent with the pattern and treatment of women's employment we have repeatedly observed. World War II had a great impact on women's relationship to the public world. "The proportion of women working increased from twenty-five percent to thirty-six percent, a rise greater than that of the preceding four decades. Wages rose, the number of wives holding jobs doubled and unionization of women quadrupled. Employers' attitudes toward hiring women remained skeptical, but since women were the only available labor force reserve, they were hired" (Baxandall, Gordon, and Reverby 1976:280). That Hobson's choice for employers gave women opportunities to move into nontraditional job categories and learn skills. "Rosie the Riveter" became a metaphor for a description of women's place in the work force during the war. Of even greater significance than the kinds of work women did during this period was the unprecedented support provided by industry and the corporate bureaucracy both to the concept of women working outside the home and to services that would facilitate the entrance into the work force not only of young, unmarried women but of married women with children. Public insistence on the place of woman in the home and the creation of an "occupation" as homemaker to keep her there, was stretched to accommodate propaganda about women's new duty in the work force. Homemaking services, including hot take-home meals, and child care services, often at the worksite, were made available to working women to induce them to leave the homes to which they had been well taught to cling.

As if on cue, such services, as well as encouragement of women to work, were withdrawn at the end of the war. Men were returning to jobs and to wives they expected to be unchanged; and the same forces that were gathered to set aside the concept of women's sphere for the war effort turned to its reestablishment as the task of the late 1940s and '50s. Middle-class women, like their mothers and grandmothers, were expected to return to homemaking with a new will. The by now conventional wisdom born in Betty Friedan's *The Feminine Mystique* is that women went home after the war because they succumbed to the imposition of a new "feminine mystique," the complex and numerous elements of which Friedan explores in her book. Magazine publishers, advertisers, ministers, and newspaper editors conspired, she argues, in the creation of a reborn cult of domesticity, called in its new incarnation, "togetherness." Perhaps so, Sheila Tobias and Lisa Anderson observe in *What Really Happened to Rosie the Riveter? Demobilization and the Female Labor Force, 1944–47*, but "what history has not yet set right is the degree to which the women were forcibly laid off their jobs in the postwar period" (1973). Among the persuasive statistics collected by Tobias and Anderson in their effort to set right the story are those indicating that while the percentage of women in the labor force increased from 27.6 in 1940 to a wartime high of 37.0 and decreased to a low of 30.0 in the postwar period (1947), by 1951 the percentage was up again to 32.7. Moreover, a number of surveys taken during and immediately after the war indicated that significant numbers of women did not regard their work as a temporary war effort:

The UAW (United Auto Workers), for example, reported that a survey done of their own membership indicated that fully 85% of the women then working wanted to continue to work after the war. The report predicted that of the 350,000 female UAW members, 300,000 would want to go on working (Statement of R. J. Thomas, president of UAW). In answer to the question, "If a job is available, will you continue to work outside your home after the war?" 98.5% of the single women and 100% of the widows answered, "Yes." Among the married women 68.7% (this is the highest proportion of married women responding positively in any of the surveys taken) said "yes." In reporting the figures R. J. Thomas . . . said the results of the study would shatter the preconceived ideas of certain industrialists and "experts" who think the majority of women workers will want to leave the labor market. (1973:16)

That they did leave, at least temporarily, is accounted for by Tobias and Anderson by a catalog of "inducements" including an end to federally funded or corporation-supported child care; reclassification of jobs women had held into "men's jobs"; refusal by unions and companies to honor seniority of women in rehiring after the postwar layoffs; and new and strengthened protective legislation. In any case, women did not all return gladly to their homes, nor to the lesser jobs and lower pay to which the many women who continued or returned to work were relegated. They fought, through equal pay suits, labor unions, and petitions to the government, to retain gains made during the war. The battle was largely lost. Even the Equal Pay Act, introduced in 1945 and again in 1946 and 1947, failed to pass, not becoming law until 1963 (Tobias and Anderson 1973:28). World War II had nonetheless been a watershed in establishing the legitimacy of work outside the home for women—especially married women and mothers. The working-class women who were, for the most part, the "Rosie the Riveters" would remain in the labor force, albeit within a widening web of myth that they were not there, that they did not need to be there, or that if they were there, it was not as breadwinners but simply to earn pin money. The perpetuation of those myths seemed only to ensure second-class status of women in the working world and to fuel the creation of the large body of "welfare mothers" and other underclass women so familiar in the modern landscape.

Betty Friedan's *The Feminine Mystique*, published in 1963, spoke to a different class of women—the middle-class women for whom the postwar dream of suburbia became a reality. Friedan's work is discussed elsewhere in this volume, but her exploration of the denouement of the dream in the decade of the 1950s is relevant here. The result of the buying of the dream, Friedan tells us, was the debilitating "problem that had no name":

It is my thesis that the core of the problem for women today is not sexual but a problem of identity—a stunting or evasion of growth that is perpetuated by the feminine mystique. It is my thesis that as the Victorian culture did not permit women to accept or gratify their basic sexual needs, our culture does not permit women to accept or gratify their basic need to grow and fulfill their potentialities as human beings, a need which is not solely defined by their sexual role. (Friedan 1970:69)

Any articulation of or objection to the new cult of domesticity in which the problem was rooted earned a woman scorn and pity by purveyors of the pop psychoanalysis that characterized the period, and which we consider in the next chapter. Only disappointment and lack of fulfillment could be the fate, women learned through fiction and sermon, of the unwomanly woman who perversely pursued a career or a paycheck instead of—exclusively—marriage and motherhood.

Of course, as our earlier discussion indicates, the female population about whom Friedan writes never included all women. Class distinctions, as in previous centuries, continued to create gulfs between women. The victims of the "feminine mystique" as she describes them were largely white and middle class. Many poor or working-class women, and particularly black women in America, continued to work, often reluctantly, to support families throughout the decades of domestic frenzy. For working-class women, Maryland Congresswoman Barbara Mikulski reminds us, the alternative to staying at home to care for a family has been "dreary hours at factories doing work that was tedious, monotonous and backbreaking, or standing on their feet long hours as shop girls" (Seifer 1973:ix). Effectively denied satisfying or lucrative work during the immediate postwar period, the dream for many such women was initiation into the world increasingly perceived as prison for middle-class women. "We dreamed of marrying white collar organization men and moving, up and out. Suburbs meant getting away from those old stereotypes" (Seifer 1973:ix). The same dream, of course, fueled the support by many black women of the new model of black femininity of the 1960s discussed earlier. Many a white feminist has been stung by the accusation that her physical participation in the women's movement was made possible by a black maid in her home. It is unlikely that such antagonisms and divisions among women will be obliterated as long as race and class inequality continues.

These are accounts of decades and centuries past. To what degree, after two major political movements aimed at achieving equality for women, has the status of women in the marketplace changed? One is tempted to answer "hardly at all," and with some grim justification when progress is measured statistically. In 1979, women earned on the average fifty-nine cents for every dollar earned by men (black females earned fifty-four cents; Hispanic females earned forty-nine cents). That discrepancy is greater than in 1955 when women earned sixty-four cents to men's one dollar. Moreover, confinement of women to female job ghettos appears to have continued virtually without deviation since those ghettos were established in the nineteenth century. In March 1979, nearly 80 percent of women in the work force were in clerical, sales, and service jobs, and in unskilled factory or plant jobs. Moreover, within the larger occupational categories, women are concentrated in certain job classifications. More than two-fifths of working women are employed in ten occupations: as secretaries, retail trade sales workers, bookkeepers, private household workers, elementary school teachers, waitresses, typists, cashiers, sewers and stitchers, and registered nurses (Eisenstein 1981:217).

The only significant change from patterns established in the last century and before is the number of women in the work force. In 1977, 56 percent of all women sixteen and over worked, including for perhaps the first time since the elimination of the home as a central production unit, a major portion (62 to 69 percent) of women in the primary and childbearing years of twenty to thirty-four. The confinement of women to traditional female jobs that we noted above is particularly acute for a growing number of women between the ages of forty-five and fifty-four who are entering the job market, many for the first time. Today, a report by the National Commission on Working Women on "Women, Work and Age Discrimination" indicates, one out of three women in the work force is forty-five years or older. Such women are frequently denied training and access to positions that are opening up for younger women. Women who married with the expectation that marriage would provide lifetime economic security have been, in discouraging numbers, thrust into the work force as "displaced homemakers."

It seems that, just as suffrage failed to change substantially the political or social position of women in the Anglo-American world, so has the new body of law mandating sex equality failed in its promise of economic equality. Since the early 1960s there has been a proliferation of legislation prohibiting discrimination in employment and education based on race, sex, religion, national origin, handicap, and most recently, age. Beginning with the Equal Pay Act of 1963 and continuing through Title VII of the Civil Rights Act of 1964 and Title IX of the Education Amendment Act of 1972 (prohibition of discrimination based on sex in educational programs, including admissions and athletics), women have been furnished with a raft of laws designed to erase the economic effects of years of oppression. The results of those laws have been disappointing. In spite of a number of famous sex-discrimination cases won by women, or settled advantageously, the decline in wages of working women cited above would seem to indicate total failure of those laws to redress discrimination. Yet the signs of success can be counted not only in "won" cases, including "comparable pay for comparable work" suits, but in statistics relating to black women. In 1955, black women earned about one-third as much as white men; by 1977, they were earning more than half as much. The earnings of black women have increased from about 50 percent of those of white women in 1955 to almost 95 percent in 1977 (Treiman and Hartmann 1981:108–9). Such statistics indicate that the law is being enforced, although not uniformly, and that, at least, discrimination is not increasing. One must, however, recognize the limitations of the law. Its chief and central limitation is that it does not address the underlying problem—the occupational segregation of women grown out of the notion of "otherness" and the ideology of women's special sphere that we have traced throughout this book. Neither equal pay for equal work nor most traditional sex-discrimination charges can reach the underlying and structural problem of a gender-segregated work force. They do not challenge a public world that seeks to simulate a private world for its women workers by confining them to service and nurturing jobs—with inferior compensation—appropriate to their satellite sphere.

A 1981 U.S. Supreme Court decision offers some hope for mitigation of this fundamental discrimination against women in the marketplace. In *County of Washington* v. *Gunther* (25 FEP Cases 1521), the Court held that women bringing sex-based wage-discrimination claims under Title VII of the Civil Rights Act of 1964 are not required to satisfy the equal work standards of the Equal Pay Act of 1961. For the first time, jobs of comparable responsibility, skill level, and effort were considered as requiring equal pay. Although the Court insisted upon the "narrowness" of the *Gunther* decision, new possibilities for breaking through the barrier of work-force gender segregation have been opened. Studies are even now being undertaken to compare and classify jobs according to such criteria as effort, skill level, responsibility, and working conditions. The degree of resistance employers will present to new salary schedules for which such studies will inevitably indicate need, or to the need for gender-conscious management of appointments and promotions in traditional men's and women's jobs to diminish gender segregation, remains to be seen.

Equity, then, as measured in annual earnings or by the presence of women in job categories across the board, still has not been achieved. Some improvements, however, have been gained. Although still few in number, women are now counted among the elite of the working-class world—the skilled trades and crafts. Bureau of Labor Statistics reports show that women are moving steadily into management, banking and finance, and buying and purchasing positions. Women are stockbrokers, attorneys, physicians, college professors, and, occasionally, politicians and corporation executives. Dramatic gains have been made in medicine and law. In 1980, one in four medical graduates and one in three law school graduates was a woman, compared with one female graduate in ten in medicine and one in nine in law at the beginning of the 1970s.

But similar progress in past decades has proved short-lived. In the 1920s, in a period of temporary and, as we shall see in the next chapter, superficial, sexual and economic freedom following World War I, women were professors, business executives, and physicians in numbers not exceeded until the late 1970s. Gains made in those early years, however, were wiped out in the years of the Great Depression. With job scarcity, it was once again a man's work world. Such work as continued to be available through the 1930s was not available to women, or at least not to married women, who were even vacated from their stronghold of long duration—classroom teaching. Called back to the work force during World War II, but only until the men returned, the pattern of expediency in employment of women that we saw as far back as the 1563 Elizabethan Statute of Artifices was confirmed in the post-War War II era, and in the 1950s and '60s described by Friedan. That pattern of expediency, as many of the events noted here confirm, was not least destructive in its power to divide women, to mask their shared bonds of oppression as women while they struggled against the oppression of class and race.

Still, the effect of the sexual economy on the black woman has in recent years won some acknowledgment. Elizabeth M. Almquist, in an excerpt from her essay "Black Women and the Pursuit of Equality," included here, points out that current patterns of labor force participation indicate more similarities than differences among black and white women in rates of participation, occupational distribution, and annual earnings. Changes within the last twenty-five years have brought black women within economic parity of white women, although they still lag far below black men and farther still below white men. Almquist notes that the occupational upgrading experienced primarily by young black women increases the generational differences among all black women. It is not likely that the lives of the large number of older black women confined to domestic work will be improved by changing patterns of labor force participation, while the position of the young black woman may continue to improve. For her, "to the extent that we can disentangle racial and sexual components in black women's employment status, the sexual component is the more decisive one" (1979:444).

Finally, beyond the obvious and painful material effects of economic discrimination on women who must support themselves and families, or who, increasingly, must contribute to insufficient family incomes, what is the product of so many years of exclusion from significant participation and mobility in the public world? Phyllis Chesler argues that a distressing effect is a disabling ambivalence about money. "Psychologically," she asserts, "female financial ambition or the female need for economic self-sufficiency is completely at odds with the female need to either *be* or *be seen* as a Lady: protected, respectable, bought at a high price by one man" (1976:19). So susceptible have women been to the pedestal myth that they often deny their involvement in any productive labor, including that of maintaining a home or rearing children. The work of centuries of myth making about women's proper sphere, of years of manipulation of women's labor according to the dictates of expediency, appear above all to have left women bewildered about their role in a world in which worth is most particularly defined in terms of production. "Women are genuinely confused," Chesler says, "by a money culture that depends on their labor completely, but does not reward them for it economically" (1976:21).

We close this chapter with an excerpt from Virginia Woolf's famous treatise on sexism, *A Room of One's Own*, in which she explores women's place in a special corner of the marketplace. For clues to an understanding of women's assumed incapacity for literary achievement, she looks to the simple conditions of women's lives. Literature, Woolf asserts is not "spun in midair by incorporeal creatures" but is "the work of suffering human beings . . . attached to grossly material things, like health and money and the houses we live in." An even more formidable set of obstacles to women's creative achievement than material circumstances—the constant distractions, the lack of space and time—are the immaterial, what Woolf calls the "notorious indifference" of the world. But the indifference that was so hard for men to bear was to women not merely indifference but hostility. We are reminded of those women writers who sought, under such names as Currer and Ellis Bell, George Eliot, and George Sand, refuge from a world hostile to their explorations. In comparison with other areas of achievement—biological or physical sciences, mathematics, philosophy or law, for example—literature provides us with a great many examples of women who, in spite of oppressive institutions and attitudes, created enduring art. The list includes such major contributors as Jane Austen, Charlotte and Emily Bronte, George Eliot, and, of course, Virginia Woolf. And yet, might even this list have been longer had circumstances been more favorable? Literary achievement requires few special tools or acknowledgments. But it does demand free access to the world outside the home. Even Charlotte Bronte could claim that she had been denied the "facilities for observation . . . a knowledge of the world," which gave the work of such writers as Thackeray and Dickens "an importance, variety, depth greatly beyond what I can offer" (quoted in Olsen 1978:41). Success in literary creation, Woolf argues, for all its "private" quality, is made at least as difficult an achievement for women by their problematical relationship to the public world as is success in any part of the marketplace.

Are women writers in the twentieth century, like Shakespeare's "sister" or Charlotte Bronte, denied access to the outside world? In her now classic essay, "One Out of Twelve: Writers Who Are Women in Our Century,"[1] Tillie Olsen reaches conclusions similar to Woolf's. For clues to an understanding of women's "inferior" capacities for achievement, Olsen looks not to age-old arguments based upon biological differences but to the created human structures, the "punitive difference in circumstance, in history, between the sexes" (1978:27). Even contemporary women, Olsen tells us, live in a world which insists that creative achievement is opposed to womanly fulfillment and have been required to make a choice not imposed on men. Yet Olsen views with ambivalence the assumption by women writers in our century "as their right fullness of work *and* family life," for, if the fundamental human structures remain unchanged, their work will necessarily be "impeded, lessened, partial" (1978:32).

As we continue to examine the sexual economy, we will be repeatedly reminded that few aspects of women's lives remain undetermined by external forces.

---

1. On the basis of her informal examination of college and university course bibliographies, textbooks, anthologies, and critical reviews, Olsen concludes that the ratio of women to men writers of distinction is one to twelve.

Elise Boulding made a major contribution to the study of women with the publication of her history of women, The Underside Of History: A View of Women Through Time *(1976). In this precursor to that ambitious work, Boulding reveals the complex interrelationships of social, legal, and familial constraints that over the centuries have narrowed the power, influence, and as a result, economic independence of women. Like many other writers represented here, Boulding points to the nineteenth century as the sad "end of an era." It was the period when the many alternatives to economic dependency for women ended in a flush of sanctimonious and oppressive ideology about "woman's place."*

FAMILIAL CONSTRAINTS ON WOMEN'S WORK ROLES

Elise Boulding

The nature of the familial constraints on woman's role as worker in every type of human society is perhaps best captured by the triple role concept of "breeder-feeder-producer." From the earliest and simplest hunting and gathering folk to the most industrialized society of the twentieth century, the breeding of babies[1] and the feeding of humans of all ages is almost exclusively the work of the woman,[2] above and beyond other productive processes she is engaged in. In addition, the woman participates in certain producer roles, usually but not always differentiated from male producer roles.

It should be clear that all three categories in the breeder-feeder-producer triad are in fact producer roles, but I am distinguishing between the first two categories, which are assigned to women only, and the third, which is divided between women and men. In a subsistence society, the producer role exists primarily to create material for domestic consumption. It is only when trading begins that sticky questions about the agents and measurements of production arise.

Some of the material in this article is taken from *The Underside of History: A View of Women through Time* (Boulder, Colo.: Westview Press, 1976, in press). I wish to thank my associate, Dorothy Carson, for assistance in preparing this manuscript.

1. I include in the concept of breeding both the bearing of children and caring for them until they are self-sufficient. The biological aspect of childbearing is only one component of breeding thus defined.

2. Men may prepare special feast foods, but in no society is the preparation of food for consumption in the home the regular daily work of men.

Woman's production is normally noticed by statisticians only when it leaves the home. Man's production is more apt to be noticed whether it leaves the home or not.

At the simplest level the producer roles for women outside the breeder-feeder complex have to do with the gathering or growing of food, carrying water and fuel to the hearth, erection of shelters, making domestic utensils and clothing, and the creation of ceremonial objects. The triple role tends to give women more hours of work in a day than men, although this is not universally true. We will begin by examining the working day of women in different kinds of societies.

Different Work Settings for Women through History

Hunting and Gathering Societies

In hunting and gathering societies the producer role of the male is encompassed by hunting and the making of tools associated with hunting. These activities consume all of his working hours and generally provide about 20 percent of the food of the band.[3] Hunting has been described as a high-risk, low-yield activity, in contrast to food gathering as a low-risk, high-yield activity.[4] Women seem to be able to provide the other 80 percent of the band's food through gathering activities and still carry out the breeder-feeder roles, the procuring of water and fuel, building of shelters, making of utensils, etc. They also catch small game close to the campsite with their bare hands, but do not run great distances after game—an impractical proposition with small children to care for. It is sometimes said that the hunting and gathering way of life is the only leisure society we know of. Reports from many of the 250 hunting and gathering bands extant today indicate that women and men work shorter hours than in any other type of society and have more time for ceremonies and celebrations.[5]

Due to the constraints of the nomadic life, there is a strict limitation on family size. Hunting and gathering bands manage zero population growth through a combination of abortion, infanticide, and infant mortality. In this leisure society there are few sex-differentiated reward systems. Women and men have different ceremonial roles but participate equally in ceremonials and band decision making, including decisions about marriages. There is no accumulation of resources to serve as a power base for individuals of either sex, and monogamy is the rule. Although it is said that twenty hours

3. Richard B. Lee and Irven DeVore, eds., *Man the Hunter* (Chicago: Aldine Publishing Co., 1968).
4. Ibid.
5. Ibid.

of work per person per week may meet all maintenance needs, it is not clear whether the anthropologist observers have actually clocked the full working time of women around the campfire after the food has been brought there. There is probably a component of "invisible" work which needs to be more accurately recorded before this way of life disappears. It is also difficult to clock time spent in care of small children. When are they being "cared for," and when is interaction with them pure recreation and enjoyment? When all these considerations are taken into account, the chances are that even in this most egalitarian of all types of human societies the women are "working" longer hours than men.

The Early Agrovillages

Agriculture probably emerged out of discoveries of stands of wild grain at revisited campsites—stands that represented accidental harvests of the previous year's gathering activities. This was clearly women's work and still is wherever simple digging-stick type of planting in the slash-and-burn cultivation pattern is found, notably in Africa. In the agrovillage existence that developed when people began settling down near good supplies of wild grain, and planting their own crops besides, the work load began to shift more heavily toward women. Men in these agrovillages were still contributing their share of the food through hunting. Because of game scarcity by 12,000 B.C., the contributions of the now sedentary hunters, even with improved tools, were probably kept to 20 percent of the total food supply. Men would be gone for days at a time in pursuit of game, and women's producer roles in the agrovillage multiplied. The herding pattern for men, which was an offshoot of hunting, involved similar movement patterns, although it may have increased the economic contribution of men to family sustenance. With settlement came buildings, courtyards, the making and accumulation of domestic objects and ceremonial materials. The following outline summarizes women's daily activities in the agrovillage based on my interpretation of archeological evidence in the Near East from 10,000 to 6000 B.C., plus more contemporary anthropological evidence.

1. The hearth
    a) Cooking
    b) Feeding family
    c) Care of small infants (carried out concurrently with all other activities during day and night)
    d) Childbearing (one of primary productive processes of women, carried out concurrently with all other activities during day and night)
    e) Cleaning and maintenance of hearth

2. The courtyard
    a) Production processes
        (1) Food: processing of foods to be cooked (sometimes cooking and baking also done in courtyard, combining 1 and 2*a*)
        (2) Crafts: sewing, weaving, basket and pottery making, stoneware and implement making, jewelry, production of cosmetics
        (3) Building activities: houses, cult centers, etc.
    b) Social organization
        (1) Council meetings
        (2) Ritual and ceremony preparations
        (3) Teaching of children
        (4) Other village affairs
3. The fields
    a) Gathering fruit and nuts
    b) Clearing fields (with help from men)
    c) Planting, cultivating, and harvesting food
    d) Caring for sheep and goats
    e) Colleting fuel for hearth fires
    f) Collecting material for building
    g) Carrying water to the courtyard and hearth

These first agrovillages had populations of from 100 to 200 people. If the work load assigned to women seems improbably heavy, compare it with the summary of workloads for women (table 1) based on surveys of women engaged in subsistence agriculture in Africa today.[6]

I suggest that the point of transition from these early agrovillages (such as Eynan, Jarmo, Hacilar) to the large trading towns (like Jericho, Beidha, Catal Huyuk) was the point at which the woman's economic contribution started to "weigh" less than the man's, even though the sheer quantity of productive labor was greater. Initially, the egalitarianism of the hunting and gathering society must have carried over into the earliest agrovillages. The sheer fact of the continuing presence of women and long absences of men may have given rise to occasional examples of a "rule of women" during this first village life. Aberle suggests that matriliny arises in situations where there are all-women work groups, where women control the residence bases, and where there is "a certain range of productivity and

6. The data base for discussion on the interrelations between the integration of women in development, their situation, and population factors in Africa is the Regional Seminar on the Integration of Women in Development, with Special Reference to Population Factors, held by the Economic Commission for Africa of the United Nations Economic and Social Council in Addis Ababa, May 1947, mimeographed report (New York: United Nations, 1974).

Table 1

Participation by Women in the Traditional Rural and Modernizing
Economy in Africa

Responsibility	Unit of Participation*
A. Production/supply/distribution:	
1. Food production	0.70
2. Domestic food storage	0.50
3. Food processing	1.00
4. Animal husbandry	0.50
5. Marketing	0.60
6. Brewing	0.90
7. Water supply	0.80
8. Fuel supply	
B. Household/community:	
1. Household:	
a) Bearing, rearing, initial education of children	1.00
b) Cooking for husband, children, elders	1.00
c) Cleaning, washing, etc.	1.00
d) Housebuilding	0.30
e) House repair	0.50
1. Community:	
Self-help projects	0.70

Source: Mimeographed report of the Regional Seminar on the Integration of Women in Development (in 6 above). Data base from "The Changing and Contemporary Role of Women in African Development (1974): "Country Reports on Vocational and Technical Training for Girls and Women" (1972–74): studies, mission reports, discussions, all available from the United Nations. As noted in the text, units of participation should be determined first for areas within countries, then on the national level, then for Africa.

* Estimates are given in terms of the unit of participation for women's labor, i.e., women as a percentage of the total population in a given activity.

a certain range of centralization—ranges narrower than those of either patrilineal or bilateral systems."[7]

The Trading Towns

Women's range of productivity increasingly narrowed as men, during their hunting journeys, began locating sources of flint and other materials valued for tools and for ceremonials. This immediately gave them a competitive advantage over stay-at-home women. The first specialization between villages, according to the archaeological

7. David F. Aberle, "Matrilineal Descent in Cross-cultural Perspective," in *Matrilineal Kinship*, ed. David M. Schneider and Kathleen Gough (Berkeley: University of California Press, 1974), pp. 655–730. I agree with him that matriliny is not a general evolutionary stage but only arises under certain conditions. Not all agrovillage development would follow the pattern I am suggesting.

evidence, appears when hunters (some from agrovillages, some of them probably still nomadic) begin supplying other villages with flint and receiving craft and food products in return. Women are not able to work the trading networks to the extent the men are, because they are too busy with production for family consumption. Some of the craft products of women enter the trading networks, but by and large the diversity of women's tasks prevents specialization. Thus, when their products do enter the market they are marginal, and probably do not command "prices" comparable with those of the male specialists in the new stone and bone shops of the later trading towns.

The Rise of Urban Civilization

By the time major urban centers in Sumer and Egypt arose, a system of social stratification had developed that complicates the picture. In Sumerian Erech, 4000 B.C., there were few distinctions between rich and poor. There were "street scribes" available to any woman or man for business purposes, and there were no great differences in housing style and size. By 2500 B.C., however, nomadic incursions, wars, and gifts of land and booty from kings to their supporters had created an aristocracy based in the palace, the temple, and the landed estates. On the new urban scene there were large palace-temple complexes, rich landholders, and elaborate tables of law. From there a certain class of women—the aristocracy—became visible and would remain visible until the industrial revolution. Women in the scribal and small-merchant class, on the contrary, became invisible, working-class women somewhat less so. Thus, while the emergence of early trading towns tipped the scales against recognition of the productive role of the mass of women, the first urban civilizations finished the process.

The Role of Law in Redefinition of Women's Work

The emergence of law contains the emergence of the concept of the male-headed household and of the administration of property by the male. The earlier, more fluid, clan rights to land and property that left resources available to the women and men who were prepared to work with them were tranformed into rigidly spelled out male rights. This was no simple process; as late as 1751 B.C. the Code of Hammurabi contained sixty-eight sections on family and women, fifty on land and territory (dealing with clan rights), and seven on priestesses. While descent of the elites was usually recorded in government records through the male, a woman was sometimes named and descent traced through her. Women sometimes also appear in land deeds as heads of households and as donors and recipients of ritualized food offerings. They are recorded as doing long-distance trading under their own names. Ancient legal records show that the women of the elite often fought successfully to keep their rights to land under the new system that in principle recorded land in the name of males only. No study has been made of the percentage of women holding land in their own name throughout history, but in Europe from A.D. 900 to 1200 it was sometimes as high as 18 percent. When land administered by women on behalf of children is included, the figure was as high as 25 percent.[8] The amount of attention given to women's rights, both in Egyptian and Sumerian law,[9] and the numerous references in contemporary documents to court battles fought by women in Greece and Rome, indicate that declaring the male the legal head of the household and building legal and administrative practices around him never fully covered the real-life economic and social exigencies with which women and men had to deal. What the male head of household device did do, however, was to make second-class citizens of the great mass of middle- and working-class women, who had no independent power base as the women of the elite did. By defining them as subsidiary household members, it became possible to avoid the issue of equal work for equal pay. This mainly affected working-class women, since the scribal and small-merchant class—the urban bourgeoisie of the ancient civilizations—were as apt to promote women as display objects as their brothers centuries later. Middle-class urbanites in the Mediterranean civilizations enclosed their women from the beginning. Europe, ancient and modern, followed suit.

There were two classes of "working women," then, from about 2000 B.C. on: the wealthy overseas merchants and the estate and temple administrators on the one hand, and, on the other, the poor women who worked in textile workshops, ran the corner bakery and brewery, and provided the upper classes with much the same range of domestic, health, and beauty services that working women do today. The occupational roles for women in the Age of Pericles can be classified in the following way.[10]

1. Occupations for women slaves (there were an estimated

8. David Herlihy, "Land, Family, and Women in Continental Europe, 701–1200," *Traditio* 18 (1962): 89–120.

9. Steffan Wenig, *Women in Egyptian Art* (New York: McGraw-Hill Book Co., 1970); Samuel Noah Kramer, *The Sumerians: Their History, Culture, and Character* (Chicago: University of Chicago Press, 1963).

10. This listing represents a synthesis of information about Greek women from a great variety of sources, including material summarized in Evelyne Sullerot, *Histoire et sociologie du travail féminin* (Paris: Société Nouvelle des Editions Gonthier, 1968).

90,000 women slaves in Athens in the fourth century according to Wallon's *Histoire d'esclavage*)

a) Food processing: threshing grain, grinding flour

b) Agricultural work in the fields

c) Mining: gold and silver mining; separating metal from slag, washing metal; transporting ore from underground corridors of mines to the surface

d) Textile workers: all operations connected with carding, spinning, and weaving carried on by women in workshops —no indication whether these were state owned or privately owned. Weaving also carried on as cottage industry in private homes

e) Variety of craft production carried on as cottage industry in private homes

f) Domestic service

2. Occupations open to free women

a) Agriculture, unspecified except for "fieldwork"

b) Textile work as above

c) Trade: selling of vegetables, processed foods, baked goods, other home-manufactured products, unspecified. Selling of cloth, garments, headdresses

d) Innkeeping

e) Being a courtesan (combination intellectual, artist, and entertainer)

f) Running schools for courtesans

g) Midwifery, nursing

h) Music

i) Dancing

j) Vase painting

3. Occupations specifically forbidden to women

a) Medicine (there are records of illegal practice and punishment of women practitioners)

4. Occupations possible but not encouraged

a) Scribe; schools for women are rare (ex. Sappho) but if a woman could write she was not forbidden to exercise her skill.

Poor working women had several disadvantages compared with men from the beginning. They had to compete with slave labor for one thing.[11] Most of the textile workshops in Egypt and Greece were operated by female slave labor, and many services were rendered by

11. Free men had so many other advantages in ancient societies that the existence of male slaves did not affect their situation to the extent that female slaves affected the situation of free women (see William L. Westermann, *The Slave Systems of Greek and Roman Antiquity* [Philadelphia: American Philosophical Society, 1955]).

slave women in the Mediterranean cities. Since slaves were only given subsistence, a double force operated to give free women pittance wages: (1) the availability of slave labor and (2) the fiction of male head of household. The woman supposedly had someone to support her, and so her wages needed only be supplemental.

Characteristic Constraints on the Woman Worker

In the foregoing analysis, I have traced the work settings for women in hunting and gathering societies, the early agrovillages, the trading towns, and in the first urban civilizations. From the first urbanism until the industrial revolution, it is my view that there were no substantial differences in the work situation for women. The following discussion of the social, legal, and familial constraints on women will apply primarily but not exclusively to the Western world from Greek and Roman times onward.

The Male Head of Household Fiction

One of the most enduring constraints is the male head of household concept. I have labeled the term a fiction, for, while a careful study still needs to be done, it appears that in any setting—urban or rural—in any period of history for which data is available, one fifth to one-half of the heads of households were women. Many of these women were rearing children without male partners because of widowhood, desertion, divorce, or because they were plural wives infrequently visited by the husband and with full responsibility for the care and feeding of their children.[12] Some were never-married women who had been driven by poverty to sell sexual services and who raised children with minimal resources. Or they were never-married women who had chosen an independent way of life as entertainers, intellectuals, or merchants (variously labeled hetaira, courtesans, and prostitutes); they might or might not have chosen to raise children of their own. Most of these women, except for the wealthy and the independent entrepreneurs, had to struggle to make ends meet. They had to accept the low wages established through the fiction of male support and the reality of the competition of slave labor.

What family arrangements did women heads of household make for the care of their children while they were at work? Women in great poverty had to leave children without care to run the streets or

---

12. A common situation in parts of Africa today (see Ester Boserup, *Woman's Role in Economic Development* [London: George Allen & Unwin, 1970]: out of print, but reissued as a paperback [New York: St Martin's Press, 1974]).

locked them in airless rooms. Probably the institution of the neighbor who takes in children for a few pennies is as ancient as the urban working woman. For the most part, however, what care such children received throughout the Christian Era came from women who chose celibacy rather than motherhood, the women of the religious orders. They ran the soup kitchens, the orphanages, and the schools for the very poor. When many of the earlier religious orders declined and before the nineteenth-century growth in religious service orders began, the plight of children of the poor became desperate. In 1770 thousands of children of Parisian working mothers were rounded up from the streets by the "authorities" to be deported as labor for overseas settlements.[13] Only the mass exodus of their mothers from their places of work stopped this roundup. Indeed, it was around the problems of these "ragged children," as the British called them, that the nineteenth-century philanthropic and social service movements developed. For the women heads of household who were the mothers of these children, however, there was never much more than pious exhortation to "stop sinning." They were fallen women in the eyes of the middle and upper class, not working women with family responsibilities. That notion continues even today.

Familial Division of Labor

Rural areas. The division of labor between women and men in rural areas throughout the world has varied depending on the scale of agriculture. With cash cropping and plantation agriculture comes the development of labor-saving machinery and the dominance of the male.[14] In developing countries, the development of large-scale agriculture usually puts heavier work loads on women in terms of working hours because they are required to weed and carry water to the cash-crop fields while still growing food in their own plots to feed the family. Since the breeding-feeding activities are not counted as productive labor, the wages of Third World women agriculturalists are often of some indeterminate minus quantity. That is, they subsidize, even more than other working women, the men of their households and of their community. In a society with large-scale urban migration, the women are usually left behind to do the farming. Rarely do they share the urban wages of male family members, although these wages may be invested in buying more land for the woman to farm.

In Europe during the Middle Ages the situation of farm women varied. There was the prosperous but hardworking peasant household where length of working hours was perhaps fairly equally

13. George Rude, *The Crowd in History, 1730–1848* (New York: John Wiley & Sons, 1964).
14. See Boserup.

divided. On the other hand, there were the widows who had an incredible work load because they were compelled to render, unaided, feudal services that were shared in husband-wife households.[15] There was also the desperate situation of laboring women without partners who sometimes died, with their babies, of exhaustion and starvation in the very fields that were yielding unprecedented harvests.[16]

Wave and labor differentials in rural areas. With the decline of the feudal estates in the later Middle Ages, the new phenomenon of detached wage labor began in rural areas. Here the outlines of women's subservient economic situation as wage laborer became clear. The state tried to establish control over manpower movements but in effect controlled the movement of women. The 1563 Elizabethan Statute of Artifices, for example stated: "By this Act [the Statute of Laborers] every woman free or bound, under 60, and not carrying on a trade or calling, provided she had no land, and was not in domestic or other service, was liable to be called upon to enter service either in the fields or otherwise, and if she refused, she was imprisoned until she complied: whilst all girls who for twelve years had been brought up to follow the plough, were not allowed to enter any other calling, but were forced to continue working in the fields."[17]

Men continued to move to get jobs, but women with family responsibilities felt the full force of the compulsion to work in the fields and took home piecework which they could do while still caring for children. With the unity of capital and labor gone, the only limit set on the exploitation of the poorest class of laboring women was death by starvation. That grim scenario became more fully developed in the next century.

It is with the appearance of wage labor that the manifestations of wage differentials (which may in fact have existed all the time) became visible. Because of their immobility women have no bargaining power and so suffer wage discrimination everywhere. In 1422 the scholars of Toulouse paid women grape pickers half what they paid the men, who only had to carry the full baskets back to the college cellar. (The monks of Paris did the same.)[18] Women construction workers who worked side by side with men in building the College of Toulouse were paid far less than the men for the same labor.[19] Not even the labor shortage resulting from the Black Death improved

15. For an incredible account of the work load under feudalism, see G. Duby, *Rural Economy and Country Life in the Medieval West*, trans. C. Pasten (London: E. Arnold, 1968).

16. Julia O'Faolian and Laura Marines, eds., *Not in God's Image: A History of Women in Europe from the Greeks to the Nineteenth Century* (New York: Harper & Row, 1973).

17. Arthur Rackham Cleveland, *Woman under the English Law* (London: Hurst, 1896). p. 76.

18. Sylvia L. Thrupp, *Changes in Medieval Society Europe North of the Alps, 1050–1500* (New York: Appleton-Century-Crofts, 1964), pp. 240–41.

19. Ibid., p. 244.

women's wages; they remained substantially the same on the Continent for nearly 100 years.[20] The supposed labor shortages from the Black Death did not help the laboring poor in England, either.[21] While this could be interpreted as reflecting widespread underemployment in the previous century, one could also say that laborers in that century had "shorter hours, better working conditions." Fourteenth-century workers had to work longer and harder for the same pay, especially women.

The opportunities for the woman of the rural upper classes were limited only by her abilities; entrepreneurship was rewarded. With plenty of hands to help, the breeding-feeding role posed no problem to her. During the Middle Ages and as a result of the absence of men in crusades, there may have been an increase in the number of women in landholding and public roles, but the basic pre-Crusade participation level was already high, as the Herlihy study shows.[22]

Urban areas. It is difficult to construct a clear picture of the situations of urban middle-class women. The enclosure concept that I have emphasized is only part of the picture. In addition to the unknown number of women who had no significant activities beyond supervision of children and servants, there were women who acted as partners in their husbands' enterprises, including trading. It is hard to determine how many of the women who became known as successful traders in their own right began as partners with their husbands and expanded the business after widowhood. The well-to-do middle-class woman trader was a familiar figure in all the port cities of the Mediterranean from Phoenician times on. Many of the first converts to Christianity were well-to-do women merchants who put their homes and their wealth at the disposal of the early Christian communities. The wealthiest Greek trader in Byzantium in the Middle Ages was a woman,[23] and women traders were major figures in Bristol in the 1400s.[24] These were all middle-class women whose enterprise and ability enabled them to "earn" the help they needed to free themselves from the burdens of the breeder-feeder role.

Somewhere on this continuum of producer roles for the urban middle-class woman, which runs the gamut from the almost totally non-productive display wife through the independent trader, there exists the craft partner, the woman who was jointly engaged with her spouse in home-workshop production as a member of a craft guild.

20. E. Perroy, as quoted in Thrupp, p. 244.
21. Philip Ziegler, *The Black Death* (New York: John Day Co., 1969; reprint ed., Baltimore: Penguin Books, Pelican Books, 1970), pp. 240–59.
22. See n. 8 above.
23. Philip Sherrard, *Byzantium* (New York: Time, Inc., 1966).
24. Eileen Power and M. M. Postan, *Studies in English Trade in the Fifteenth Century* (London: George Routledge & Sons, 1933).

Where this kind of economic partnership existed, there may have been considerable sharing of the child-care part of the breeder role with the spouse. The craft-guild tradition, which began in the Mediterranean before the Christian Era, was one of husband-wife partnership which involved both more equality in the producer roles and more joint involvement with the children. The dividing line between teaching and nurturance faded away when both spouses were engaged in the craft role. In addition, every craft-guild household had outside children of the age of seven and up in an apprentice relationship. Even in non-craft-guild families it was common to send one's own children out to other households in the community and take others' children into one's home to rear. This practice seems to have been a combination of mutual boarding out, a way of getting extra household help, and a device for involving others in the education of one's children.[25] Because people were raising each others' children, men became more involved in the process than they might have been had children stayed in their own home.

The whole history of the craft-guild movement in England and on the Continent (though more so in the former than the latter) is a history of the involvement of women in the productive process in partnership roles with men. (There is less information about the relative roles of father and mother in relation to children and production in rural settings.) It may well be that the small-scale craft-guild enterprise that predated the industrial revolution provided the setting of a more egalitarian, less exploitative work and parenting partnership than any other kind of work setting.

Household Size and Familial Restraints

In the sixteenth century, the process of pushing women back inside their families denying them economic and other extradomestic involvements, gained momentum. Household size became an important constraint and should be considered. Recent studies of local records in various parts of Europe reveal the surprising fact that household size has changed very little from the Middle Ages to the present.[26] Apart from the great manor houses of the nobility and the homes of rich merchants, most people lived in families with an average size of 4.75 persons per family, plus a servant.[27] Not only were families small, but the marriage age for women and men was beginning to rise. For European women in the 1500s the average age at

25. Peter Laslett, ed., *Household and Family in Past Time* (Cambridge: Cambridge University Press, 1972).
26. Ibid.
27. These "servants," it turns out, are not servants in the contemporary sense of the word but rather children of neighboring families in the same parish.

marriage was about twenty-one, rising in succeeding centuries to twenty-five and twenty-eight. Furthermore, because multigenerational families were very much the exception, most women were confined to very small domestic spaces in small families before and after marriage. While women certainly had larger households during their childbearing years, high infant death rates and the practice of older couples and widows maintaining their own separate quarters left women in increasing domestic isolation as they lost freedom of movement in other spheres.

The tension level between mothers and daughters was apparently very high in this period. There are many mentions of brutal child rearing, and particularly of mothers beating daughters who resisted parental marriage plans. Even the gentle peace queen, Margaret of Navarre, beat her daughter daily for weeks on end to make her agree to a politically designed marriage choice. Agnes Paston of the lively Paston family, known for its voluminous intrafamily correspondence and numerous lawsuits, beat her daughter so badly that "her head was broke in 2 or 3 places." Lady Jane Gray's mother beat her. Since the records all refer to mothers, not fathers, beating their daughters, and this in the context of an otherwise "good" family life, it would seem that women of this period were subject to severe emotional pressure which they relieved by child beating. Sending daughters out to other families as servants was one of the few available means of relieving the strain, but this required reciprocity and acceptance of someone else's daughter into the home. The disappearance of convents in England and in many places in Europe,[28] and the closing down of other occupational options for women, made marriage arrangements increasingly important and also made marriages harder to achieve. Mothers bore the brunt of these problems in terms of pressure to get their daughters out of their small households.

The effect of a lowering status of women on mother-daughter relations is a subject that needs much more attention. Obviously not all mothers beat their daughters, and when there were beatings they do not seem to have led to ruptured relations. There was, rather, some continued expression of affection between mothers and daughters in later life. Women seem to have fled from confining extended family situations whenever possible. This is supported by the fact that in the 1500s, even with housing shortages, 16 percent of all English households in the 100 communities Laslett examined were headed by

28. The pressure on mothers to get rid of daughters also existed in the Middle Ages at the height of convent life, and many daughters were beaten half to death by mothers who were trying to force them into convents against their wills. There are interesting records of lawsuits of nuns who claimed that they had been forced to take vows by their parents (see O'Faolian and Martines, pp. 270–75).

women.[29] Of these, 12.9 percent were widows, 1.1 percent single females, and 2.3 percent "unspecified females" in humble households, as well as estates. There are many references to the joy with which women set up their own households after widowhood and the vigor with which they resisted courting by amorous widowers. The extended family togetherness we nostalgically refer to as part of our golden past simply did not exist in the European heritage, and there is some evidence that it never really existed on a large scale anywhere.

More important, perhaps, the picture of women that emerges from this material is a useful corrective to the popular misconception that women have throughout history submissively endured everything. They endured a great deal, but they were not necessarily submissive.

Alternatives to Familial Roles

During the entire historical period from 500 B.C. to the industrial revolution, there were important alternatives for women to being the wife/mother in a male headed household or the family-burdened female head of a household. One alternative was celibacy. The nun role has existed from early times in Hinduism, in Buddhism, and finally in Christianity and Islam. Although religious orders for women took different forms in Asia, the Middle East, and Europe, the basic pattern of an alternative role that did not involve the breeder-feeder function was present in all these societies. Between A.D. 500 and 1400 there was an extraordinary flowering of convent culture in Europe. This culture produced science, art, and literature, and a social service infrastructure in the fields of health, education, and welfare unparalleled until the nineteenth century. While nuns were in one sense isolated within the male-dominant structure of the Catholic church, in another sense they lived in protected niches within which they could be free. And if the price they paid for that freedom was celibacy, there is real evidence of the creativity and joy of convent life in those centuries (as well as before and since). The nineteenth and twentieth centuries have seen a second explosion of creativity through celibacy, partly within religious orders and partly outside of them. Today, there are approximately 2 million nuns in the world from all the major religious traditions.

In addition to the celibacy in the convent, there was the beguinage[30]—an urban secular commune for rural women migrants

29. Laslett, p. 147.
30. This was a religiously based social movement, but the women were *not* in religious orders (see Ernest W. McDonnell, *The Beguines and Beghards in Medieval Culture* [New York: Octagon Books, 1969]).

to the city during the major urban migrations of the 1200s and 1300s. Invented by women, the beguinages were so successful that they were seen as serious threats to some of the existing craft guilds and were persecuted by them. Besides the beguines there were also hermitesses—women solitaries who lived in huts by bridges, on the edges of towns, and in forest solitudes all over England and, to a lesser extent, in Europe. These were a special class of independents in the Middle Ages—able to support themselves through their knowledge of human nature and folk medicine. With no institutional protection of any kind, most of them were burned as witches during the height of the medieval witch mania. Last, there were the vagabonds, the hardworking fun-loving women who moved partnerless through the Middle Ages, always able to pick up the pennies they needed at a fair or celebration of some kind. When they were willing to settle in a town, they were not infrequently supported by town councils, glad to have resident entertainers for the community. Besides being entertainers, they ran the soup kitchens and the first-aid stations in wars, including the Crusades. They were good soldiers when they were needed as fighters. Altogether, they were a social category for which we would have no labels today. Marriage was not on their agenda, and at times up to one-fourth of the women of Europe belonged in their company.

The End of an Era

During the late 1500s and the 1600s many of the phenomena described above began to disappear. The craftwomen, the celibates, and the vagabonds all declined in numbers and status. In the guilds in particular there was a rapid loss of rights and statuses for women. Men were feeling the pressure of women as competitors in the labor market and successfully pressed for their expulsion from guild after guild. This transition era intiated the prolonged suffering of both rural and urban female laborers as they were squeezed out of secure medieval work statuses. The hermitess or vagabond of the fourteenth century became the work-deadened automaton of the seventeenth and eighteenth centuries. Rural laboring women went hungry, and the children of women in the factories were rounded up like cattle. Married and single women alike were trapped by the formula of "supplemental" pittance wages for women.

This was also the period when the gentlewoman in straitened circumstances appeared—the middle-class woman without training and resources who could not enter domestic service because of her social status. She became a governess or a companion in homes of slightly better off middle-class people, working for little more than bread and board, often in a position close to that of the household slave of Greek and Roman times. Just below her in station was the domestic, even more of a household slave. By the 1700s, these women began to emigrate overseas to new hardships, but also to new opportunities.

It is this period that witnessed the emergence of the Marxist analysis of the situation of women. Women and men alike, whether Saint-Simonians or anarchist socialists or Marxian socialists, all saw the necessity for society to deal with the burden of the breeder-feeder role that entrapped women by providing child care and domestic maintenance for everyone. However, no one looked back to the time when men had shared part of the breeder-feeder role. Everything (except biological childbearing) was to be taken over by the state. If this proposal asked nothing of men, it had the virtue of helping married and single women heads of household equally.

Since no socialist state could afford to duplicate the individualized breeder-feeder role of women as a public service, and no capitalist state wanted to, it was easy to turn this task back to women in the end. The famous Ellen Key "return to matriarchy movement" to restore full legal head of household rights to women independently of marital status has to be seen in that context. Indeed, all the nineteenth-century utopian movements from Brook Farm to New Harmony left women's roles unchanged. Only the Shakers and the Mormons offered something different; the former the freedom of celibacy, the latter the freedom of co-wives with whom to share farm labor. Both attracted women in droves.

It was a hard century for working women, and it was an unsettling one for middle-class women who had been led to expect something different—some kind of equality. All the women-triggered social reform movements of the nineteenth century and all their concrete achievements—protective legislative enactments and new types of social service institutions—could not take the edge off the bitterness of unacknowledged colleagueship. Women were invited, welcomed, urged into the labor force—but at bargain prices; working was to be an avocation. The breeder-feeder role was here to stay as the unremitting background rhythm to all other activities of women. Even in the socialist countries, where women were the most needed and most welcomed into the labor force, they were expected to carry on the same breeder-feeder role at home after hours.

The decades following industrialization saw drastic changes in the lives of Western women and in attitudes toward them. In the larger work from which the following selection is taken, Sheila Rothman traces those changes as they occurred in the nineteenth century. She explores the reasons why technology, new educational opportunities, and an expanding marketplace failed to free women in that promising new century and resulted rather in increased rigidity in attitudes toward and opportunities for women. Coming to by now familiar conclusions, Rothman analyzes the tensions between ideology and reality that divided women for centuries and that only intensify in the newly industrialized world.

WOMEN'S SPECIAL SPHERE

Sheila Rothman

FROM *Woman's Proper Place*

The closing decades of the nineteenth century present two contradictory and yet authentic images. In the first instance, the period appears to be remarkably open and fluid, filled with marvelous innovations and technological advances. Over these thirty years, America did become modern. Industrial production transformed the economic life of the nation: large-scale corporations distributed mass-produced goods to national markets over an elaborate network of railroads. Americans in unprecedented numbers began to move to the cities. A restless energy drove them from the countryside and the small towns to the new urban centers. At the same time, great numbers of Europeans, particularly Eastern Europeans, migrated to take their chances in a New World. A sense of ambition and adventure seemed to pervade every place and enterprise. But these same decades were no less marked by constraints and restrictions. The gap between the rich and the poor widened, the distance between mansion and tenement becoming so great that only a very lucky few could ever bridge it. The discipline of work took on a new relentlessness: the factory machine and the office routine imposed their own kind of tyranny. Thus one vacillates, properly, between a sense of opportunity and creativity and a sense of fixity and rigidity.[1]

1. David Potter, *People of Plenty* (Chicago, 1954); Robert Wiebe, *The Search for Order 1877–1920* (New York, 1967); and Stephen Thernstrom, *Poverty and Progress* (Cambridge, Mass., 1964).

Although many of these images come from the world of men, the same tension predominated in the world of women. In a variety of ways, technological innovations transformed women's lives and particularly the lives of middle-class, urban women. Technology liberated them from much of the drudgery of household tasks. The appliances that electricity powered freed women from traditional and incredibly onerous household chores. Further, new types of institutions for women, particularly the women's colleges, came into existence during these years, providing an altogether novel kind of experience. Still further, new occupations opened up to women, especially in offices and department stores, while the number of teaching positions in the public schools increased. Finally, this era witnessed the vigorous and energetic activities of women's clubs; benevolent-minded women set out to reform the almshouses and eliminate the saloon. As the Woman's Christian Temperance Union (WCTU) motto proclaimed: "Woman will bless and brighten every place she enters, and will enter every place."

Yet again, in each of these instances, liberation seems to be only part of the story. A very special ideology defined women's proper social roles in narrow and restricted ways. Ideas that we may label "virtuous womanhood" dominated their lives, closing off opportunities, fostering a sex-stereotyping of jobs, and ruling out options. Both in the private and public arena—in the home, in the club, and in the workplace—women's actions had to be consistent with moral sensibility, purity, and maternal affection, and no other code of behavior was acceptable. Hence, to understand the experience of women in the post-Civil War decades, particularly as it helped to shape social policy by women and on behalf of women, requires a full appreciation of the interaction between opportunity and obligation, between social reality and ideology. . . .

The contrast between opportunity and rigidity, innovation and fixity . . . characterized the world of working women. To many observers, women were enjoying an unparalleled freedom to enter traditional professions and to hold newly created positions in an expanding economy. And yet, their actual distribution in the labor force and their chances for promotion do not bear out such optimistic pronouncements. In fact, the late nineteenth century began a sex-stereotyping of occupations that would persist through most of the twentieth century. This was the moment when typists, stenographers, department store clerks, and school teachers all became prototypically female.

The definition of what constituted a woman's occupation owed much to purely market forces. Employers hired women when men, because of their social class or education, were either unwilling or unable to fill the positions—or, put another way, when women made up the cheapest available and suitable labor pool. Yet the prevailing concepts of virtuous womanhood . . . had an impact, too; they helped to buttress and support this process of selection and labeling. Notions of when women could properly work and what they could properly do contributed in critical ways to legitimating distinctions that were frankly discriminatory. . . .

Although one could find a woman here or there in many job categories, most women were grouped into a select few. College graduates ended up as school teachers (of those 815 Vassar graduates, 805 worked at some time as teachers). Women with less education entered offices; those with still less, retail stores. (In 1870 the number of women in offices and stores was 10,798 or under 1.0 percent of the women employed in nonagricultural jobs; by 1900 the number had risen to 394,747 or 9.1 percent of the total.) And no matter what the job, women remained at the lower end of the ladder. In the public schools they were the classroom teachers, not the principals or superintendents; in offices, they made up the ranks of typists and stenographers, not the executives; in the retail stores, they were the clerks and cashiers, not the floorwalkers or managers. In other words, the job that a woman first assumed was generally the one that she kept as long as she worked. Men had careers, rising from clerks to become managers, from teachers to become principals; women remained locked in the same position. Once a typist, always a typist; once a clerk, always a clerk. Indeed, the job discrimination that they suffered was so obvious, the situation that they confronted so bleak, that the point that needs explaining is why some jobs opened up for women at all.

By the same token, even the staunchest proponents of women's work wanted them—and everyone else—to think of labor essentially as a temporary state (something to do until the right man came along), as a form of insurance (something to do if an emergency arose), or, in a still more restricted way, as a last resort (something to do if the sex ratio remained grossly imbalanced). A woman's job skills were to improve her marital choices, to allow her and her husband to sleep more securely, and to demonstrate her moral worth through self-support under the most trying circumstances. But a woman was not to work in order to advance a career. In fact, these postulates assumed a self-fulfilling quality. Encouraged to think of themselves in some sense or other as part-time workers, women did not generally expect or press for promotion and equal pay. So, too, employers defined women as temporary workers and were accordingly reluctant to advance them or to raise their salaries. The graduate and professional schools also took refuge in this argument (more or less honestly). Why invest in so expensive a training program for a woman if she would only practice law or medicine temporarily? Again, what now seems most puzzling is that *any* job actually became a woman's job.

The dynamic that operated in the post-Civil War decades to create new and exclusive positions for women emerges with special clarity in white-collar occupations. An expanding and modernizing economy did increase the number of clerical and office jobs, particularly for typists and stenographers—and it was women who filled them. In the 1870s, men typically worked as stenographers and scriveners; women composed less than 5 percent of this group. By 1900, the women held fully three-quarters of these jobs.[2]

The change began with the typewriter. It altered both the style of office work and the composition of the office staff. Although the Remington Company developed the first writing machines in 1874, typewriters were not sold in significant numbers until the 1880s. They remained a novelty, mostly because few people had the necessary skills to use them. Remington soon understood that to market its product it would have to train operators; only when typists, like spare parts, were available on demand would businesses invest in the machines. The company therefore opened typewriting schools in the large cities and established an employment bureau as an adjunct to each of them. The strategy worked well. By 1890, Remington could barely keep up with orders for machines and demands for operators. Between 1897 and 1902 it supplied New York City alone with 25,262 typists, and Chicago with 23,368.[3]

Nearly all of Remington's students were women. One of the designers of the machine even boasted that its most important achievement "was to allow women an easier way to earn a living." But why did Remington's schools recruit—and recruit successfully—among women? Because the company recognized that a typist had to "be a good speller, a good grammarian and have the correct knowledge of the use of capitals and the rules of punctuation."[4] Where might it find a ready source of labor with such educational qualifications? Lower-class men did not have the literacy skills necessary for the job; skilled male workers were well paid in other positions. Middle-class men with high school educations had still more opportunities

2. May Allison, *The Public Schools and Women in Office Service* (Boston, 1914), p. 6.

3. For the early history of the typewriter see Richard N. Current, *The Typewriter and the Men Who Made It* (Urbana, Ill., 1954); Bruce Bliven, *That Wonderful Writing Machine* (New York, 1954). For the role of the Remington Company as an employment agency, see *The Typewriter and Phonographic World*, 20 (1902), p. 125.

4. Arthur T. Foulke, *Mr. Typewriter* (Boston, 1961), p. 79; G. Shankland Walworth, "How to Get a Situation," in *The Typewriter and Phonographic World*, 18 (Oct. 1901), p. 191; Anna Wade Westabrook, "Young Ladies as Stenographers and Typewriters," *The Typewriter and Phonographic World*, 6 (Feb. 1891).

for responsible and upwardly mobile employment elsewhere. Recognizing that men were either ineligible or uninterested, the company then turned to women, to the large pool of female high school graduates.

The high school system had only recently come to hold a significant place in urban educational systems, and its new popularity was linked in part to its filling up a young girl's time. "Boys drop out of high school," as one superintendent explained, "some [to] go to college; others because they get tired of school; others to engage in business; and still others because they had formed bad associations; but the girls remain and graduate if not obliged to quit."[5] Put another way, boys had options (to go to college or into business); girls did not, so they stayed on to graduate. But what were they to do when commencement finally came? For many of them, as we shall see, a teaching position was the answer. But over the 1870s and 1880s, competition so increased that a sizable number of girls could no longer find open posts. There was always the factory, but that was a last resort. Clearly, work at the typewriter in an office was a far more attractive option. The girls could remain in a middle-class, respectable setting, one that was clean, well lit, quiet, and safe. The typewriter was an easy machine to run, and the wages paid were no lower than those of skilled female machine operators. How much better, then, to be a typewriter (as these girls were called) than a factory worker. This fact of life gave Remington and other companies like Royal their labor supply.

Given the desirability of this sort of office work, the manufacturers, the commercial schools, and soon the high schools themselves, rushed to train girls at typewriting. In the early 1880s, one commercial school, Prospectus, still had to concede that "it was an uncommon thing to find a girl living in a respectable home and moving in good society who would not consider herself somewhat degraded by going into a business office and earning a living. And more than that, her father and brother—if she had them—would feel it would be greatly to their discredit to permit such a thing."[6] But by the 1890s, views had changed. The mayor of New York could now tell the graduating class at the Packard Commercial School, "You will lift the tone of those offices...and win the lasting respect of your associates. The men around you will grow nobler and better." He assured them that the women working in his office had not only made it a finer place, but "they have made me better, and there is

---

5. In 1891, for example, there were 239,556 high school graduates in the United States, 60 percent of whom were women; U.S. Commissioner of Education, *Report*, 1891–92, p. 686; Board of Education, Kansas City, Missouri, *Sixteenth Annual Report*, 1887, p. 24.
6. Packard's Business College *Prospectus* 1897–1898, pp. 17–18.

not a person about the office who has not been improved by the presence of the ladies."[7]

From the employers' perspective, women were perfectly suited
to be "typewriters." The temporary nature of the work commitment
posed no problem; if one operator left to be married, a call to the
Remington Company quickly produced another. And since each typing
assignment was discrete, the continuity of service of any particular
operator was unimportant. Another typist could just as well copy the
next letter or bill. Further, wages could be kept low—office managers recognized that their working conditions were superior to those
in the factory. Finally, the women's presence did not threaten the
ambitions of the men in the office. They could be added to the staff
with a minimum of trouble. . . .

The department stores, which revolutionized the buying habits
of one class of women, also provided novel employment opportunities
for another. As they proliferated, so did the number of women employed as cash girls, saleswomen, and cashiers. Because middle-class
men (and in this case, middle-class women, too) did not want these
low-paying and tedious jobs, and because store owners considered
lower-class men unsuitable, it was lower-class women who filled
them.

In the pre-Civil War decades, men had typically worked as
clerks in small retail stores, doing the bargaining and selling, and
even purchasing the merchandise. To be a clerk in a dry goods shop
was a position of some responsibility. The post-Civil War department store, however, with its "one price" formula and specialized
buying staff, made the sales clerk's job into a menial position. Department stores actually prided themselves on the passive and
routine quality of the help. One general manager boasted that his
"salespersons do not urge the customer to buy, and dilate upon the
beauties of his wares. They simply ask the customer what he or she
wants, and make a record of the sale."[8] The stores generally did not
pay their clerks a commission on sales, reducing in still another way
the possible returns from the position. Under these circumstances,
middle-class men preferred to look elsewhere for jobs that valued
their initiative or allowed more responsibility and better prospects
for advancement.

But young women whose only other choice was factory work or
domestic service found the department store a very attractive option.
Since it was designed to attract middle-class women as customers,
the store was far cleaner and more pleasant than a factory. The work

7. Packard Commercial School *Graduation Exercises* (1895), p. 15. See also Jessica Kemm,
Women as Stenographer/Typist: 1880–1900, unpublished paper (1976), pp. 6, 12.
8. John S. Steck, "Storekeeping in New York City," *Arena*, 22 (August 1899), p. 179.

was also less tiring. However demanding the customer might be, the machine was much more ruthless. A department store clerk was much less isolated than a domestic. (Indeed, more than one reformer worried that salesgirls met *too many* people.) And even the most dictatorial company rules and autocratic managers were mild in comparison to the regimen that middle-class housewives imposed on their maids.

Department store employment created its own hierarchy. The youngest workers, those around fourteen years old, took their first jobs as cash girls and moved up to become wrappers and stock girls. Each promotion carried a slight increase in pay—a stock girl earned between $2 and $3 a week, less than an unskilled factory worker. The cash girls raced between salesclerks and cashiers, delivering payments and bringing back change. (In the twentieth century the pneumatic tube and then the computerized cash register would take over this job.) The wrapper "artfully" packaged the merchandise, and the stock girl "neatly" replenished the shelves. At age 16, usually after two years of service, a girl might become a salesclerk (receiving $6 to $7 weekly, better than an unskilled factory worker and the same as a typist). Clerks who proved both "intelligent and responsible" went on to become cashiers (earning $8 to $10 a week).[9]

Owners preferred to hire women for all these positions, so that three-quarters of department store employees were female. They believed that women were more honest than men. In an establishment with two or three thousand workers, owners and managers—unlike their counterparts in a retail shop—could not expect to oversee every detail. "Honesty on the part of employees," one observer reported, "must of necessity be taken for granted." Therefore, as one manager told Helen Campbell, an investigator of conditions of women's work, "We don't want men; we wouldn't have them even if they came at the same price. No, give me a woman every time. I've been a manager thirteen years, and we never had but four dishonest girls, and we've had to discharge over forty boys in the same time."[10]

Women also seemed easier to discipline and manage. "Boys smoke and lose at cards," Helen Campbell learned, "and do a hundred things that women don't and they get worse instead of better." The girls, drilled in obedience and politeness in an almost military manner, proved tractable. "We want it said of our employees that

9. Samuel Hopkins Adams, "The Department Store," *Scribner's Magazine*, 21 (June 1897); Anonymous, "A Salesgirl's Story," *Independent*, 54 (July 31, 1902), pp. 1815–1821; Hower, *Macy's*, pp. 194–199; Helen Campbell, *Darkness and Daylight* (Hartford, Conn., 1892), pp. 256–259.

10. Adams, "Department Store," p. 19; Helen Campbell, *Prisoner of Poverty* (Boston, 1887), p. 173.

they are a credit to the house," the Siegel and Cooper Company told its workers. "Be civil and polite to your superiors. Should those in authority not be civil to you, OBEY." The store's manual went on to establish the following rules:

THINGS NOT TO DO

Do not stand in groups.
Do not chew gum, read books, or sew.
Do not giggle, flirt, or idle away your time.
Do not walk together through the store.
Do not be out of your place.
Do not be late at any time.
Do not take over fifteen minutes on a pass.
Do not make a noise when going up in elevators.
Do not push when going into elevators, but always stand in line.
Do not talk across aisles, or in a loud voice.
Do not gossip; mind your own affairs and you will have
enough to do.
Do not sit in front of the counter. . . .

In the department store, as in the office, the women's jobs were the dead-end jobs. Girls did not rise from clerical positions to become floorwalkers; they did not earn promotions to become buyers or assistants to the managers. They could move from cash girl to cashier, but never beyond that. Had the position held out more promise, it might well have become the preserve of middle-class men. So once again, opportunity for women in the post-Civil War decades came in a very particular way: through novel job openings that were preferable to factory work but that led nowhere.

For all the availability of novel types of employment, teaching remained women's primary role in the work force. Large numbers of women had entered the profession in the pre-Civil War decades, and the dynamic that first made teaching a woman's job continued to operate through the post-Civil War period. In schools, as in offices and factories, women did what men would not or could not do.

No sooner were public schools founded in the 1820s than a seemingly endless number of complaints began to circulate about the unsatisfactory nature of the teaching staffs. School reformers had assumed that educated, sober, and even refined middle-class men would make a career of teaching the young. Instead, the male teachers either were poorly educated or were using the post as a stepping-stone to another career; many would-be lawyers, for example, supported themselves by classroom teaching. In 1837, George Emerson, one of Massachusetts' most distinguished educators, drew a discouraging portrait of the average teacher for the state legislature.

Public school teachers, he contended, were either "young men in the course of their studies, teaching from necessity, and often with a strong dislike for the pursuit," or they were "mechanics and others wanting present employment," or "persons who, having failed in other callings, take to teaching as a last resort with no qualifications for it, and no desire of continuing in it longer than they are obliged by absolute necessity." Emerson believed that local boards were "baffled by the want of good teachers; that they have been sought for in vain; the highest salaries have been offered, to no purpose; that they *are not to be found* in sufficient numbers to supply the demand." As a remedy, he proposed a system of state normal schools. Emerson's ideal teacher was "to know *how* to teach," to "have a thorough knowledge of whatever he undertakes to teach," and to have such an "understanding of *the ordering and discipline* of a school, as to be able at once to introduce system, and to keep it constantly in force."[11] He insisted that the state normal school would inculcate just such traits in its students. Graduates would be able to fulfill the seemingly masculine task of ordering and disciplining a classroom.

But it was women, and not men, who flocked to the normal schools. The men found better opportunities elsewhere. "When we consider the claims of the learned professions," explained Catharine Beecher, "the excitement and profits of commerce, manufactures, agriculture, and the arts; when we consider the aversion of most men to the sedentary, confining, and toilsome duties of teaching and governing young children; when we consider the scanty pittance that is allowed to the majority of teachers; and that few men will enter a business that will not support a family, when there are multitudes of other employments that will afford competence, and lead to wealth; it is chimerical to hope that the supply of such immense deficiencies in our national education is to come from that sex." Yet, the very reasons that made teaching so unattractive to men made it more suitable and appealing for women. "It is woman," Beecher continued, "fitted by disposition, and habits, and circumstances for such duties, who, to a very wide extent, must aid in educating the childhood and youth of this nation; and therefore it is, that females must be trained and educated for this employment." In following a teaching career, a woman helped herself as well as improved society. "Most happily," concluded Beecher, "the education necessary to fit a woman to be a teacher, is exactly the one that best fits her for that domestic relation she is primarily designed to fill."[12]

11. "Memorial of the American Institute of Instruction to the Legislature of Massachusetts in Normal School," January 1837, in Henry Barnard, *Normal Schools and Other Institutions* (Hartford, Conn., 1851), pp. 85–87.

12. Catharine E. Beecher, *An Essay on the Education of Female Teachers* (New York, 1835), p. 18.

The fit between women and teaching seemed no less ideal to local school boards. Women not only were willing to work for low salaries but, in the absence of competing opportunities, composed a very pliable staff. Thus, one Ohio school superintendent confidently told his fellow educators: "As the business of teaching is made more respectable, more females engage in it, and the wages are reduced. Females do not...expect to accumulate much property by this occupation; if it affords them a respectable support and a situation where they can be useful, it is as much as they demand. I, therefore, most earnestly commend this subject to the attention of those counties which are in the habit of paying men for instructing little children, when females would do it for less than half the sum, and generally much better than men can."[13] . . .

Women heeded the message. Perhaps they did so in a spirit of resignation, recognizing that business and the professions were closed to them. Or perhaps, in keeping with the precepts of virtuous womanhood, they were most comfortable in the role of moral counselor and teacher to the young. "There are more reasons," insisted Marion Harland, "for the press of women who are obliged to earn a livelihood, into the profession of teaching than the one usually assigned and accepted, namely, that it is an eminently respectable occupation and involves little physical drudgery. It is the nature of being of the mother-sex to gather together into her care and brood over and instruct creatures younger and feebler than herself."[14] Or perhaps women calculated that teaching wages were the best available for the least onerous work. The salaries were higher than factory girls earned and identical with those of stenographers. In all events, women crowded into teaching jobs.

Despite their numerical dominance in the teaching ranks and seemingly natural suitability for the jobs, female teachers suffered the same kind of discrimination in school systems that their counterparts did in offices and department stores. School boards paid men more than women for carrying out the same assignments ($35 a week compared to $14). As the Massachusetts Board of Education reported in 1893, women's wages, when contrasted with men's, "are so low as to make it humiliating to report the two in connection. Moreover, the advance in the wages of male teachers in ten years has been at the rate of 36.2 percent, while that for female teachers has been at the rate of 14.8 percent."[15] Even more important, the men

---

13. Thomas Woody, *History of Women's Education in the United States*, I (New York, 1929), p. 491.
14. M. Carey Thomas, "The College Woman of the Present and Future," *McClure's Syndicate* (1901), p. 3; Harland, *Eve's Daughters*, p. 271.
15. Massachusetts Board of Education, *57th Annual Report*, 1893, p. 70.

held practically all the influential and well-paying administrative positions. (Probably the boards hired men as school teachers so as to be able to promote them up the ranks to run the system). If men composed only a small minority of classroom teachers, they made up a heavy majority of the principals and superintendents. "There is some slight relief from . . . the steady falling off of male teachers," declared the Massachusetts Board of Education, "in the fact that it is more than compensated for in the number of male teachers transferred to the ranks of school superintendents." Put another way, women with similar credentials remained elementary and secondary school teachers. "While 67 percent of all the teachers in the country are women," one investigator reported to the Association for the Advancement of Women in 1888, "less than 4 percent of those who direct what shall be taught and teaching what shall be done are women." Women were permitted to teach children in every state of the union, but in only 13 states were they even eligible to hold all school offices. In 1900, only two women held the position of state superintendent of schools and only twelve were superintendents of city school systems.[16] . . .

In the world of work as elsewhere, new opportunities were counterbalanced, if not quite canceled out, by restrictions and qualifications. The post-Civil War decades created many types of novel settings for women, and yet within each of them women had to know their very special place.

16. Ibid., p. 70; May Sewall, "Women as Educators," in Association for the Advancement of Women, *Proceedings* (1888), pp. 126–127; U.S. Commissioner of Education, *Report*, 1900–1901, II, pp. 2406–2407.

Although life was hard for the many thousands of Eastern European Jews who immigrated to America between 1880 and 1910, employment of married women was not new to them. The traditional division of roles by sex in Jewish culture ideally included a working wife in active exchange with the world and a husband engaged in Jewish study, sheltered from worldly concerns. For the wives described in the following selection, however, the goal was survival of the family, not a husband's scholarship.

HOMEWORK AND THE DEVELOPMENT OF THE FACTORY SYSTEM

Charlotte Baum
Paula Hyman
Sonya Michel

FROM *The Jewish Woman in America*

The popularity of ready-made clothing was growing, coincidentally, as immigration from Eastern Europe increased, so Jews who had already had some experience in the needle trades found their skills in demand. As the industry grew, production became more specialized; in the beginning, all work was done in one shop, but it gradually became more expedient to break manufacturing down into a number of tasks, some of which would be given out to contractors. Designing, patternmaking, and cutting usually remained inside the shop, where they could be closely supervised, but other processes—basting, sewing, felling, and finishing—were contracted out.

Competition among contractors was fierce. They were continually seeking ways to reduce their overhead so they could underbid one another. One way to do this was to parcel out work to subcontractors who hired the freshest of greenhorns who were willing to work for the lowest wages. Turnover was fairly rapid, for greenhorns soon learned and they moved up to another level of production, but the subcontractors were usually able to replace them easily.

Contractors picked up bundles of cut garments from "inside shops" and turned them over to subcontractors, who usually had sweatshops in their own homes. There two or more people worked on the bundles, and the family was often pressed into service as well. And bundles were also farmed out to housewives who worked on them in their own homes. The subcontractor himself worked along with his hirelings, suffering from the same long hours and close conditions. Since the margin of profit was very low, he often made little more than those in his employ.

Work was paid by the piece. Women working at home alternated paid tasks with their normal household routine. They would set up their sewing machines, spread out the bundles, and between cleaning, shopping, making meals, and caring for their children and any boarders, they managed somehow to complete their work, often pedaling and stitching far into the night. In one story written about this period, a little girl describes her mother's life:

"She ain't got no friends. She ain't got time she should have 'em. She sews all times. Sooner I lays me und the babies on the bed by night my mamma sews. Und sooner I stands up in mornings my mamma sews. All, *all*, ALL times she sews."

Although most women deplored their long hours and low pay, they were grateful to earn the money their families so desperately needed, and availed themselves of every opportunity to get this type of homework. Contractors and manufacturers were able to play willing homeworkers off against disgruntled factory workers seeking to organize and obtain better wages and working conditions. Despite the fact that homework created a breach in labor solidarity, it operated favorably, in the short run, for women who had to continue to share financial responsibilities with their husbands even after they had children. The development of the factory system and the enactment of anti-sweating laws, while benefiting the shopworkers, most of whom were young, unmarried women, actually penalized homeworkers, for it divided the home from the workplace, and kept women out of occupations that had previously provided them with a source of vital income.

As homework became scarcer, a small proportion of mothers tried to make arrangements for the care of their children so they would be free to work in the shops. Of course, there was little day care available to them: more often, these women relied on a female relative or neighbor to look after their children, or even left younger ones in the care of older siblings.

Whatever their hesitations were about leaving children under less than optimal conditions, many women could not afford to pass up opportunities to work, for production in the garment industry was sporadic and between the busy seasons were long periods of idleness. A scene described by Samuel Ornitz in *Bride of the Sabbath* was probably not unusual: a destitute mother who was nursing an infant when it became "busy by cloaks" had her older son bring the baby to her at work. The boy would carry his sister and a pot containing his mother's dinner up five flights to the factory loft.

Mamma nursed the baby and ate at the same time. She ate mechanically, too tired to taste the food. Between mouthfuls she kissed the baby's head. When the baby was satisfied, she was too, and handed the boy the baby and the pot. Then, without looking at them again, she went back to work, pedaling like mad. . . .

Through the 1960s and into the 70s, the feminist movement, in spite of the wide-ranging political spectrum it represented, was seen by many black women as middle class in orientation and as composed of just those white women who had participated in the oppression of black women, especially in their roles as household workers. The issue was complicated by a strain of the black liberation movement that saw black men as emasculated by slavery and racism and particularly in need at that time of the emotional support of black women. In recent years, there has been considerable diminishing of that disaffection and steadily increasing involvement of black women in the women's movement. Elizabeth Almquist would see a significant reason for that change in the realities of a labor market in which, for black women, sex has emerged as a factor of greater importance in their status and remuneration than race.

BLACK WOMEN AND THE PURSUIT OF EQUALITY

Elizabeth Almquist

Social scientists who study employment patterns have rarely considered the situation of black women. Even the very recent research that measures sex discrimination tends to overlook black women.[1] In the past, researchers have compared black women to white women and black men to white men. This stress on racial factors that hamper achievement obscures the sex discrimination that affects black women very seriously. The material that follows (1) compares employed black and white women to show the increasing similarity between their patterns of labor force participation and the way in which they are the common victims of sex discrimination at work; (2) compares black women with black men to indicate the extent to which black women are disadvantaged in relation to their brothers and husbands; and (3) compares all three groups of minority workers

1. When such research is based on sample surveys, the numbers of black women included are often too small to yield reliable conclusions. But in other cases, where appropriate numbers were available, researchers have simply avoided making comparisons among groups that would reveal the seriousness of sex discrimination. Several of the issues are described in Elizabeth M. Almquist, "Social Science Research on Women and Wage Discrimination: The Missing 40 Percent and the Missing Perspective," paper presented at the American Sociological Association Annual Meetings, Chicago (1977).

Research for this essay was supported in part by a multidisciplinary grant from the Administration on Aging to the Center for Studies in Aging of North Texas State University.

to white men to show that the disadvantaged position of black women is currently more a function of their being female than of being black.

In the stress on racial differences, the many similarities between black and white women have gone unrecognized. In reality, black and white women today have nearly identical patterns of labor force participation. Changes over the last 25 years have brought them ever closer together. The similarities between the two groups occur in several areas: rates of labor force participation, occupational prestige, education, and earnings. In most of these, black women have been improving their status while white women have changed very little. For labor force participation rates, however, the situation is reversed: white women are becoming similar to black women. Twenty-five years ago, all categories of black women had markedly higher labor force participation rates than white women did. While the rates of all women have been increasing, so many more white women than black are entering the labor force that their rates are approaching parity. By 1977, 48 percent of whites and 51 percent of blacks were paid employees.[2]

Increasing similarities are most apparent in occupations. Black women are now entering jobs that white women have long dominated. In 1965, only 24 percent of employed black women but 62 percent of employed white women were white collar workers. In 1977, the figures were 46 and 66 percent respectively. In 1965, 55 percent of black women were service workers (including 30 percent who were private household workers) and only 12 percent were secretaries or clerks. Twelve years later, black service workers had declined to 35 percent (only 9 percent remained as household domestics), while 26 percent were clerical workers.[3]

Another way to illustrate the growing similarity between black and white women is to consider the degree of overlap between their distributions in the eleven major occupational categories. In 1965, the overlap was small; 60 percent of black women were in the same occupational categories as white women and 40 percent were in different ones. By 1977, 79 percent were in the same categories and only 21 percent were in different categories.[4] Again, this change was achieved mainly by black women moving into jobs traditionally held by white women.

Black women are also closing the gaps between themselves and white women in earnings. In 1959, prime age black women workers

2. *Employment and Earnings*, January 1978, p. 142.
3. The 1965 figures are from *A Statistical Portrait*, Table 13–16, p. 74; and the 1977 figures are from *Ibid.*, p. 152.
4. *Ibid.*

Table 1

Indicators of Labor Force Status by Sex and Race

Race-sex group	Average in 1959	Average in 1974	Increase 1959–1974
	Years of school completed		
White males	11.2	12.9	+ 1.7
Black males	8.5	11.2	+ 2.7
White females	11.4	12.6	+ 1.2
Black females	9.5	11.4	+ 1.9
	Occupational prestige★		
White males	37.2	44.3	+ 7.1
Black males	18.9	27.7	+ 8.8
White females	38.1	44.8	+ 6.7
Black females	20.1	33.3	+13.3
	Annual earnings		
White males	$10,638	$13,432	+2794
Black males	5,473	9,137	+3664
White females	4,762	5,760	+ 998
Black females	2,954	5,652	+2698
	Hours worked per year		
White males	2,145	2,184	+ 39
Black males	1,852	1,910	+ 58
White females	1,614	1,617	+ 3
Black females	1,453	1,651	+198
	Hourly earnings		
White males	$4.96	$6.15	+$1.19
Black males	2.96	4.78	+ 1.82
White females	2.95	3.56	+ .61
Black females	2.03	3.42	+ 1.39

Source: Adapted from Reynolds Farley, "Trends in Racial Inequalities: Have the Gains of the 1960s Disappeared in the 1970s?", *American Sociological Review*, 42 (1977), 422–30. Data refer only to persons aged 25 to 54 who reported earnings and hours worked per year.

★ Occupational prestige scores are derived by asking people to evaluate individual occupations according to how "good" or "poor" they think the job is. Many female occupations may receive high prestige scores because respondents believe the occupation is "good" for a woman's job.

(25–54 years) earned only 62 percent of the amount white women did; by 1974, the figure had risen to 98 percent (see Tables 1 and 2). In 1974, white women earned just $108 more per year than black women. Reynolds Falley[5] found that this very small difference is more than accounted for by three facts: more black women than white live in the South where wages are lower than in other regions; black women have completed fewer years of schooling (11.9 vs.

5. "Trends in Racial Inequalities: Have the Gains of the 1960s Disappeared in the 1970s?" *American Sociological Review*, 42 (1977), 422–30. Data based on people who were employed and between ages 25 and 54.

Table 2

Black Women's Labor Force Status Expressed as a Percentage of the Labor
Force Status of White Men, Black Men and White Women

Race-sex group used in comparison	Percentage in 1959	Percentage in 1974	Percent change 1959–1974
Years of school completed			
White males	85%	92%	+ 7
Black males	112	106	− 6
White females	83	94	+11
Occupational prestige			
White males	54%	75%	+21
Black males	131	120	−11
White females	53	74	+21
Annual earnings			
White males	28%	42%	+14
Black males	54	62	+ 8
White females	62	98	+36
Hours worked per year			
White males	68%	76%	+ 8
Black males	78	86	+ 8
White females	90	102	+12
Hourly earnings			
White males	41%	56%	+15
Black males	69	71	+ 2
White females	69	96	+27

Source: Adopted from Reynolds Farley, "Trends in Racial Inequalities: Have the Gains of
the 1960s Disappeared in the 1970s?", *American Sociological Review*, 42 (1977), 422–30. Data
refer only to persons aged 25 to 54 who reported earnings and hours worked per year.

12.6); and they have lower occupational prestige than whites (33 vs.
45 on a 100 point scale of prestige). These gaps are somewhat larger
than the gap in earnings between black and white women. How then
do black women manage to come so close to white women when they
bring home the paychecks?

Paula Hudis[6] also found regional, occupational, and educational
differences between the two groups of women, but she argued that
black women compensate by working longer hours and by remaining
in the labor force steadily rather than interrupting employment for
long periods after childbearing. Hudis also suggests that black
women may travel further to work and search more aggressively for
jobs that yield higher pay.

Black women are closing the gaps between themselves and white
women because they are achieving progress while white women are

6. "Commitment to Work and Wages: Earnings Differences of Black and White Women,"
Sociology of Work and Occupations, 3 (1976), 127–45.

virtually standing still. Between 1959 and 1974, white women made the smallest gains in education, occupational prestige, and earnings of the four race-sex groups. Black women made the largest gains of any of the four groups in occupational prestige, but they were considerably outdistanced by black males in education and by both black and white males in earnings increases (see Table 1).

In 1974, black women still had slightly higher educational attainment and job prestige than black men, but the distance between them was smaller than in 1959. Yet in 1974, women were earning only 62 percent as much as black men were earning in terms of annual earnings and 71 percent as much as black men in hourly earnings. How can this paradox be true? Why do women who have higher educations and higher occupational prestige earn so much less than black men? There are several reasons. One is that occupational prestige is a relatively poor predictor of earnings. A high prestige score does not necessarily produce a large paycheck. More importantly, segregation of jobs by sex and the consequent crowding of women into a smaller number of occupations means that black women are concentrated in lower paying jobs than are black men. Black men are much more likely to be high status professionals, business executives, and crafts workers than black women are. These occupations pay more than the secretarial and service jobs in which women are concentrated. Overall, black women are much more similar to white women in occupational distribution than they are to black men. Again using the eleven major occupational categories, the overlap between black women and black men is only 58 percent. Fully 42 percent of the women are in different job categories from black men.[7]

Sex segregation and the subsequent low pay of black women is especially apparent in the professional fields. Like white women, black women are underrepresented in the high paying professions and overrepresented in the low paying professions. Women are 46 percent of the total black professionals, yet they are only 7 percent of the engineers, 14 percent of the lawyers, 24 percent of the physicians and dentists, and 25 percent of the life and physical scientists. On the other hand, women are 79 percent of the black librarians, 97 percent of the nurses, and 78 percent of the non-college teachers.[8]

The other important reason that black women have lower wages than black men is sex discrimination in pay. In the workplace, discrimination against black women is much more sexual than racial. This point has been demonstrated statistically in other pieces of research,

7. *Employment and Earnings*, January 1978, p. 152.
8. Unpublished data for 1977 annual averages, Bureau of Labor Statistics.

but it is an idea that is strongly resisted, even by trained social scientists.[9]

The impact of sex discrimination on black women can best be seen by including white men and making comparisons among the four race-sex groups. In one study based on 1970 statistics,[10] the earnings that were lost due to wage discrimination were estimated by controlling for education, occupation and region. The first two comparisons involved race discrimination. It was found that black males lost $1,772 in comparison to white males and that black women lost nothing because of wage discrimination when compared to white females. These racial comparisons show that black males, but not females, suffer earnings losses when compared with their white counterparts. The second set of comparisons involved sex discrimination. When compared to black males, black women lost $2,501 while white women lost $4,570 when compared to white males. These losses from sex discrimination clearly exceed those from racial discrimination. These findings point to a very clear conclusion: To the extent that we can disentangle racial and sexual components in black women's employment status, the sexual component is the more decisive one.

When we look at the labor force patterns over the past 25 years, another conclusion seems well established: Racial inequalities have declined over time, but sexual inequalities have persisted or even increased. While black women's status has improved both relatively and in absolute terms, black male status has improved even faster. Black women have very nearly caught up with white women. The major question is whether black women will be stopped in their progress and stay at the same level that white women have now achieved or whether both groups of women will surge ahead to achieve equality with men. The outlook is not optimistic. With racial barriers to equality crumbling, sexual barriers seem to be standing firm.

Much of the material discussed thus far has presented only the average characteristics of black women as a group, and most of the detailed labor force data pertains only to women aged 25–54. There are enormous variations around the average—not all black women are poor and not all black women work for pay. For example, age is a critical factor. The increasing similarity between black and white women is especially strong for those under 35. Concomitantly, there

9. More details are included in Almquist, "Social Science Research on Women and Wage Discrimination," but see also Elizabeth M. Almquist, "Women in the Labor Force," *Signs: Journal of Women in Culture and Society*, 2 (1977), 843–55.

10. Elizabeth M. Almquist, "Untangling the Effects of Race and Sex: The Disadvantaged Status of Black Women," *Social Science Quarterly*, 56 (1975), 116–28.

are major generational differences among blacks. The 70-year-old woman who had only a few years of schooling, who spent her entire working life as a domestic and who now subsists on the minimal benefits from old-age assistance has different needs and interests than the highly educated, 30-year-old lawyer who is a political activist and community organizer.

The special age-occupation mix for black women becomes especially poignant when we recognize that historically black women were confined to few roles other than that of domestic worker. That black women have only recently begun to escape this confinement is revealed in these figures: In 1970, among black women workers who were 65 years old or older, one-half were domestics. Among those aged 45–64 one out of three were maids. Among those who are 35–44 years old, one out of six; among those aged 25–34, one out of ten; and finally among those aged 20–24, only one out of eighteen.[11] It is apparent that when we speak of changes in the labor force—occupational upgrading, the movement of black women into white collar jobs, increases in earnings—it is primarily younger women who are reaping these benefits. In the meantime, there remains a large cadre of older black women whose lives are scarcely improved by the changes that are occurring now.

11. U.S. Bureau of the Census, 1973, *Census of Population: 1970*, Subject Reports, Final Report PC(2)–1B, *Negro Population*.

Virginia Woolf's feminist treatise A Room of One's Own
*has become a central literary document to the contemporary
women's movement. In the following selection from that
work, Woolf gives graphic dimension to the iron constraints
on creative work by women imposed by the sexual economy.
Shakespeare's sister, with a gift perhaps equal to the Bard's
own, would have been "an unhappy woman, a woman at
strife against herself. All the conditions of her life, all her
own instincts, were hostile to the state of mind which is
needed to set free whatever is in the brain." Little better,
Woolf concludes, is the situation of the gifted modern
woman.*

SHAKESPEARE'S SISTER

Virginia Woolf

FROM *A Room of One's Own*

It would have been impossible, completely and entirely, for any woman to have written the plays of Shakespeare in the age of Shakespeare. Let me imagine, since facts are so hard to come by, what would have happened had Shakespeare had a wonderfully gifted sister, called Judith, let us say. Shakespeare himself went, very probably—his mother was an heiress—to the grammar school, where he may have learnt Latin—Ovid, Virgil and Horace—and the elements of grammar and logic. He was, it is well known, a wild boy who poached rabbits, perhaps shot a deer, and had, rather sooner than he should have done, to marry a woman in the neighbourhood, who bore him a child rather quicker than was right. That escapade sent him to seek his fortune in London. He had, it seemed, a taste for the theatre; he began by holding horses at the stage door. Very soon he got work in the theatre, became a successful actor, and lived at the hub of the universe, meeting everybody, knowing everybody, practising his art on the boards, exercising his wits in the streets, and even getting access to the palace of the queen. Meanwhile his extraordinarily gifted sister, let us suppose, remained at home. She was as adventurous, as imaginative, as agog to see the world as he was. But she was not sent to school. She had no chance of learning grammar and logic, let alone of reading Horace and Virgil. She picked up a book now and then, one of her brother's perhaps, and read a few pages. But then her parents came in and told her to mend the stockings or mind the stew and not moon about with books and papers.

They would have spoken sharply but kindly, for they were substantial people who knew the conditions of and life for a woman and loved their daughter—indeed, more likely than not she was the apple of her father's eye. Perhaps she scribbled some pages up in an apple loft on the sly, but was careful to hide them or set fire to them. Soon, however, before she was out of her teens, she was to be betrothed to the son of a neighbouring wool-stapler. She cried out that marriage was hateful to her, and for that she was severely beaten by her father. Then he ceased to scold her. He begged her instead not to hurt him, not to shame him in this matter of her marriage. He would give her a chain of beads or a fine petticoat, he said; and there were tears in his eyes. How could she disobey him? How could she break his heart? The force of her own gift alone drove her to it. She made up a small parcel of her belongings, let herself down by a rope one summer's night and took the road to London. She was not seventeen. The birds that sang in the hedge were not more musical than she was. She had the quickest fancy, a gift like her brother's, for the tune of words. Like him, she had a taste for the theatre. She stood at the stage door; she wanted to act, she said. Men laughed in her face. The manager—a fat, loose-lipped man—guffawed. He bellowed something about poodles dancing and women acting—no woman, he said, could possibly be an actress. He hinted—you can imagine what. She could get no training in her craft. Could she even seek her dinner in a tavern or roam the streets at midnight? Yet her genius was for fiction and lusted to feed abundantly upon the lives of men and women and the study of their ways. At last—for she was very young, oddly like Shakespeare the poet in her face, with the same grey eyes and rounded brows—at last Nick Greene the actor-manager took pity on her; she found herself with child by that gentleman and so—who shall measure the heat and violence of the poet's heart when caught and tangled in a woman's body?—killed herself one winter's night and lies buried at some cross-roads where the omnibuses now stop outside the Elephant and Castle.

That, more or less, is how the story would run, I think, if a woman in Shakespeare's day had had Shakespeare's genius. But for my part, I agree with the deceased bishop, if such he was—it is unthinkable that any woman in Shakespeare's day should have had Shakespeare's genius. For genius like Shakespeare's is not born among labouring, uneducated, servile people. It was not born in England among the Saxons and the Britons. It is not born today among the working classes. How, then, could it have been born among women whose work began, according to Professor Trevelyan, almost before they were out of the nursery, who were forced to it by their parents and held to it by all the power of law and custom? Yet genius of a sort must have existed among women as it must have existed among the working classes. Now and again an Emily Brontë or a Robert Burns blazes out and proves its presence. But certainly it never got itself on to paper. When, however, one reads of a witch being ducked, of a woman possessed by devils, of a wise woman selling herbs, or even of a very remarkable man who had a mother, then I think we are on the track of a lost novelist, a suppressed poet, of some mute and inglorious Jane Austen, some Emily Brontë who dashed her brains out on the moor or mopped and mowed about the highways crazed with the torture that her gift had put her to. Indeed, I would venture to guess that Anon, who wrote so many poems without signing them, was often a woman. It was a woman Edward Fitzgerald, I think, suggested who made the ballads and the folksongs, crooning them to her children, beguiling her spinning with them, or the length of the winter's night.

This may be true or it may be false—who can say?—but what is true in it, so it seemed to me, reviewing the story of Shakespeare's sister as I had made it, is that any woman born with a great gift in the sixteenth century would certainly have gone crazed, shot herself, or ended her days in some lonely cottage outside the village, half witch, half wizard, feared and mocked at. For it needs little skill in psychology to be sure that a highly gifted girl who had tried to use her gift for poetry would have been so thwarted and hindered by other people, so tortured and pulled asunder by her own contrary instincts, that she must have lost her health and sanity to a certainty. No girl could have walked to London and stood at a stage door and forced her way into the presence of actor-managers without doing herself a violence and suffering an anguish which may have been irrational—for chastity may be a fetish invented by certain societies for unknown reasons—but were none the less inevitable. Chastity had then, it has even now, a religious importance in a woman's life, and has so wrapped itself round with nerves and instincts that to cut it free and bring it to the light of day demands courage of the rarest. To have lived a free life in London in the sixteenth century would have meant for a woman who was poet and playwright a nervous stress and dilemma which might well have killed her. Had she survived, whatever she had written would have been twisted and deformed, issuing from a strained and morbid imagination. And undoubtedly, I thought, looking at the shelf where there are no plays by women, her work would have gone unsigned. That refuge she would have sought certainly. It was the relic of the sense of chastity that dictated anonymity to women even so late as the nineteenth century. Currer Bell, George Eliot, George Sand, all the victims of inner strife as their writings prove, sought ineffectively to veil themselves by using the name of a man. Thus they did homage to the convention, which if not implanted by the other sex was liberally encouraged by them (the chief glory of a woman is not to be talked of, said Pericles, himself a much-talked-of man), that publicity in women is detestable. Anonymity runs in their blood. The desire to be veiled still possesses them. They are not even now as concerned about the health of their fame as men are, and, speaking generally, will pass a tombstone or a signpost without feeling an irresistible desire to cut their names on it, as Alf, Bert or Chas. must do in obedience to their instinct, which murmurs if it sees a fine woman go by, or even a dog, Ce chien est à moi. And, of course, it may not be a dog, I thought, remembering Parliament Square, the Sieges Allee and other avenues; it may be a piece of land or a man with curly black hair. It is one of the great advantages of being a woman that one can pass even a very fine negress without wishing to make an Englishwoman of her.

That woman, then, who was born with a gift of poetry in the sixteenth century, was an unhappy woman, a woman at strife against herself. All the conditions of her life, all her own instincts, were hostile to the state of mind which is needed to set free whatever is in the brain. But what is the state of mind that is most propitious to the act of creation, I asked. Can one come by any notion of the state that furthers and makes possible that strange activity? Here I opened the volume containing the Tragedies of Shakespeare. What was Shakespeare's state of mind, for instance, when he wrote *Lear* and *Antony and Cleopatra?* It was certainly the state of mind most favourable to poetry that there has ever existed. But Shakespeare himself said nothing about it. We only know casually and by chance that he "never blotted a line." Nothing indeed was ever said by the artist himself about his state of mind until the eighteenth century perhaps. Rousseau perhaps began it. At any rate, by the nineteenth century self-consciousness had developed so far that it was the habit for men of letters to describe their minds in confessions and autobiographies. Their lives also were written, and their letters were printed after their deaths. Thus, though we do not know what Shakespeare went through when he wrote *Lear*, we do know what Carlyle went through when he wrote the *French Revolution*; what Flaubert went through when he wrote *Madame Bovary*; what Keats was going through when he tried to write poetry against the coming of death and the indifference of the world.

And one gathers from this enormous modern literature of confession and self-analysis that to write a work of genius is almost always a feat of prodigious difficulty. Everything is against the likelihood that it will come from the writer's mind whole and entire. Generally material circumstances are against it. Dogs will bark; people will interrupt; money must be made; health will break down. Further, accentuating all these difficulties and making them harder to bear is the world's notorious indifference. It does not ask people to write poems and novels and histories; it does not need them. It does not care whether Flaubert finds the right word or whether Carlyle scrupulously verifies this or that fact. Naturally, it will not pay for what it does not want. And so the writer, Keats, Flaubert, Carlyle, suffers, especially in the creative years of youth, every form of distraction and discouragement. A curse, a cry of agony, rises from those books of analysis and confession. "Mighty poets in their misery dead"—that is the burdern of their song. If anything comes through in spite of all this, it is a miracle, and probably no book is born entire and uncrippled as it was conceived.

But for women, I thought, looking at the empty shelves, these difficulties were infinitely more formidable. In the first place, to have a room of her own, let alone a quiet room or a sound-proof room, was out of the question, unless her parents were exceptionally rich or very noble, even up to the beginning of the nineteenth century. Since her pin money, which depended on the good will of her father, was only enough to keep her clothed, she was debarred from such alleviations as came even to Keats or Tennyson or Carlyle, all poor men, from a walking tour, a little journey to France, from the separate lodging which, even if it were miserable enough, sheltered them from the claims and tyrannies of their families. Such material difficulties were formidable; but much worse were the immaterial. The indifference of the world which Keats and Flaubert and other men of genius have found so hard to bear was in her case not indifference but hostility. The world did not say to her as it said to them, Write if you choose; it makes no difference to me. That world said with a guffaw, Write? What's the good of your writing?

Our study of the origins and perpetuation of the sexual economy has led us persistently to the real or perceived biological differences between women and men that have provided focus and rationale for women's oppression throughout history. Earlier chapters have explored the means by which woman, appearing to be in the "iron grasp of the species" (de Beauvoir 1952:27), was deemed by man a different and therefore, by the male normative standard, lesser being, incapable of humanity in her own right, and sorely in need of protection. While that view has been moderated in at least the last century, and few people would suggest today that woman arrange her daily activities around the demands of her uterus, she has not yet

CHAPTER 5

The Personal as Political

been released from the bonds of what Juliet Mitchell has called the biohistorical fact of women's existence. A dogged focus on a woman's sexuality and fertility, in fact, has been a constant over the centuries as women have been moved into and out of the male-appropriated world according only to a law of expediency. As recently as the mid-twentieth century, women took seriously the warning of the media that "a separate identity . . . must be exorcised to win or keep the love of husband and child" (Friedan 1970:40). If the feminist movements of the nineteenth and twentieth centuries have done much to loosen the bonds, they have fallen far short of releasing women from them.

Nor are the bonds easily perceived by many, perhaps most, women. To the less than critical eye, great strides appear to have been made toward freeing the modern Western woman to make her own decisions. Technology, particularly in regard to birth control, has given her the potential for considerable control over the functions of her body. She has freedom to choose from among a number of life styles and occupations and is somewhat more free than formerly in the exercise of sexual preference. There is much evidence to suggest that such personal freedom is, however, largely illusory, that what appears as self-determination is, rather, politically conditioned response. Certainly the sociopolitical and economic structures developed in the eighteenth and nineteenth centuries remain essentially unchanged in the twentieth century. Nor does it seem that the power of those structures to limit or direct choices that might be construed as purely personal—when and whom to love, to marry, whether and how often to bear children, the choice of a life-work, how even to grow old—has diminished. For insofar as those "personal" decisions derive from female biology and have been shaped over the centuries as cultural vocations, they are not personal but political responses. An examination of the relationship between what truly is personal and what political demands that we return to those crucial years preceding and immediately following industrialization to retrace in this additional context the development of the new bourgeois family and the consequent reordering of the female role within the new family and society.

The patriarchal family has been the primary mode of social organization for most of recorded history. Indeed, it can be argued that in one form or another the nuclear family has been the normative standard for many hundreds of years. Nevertheless, the nuclear family as we know it bears little resemblance to that of even two hundred years ago. In *Centuries of Childhood: A Social History of Family Life*, Philippe Ariès traces the evolution of the medieval family to the modern family, arguing that the idea of the family has become "a value, a theme of expression, an occasion of emotion" only in very recent times (1962:404). Under the "ancien régime" the family was identified either as a production unit or with an estate and a reputation; little emotional investment seems to have been made in children, who were important primarily as workers or to ensure the transmission of property. In the medieval family, claims Ariès, children were viewed as adults in miniature, members, like servants, of a larger patriarchal household. Education for even the sons of the lord of the manor was rudimentary by most standards, consisting often, like that of peasants, of apprenticeship in the homes of others. However, the advent of commercial capitalism in Western Europe in the sixteenth and seventeenth centuries was accompanied by the development of the notion of childhood and adolescence as distinct life stages and by an emphasis on the importance of education. The family as a separate and autonomous unit thus began to take shape. But the seventeenth-century family, though indeed nuclear, was still not at all the modern family. It was distinguished from the latter, Ariès tells us, by the enormous amount of sociability it retained. The workplace, as we know, had not yet been separated from the household; women were essential to production, although, as we learned, their work evolved more and more as an adjunct to men's work. Both fathers and mothers were available to participate in childrearing. Children received training, discipline, and nurturance from both parents, as well as from other adults living within the patriarchal household, from older siblings, from servants or apprentices, and perhaps from clerics. But of special significance in the unprecedented interest in the child is that, although the mother tended the infant, it was the father who was expected to assume the major responsibility for socialization after the child reached what was considered an educable age. Indeed, the earliest treatises on the cultural and social education of children, such as Rousseau's *Emile*, were written by men and addressed specifically to fathers.

Nor did fathers under industrial capitalism relinquish immediately their duty to socialize and educate their children. One of the early arguments in support of child factory labor was that, with his children nearby, the father could continue to perform his appropriate role. As the age of industrial capitalism progressed in the eighteenth and nineteenth centuries, however, conditions were created for the economic dislocation of women in the ultimate separation of the household from production and the subsequent establishment of the mother's exclusive responsibility for child care and socialization.

While there is widespread agreement among feminists on the oppressive effect of the family on women since the advent of industrial capitalism, there are significant differences in analyses of that effect as well as of the sources of the family's oppressiveness. Juliet Mitchell, in an excerpt from her analysis of *Woman's Estate*, included here, sees the family as part of a complex of separate but interdependent structures that together form the unity that is "woman's condition." Citing production, reproduction, sexuality, and the socialization of children as the "key structures of women's situation," Mitchell inveighs against the notion that the contemporary form and composition of those structures represent natural conditions of humanity. Rather, she argues, each, in the particular composition it reflects at a given point in history, is a cultural creation. The family itself has about it nothing inevitable, no more than does the character or role of women. In her work, Mitchell undertakes the painstaking task she claims must be performed if women are to be liberated; she begins "to uncoil this ideological concept of [the family and woman's] permanence and of their unification into a monolithic whole, mother and child, a woman's place . . . her natural destiny."

Mitchell, while, as she says, asking feminist questions and

trying to come up with Marxist answers, regrets the fundamental failure of socialist theoreticians to see women's condition as a separate unity and to differentiate its structures. In this failing, socialists have historically never confronted the full oppression of women, and she perceives in that failure their acceptance of the myth of the family as monolith. While seeing the modern family as a creation of capitalism, they have failed to see the complex interweaving of that structure called family into the whole cloth of contemporary human life. Given their limited vision, the most commonly formulated socialist solution is invariably inadequate. For the family will not, she asserts, be eliminated by full inclusion of women in the work force, nor will women's liberation be won by socialist effort on behalf of the working class—even after women are fully a part of that working class.

One Marxist critic, Eli Zaretsky, in *Capitalism, the Family and Personal Life*, agrees with Mitchell that a modern conception of the family, with its ideological baggage of idealized motherhood, child-centeredness, and legend of the home as refuge from a cruel marketplace, is essential to the contemporary incarnation of the sexual economy. He regrets with her also the failure of socialist theory heretofore to apply its analysis to woman's condition as it has been defined by Mitchell. Zaretsky takes issue, however, with her conclusion that socialist analysis is by definition inadequate, that it suffices only to decode "economic and ideological activity" and excludes "an understanding of women's oppression and of social life generally—the emotions, sexuality, infancy and childhood and the instinctual life of both sexes" (1976:22). To decode the latter, which Zaretsky calls in his book the "private sphere" and which has come to be sharply differentiated in the post-World War I era as "personal life," Mitchell has turned to psychoanalytic theory, albeit "in conjunction with the notions of ideology already gained by dialectical materialism"

(1973:xx). Mitchell establishes as her point of departure in this effort a particular interpretation of Freud by Jacques Lacan that has been drawn upon by feminist subgroups of the French Woman's Liberation Movement, the "Psychoanalyse et Politique." "They would use psychoanalysis for an understanding of the operations of the unconscious. Their concern is to analyse how men and women live as *men and women* within the material conditions of their existence—both general and specific" (1973:xx). That formulation, Zaretsky complains, threatens to sustain the very dualism between the marketplace and the family that Mitchell criticizes so well. As an alternative, Zaretsky offers a historical analysis of the development of the contemporary concept of "personal life" that insists on the continuing roles of industrial capitalism in shaping that newfound personal life, of the contemporary concept of the family on which the personal depends so heavily, and of women's circumscribed conceptual place within sanctioned personal life and the family. The "split" so familiar to us today between the places we occupy in the social division of labor and our "personal" lives is a result, Zaretsky argues, of the "'split' between the socialized labour of the capitalist enterprise and the private labour of women in the home" (1976:31). Tracing the changes that occurred when the home ceased to be a productive unit (see Chapters 3 and 4, this volume), Zaretsky reminds us of the sense of alienation suffered by workers whose work ceased to be of their own definition. For the first time, an inner world of personal feeling was separated from work, from production. The result has been the development of an "ethic of personal fulfillment" and a "search for personal meaning [much of which] takes place within the family" (1976:30). Zaretsky charges psychoanalysis and psychology with feeding this pointless search by assuming that personal life

is governed by its own internal laws (for example, the psychosexual dynamics of the family, the "laws" of the mind or of "interpersonal relations") rather than by the "laws" that govern society as a whole. And they encourage the idea that emotional life is formed only through the family and that the search for happiness should be limited to our "personal" relations, outside our "job" or "role" within the division of labour. (1976:31)

He concludes that "the dichotomies that women's liberation first confronted—between the 'personal' and the 'political,' and between the 'family' and the 'economy'—are rooted in the structure of capitalist society" (1976:31). Both Mitchell's and Zaretsky's work furnish us with signposts into territory that must be explored if the most recent and sophisticated oppression of women is to be understood. A major contribution of these important writers, and of other modern feminist theorists whom we consider here, is the exposure not only of the deep penetration of the private sphere by the ideology of industrial capitalism and by the assumptions and techniques of mass technological society, but of the virtual invention by those forces of that sphere in a form that has assured continuation and elaboration of the sexual economy since World War I.

As we have seen in earlier chapters, and as Zaretsky confirms, woman's role in the productive unit that was the home and family before the industrial revolution was clearly defined. There is danger, as we shall see, of falsifying the historical reality of women's lives by imagining real equality in the shared labor of men and women in preindustrial times. This much is true: the oppression of women under the patriarchal system was grounded in material conditions of preindustrial society and was not a product of the industrial revolution. The work performed by women in those earlier times was, as we explored it in Chapter 4, endless and backbreaking. Given those qualifications, it is still the case that the industrial revolution was a watershed in the evolution of "women's place." In the preindustrial period, woman's work complemented (indeed, probably exceeded) men's, and was needed and valued. When men left the home after the industrial revolution, the nature of women's work changed rapidly. Industrialization not only drew men and women from the farms, but it produced for them goods that they had formerly produced for themselves. Gradually, a market economy emerged in which work was done in exchange for cash, and a family's needs were purchased in ever increasing proportion. That alteration meant little for many working-class women, particularly unmarried ones, who, as Ehrenreich and English point out in *For Her Own Good*, simply "followed their old 'woman's work' into the factory system—making the textiles, clothing, and soap which had once been made in the home" (1979:130). It meant even less to immigrant women, who went from boats to sweat shops as the century wore on. But for the "over 95 percent of married women [who] remained, like their mothers before them, at home, seemingly untouched by the industrial and social revolution sweeping through American life" (1979:129), drastic change occurred. Technology increasingly reduced the work of family survival in the home. Rather than the real liberation into the world of men some feminists anticipated as a result of the rapidly decreasing number of things to do in the home, a new element in the sexual economy was created to close off the uncovered escape routes. As we learned from Mitchell, transformation of only one structure in women's estate will be neutralized by the reinforcing of one or more of the other structures. In this case, transformation of production was rendered ineffective by the impact of capitalist social organization on individual persons and by the efforts of new corporate bureaucrats to preserve largely unchanged the structures of sexuality, reproduction, and socialization of children as a woman's situation of benefit to them. To preserve those structures under the new material conditions of life would require a redefinition of the home and of women's role in it and in the family. That redefinition, as Zaretsky begins to discuss it, is in large measure the subject of this chapter. Maintained outside the marketplace—in official myth if not entirely in reality—women were assigned a responsibility for the personal life of working men that gained increasing importance as the oppressive quality of life and work under industrial capitalism intensified.

Women's role as guardian of private life included changed and expanded "housework" responsibilities. Ehrenreich and English describe the creation in the late nineteenth and twentieth centuries of new forms of housework as women's work and as women's only sanctioned channel (beyond motherhood) for "personal expression." They explore the appointment of women as guardians of the ideal of domesticity and of the home, which was for some time, as Zaretsky and others have observed, regarded across class lines as the single retreat for the male worker where some vestige of control over his life remained.

Both the nature of housework and standards of accomplishment were altered, Ehrenreich and English maintain, when the pressures of home production were eliminated by industrialization. A "domestic void" was created for urban middle-class women, and a sense that something was missing in their lives. Rather than serve as a point of departure for the pursuit of new opportunities outside the home, however, the void was filled with newly invented women's work. A new era of "domestic science" was born, a product of the "germ theory of disease," of new industrial scientific management techniques, and of the immediate need to give women with free time and a sense of something missing in their lives renewed purpose within the approved sphere. "Here at last," the authors of *For Her Own Good* observe of the new field of domestic science, "was a challenge suitable to the energy and abilities of educated women." And nowhere was the challenge more stimulating than in the battle against the newly discovered Germ. Ehrenreich and English quote Helen Campbell, author of *Household Economics*, who "described how the old domestic crafts had gradually been taken over by men, but cleaning 'can never pass' from women's hands. 'To keep the world clean,' she exulted, 'this is the one great task for women'" (1979:158–59).

Concomitant with this elaboration of that special sphere for women discussed in earlier chapters came their expulsion from the public world, which Ann Douglas has called "feminine disestablishment." In America, Douglas tells us, it began in colonial times when women "lost a significant number of their legal privileges, among them the right to vote," and "vanished from a number of occupations . . . printers, blacksmiths, arms-makers, proprietors of small business concerns." Although these early events prefigured a later widespread condition for women, it was the case for the great majority of women in America that "disestablishment" waited until some time after the Civil War.

For the countless girls who moved from a life of labor on a farm to a life of labor in a factory, for the feminine immigrants who came in increasing numbers straight from a ship to a northern sweatshop or a midwestern frontier, for the thousands of enslaved black women who served King Cotton, disestablishment clearly had little or no meaning. (1977:49)

Douglas focuses in her work on the northern middle-class woman in the United States whose life, like that of her middle-class British counterpart, would have a profound effect on the shaping of social policy and thereby the oppression suffered by later generations of women in all classes as the notion of private or personal life and women's role in it became a more pervasive control strategy of modern capitalism. Inevitably, personal life—especially home and family—would be seen as inadequate compensation for the alienated and powerless lives to which most people have submitted in a post-industrial age. In fact, the home and family itself, and woman as their personification, would be held responsible for much of the alienation and frustration that would be acknowledged in the mid-twentieth century.

The seeds for the later, overt denigration of women were planted in this period of "disestablishment." One such seed was the modern cult of motherhood. Sociologist Jessie Bernard, in *The Future of Motherhood* (1974), explores the political implications of the new emphasis on motherhood that became an important element in the evolving concept of woman's place. Focusing on the effects of industrialization and urbanization, Bernard also identifies the wife and mother as the center of the single refuge from an industrial age characterized by intense and unrestrained competitiveness. It follows, she points out, that if the woman were to be the priestess of this "secular temple . . . she herself had to be protected from the outside world, isolated from it, immured in a walled garden." The political ramifications of this isolation, as well as of the single acknowledged vocation for women, are manifest. Having forced women into an isolation with their children unknown in most cultures, Western and particularly American "experts" began to blame mothers for psychological dislocations, particularly in their male children. In the pattern of ambivalence with which we have by now become thoroughly familiar, the Great Mother archetype became the Terrible Mother archetype, and "whatever was wrong in society, it had to be the mother's fault" (1974:15). Restrained from achieving power, influence, or even participation in the world beyond home and family, women were maligned for their real or imagined attempts to wield power or influence, or to participate through their husbands and children.

The blame for personal and social failures visited upon women was at its keenest in the 1940s and '50s. Those were the years in which disciples of Freud decried the "lost woman," the modern woman whose reach extended beyond the newly defined components of feminine psychology—passivity, narcissim, and masochism—and who thus doomed herself to unhappiness in the male world. In their depiction of that male world, the architects of "feminine psychology" (Helene Deutsch is perhaps foremost in the field) were drawing upon distinctions between public and private life, the workplace and home, man's place and woman's place, that were not merely Freudian. They were distinctions carefully nurtured by a preceding generation of industrialists and corporate bureaucrats, whom Stuart Ewen calls *Captains of Consciousness* (1976).

The captains of consciousness created, Ewen claims, a private life for the working class predicated on escape from the public world in which they had but little impact, on self-absorption, and on consumerism. In part, the objective was to create the market of eager consumers necessary to sustain a capitalist economy, but also, by providing real or imagined satisfactions outside the workplace, to soften the alienating effect of work transformed both by capitalism and technology. In large measure, the effort was designed, Ewen tells us, to create the illusion of self-determination as well as of pleasure. Women were losers on both counts. As distracting objects of sexual pleasure for dissatisfied male workers, women's usefulness was, as always, boundless. That was particularly so in the context of loosening attitudes toward sexuality that prevailed during the 1920s in counterpoint to the domestic expectations imposed on women. Life as a flapper, like life as "mistress" of the walled garden called home, or as chief consumer in the marketplace, was a facsimile of the autonomy and freedom hoped for by earlier generations of feminists. This beginning cult of the personal so familiar to us now in the

1980s, a cult whose development has been heavily dependent on modern techniques of advertising, was perhaps more responsible than any other factor for the virtual disappearance of feminist activity after suffrage in 1920. "[The] logic of contemporaneous advertising read," Ewen tells us, that "one can free oneself from the ills of modern life by embroiling oneself in the maintenance of that life" (1976:44). Consumption, Ewen argues, not only diverted men and women from the monotony and purposelessness of their lives in industrial society but it created a superficial sense of change that forestalled the possibility of deeper changes in the relationship between individuals and the corporate structure (Ewen 1976:85). In one chapter in *Captains of Consciousness*, "Consumption and the Ideal of the New Woman," Ewen describes the way in which, in the immediate postsuffrage period, "the feminist demand for equality and freedom for women was appropriated into the jargon of consumerism," and the identification of women with the home that was to survive as the *bête noir* of a second generation of feminists was sustained. An example of the former cited by Ewen was a 1929 advertising campaign to induce women to smoke cigarettes in public. Advertiser Edward Bernays was hired by the American Tobacco Company to undertake the campaign.

Utilizing the feminist motif, and enlisting the support of "a leading feminist," Ruth Hale, Bernays had a contingent of cigarette-puffing women march in the 1929 Easter parade, down Fifth Avenue in New York. "Our parade of ten young women lighting 'torches of freedom' on Fifth Avenue on Easter Sunday as a protest against women's inequality caused a national stir," Bernays proclaimed. "Front-page stories in newspapers reported the freedom march in words and pictures." (1976:160–1)

For women, the blind of consumerism and the larger diversion of "personal life" at the turn of the century and beyond were simply elaborations of the myth making that had characterized the feminine experience for generations.

More than thirty years later, a new generation of feminists began the long struggle to debunk the myths that had diverted their mothers and grandmothers from nineteenth-century feminism's promise of self-determination for women. Unwilling to accept the by now traditional appointments as guardians of the private world or custodians of men's personal happinesss, radical feminists began a period of intense examination of their personal lives. Primarily through the consciousness-raising sessions and "rap groups" that we explore more fully in a later chapter, radical feminists of the 1960s and early '70s began to explore the power relations and political implications of such "personal" experiences as sexual relations, love, marriage, friendship, childbirth and childbearing, health, household division of labor, abortion, and divorce. As we shall see, this burgeoning understanding of the relationship of the personal to the political was destined a decade later to deteriorate into a new absorption in personal satisfaction and achievement with little understanding of the structural limitations that continued to be imposed by the sexual economy. For a while, however, a heady confidence in the power of change in the way we *think* to affect the way things *are* prevailed in the women's movement.

In an excerpt from her essay "Sex and Power: Sexual Bases of Radical Feminism," included here, the veteran feminist Alix Kates Shulman traces early radical feminist ideas about female sexuality and its relationship to the sexual economy and captures the flavor of that early confidence. The lifting of the taboo against open discussion of female sexuality, described by Shulman, deepened, at least temporarily, women's understanding of the political dimensions of sexual relations. Unfortunately, the new understanding of sexual possibilities for women led ultimately to a concentration on sexual satisfaction and performance as an additional diversion from political analysis, and to a pseudo liberation similar to the sexual "freedom" of the 1920s. Moreover, this era of "sexual liberation" for women appears to have brought in its train new myths to which women learn to aspire. While there has been a healthy dispersion of knowledge about women's high capacity for the achievement of sexual arousal or orgasm, most clinicians have chosen to measure capacity, achievement, and inclination against the normative standards of male sexuality. Thus, sexual inhibition, for example, has been assumed to derive in women from psychological conflict.

In a study of "Sexuality as a Mainstay of Identity: Psychoanalytic Perspectives," Ethel Spector Person examines the difference in the expression of male and female sexuality within our culture and finds that the male model of sexuality, emphasizing performance and achievement, has led to "an almost fanatic preoccupation with the achievement of orgasm, multiple orgasms and vaginal orgasms" (1980:624). While confirming the studies that have demonstrated a "muting of female erotic impulsivity" relative to that exhibited by men, Person insists that a woman's lack of responsiveness to or concentration on genital sexuality is not in itself pathological. "This is not to deny," she claims, "that previously 'frigid' women may experience ego expansion when they achieve orgasm for the first time or that many women clinically have significant areas of repressed sexuality. . . . It is to argue that one must demonstrate repression rather than assume it, that periodic asexuality and anorgasmia seem consonant with mature ego development in women, and that one ought not dictate a tyranny of active sexuality as critical to female liberation" (1980:624–25). The available literature on the nature of female sexuality is, at this writing, inconclusive. Much further research is needed before we can determine whether the difference in the primacy of genital sexuality between men and women can be attributed to biological or cultural factors. It is nonetheless true, as feminist scholars have so abundantly illustrated, that sexuality under patriarchy has become a means for the expression of power and dominance that the current ambiance of sexual freedom has not mitigated. It remains for feminists to envision a world in which sexuality is disentangled from power contaminants. One does not become sexually liberated, as the past two decades of feminist energy have shown, merely by becoming sexually active. Sexual liberation is deficient as social critique or as public policy, as Person points out:

> At its worst, sexual liberation is part of the cult of individuality which only demands legitimization of the expression of the individual's needs, what appears to be her raw "impulse" life, against the demands of society without considering a political reordering of the social order itself. The achievement of the conditions necessary to female autonomy is a precondition for authentic sexual liberation. (1980:629)

The pressures and constraints on female sexuality created by the patriarchy are certainly substantial, but there is perhaps no area of "personal life" on which the sexual economy exerts its presence so heavily as that of reproduction. According to Zillah Eisenstein, "the struggle to control women's reproductive activity and the limiting of her choices related to the institution of motherhood reflects the centrality of patriarchy to Western society. The successful control of the struggle lays the basis for the survival of patriarchal society" (1981:224). By controlling women's struggles for reproductive freedom and the potential power of women in that freedom, Eisenstein argues, the state may salvage the nuclear family and preserve the distinction between the public (men's) and private (women's) spheres that are essential to the preservation of the patriarchy.

Sharing Eisenstein's conviction that reproduction operates "'at the core of social life' as well as within and upon women's individual bodies," Rosalind Pollack Petchesky offers a theory of reproductive freedom that includes two essential requirements: It must be grounded in the right to "bodily self-determination," and it must take into account the "social position of women and the socially determined needs which that position generates." Space does not permit us to reprint here in full Petchesky's article "Reproductive Freedom: Beyond 'A Woman's Right to Choose.'" Thus we have regretfully omitted her analysis of the political and theoretical origins of these two ideas. In the excerpt that follows, Petchesky argues that while a preeminent need for control of one's body, cutting across race and class divisions, must inform a feminist theory of abortion, that need does not confer an abstract or absolute right. Any such right, rather, must take into account the "historical contingency of the conditions" under which women must make reproductive decisions. We live in a world in which no substantial responsibility for a child is assumed by anyone but the parent, usually the mother. It is possible to imagine a world in which this would not be so, in which public policy would provide the support essential to distribute the burdens and responsibilities of child care as they currently exist, and in which, therefore, a woman's individual right to control her reproductive life might be tempered by collective needs and rights. Petchesky cautions us, however, against assuming that "an accretion of reforms," in the absence of total transformation of the position of women, will lift those burdens.

It is in the work of such feminist theorists as Person, Eisenstein, and Petchesky that the myth of private life so essential to the operation of the sexual economy becomes transparent. To deepen our understanding of the ways in which the myth has operated in human experience, we might turn to literary examples such as Tillie Olsen's classic short story, "I Stand Here Ironing." In that moving autobiographical piece, a mother recalls her struggle and her failures in the mothering of her eldest daughter, all she "did or did not do, with what should have been and what cannot be helped" (1961:1–2). Facing the injunction of an "expert"—a school counselor—that she "explain" her troubled daughter, the narrator mentally relives as she irons the growing-up years of that child. She recalls the depression, the war, the poverty, and the loneliness, her own youth and helplessness as she sought to provide for herself and the child after being abandoned by her husband. At the end, she refuses to "total it all," for an accounting of the years she spent rearing that troubled child would not add up to the person either of them had become. The reality of their struggle to survive, while shared by many women and their children, reflected no ideal of motherhood, of sheltering home, of nurturing personal relationships. Olsen's masterful story illuminates the moral issues, defined by Petchesky, growing out of the "historically and culturally defined position that women find themselves in through motherhood." The impact of this story derives especially from the narrator's understanding of the context in which her mothering took place and of her unwillingness to bear guilt for failures made inevitable by a world that denies her the support she needs to provide for her children the "soil of easy growth."

"The Mother," a poem by Gwendolyn Brooks, is, like Olsen's "I Stand Here Ironing," full of the complexity of woman's "choices" in the current social order and the complexity of the mind of a woman who grasps the narrowness of her possibilities. In "The Mother" we have a woman for whom the establishment of the legal right to abortion will not ensure freedom of choice. As Petchesky and others remind us, not until our most basic social and economic institutions are transformed will women be able to exercise genuine reproductive freedom. The mother in Brooks' poem cannot forget the abortions she has had, her "dim killed children." "If I poisoned the beginnings of your breaths," she tells her lost unborn, "believe that even in my deliberateness I was not deliberate" (1971).

As in all our discussions of the personal as political, it is important not to lose sight of the class and race distinctions that shape and define women's treatment by and responses to the sexual economy. For members of the dispossessed underclass, the inevitable hope vested in children assumes a special poignancy. In the virtual absence of the institutional or economic privilege that might provide the "soil of easy growth," reproductive freedom may take on different meaning. In the first of his five-volume work, *Children of Crisis*, Robert Coles provides a glimpse of that difference. A black female tenant farmer from Georgia speaks to Coles of the yawning gulf of understanding between her world and that of the white, middle-class "family planner" who would effect the poor woman's release from childbearing:

To me, having a baby inside me is the only time I'm really alive. I know I can make something, do something, no matter what color my skin is, and what names people call me. When the baby gets born . . . you feel there must be some hope, some chance that things will get better; because there it is, right before you, a real, live, growing baby. (1967:368–69)

So skillfully have the most personal elements of a woman's life been conscripted into the service of the sexual economy that women have believed themselves in possession all along. Having explored earlier the political ramifications of reproductive freedom, we turn now to the interventions of an almost exclusively male medical establishment into control over and knowledge about women's bodies. The nineteenth-century notion of innate female frailty discussed in the preceding chapter, with roots in the separation of home and work-place, provided substance and rationale for the "professionalization" of gynecology and obstetrics. That century's medical theory, borne heavily by white, middle-class women, that a woman's entire being— her emotional, psychological, intellectual, and sexual life—is inex-tricably tied to the demands of the uterus continues in a somewhat modified form to shape twentieth-century medical interventions. Women's normal life processes now, as in the nineteenth century, often still are deemed pathological by those to whom women's health has been entrusted.

Several feminist writers—Ehrenreich and English (1979), Adrienne Rich (1976), and Suzanne Arms (1975)—have described the emergence of gynecology and obstetrics as disciplines within an exclusively male medical establishment, the consequent purging of the woman healer and midwife, and the ultimate stripping from women of control over and knowledge about their bodies. The purge took place throughout the industrialized Western world, but with particular strength in America where the development of gynecologic practice was not unrelated to women's growing and active dissatisfac-tion with their "proper sphere."[1] In addition, American gynecolo-gists, claims G. J. Barker-Benfield, were typical of the American men described by de Tocqueville in their "mad impatience, addiction to change, and ferocious competitiveness with other men—and a para-doxical dependence upon them for judgment of success" (1976:120).

---

1. Christopher Lasch claims that women's anger against men for imposing on them repeated pregnancies led them to acceptance of male medical attendance in childbirth. Even though it eroded the traditional prerogatives of women, "the redefinition of pregnancy as a disease helped women in their campaign for voluntary motherhood by raising the cost of pregnancy to their husbands—not only the financial cost but the emotional cost of the doctor's intrusion into the bedroom, his usurpation of the husband's sexual prerogatives" (1980:27).

Obstetrics and gynecology, the most rapidly developing medical specialties in late-nineteenth-century America, were firmly grounded in the notion of the perversity of the uterus. The new teaching hospitals stressed the physiological origins of women's disorders, placing upon the medical practitioner the obligation to treat not only physical but psychological and moral symptoms of illness as well. Gynecological activity, characterized, Barker-Benfield claims, by "flamboyant, drastic, risky, and instant use of the knife" (1976:90), included great numbers of ovariotomies, clitoridectomies, and hysterectomies, performed to cure a host of behavioral as well as physical ills, from menstrual pain to "erotic tendencies" or "simple cussedness." Nor was the surgeon's knife wielded only on the wives and dependents of men who could afford to pay for such services; the charity hospitals, to which the medical schools attached themselves, provided medical students with a ready supply of live patients, primarily immigrant and working-class women, on whom to practice.

Current feminist research suggests that the nineteenth-century view of women as having been "made up around a uterus" persists in twentieth-century medical interventions. Deborah Larned, in an article on "The Epidemic in Unnecessary Hysterectomy," for example, claims that hysterectomies are among the most popular of the estimated two million unnecessary operations performed each year in the United States. This procedure, long accepted as a cure for uterine cancer, has been recently regarded by many gynecologists as the solution for "everything from backaches to contraception" (1978: 196). Surgeons, assuming the uterus of a woman past childbearing to be a "useless" but potentially lethal organ, are exposing women to greater surgical risks than posed by cancer itself.

While much of the medical management of women's health has been critically examined by feminists in recent years, childbirth has perhaps garnered most attention in both the popular press and among scholars. Much further research is needed before we fully understand the causes of the transition from childbirth as an exclusively female and social affair in the eighteenth century to the full acceptance of medically managed childbirth in the late 1920s and '30s. While much feminist anger has been directed against this evolution, Nancy Schrom Dye is one feminist researcher who cautions us against assuming that women were merely passive victims in a drama in which men wrested from them an essential life function and in so doing deprived them of an important expression of female bonding (1980:99). Childbirth, she reminds us, was a terrifying event from which many women turned to science for release. Indeed, women accepted the medical model of childbirth, with its promise of safer, less painful childbirth, in part as a means of mitigating those forces which, in the words of de Beauvoir, placed them in the "iron grip of the species." Women's rights advocates in the 1920s and '30s, for example, who demanded of an initially resistant medical profession the administration of drugs that created the condition known as "twilight sleep," were not, in their opinion, relinquishing control over their bodies, but were exercising their right to choose the conditions under which they would give birth. "Parturient feminists today," comments Judith Walzer Leavitt in an article on the "twilight sleep" controversy, "seeking fully to experience childbirth, paradoxically must fight a tradition of drugged, hospital-controlled births, itself the partial result of a struggle to increase women's control over their bodies" (1980:164).

While it is essential, we believe, to resist romanticizing the female-controlled model of childbirth of past centuries, one cannot but regret the loss of the social context in which the parturient woman in past centuries received comfort, love, and assistance from other women. With the final acceptance of childbirth as a medical event, pregnancy and parturition came to be seen as diseases to be cured. Not the least because of the introduction of that element of pathology into the function of women's bodies, the history of obstetrics-gynecology needs and deserves the full treatments it has received in recent years by feminist scholars. Lack of space allows us only to note here the recurrent discovery of feminist critics that the assumption of control over the health professions by men has added yet another dimension to the oppression of women. But the casting of women's biology into a pathological context is not the exclusive province of the health care professions. Indeed, the social sciences have followed the lead of medicine and psychiatry in the neglect of women's health issues and life processes except as they are deemed deviant. Prostitution and lesbianism, for example, as well as other forms of "antisocial behavior," have received extensive coverage in professional literature. At the same time, there has been until recently but scant interest in the fields of sociology or psychology in the study of menstruation, pregnancy, the birth process, or menopause as important life functions.

As new studies by feminist scholars appear, most confirm that no female life function has escaped political control within the sexual economy, even menstruation and menopause, the watersheds of the female life cycle. As has been repeatedly emphasized in this chapter, woman's assigned role as guardian of a private world created by industrial capitalism has required her reduction to the body, to her "natural being." Thus, the lesson of the menarche is that the young girl is now to be defined by her unique biology; her striving for identity must now focus on men and on motherhood. In Western societies the onset of menstruation is treated with ambivalence. As the promise of fertility, the event is heralded as a great blessing; but as the symbol of her sexuality, it is her initiation into the sexual economy, with all the limitations that implies. What the young girl often learns is that much of the freedom she shared with boys as a child is to be exchanged for her femininity.

If the onset of menstruation is the signal of her impending womanhood, it follows, then, in the conventional wisdom of the sexual economy, that menopause marks its end, leaving women empty, purposeless, and often depressed. The menopausal woman, Paula Weideger claims, in *Menstruation and Menopause* (1975), having absorbed the lesson that she is defined by her fertility, denies her sexuality and often attempts to secure her identity by living more completely for others. It is the woman who has embraced the roles of wife and mother to the exclusion of all others who becomes the primary casualty of the menstrual taboo after menopause (1975:214–16).

In her classic study of "Depression in Middle-Aged Women" (1971), sociologist Pauline Bart anticipates Weideger's conclusions. While traditional psychoanalytic theory with its notions of feminine psychology would predict that women who had failed to accept their feminine identity, including motherhood, would be most likely to suffer from depression at menopause, Bart's findings cast serious doubt on those hypotheses. Her sample of depressed, hospitalized middle-aged women, on the contrary, included a larger proportion of very devoted mothers who fulfilled the classic psychoanalytic prescription for mothering than one would expect to find in a population of middle-aged women. In fact, Bart suggests that a failure to develop a life independent of one's husband or children, and ways of relating to them other than those based on the traditional mothering role, may have contributed directly to some women's inability to cope successfully with the pressures of aging. Bart's study suggests that, in an all too familiar manner, it is largely myth useful to the sexual economy that drains purpose and meaning from the life of the postmenopausal woman.

There is evidence, in any case, that the influence of this particular myth on the reality of women's lives is diminishing. Alice Rossi, in a recent review of life-span theories, observes that

contrary to assumptions in the social sciences and medicine, menopause is rarely a crisis to women. There is more dread in the anticipation than difficulty in the experience, and far from being upset at the loss of an important biological function, most women feel a relief to have it behind them. This is not simply a matter of cessation of menses . . . many of the women in the forty-five to fifty-five age group were happy to have done not only with menstruation and its attendant annoyances, but also with the mothering of small children. (1980:20–21)

Either these and similarly positive attitudes among middle-aged women noted by Rossi mark a change in women or the myth of the empty middle-aged woman is a relic sustained by the sexual economy. In either case, the postmenopausal woman remains persistently invisible.

The paucity of female literary characters of middle age or beyond who are fully drawn characters is revelatory of social attitudes toward the aging woman. There are earth mothers who suffer and nurture—Faulkner's Dilsey, Ma Joad in Steinbeck's *The Grapes of Wrath*, Pegotty in Dickens' *David Copperfield*. There is a seemingly ceaseless supply of silly middle-aged women—Mrs. Bennet in Jane Austen's *Pride and Prejudice*, Mrs. Jellyby in Dickens' *Bleak House*. Even a humanly despairing middle-aged woman of the ilk of Virginia Woolf's Mrs. Dalloway is rarely encountered in Anglo-American literature. Yet, it is to literature, to the arts, that we must often turn both for reflections of reality and for models for the future as we examine personal lives shaped by the sexual economy.

Catherine Stimpson, former editor of the leading feminist journal *Signs*, charges feminist theorists with the task of exploring the place and extent of nature in the reconstruction of women, warning against "both the old fallacy of reducing women to their bodies and the potentially new fallacy of evading all their claims." To accomplish that task, Stimpson claims, we must use the testimony of women themselves. Women must "name" themselves and "name" the events of their lives. Then, she says, we will have reason to celebrate rather than mourn those events (1979). Such sharing and naming of events, though important adjuncts to personal autonomy, cannot suffice, however, in a society whose institutions are based on deeply entrenched and convenient notions of appropriate feminine behavior. As we have been reminded by many feminist critics, individual solutions are not solutions at all. A woman's possible choices must be assessed within the context of institutions not of her shaping. Real self-determination and the celebration of life held out by Stimpson wait upon the overthrow of the sexual economy.

The analysis of women's position by Juliet Mitchell from which the following selection is taken was an important contribution to the canon of feminist theory. Mitchell questions the widely accepted notion of the historical inevitability of the nuclear family, from which it follows that woman's role in reproduction is the "complement" of man's role in production. The liberation of women, Mitchell finds, will be achieved only if all four structures common to all women—production, reproduction, socialization of children, and sexuality—are transformed.

THE POSITION OF WOMEN

Juliet Mitchell

FROM *Woman's Estate*

The key structures of woman's situation can be listed as follows: Production, Reproduction, Sexuality and the Socialization of Children. The concrete combination of these produce the "complex unity" of her position; but each separate structure may have reached a different "moment" at any given historical time. Each then must be examined separately in order to see what the present unity is, and how it might be changed. The notes that follow do not pretend to give a historical account of each sector. They are only concerned with some general reflections on the different roles of women and some of their interconnections.

I. Production

The biological differentiation of the sexes into male and female and the division of labour that is based on this have *seemed*, throughout history, an interlocked necessity. Anatomically smaller and weaker, woman's physiology and her psycho-biological metabolism appear to render her a less useful member of a work-force. It is always stressed how, particularly in the early stages of social development, man's physical superiority gave him the means of conquest over nature which was denied to women. Once woman was accorded the menial tasks involved in maintenance while man undertook conquest and creation, she became an aspect of the things preserved: private property and children. Marx, Engels, Bebel, De Beauvoir—the major socialist writers on the subject—link the confirmation and continuation of woman's oppression after the establishment of her physical inferiority for hard manual work with the advent of private property. But woman's physical weakness has never prevented her from performing work as such (quite apart from bringing up children)—only specific types of work, in specific societies. In Primitive, Ancient, Oriental, Medieval and Capitalist societies, the *volume* of work performed by women has always been considerable (it has usually been much more than this). It is only its form that is in question. Domestic labour, even today, is enormous if quantified in terms of productive labour.[1] It has been calculated in Sweden, that 2,340 million hours a year are spent by women in housework compared with 1,290 million hours in industry. The Chase Manhattan Bank estimated a woman's overall working week averaged 99.6 hours. In any case women's physique alone has never permanently or even predominantly relegated them to menial domestic chores. In many peasant societies, women have worked in the fields as much as, or more than, men. . . .

This is pre-eminently woman's condition. For far from woman's *physical* weakness removing her from productive work, her *social* weakness has in these cases evidently made her the major slave of it.

This truth, elementary though it may seem, has nevertheless been constantly ignored by socialist writers on the subject, with the result that there is an unfounded optimism in their predictions of the future. For, if it is just the biological incapacity for the hardest physical work which has determined the subordination of women, then the prospect of an advanced machine technology, abolishing the need for strenuous physical exertion, would seem to promise, therefore, the liberation of women. For a moment industrialization itself thus seems to herald women's liberation. Engels, for instance, wrote:

The first premise for the emancipation of women is the reintroduction of the entire female sex into public industry. . . . And this has become possible only as a result of modern large-scale industry, which not only permits of the participation of women in production in large numbers, but actually calls for it and, moreover strives to convert private domestic work also into a public industry[2].

What Marx said of early industrialism is no less, but also *no more* true of an automated society:

---

1. Apologists who make out that housework, though time-consuming, is light and relatively enjoyable, are refusing to acknowledge the dull and degrading routine it entails. Lenin commented crisply: "You all know that even when women have full rights, they still remain factually downtrodden because all housework is left to them. In most cases housework is the most unproductive, the most barbarous and the most arduous work a woman can do. It is exceptionally petty and does not include anything that would in any way promote the development of the woman." (*Collected Works*, vol. XXX, p. 43.)

2. Friedrich Engels: *The Origin of the Family, Private Property, and the State*, II, pp. 233, 311.

...it is obvious that the fact of the collective working group being composed of individuals of both sexes and all ages, must necessarily, *under suitable conditions*, become a source of human development; although in its spontaneously developed, brutal, capitalist form, where the labourer exists for the process of production, and not the process of production for the labourer, that fact is a pestiferous source of corruption and slavery.[3]

Industrial labour and automated technology both promise the preconditions for women's liberation alongside man's—but no more than the preconditions. It is only too obvious that the advent of industrialization has not so far freed women in this sense, either in the West or in the East. De Beauvoir hoped that automation would make a decisive, qualitative difference by abolishing altogether the physical differential between the sexes. But any reliance on this in itself accords an independent role to technique which history does not justify. Under capitalism, automation could possibly lead to an ever-growing structural unemployment which would expel women (along with immigrants)—the latest and least integrated recruits to the labour force and ideologically the most expendable for a bourgeois society—from production after only a brief interlude in it. Technology is mediated by the total structure, and it is this which will determine woman's future in work relations. It is the relationship between the social forces and technology that Firestone's "ecological" revolution ultimately ignores.

Physical deficiency is not now, any more than in the past, a sufficient explanation of woman's relegation to inferior status. Coercion has been ameliorated to an ideology shared by both sexes. Commenting on the results of her questionnaire of working women, Viola Klein notes: "There is no trace of feminine egalitarianism—militant or otherwise—in any of the women's answers to the questionnaire; nor is it even implicitly assumed that women have a "Right to Work."[4] Denied, or refusing, a role in *production*, woman does not even create the preconditions of her liberation. But even her presence in the work force does not erode her oppression in the family.

2. The Reproduction of Children

Women's absence from the critical sector of production historically, of course, has been caused not just by their assumed physical weakness in a context of coercion—but also by their role in reproduction. Maternity necessitates withdrawals from work, but this is not a decisive phenomenon. It is rather women's role in reproduction which

3. Karl Marx: *Capital*, I, p. 394.

4. Viola Klein: "Working Wives,' *Institute of Personnel Management Occasional Papers*, no. 15, 1960, p. 13.

has become, in capitalist society at least, the spiritual "complement" of men's role in production. Bearing children, bringing them up, and maintaining the home—these form the core of woman's natural vocation, in this ideology. This belief has attained great force because of the seeming universality of the family as a human institution. There is little doubt that Marxist analyses have underplayed the fundamental problems posed here. The complete failure to give any operative content to the slogan of "abolition" of the family is striking evidence of this (as well as of the vacuity of the notion).

The biological function of maternity is a universal, atemporal fact, and as such has seemed to escape the categories of Marxist historical analysis. However, from it is made to follow the so-called stability and omnipresence of the family, if in very different forms.[5] Once this is accepted, women's social subordination—however emphasized as an honourable, but different role (cf. the equal-but-"separate" ideologies of Southern racists)—can be seen to follow inevitably as an *insurmountable* bio-historical fact. The causal chain then goes: maternity, family, absence from production and public life, sexual inequality.

The lynch-pin in this line of argument is the idea of the family. The notion that "family" and "society" are virtually co-extensive or that an advanced society not founded on the nuclear family is now inconceivable, despite revolutionary posturings to the contrary, is still widespread. It can only be seriously discussed by asking just what the family is—or rather what women's role in the family is. Once this is done, the problem appears in quite a new light. For it is obvious that woman's role in the family—primitive, feudal or bourgeois—partakes of three quite different structures: reproduction, sexuality, and the socialization of children. These are historically, not intrinsically, related to each other in the present modern family. We can easily see that they needn't be. For instance, biological parentage is not necessarily identical with social parentage (adoption). Thus it is essential to discuss not the family as an unanalysed entity, but the separate *structures* which today compose it but which tomorrow may be decomposed into a new pattern.

As I have said, reproduction is seen as an apparently constant atemporal phenomenon—part of biology rather than history. In fact this is an illusion. What is true is that the "mode of reproduction" does not vary with the "mode of production"; it can remain effectively the same through a number of different modes of production.

---

5. Philippe Ariès in *Centuries of Childhood*, 1962, shows that though the family may in some form always have existed it was often submerged under more forceful structures. In fact according to Ariès it has only acquired its present significance with the advent of industrialization.

For it has been defined till now by its uncontrollable, natural character and to this extent has been an unmodified biological fact. As long as reproduction remained a natural phenomenon, of course, women were effectively doomed to social exploitation. In any sense, they were not "masters" of a large part of their lives. They had no choice as to whether or how often they gave birth to children (apart from precarious methods of contraception or repeated dangerous abortions); their existence was essentially subject to biological processes outside their control. . . .

3. Sexuality

Sexuality has traditionally been the most tabooed dimension of women's situation. The meaning of sexual freedom and its connection with women's freedom is a subject which few socialist writers have cared to broach. "Socialist morality" in the Soviet Union for a long time debarred serious discussion of the subject within the world communist movement. Marx himself—in this respect somewhat less liberal than Engels—early in his life expressed traditional views on the matter:

. . . the sanctification of the sexual instinct through exclusivity, the checking of instinct by laws, the moral beauty which makes nature's commandment ideal in the form of an emotional bond—(this is) the spiritual essence of marriage.[6]

Yet it is obvious that throughout history women have been appropriated as sexual objects, as much as progenitors or producers. Indeed, the sexual relationship can be assimilated to the statute of possession much more easily and completely than the productive or reproductive relationship. Contemporary sexual vocabulary bears eloquent witness to this—it is a comprehensive lexicon of reification— "bird, fruit, chick . . ." Later Marx was well aware of this: "*Marriage . . .* is incontestably a form of *exclusive private property.*"[7] But neither he nor his successors ever tried seriously to envisage the implications of this for socialism, or even for a structural analysis of women's conditions. Communism, Marx stressed in the same passage, would not mean mere "communalization" of women as common property. Beyond this, he never ventured.

Some historical considerations are in order here. For if socialists have said nothing, the gap has been filled by liberal ideologues. Fairly recently, in his book, *Eros Denied*, Wayland Young argues that

6. Karl Marx: "Chapitre de Mariage," *Oeuvres Complètes*, ed. Molitor *Oeuvres Philosophiques*, I, p. 25.
7. Karl Marx: *Private Property and Communism*, p. 153.

western civilization has been uniquely repressive sexually, and, in a plea for greater sexual freedom today, compares it at some length with oriental and ancient societies. It is striking, however, that his book makes no reference whatever to women's status in these different societies, or to the different forms of marriage-contract prevalent in them. This makes the whole argument a purely formal exercise—an obverse of socialist discussions of women's position which ignore the problem of sexual freedom and its meanings. For while it is true that certain oriental or ancient (and indeed primitive) cultures were much less puritanical than western societies, it is absurd to regard this as a kind of "transposable value" which can be abstracted from its social structure. In effect, in many of these societies sexual openness was accompanied by a form of polygamous exploitation which made it, in practice, an expression simply of masculine domination. Since art was the province of man, too, this freedom finds a natural and often powerful expression in art—which is often quoted as if it were evidence of the total quality of human relationships in the society. Nothing could be more misleading. What is necessary, rather than this naive, hortatory core of historical example, is some account of the co-variation between the degrees of sexual liberty and openness, and the position and dignity of women in different societies. . . .

4. Socialization of Children

Woman's biological "destiny" as mother becomes a cultural vocation in her role as socializer of children. In bringing up children, woman achieves her main social definition. Her suitability for socialization springs from her physiological condition: her ability to produce milk and occasional relative inability to undertake strenuous work loads. It should be said at the outset that suitability is not inevitability. Several anthropologists make this clear. Lévi-Strauss writes:

In every human group, women give birth to children and take care of them, and men rather have as their speciality hunting and warlike activities. Even there, though, we have ambiguous cases: of course, men never give birth to babies, but in many societies . . . they are made to act as if they did.[8]

Evans-Pritchard's description of the Nuer tribe depicts just such a situation. Margaret Mead comments on the element of wish-fulfilment in the assumption of a *natural* correlation of femininity and nurturance:

---

8. Claude Levi – Strauss: "The Family," in *Man, Culture and Society*, ed. H. L. Shapiro, 1956, p. 279.

We have assumed that because it is convenient for a mother to wish to care for her child, this is a trait with which women have been more generously endowed by a careful teleological process of evolution. We have assumed that because men have hunted, an activity requiring enterprise, bravery and initiative, they have been endowed with these useful attitudes as part of their sex-temperament.[9] . . .

Family Patterns

This ideology corresponds in dislocated form to a real change in the pattern of the family. As the family has become smaller, each child has become more important; the actual *act* of reproduction occupies less and less time, and the socializing and nurturance process increases commensurately in significance. Contemporary society is obsessed by the physical, moral and sexual problems of childhood and adolescence. Ultimate responsibility for these is placed on the mother. Thus the mother's reproductive role has retreated as her socializing role has increased. In the 1890s in England a mother spent fifteen years in a state of pregnancy and lactation: in the 1960s she spent an average of four years. Compulsory schooling from the age of five, of course, reduces the maternal function very greatly after the initial vulnerable years.

The present situation is then one in which the qualitative importance of socialization during the early years of the child's life has acquired a much greater significance than in the past—while the quantitative amount of a mother's life spent either in gestation or child-rearing has greatly diminished. It follows that socialization cannot simply be elevated to the woman's new maternal vocation. Used as a mystique, it becomes an instrument of oppression. Moreover, there is no inherent reason why the biological and social mother should coincide. The process of socialization is, in itself, invariable—but the person of the socializer can very. Observers of collective methods of child-rearing in the kibbutzim in Israel note that the child who is reared by a trained nurse (though normally maternally breast-fed) does not suffer the back-wash of typical parental anxieties and thus may positively gain by the system. This possibility should not be fetishized in its turn (Jean Baby, speaking of the post-four-year-old child, goes so far as to say that "complete separation appears indispensable to guarantee the liberty of the child as well as the mother."[10] But what it does reveal is the viability of plural forms of socialization—neither necessarily tied to the nuclear family, nor to the

9. Margaret Mead: "Sex and Temperament," in *The Family and the Sexual Revolution*, pp. 207–8.
10. Jean Baby: *Un Monde Meilleur*, Maspero, 1964, p. 99.

biological parent, or rather to *one* of the biological parents—the mother.

Conclusion

The lesson of these reflections is that the liberation of women can only be achieved if *all four* structures in which they are integrated are transformed—Production, Reproduction, Sexuality and Socialization. A modification of any of them can be offset by a reinforcement of another (as increased socialization has made up for decreased reproduction). This means that a mere permutation of the form of exploitation is achieved. The history of the last sixty years provides ample evidence of this. In the early twentieth century, militant feminism in England and the U.S.A. surpassed the labour movement in its violence. The vote—a political right—was eventually won. None the less, though a simple completion of the formal legal equality of bourgeois society, it left the socio-economic situation of women virtually unchanged. The wider legacy of the suffrage was practically nil: the suffragettes, by and large, proved unable to move beyond their own initial demands, and many of their leading figures later became extreme reactionaries. The Russian Revolution produced a quite different experience. In the Soviet Union in the 1920s, advanced social legislation aimed at liberating women above all in the field of sexuality; divorce was made free and automatic for either partner, thus effectively liquidating marriage; illegitimacy was abolished, abortion was free, etc. The social and demographic effects of these laws in a backward, semi-literate society bent on rapid industrialization (needing, therefore, a high birthrate) were—predictably—catastrophic.[11] Stalinism soon produced a restoration of traditional iron norms. Inheritance was reinstated, divorce made inaccessible, abortion illegal, etc.

The State cannot exist without the family. Marriage is a positive value for the Socialist Soviet State only if the partners see in it a lifelong union. So-called free love is a bourgeois invention and has nothing in common with the principles of conduct of a Soviet citizen. Moreover, marriage receives its full value for the State only if there is progeny, and the consorts experience the highest happiness of parenthood. (From the official journal of the Commissariat of Justice in 1939.[12])

Women still retained the right and obligation to work, but because these gains had not been integrated into the earlier attempts

---

11. For a fuller account of this see Chapter IV A of Kate Millet's *Sexual Politics*.
12. *Sotsialisticheskaya Zakonnost*, 1939, no. 2, cit. N. Timasheff: "The Attempt to Abolish the Family in Russia," in *The Family*, ed. N. W. Bell and E. F. Vogel, 1960, p. 59.

to free sexuality and abolish the family no general liberation has occurred.

In China, today there is still another experience. At this stage of the revolution all the emphasis is being placed on liberating women in *production*. This has produced an impressive social promotion of women. But it seems to have been accompanied by a tremendous repression of sexuality and a rigorous puritanism (rampant in civic life). This corresponds not only to the need to mobilize women massively in economic life, but to a deep cultural reaction against the brutality, corruption and prostitution prevalent in Imperial and Kuo Ming Tang China (a phenomenon unlike anything in Czarist Russia). Because the exploitation of women was so great in the *ancien régime* women's participation at village level in the Chinese Revolution was uniquely high. As for reproduction, the Russian cult of maternity in the 1930s and 1940s has not been repeated for demographic reasons: indeed, China may be one of the first countries in the world to provide free State authorized contraception on a universal scale to the population. Again, however, given the low level of industrialization and fear produced by imperialist encirclement, no all-round advance could be expected.

Probably it is only in the highly developed societies of the West that an authentic liberation of women can be envisaged today. But for this to occur, there must be a transformation of *all* the structures into which they are integrated, and all the contradictions must coalesce, to explode—an *unité de rupture*. A revolutionary movement must base its analysis on the uneven development of each structure, and attack the weakest link in the combination. This may then become the point of departure for a general transformation. What is the situation of the different structures today? What is the concrete situation of the women in each of positions in which they are inserted?

As Shulman observes in a section of this article not reprinted here, ideas about female sexuality were critical to the development of the second stage of feminism in the late 1960s and early '70s. Feminists saw their sexuality as important keys to their oppression and their potential liberation, as did hostile onlookers. Shulman recalls that at early feminist demonstrations, epithets flung at demonstrators were predominantly sexual: "we were called dykes, whores and beasts, as well as commies, bitches, and nuts" (1980:596). In the following pages, Shulman traces early feminist ideas about sex and evaluates them in the larger context of the personal as political.

SEX AND POWER: SEXUAL BASES OF RADICAL FEMINISM

Alix Kates Shulman

What were the early radical feminist ideas about sex? Naturally, as WLM was a political movement the new attention directed by radical feminists to our sexuality had to do with power; with taking for ourselves the control of our lives and our bodies that men—through the laws, customs, and other institutions of a male-ruled society—had appropriated. The feminist movement for reproductive freedom, the women's self-help movement from California, the broader women's health movement—of which the Boston collective's best-selling *Our Bodies, Ourselves* was a product and a source—all organized around the idea of reclaiming for ourselves control over our very bodies. So with the new feminist analysis of sexuality.[1] Perceiving sexual relations as but one aspect of the power relations between men and women, early radical feminists questioned traditional definitions of women's sexuality, of women's "nature," of sexual satisfaction and health (conceived as heterosexual) on the grounds that such definitions, as propounded by men, tended to justify the sexual exploitation of women by men. "If sexual relations were not pro-

[Signs: Journal of Women in Culture and Society, 1980, vol. 5, no. 4] Permission to reprint this article may be obtained only from the author.

1. Important pre-WLM feminist analyses of female sexuality included Ruth Herschberger's *Adam's Rib* and Mary Jane Sherfey's 1966 paper for the *Journal of the American Psychoanalytic Association*, "The Evolution and Nature of Female Sexuality," based on her studies of multiple orgasm in women. After WLM was launched, *Adam's Rib* was reissued in paperback by Harper and Row, and Sherfey's essay was published in *Sisterhood Is Powerful* as "A Theory of Female Sexuality" and later expanded into a book.

grammed to support political ends—that is, male oppression of the female—then the way would be clear for individuals to enter into physical relations not defined by roles, nor involving exploitation. Physical relations (heterosexual and homosexual) would be an extension of communication between individuals and would not necessarily have a genital emphasis," read a 1969 position paper put out by "The Feminists: A Political Organization to Annihilate Sex Roles."[2]

"We must begin to demand that if certain sexual positions now defined as 'standard' are not mutually conducive to orgasm, they no longer be defined as standard. New techniques must be used or devised which transform this particular aspect of our current sexual exploitation,"[3] proclaimed Anne Koedt in her famous essay, "The Myth of the Vaginal Orgasm," published in 1968 in *Notes from the First Year* and expanded the following year. Though Koedt focused on technique, the point of her article was clearly political. She was concerned not only with the true facts about female orgasm, then under scrutiny by sexologists, but with exposing the distortion of those facts into the "myth" of the vaginal orgasm:

Today, with extensive knowledge of anatomy . . . . there is no ignorance on the subject [of female orgasm]. There are, however, social reasons why this knowledge has not been popularized. We are living in a male society which has not sought change in women's role. . . . The establishment of clitoral orgasm as fact would threaten the heterosexual institution. For it would indicate that sexual pleasure was obtainable from either men *or* women, thus making heterosexuality not an absolute, but an option. It would thus open up the whole questions of *human* sexual relationships beyond the confines of the present male-female role system.[4]

This analysis was continued by Ti-Grace Atkinson, a founder of The Feminists, the early antimarriage group which limited to one-third of its membership those women who lived with men. In "The Institution of Sexual Intercourse," in *Notes from the Second Year*, Atkinson analyzed sexual intercourse itself as a "political institution," analogous to the institution of marriage, which serves the needs of reproduction and often the sexual desires of men but not necessarily those of women. Atkinson coolly proposed that we try to "discover what the nature of the human sensual characteristics are from the point of view of the good of each individual instead of what we have now, which is a sort of psychological draft system of our sexualities." Never reducing sexual relations to mere technique,

---

2. *Notes from the Second Year: Women's Liberation, Major Writings of the Radical Feminists*, ed. Shulamith Firestone (New York: New York Radical Feminists, 1970), p. 114.

3. Anne Koedt, "The Myth of the Vaginal Orgasm," reprinted in *Voices from Women's Liberation*, ed. Leslie Tanner (New York: New American Library/Mentor Books, 1970), p. 159.

4. Ibid., pp. 161 and 166.

Atkinson elaborated the insight that orgasm is not everything by observing that what lovers add to the sexual experience "cannot be a technique or physical improvement on that same auto-experience" but "must be a psychological component."[5]

Carrying the feminist rebellion against the sexual exploitation of women a step further still, Dana Densmore of Boston's Cell 16 proposed a reordering of women's priorities away from the· sexual altogether. After all, the belief that sexual love of man is the core of woman's aspirations—or is even necessary for fulfillment—justifies woman's exploitation and keeps her enthralled. In her powerful 1969 essay, "On Celibacy," which appeared in the first issue of *No More Fun and Games*, the journal associated with Cell 16, Densmore wrote:

We must come to realize that we don't need sex, that celibacy . . . could be desirable, in many cases preferable to sex. How repugnant it is, after all, to make love to a man who despises you, who fears you and wants to hold you down! Doesn't screwing in an atmosphere devoid of respect get pretty grim? Why bother? You don't need it. . . . This is a call not for celibacy but for an acceptance of celibacy as an honorable alternative, one preferable to the degradation of most male-female relationships. . . . Unless you accept the idea that you don't need [men], don't need sex from them, it will be utterly impossible for you to carry through, it will be absolutely necessary for you to lead a double life, pretending with men to be something other than what you know you are. . . . If we are going to be liberated we must reject the false image that makes men love us, and this will make men cease to love us. . . . An end to this constant remaking of ourselves according to what the male ego demands! Let us be ourselves and good riddance to those who are then repulsed by us![6]

Writing on "Lesbianism and the Women's Liberation Movement," Martha Shelly, an early Radicalesbian, pursued Densmore's argument down another path:

To me, lesbianism is not an oddity of a few women to be hidden in the background of the Movement. In a way, it is the heart of the Women's Liberation Movement. In order to throw off the oppression of the male caste, women must unite—we must learn to love ourselves and each other, we must grow strong and independent of men so that we can deal with them from a position of strength. The idea that women must teach men how to love, that we must not become manhaters is, at this point in history, like preaching pacifism to the Vietcong. Women are . . . told to be weak, dependent and loving. That kind of love is masochism. Love can only exist between equals, not between the oppressed and the oppressor.[7]

5. Ti-Grace Atkinson, "The Institution of Sexual Intercourse," in *Notes from the Second Year*, pp. 45–46.

6. Tanner, pp. 264–68.

7. Martha Shelly, "Lesbianism and the Women's Liberation Movement," in *Women's Liberation: Blueprint for the Future*, ed. Sookie Stambler (New York: Ace Books, 1970), p. 127.

Thus, the price of maintaining sexual relations with men in a sexist society sometimes seemed too high to pay for many radical feminists, just as the price of motherhood in a sexist society has made many women reasonably decide to forgo that experience as well. But most radical feminists, rather than renounce heterosexuality, advocated struggle to change its basis. (Many considered separatism a cop-out.) In *The Dialectic of Sex*, Shulamith Firestone, shrewdly analyzing prevailing heterosexual relations, tried to specify the price women pay for male love. In the chapter on "Love," she describes love as requiring "mutual vulnerability or it turns destructive: the destructive effects of love occur only in a context of inequality." But because men and women are not equal, love is destructive for women. While "a man must idealize one woman over the rest in order to justify his descent to a lower caste,"[8] it is different for women:

In their precarious political situation, women cannot afford the luxury of spontaneous love. It is much too dangerous. The love and approval of men is all-important. To love thoughtlessly, before one has ensured return commitment, would endanger that approval. . . . In a male-run society that defines women as an inferior and parasitical class, a woman who does not achieve male approval in some form is doomed. . . . But because the woman is rarely allowed to realize herself through activity in the larger (male) society—and when she is, she is seldom granted the recognition she deserves— it becomes easier to try for the recognition of one man than of many; and in fact this is exactly the choice most women make. Thus once more the phenomenon of love, good in itself, is corrupted by its class context: women must have love not only for healthy reasons but actually to validate their existence.[9]

To this end, women must subordinate their true feelings, cultivate sex appeal, aspire to meet beauty standards, inhibit sexual spontaneity, and even fake orgasms—anything to catch a man. It is less this behavior many radical feminists deplored than the condition of unequal power and vulnerability between the sexes that makes such behavior seem necessary for survival. As Jennifer Gardner wrote in the essay "False Consciousness" that was published in the California journal *Tooth and Nail*, "Our oppression is not in our heads. We will not become unoppressed by 'acting unoppressed.' Try it—if you have the economic independence to survive the consequences. The result will not be respect and support. Men will either not like you—you are a bitch, a castrator, a nag, a hag, a witch; or they will accuse you of not liking them."[10] As Kathie Sarachild wrote, observing the dou-

8. Shulamith Firestone, *The Dialectic of Sex: The Case for Feminist Revolution* (New York: Bantam Books, 1970), pp. 130–31.
9. Ibid., p. 138.
10. Jennifer Gardner, "False Consciousness," reprinted in *Notes from the Second Year*, p. 82.

ble nature of sex and power, "For most of history sex was, in fact, both our undoing and our only possible weapon of self-defense and self-assertion (aggression)."[11]

That some women seem to be able to have satisfactory sexual relations with men is as much beside the point, given sexism, as that some manage to gain economic security: sexual (and economic) injustices nevertheless prevail. From the point of view of radical feminism, which addresses the problems of the many, not of the privileged few, even the best "individual solutions" will be chancy, for unless a woman is strong and independent her solution can disintegrate when she alienates her male protector, which happens to many women simply by aging. (The early feminist group, OWL, Older Women's Liberation, defined "older" as thirty and up—by prevailing sexist standards a ridiculous cut-off age for men but a realistic one for women considered as sex objects.) Irene Peslikis placed at the head of her list of "Resistances to Consciousness": "Thinking that our man is the exception and, therefore, we are the exceptions among women. . . . Thinking that individual solutions are possible, that we don't need solidarity and a revolution for our liberation."[12] As for those "personal solutions" which do not depend on male protection but involve withdrawal from men, women who choose them are subject to all the sanctions, reprisals, and punishments traditionally dealt to women without men under male supremacy. "Until we have a movement strong enough to force change," wrote Firestone in *Notes from the Second Year*, "we will have to accommodate ourselves as best we can to whichever . . . adjustment each of us can best live with," never forgetting, however, as Anne Koedt wrote in *Notes from the First Year*, "to go to the root of the problem rather than become engaged in solving secondary problems arising *out* of [woman's] condition." Just as women without control over reproduction will feel sexual anxiety, so women without control over conditions for their survival will also suffer sexual anxiety. From the beginning, radical feminists had differing analyses of sexuality, but all agreed that sexual relations were deeply affected by the general power relations prevailing between the sexes, that the way to change sexual relations was through solidarity and struggle to change the power relations, and that the way to discover how these relations oppressed women was through consciousness raising.

Like many other radical feminists at that time, impressed by how quickly our ideas were spreading and how much activity they

11. Kathie Sarachild, "A Program for Feminist Consciousness Raising," in *Notes from the Second Year*, p. 78.

12. In *Sisterhood is Powerful*, ed. Robin Morgan (New York: Random House, 1970), p. 337.

generated among ourselves, I was optimistic about the effect of our movement. Our intense examination of our personal experience for its social and political significance even helped me to develop as a writer. It was hardly an accident that the first article I wrote for publication in 1969, called "Organs and Orgasms," was on sex.[13] In it I cited case after case of the injustice done to women by bias in the very terminology of sex and suggested that a solution to our sexual problems might be advanced by reexamining our assumptions, definitions, and beliefs about sexuality from a woman's point of view. It was not that I discounted the importance of political struggle, but I believed we would have to change the way we *think* before we could change the way we live. The ideas of the movement were spreading so fast that it seemed to many of us in those days that it would not be difficult to organize masses of women to revolt. (Firestone thought it would take "several more years" to build a strong enough movement to "force change.") When the first mass August 26 Woman's March was held in large cities all over country in 1970 to commemorate the fiftieth anniversary of the women's suffrage amendment and to demonstrate our power—as thousands and thousands of women marched to demand their rights—it looked as if we might win with ease. And in the years immediately following, our hopes rose as the ERA passed through Congress for the first time since its introduction fifty years before; as the Supreme Court ruled that abortion, at least in the first trimester, was a woman's right; as suits for equal pay were launched against large corporations; as prestigious all-male colleges, professions, and institutions considered admitting women.

However, even then a powerful resistance was organizing. After a few years had passed, almost everything remained to be done. People spoke differently but acted pretty much as they always had. Following our initial success came a certain foreboding. Alice Paul, the veteran suffragist who had witnessed the defeat of feminism once, warned against allowing a time limit to be attached to the ERA; but, heedless of history as Americans—especially the young—tend to be, too ready to project our own changed consciousness onto the world, feminists failed to heed her. In time it became clear that our expectations, like my own sex article, were too optimistic; we had changed only the surface of what was wrong. Even if every woman acknowledged the injustice of sexism and every man understood about the role of the clitoris in female orgasm, sexual strife would continue, for the sexual arrangements of the world were still based on unequal power. Organized antifeminism followed each of the movement's

---

13. Alix Kates Shulman, "Organs and Orgasms," in *Woman in Sexist Society*, ed. Vivian Gornick and B. K. Moran (New York: Basic Books, 1970), p. 198.

successes in changing public consciousness. Movement or no movement, feminist feelings were not given public expression, our testimony was not considered "expert," our power in the world of public decisions remained minuscule. The heart of our sexual dissatisfaction with men was still that without power women were forced to sell it or forgo it, and we were still powerless. Even if we objected to Miss America standards we still had to be judged by them in our daily lives and then be tossed on the junk heap when we no longer measured up. Reexamining everything, even achieving *perfect understanding*, was not going to be enough to enable us to change the relations between the sexes, because sex had to do with power and those with power were not about to smile sweetly and give it up. A long, difficult struggle would have to follow understanding.

This is not to discount the considerable political gains we did make during the seventies in the fight for sexual justice. Of all the movements that emerged in the sixties, the WLM was the one that most securely became a mass movement in the seventies. Out of those early efforts grew changed attitudes and laws regarding women's work, reproductive freedom, physical abuse, and vast changes in notions of family. But many of the changes are extremely vulnerable to the growing antifeminist backlash, and if we stop far short of our original goals we may lose the gains we have won. It happened to the women in the first wave—they gained certain important but only partial victories, and they were defeated and silenced for decades. It could happen to us if we let up the pressure or lose sight of our original goals. If consciousness can be changed once, twice, it can be changed again. We are experiencing a strong move to the right. Sterilization abuse, hormone abuse are on the *rise*. The gap between average male and female income is *larger* that it was a decade ago. If abortions were outlawed again, if women were pushed back out of the work force, if we returned to viewing sex as an exclusively private matter affecting each person in isolation rather than a political matter affecting all of us, it could happen again. Just as frightening as the organized political backlash, which at least we know how to fight, is the backsliding of consciousness, the erosion of radical feminist ideals. The radical feminist critiques of sexuality and sexual repression, originally presented as aspects, or examples, of a much larger male domination of women but hardly as leading by themselves to solutions, have been diverted into concern with mere sexual technique or increased activity. Co-optation and tokenism have made it easier for people to deny that anything is still drastically wrong between the sexes. Again and again it is claimed that women have won sexual equality because the family is in a state of flux and chaos; that since the pill there is no longer any double standard—as if fear of pregnancy (which persists in any case) were the sole source of women's sexual anxiety. People say we are equal because a relatively small number of women are in positions of token power. (As with all "individual solutions," token power is different from real power, because as soon as the women who have it refuse to play the game they will lose their positions; knowing this, they are mostly supporters of the men to whom they owe their power.) But these facts only disguise the true situation of women's continued powerlessness.

A new generation does not know that ten years ago what are now our basic demands were unspoken, many even unmentionable. The ideas of women's liberation that were so recently shocking, thrilling, and liberating are already put down by many of the young as old hat and boring and by the old as a fad that is passe, obliterated in the swing of the pendulum. The presentation of feminism in the mass media has trivialized the movement's goals; in the name of "liberation" courses for women too frequently teach self-promotion instead of understanding and changing sexism in society; books on sexuality too often focus on technique and, worse, on how women may make themselves more sexually appealing to men, teaching us to blame the victim rather than on how to end victimization. The renewed search for personal solutions to collective problems is as arid today as it was a decade ago. Personal solutions to sexual problems center on finding the right partner or the right attitude or the right technique—at best chancy, at worst harmful, since they obscure the power relations inherent in sexual relations.

Several years back some of the women from the earliest movement days got together to discuss the changes that had occurred in their own sex lives since the movement began. All agreed that sex had changed for them, but very few thought it had really improved. True, some of them were now able to specify what they wanted their sex partners to do, but in some relationships the man resented the woman's desires. Several women who had changed from nonorgasmic to regularly orgasmic were sorry to find that nevertheless they were unhappy in love. Some of the women who had become lesbians found themselves facing a whole new set of problems and anxieties in a world that punishes homosexuality.[14] One woman grieved that since she no longer "played the game" she was no longer interested in sex at all and another that no one wanted her.

---

14. Sydney Abbott and Barbara Love observe that lesbians "suffer the oppression of all women but are not eligible for any of the rewards. . . . Fear of punishment creates tremendous anxiety, even though punishment may not occur" ("Is Women's Liberation a Lesbian Plot?" in Gornick and Moran, pp. 443 and 445).

Not even the most ardent feminist can claim to be "liberated" in a sexist society. "Sexual liberation" can mean nothing unless it includes the freedom to reject or enter into sexual relationships fearing neither exploitation nor punishment. But sexual exploitation and punishment still threaten every woman. The denial of complete reproductive freedom, the total responsibility for child rearing, the psychological intimidation of rape victims are all punishments·for the sexually active woman. The threat of job loss, ridicule, rejection, isolation, and even rape are punishments threatening the woman who refuses sex.

As the radical ideas of feminism, developed under the powerful insight that the personal is political, are absorbed by institutions adept at deflecting change through co-optation, and as our radical programs come under direct attack by an increasingly vocal conservative backlash, our awareness of the political dimension of sexual relations, with its powerful potential for change, is in danger of being lost. Conceiving sexual liberation apart from feminist liberation can land us where women have too often landed—not with more real freedom but with new pressures to put out or to withhold. Our only recourse is to deepen our radical insights about the connections between sex and power and build a political movement which can put insight into action.

Few issues have so divided women, including feminists, as that of abortion. While most feminists subscribe to the idea that abortion is a "woman's right," there are substantial differences regarding the origins of that right, under what circumstances it may be justifiably exercised, and under what circumstances it may be morally or socially wrong. In the following pages excerpted from her longer article, Petchesky examines the tensions between the liberal feminist view that women should enjoy unmitigated individual reproductive freedom and the Marxist perspective that demands cognizance of "the social position of women and the socially determined needs which that position generates." Petchesky cautions us that these tensions may and perhaps never should be resolved.

REPRODUCTIVE FREEDOM:
BEYOND "A WOMAN'S RIGHT
TO CHOOSE"

Rosalind Pollack Petchesky

Two essential ideas underlie a feminist view of reproductive freedom, ideas that have recurrently been implicit in all historical situations in which abortion, birth control, child care, maternity care, and the status of unmarried mothers and their children have become objects of political conflict. On the broadest level, these two ideas reflect the long-standing tension in feminist theory between an emphasis on *equality* and an emphasis on women's *autonomy*. The first is derived from the biological connection between women's bodies, sexuality, and reproduction. It is an extension of the general principle of "bodily integrity," or "bodily self-determination," to the notion that women must be able to control their own bodies and procreative capacities—that is, the reproductive and sexual uses to which their bodies are put. The second is a "historical and moral argument" based on the social position of women and the socially determined needs which that position generates. It states that, insofar as women, under the existing division of labor between the sexes, are the ones most affected by pregnancy, since they are still the ones responsible

[Signs: Journal of Women in Culture and Society, 1980, vol. 5, no 4] © 1980 by The University of Chicago. 0097–9740/80/0504–0006$01.00

A revised version of this article will appear as an introduction to Rosalind Petchesky's forthcoming book, *Reproductive Freedom: The Social and Political Dimensions of Abortion* (tentative title), to be published in fall 1984 by Longman Inc.

for the care and rearing of children, it is women who must decide about contraception, abortion, and childbearing.

It is apparent that these two ideas grow out of different philosophical traditions and have very different, sometimes contradictory, reference points and political priorities. The first emphasizes the *individual* dimensions of reproduction, the second the *social* dimensions. The first appeals to a "fixed" level of the biological person, while the other implies a set of social arrangements, a sexual division of labor that has developed historically and may therefore be changed under new conditions. Finally, one is rooted in the conceptual framework of "natural rights," while the other invokes the legitimating principle of "socially determined needs"; from this perspective, their links are to a liberal feminist and a Marxist tradition, respectively. . . .

My argument is that reproductive freedom—indeed, the very nature of reproduction itself—is irreducibly social and individual at the same time; that is, it operates "at the core of social life" as well as within and upon women's individual bodies. Thus, a coherent analysis of reproductive freedom requires a perspective that is both Marxist and feminist.[1] This dual perspective is also necessary on the level of political practice. For even if it were true, as some "right-to-lifers" have charged, that the women's movement is self-contradictory in demanding both control by women over reproductive matters and greater sharing of responsibility for such matters between women and men, it is also true that both these goals are indispensable to a feminist program for reproductive freedom. We have to struggle for a society in which responsibility for contraception, procreation, and child rearing is no longer relegated to women primarily; and, at the same time—as long as there is any connection between sex, reproduction, and women's bodies—we have to defend the principle of control over our bodies and our reproductive capacities. In the long run, we have to ask whether women's control over reproduction is what we want, whether it is consistent with equality; in the short run, we have never experienced the concrete historical conditions under which we could afford to give it up. . . .

Controlling Our Bodies

Reproduction affects women as women, in a way that transcends class divisions and that penetrates everything—work, political and community involvements, sexuality, creativity, dreams. Linda Gordon

---

1. I am indebted to Zillah Eisenstein for this important clarification.

illustrates this point with reference to the conditions that generated the nineteenth-century birth control movement:

The desire for and the problems in securing abortion and contraception made up a *shared female experience*. Abortion technique was apparently not much safer among upper-class doctors than among working-class midwives. The most commonly used contraceptives—douches, withdrawal—were accessible to women of every class. And what evidence there is of the subjective experience of women in their birth-control attempts also suggests that the desire for spaced motherhood and smaller families existed in every class, and that the desire was so passionate that women would take severe risks to win a little space and control in their lives. *The individual theory and practice of birth control stems from a biological female condition that is more basic even than class.*[2]

It is surprising to find Gordon reverting to a "biological female condition" in the midst of an analysis of the social construction of women's reproductive experience. Yet it reminds us that the "bodily integrity" principle has an undeniable biological component, inseparable from its social and moral aspects. As long as women's bodies remain the medium for pregnancies, the connection between women's reproductive freedom and control over their bodies represents not only a moral and political claim but also, on some level, a material necessity. This acknowledgment of biological reality should not be mistaken for biological determinist thinking about women; my point is simply that biology is a *capacity* as well as a limit.[3] The fact that it is women who get pregnant has been the source not only of our confinement (in all senses) but, in some measure, of our (limited) power. An abundance of feminist anthropological literature reminds us that pollution rituals, fertility cults, prohibitions against abortion, as well as chastity rules imposed upon wives and daughters are signs of men's envy and fear of women's reproductive capacity—of its imagined powers, yes, but also of its reality. Indeed, the current and vituperative attack on abortion in the United States and elsewhere in the West has been interpreted by some feminists as a massive recurrence of male "womb envy."

I would be the last to romanticize the control that comes from our biological connection to childbearing, or to underestimate its repressive social aspects for women. On the other hand, women's control over their bodies is not like preindustrial workers' control

2. Linda Gordon, *Woman's Body, Woman's Right: A Social History of Birth Control in America* (Harmondsworth, Middlesex, and New York: Penguin Books, 1977), p. 70. (My italics.)

3. Cf. Sara Ruddick: "Neither our own ambivalence toward our women's bodies nor the bigoted, repressive uses men, colonizers and racists have made of biology, should blind us to biology's possibilities. On the other hand, our belief in the biological body's psychosocial efficacy may be an illusion created by the fact that the people who engage in maternal practices almost always have female bodies" ("Maternal Thinking," *Feminist Studies* [1980], in press).

over their tools; it cannot be wrested away simply through changes in technology or legal prohibitions and repression—which is why no modern society has succeeded for long in outlawing abortion or birth control, only in driving it "underground." (Even women slaves retain the capacity to abort as an act of resistance—an act that derives from powerlessness, as I shall emphasize later, but also from a residual power.) The inability of societies, and men, to regulate totally women's reproductive control, or to mediate in an absolute way women's connection to their bodies, reflects the dialectical nature of the "biological female condition."

It is important, however, to keep in mind that woman's reproductive situation is never the result of biology alone, but of biology mediated by social and cultural organization. That is, it is not inevitable that women, and not men, should bear the main consequences of unintended pregnancy and thus that their sexual and reproductive expression be inhibited by it. Rather, it is the result of the socially ascribed primacy of motherhood in women's lives. Yet it is also true that biology as it is socially mediated by male-dominant institutions affects all women in a way that cuts across class divisions. In our own period there is prolific evidence of this "shared female experience." The cutbacks in abortion funding, whose initial and hardest impact has been on low-income women, have been the spearhead of a right-wing movement to curtail abortion services and reimbursements for most working-class and middle-class women living in various states and dependent on many different health insurance plans as well. While sterilization abuse has mainly been directed at poor, Third World, and mentally disabled women, the ultimatum to well-paid women chemical workers that they get sterilized or lose their jobs has widened our perspective on this issue.[4] Indeed, the fact that female sterilization, an irreversible procedure, has become the most widely used, medically encouraged, and economically reimbursable method of contraception among all but the very young in the United States,[5] as evidence grows of the pill's dangers to women's health and abortions are restricted, raises questions about reproductive

4. "Four Women Assert Jobs Were Linked to Sterilization," *New York Times* (January 5, 1979); Rosalind Petchesky, "Workers, Reproductive Hazards and the Politics of Protection: An Introduction," *Feminist Studies* 5 (Summer 1979): 233–45; Michael J. Wright, "Reproductive Hazards and 'Protective' Discrimination," ibid., pp. 302–9; Wendy Chavkin, "Occupational Hazards to Reproduction—a Review of the Literature," ibid., pp. 310–25.

5. Committee for Abortion Rights and against Sterilization Abuse [CARASA], *Women Under Attack: Abortion, Sterilization Abuse, and Reproductive Freedom* (New York: CARASA, 1979); Rosalind Petchesky, "Reproduction, Ethics and Public Policy: The Federal Sterilization Regulations," *Hastings Center Report* 9 (October 1979): 29–42; Charles F. Westoff and James McCarthy, "Sterilization in the United States," *Family Planning Perspectives* 11 (May/June 1979): 147–52; Charlotte F. Muller, "Insurance Coverage of Abortion, Contraception and Sterilization," ibid., 10 (March–April 1978): 71–77.

"choices" for *most* women. This basic material condition of reproduction—that the two major birth control methods in current use
are, on the one hand, irreversible, and on the other hand, dangerous
to health—affects women of all classes. It is a condition set, not by
reproductive technology, but by reproductive politics—a politics
that seeks to curtail the efforts of women, as women, "to win a little
space and control in their lives" and freely to express their sexuality. . . .

And yet, the idea of "a woman's right to choose" as the main
principle of reproductive freedom is insufficient and problematic at
the same time as it is politically compelling. For one thing, this principle does evade moral questions about when, under what conditions, and for what purposes reproductive decisions—for example,
the abortion decision—should be made. Feminists writing on abortion usually have not claimed that a pregnant woman "owns" the
fetus, or that it is part of her body (although right-to-lifers and
others have interpreted the feminist position this way). On the contrary, feminists have generally characterized an unwanted pregnancy
as a kind of bodily "invasion."[6] Recognizing a situation of real conflict between the survival of the fetus and the needs of the woman
and those dependent on her, the feminist position says merely that
women must decide, because it is their bodies that are involved, and
because they still have primary responsibility for the care and development of the children born.

But determining who should decide—the political question—
does not tell us anything about the moral and social values women
ought to bring to this decision, *how* they should decide.[7] Should
women get an abortion on the grounds that they prefer a different
gender (which amniocentesis can now determine)? Such a decision,
in my view, would be blatantly sexist, and nobody's claim to "control over her body" could make it right or compatible with feminist
principles. That is, "a woman's right to control her body" is not abstract or absolute, but we have not developed a morality that is both

6. "There is no way a pregnant woman can passively let the fetus live; she must create and
nurture it with her own body, a symbiosis that is often difficult, sometimes dangerous, uniquely intimate. However gratifying pregnancy may be to a woman who desires it, for the unwilling
it is literally an invasion—the closest analogy is to the difference between lovemaking and rape.
. . . Clearly, abortion is by normal standards an act of self-defense" (Ellen Willis, *The Village
Voice* [March 5, 1979], p. 8). This is the most eloquent statement of the feminist position on
abortion I have read. Cf. Judith Jarvis Thomson's classic essay, "A Defense of Abortion" (in
The Rights and Wrongs of Abortion, ed. John Finnis et al. [Princeton, N.J.: Princeton University
Press, 1974], pp. 10, 12), who uses philosophical sleight of hand to arrive at the same
conclusion.
7. This point is made persuasively by Daniel Callahan, *Abortion: Law, Choice and Morality*
(New York: Macmillan Publishing Co., 1970), p. 494; cf. Alison Jaggar, "Abortion and a
Woman's Right to Decide," in *Women and Philosophy*, ed. Carol C. Gould and Marx W.
Wartofsky (New York: Capricorn Books, 1976), p. 347.

socialist and feminist that would tell us what the exceptions should be. Admitting that we have not fully articulated a feminist morality of abortion, however, does not imply that all or most women who get abortions do so thoughtlessly or irresponsibly. On the contrary, women who seek abortions know and experience better than anyone else the difficulty of that decision. Much more serious is the potential danger in the assertion of women's right to control over reproduction as absolute or exclusive, insofar as it can be turned back on us to reinforce the view of all reproductive activity as the special, biologically destined province of women. Here it has to be acknowledged that this danger grows out of the concept of "rights" in general, a concept inherently static and abstracted from social conditions. Rights are by definition claims that are staked within a given order of things and relationships. They are demands for access for oneself, or for "no admittance" to others, but they do not challenge the social structure itself, the social relations of production and reproduction.[8] The claim for "abortion rights" seeks access to a necessary service, but by itself it fails to address the existing social relations and sexual divisions around which responsibility for pregnancy and children is assigned. And in real-life struggles, this limitation exacts a price, for it lets men and society neatly off the hook.

The Social Relations of Reproduction

What is "reproductive freedom," from the standpoint of historical materialism? On what principle is women's struggle to secure control over the terms and conditions of reproduction based? A materialist view of reproductive freedom would justify this struggle in terms of the principle of socially determined need—that is, from this view the moral imperative itself grows out of the historically and culturally defined position that women find themselves in through motherhood. Because it is primarily women—not fathers, not doctors, not "child care specialists," not the state—who are still the ones who bear the consequences of pregnancy and the responsibility for children, the conditions of reproduction and contraception affect them directly, and in every other aspect of their lives. Therefore, it is women primarily who should have control over whether, when, and under what conditions to have children. Moreover, an emphasis on the social rather than biological basis of reproductive activity implies that such activity is once and for all removed from any "privatized" or "personal sphere" and may legitimately be claimed for political and social intervention. That intervention may take the form of mea-

---

8. Juliet Mitchell, "Women and Equality," in *The Rights and Wrongs of Women*, ed. Juliet Mitchell and Ann Oakley (Harmondsworth, Middlesex: Penguin Books, 1976), pp. 384–85.

sures to protect or regulate reproductive health—for example, to assure the safety and voluntariness of contraceptive methods, or to transform the material conditions that presently divide women's reproductive options according to class and race.

On the other hand, a materialist view of reproductive freedom recognizes the historical contingency of the conditions in which women seek reproductive control for themselves. For most of history, women's "choices" over reproduction have been exercised in a framework in which reproduction and motherhood still determine their relationship to the rest of society. A materialist (and, I would argue, feminist) view looks forward to an eventual transcendence of the existing social relations of reproduction, so that gender is not ultimately determinant of responsibility. This implies that, should existing social arrangements change—should society be transformed so that men, or society itself, bear an equal responsibility for nurturance and child care—then the basis of the needs would have changed and control over reproduction might not belong primarily to women.[9] . . .

Can we really imagine the social conditions in which we would be ready to renounce control over our bodies and reproductive lives— to give over the decision as to whether, when, and with whom we will bear children to the "community as a whole"? The reality behind this nagging question is that control over reproductive decisions, particularly abortion, has to do not only with "the welfare of mothers and children" but very fundamentally with sexuality and with women's bodies as such. The analysis emphasizing the social relations of reproduction tends to ignore, or deny, the level of reality most immediate for individual women: that it is their bodies in which pregnancies occur. Indeed, that analysis becomes false insofar as it disregards the immediate, sensual reality of individuals altogether. In order to make this connection, a theory of reproductive freedom has to have recourse to other conceptual frameworks, particularly that which has been more commonly associated with a feminist tradition and which asserts women's right to and need for bodily self-determination.

Reproductive Politics: Lessons of the Past and Visions of the Future

How do we break out of the apparent contradiction between "women's right to control" over reproduction, and their need not to

9. The position that is being presented here is obviously different from the technological determinism of Shulamith Firestone in *The Dialectic of Sex* (New York: Bantam Books, 1970). Firestone's simplistic view that women's position could be "revolutionized" by the introduction of in vitro fertilization, artificial uteruses, and other "advanced" features of reproductive technology ignores the social aspects of reproduction and the political question of who controls that technology, how control is organized socially and institutionally, and for what ends.

be defined by reproduction? How do we begin to transform the social relations of reproduction, to bring men, as potential fathers, into those relations on an equal basis? How would such a transformation affect the principle of "control over our bodies"? It is the argument of this paper that, in practice, the two ideas of reproductive freedom discussed here must both be incorporated into a revolutionary feminist and socialist politics. Despite the real tensions between these ideas—that stressing changes in the social relations of reproduction, and that stressing women's control over their bodies—neither is dispensable for feminists, and both are essential. Yet no political movement for "reproductive rights" or women's emancipation, including our own, has yet sustained this double agenda in a full, systematic, and consistent way. . . .

Strategies for establishing reproductive freedom must distinguish between different historical and political contexts. Under the conditions of advanced capitalism existing in the United States today—particularly as the right wing seeks to restore patriarchal control, through family, church, and state, over whether, how, and with whom women have children—women are compelled to defend their own control. Reproductive politics in this context necessarily become a struggle for control. Moreover, that struggle is greatly complicated by persistent class and race divisions. For most women in capitalist society, the very idea of reproductive "control" (or "choice") is unthinkable short of a vast array of social changes in health care, employment, housing, child care, etc.—changes that are themselves predicated upon a socialist revolution. In the meantime, "control" in a more limited sense may mean very different things to different groups of women (birth control information is one thing, possession of your reproductive organs and custody of your children is another). In a class- and race-divided society, "pronatalist" and "antinatalist" policies coincide (e.g., restrictions on abortion *and* involuntary sterilization), making it necessary for "reproductive rights" proponents to articulate continually that "reproductive freedom means the freedom to have as well as not to have children."[10] Because women are still subordinate economically, politically, and legally, a policy emphasizing male sharing of child rearing responsibility could well operate to divest women of control over their children in a situation where they have little else. (We are currently getting a foretaste of this danger, with increasing losses of custody fights by women, particularly lesbian mothers.) In such a defensive and reactionary context, the "collective" principle could play into the suggestions of "right-to-

10. Committee for Abortion Rights and against Sterilization Abuse [CARASA], *Women Under Attack: Abortion, Sterilization Abuse, and Reproductive Freedom* (New York: CARASA, 1979), p. 9.

lifers" that the responsibility for childbearing is too important to be left to women.

On the other hand, because the sexual division of labor around child rearing still prevails and defines women's position, a policy emphasizing improved benefits and services in order to encourage childbearing—even among single heterosexual women and lesbians—may ease the material burdens of motherhood; but it may also operate in practice to perpetuate the existing sexual division of labor and women's social subordination. . . . [In] the United States, it is easy to imagine an accretion of reforms—particularly with current fears among demographers and policymakers about the declining birthrate—such as pregnancy disability benefits, child care centers, maternity leave provisions, etc., which, if unaccompanied by demands for transforming the total position of women, particularly around child rearing, can be used to rationalize that position.[11] The point is not, of course, that present attempts to secure funded abortion, pregnancy and maternity benefits, child care services, and other reproduction-related reforms should be abandoned, but rather that those attempts must be moved beyond the framework of "a woman's right to choose" and connected to a much broader revolutionary movement that addresses all of the conditions for women's liberation.

A feminist and socialist transformation of the existing conditions of reproduction would seek to unleash the possibilities for material (economic and technological) improvements in reproduction from traditional family and sexual forms, to embed those positive material changes in a new set of social relations. Foremost among these new relations is that concerned with the care of children. As Adrienne Rich declares, men must be "ready to share the responsibilities of full-time, universal child care as a social priority"—which is to say, the responsibility for children must be dissociated from gender, which necessarily means that it becomes dissociated from heterosexuality. The writings of feminist theorists like Rich, Nancy Chodorow, and Dorothy Dinnerstein,[12] unveiling the deeply rooted cultural

11. To offset the birthrate decline in the United States, Princeton demographer Charles Westoff suggests a variation on a pronatalist incentives policy which would divide all American women into one-third who would "never have any children" and another two-thirds who "would have to reproduce at an average rate of three births per woman to maintain a replacement." While the former group would presumably be channeled into full-time employment, the latter would be drawn into their role of "breeders" through "a serious investment in childcare institutions" and other government-sponsored reproductive subsidies ("Some Speculations on the Future of Marriage and Fertility," *Family Planning Perspectives* 10 [March/April 1978]: 79–82).

12. Nancy Chodorow, *The Reproduction of Mothering* (Berkeley: University of California, 1975); Dorothy Dinnerstein, *The Mermaid and the Minotaur* (New York: Harper & Row, 1976).

and psychic bases of traditional child-rearing arrangements, help to explain why it is this aspect of presocialist patriarchy that seems most intractable in postrevolutionary societies. The changes we require are total; as Hilda Scott writes: "... no decisive changes can be brought about by measures aimed at women alone, but, rather, the division of functions between the sexes must be changed in such a way that men and women have the same opportunities to be active parents and to be gainfully employed. This makes of women's emancipation not a 'woman question' but a function of the general drive for greater equality which affects everyone.... The care of children becomes a fact which society has to take into consideration."[13]

Under different historical conditions from any that now exist, it may become possible to transcend some of the more individualist elements of feminist thinking about reproductive freedom—to move toward a conception of reproduction as an activity that concerns all of society. At the same time, the basis could be created for the genuine reproductive freedom of individuals, ending systems of domination that inhibit individuals' control over their bodies. We need to start envisioning what those conditions would be, even though they seem very far from present reality. At least three conditions would seem necessary in order for a socially based, "gender-free," and individually liberating norm of reproduction to be actualized. First, we would have to have the material prerequisites that would make having and raising children, or not doing so, a real alternative for *all* people: convenient, safe, and reliable methods of birth control; good-quality, publicly funded health care, maternal and prenatal, and child care; the elimination of reproductively hazardous environments where we work and live; and the provision of adequate jobs, incomes, housing, and education for all.[14]

But the kind of socialist and feminist transformation we want would require more than material and technological changes. It would require, second, fundamental changes in the social and sexual relations of reproduction, so that the feminist idea of collective, shared responsibility for sexuality, birth control, and child care becomes ingrained in socialist ideology and in social practice. Under conditions of socialist transformation, unlike capitalism, there is a normative basis for maintaining the principle of collective (transgender) responsibility in the activity of reproduction and child rearing, as in everything else. The historical fact that, in most actual socialist societies, birth control and child care have remained women's pri-

13. Hilda Scott, *Does Socialism Liberate Women?* (Boston: Beacon Press, 1974), p. 190.
14. See "Principles of Unity," CARASA; and "Statement of Purpose," Coalition for the Reproductive Rights of Workers" (CRROW) (both available from CARASA, 386 Park Avenue South, Room 1502, New York, New York 10016).

mary domain, both ideologically and practically, should not be taken as evidence of an inherent incompatibility between socialism and women's liberation (the view that socialism is just one form of "patriarchy"). Rather, it should be seen as one dimension, among others, in which a full socialist transformation has not been achieved. The formal arrangements through which these transformed social relations would be expressed have not begun to be imagined. Between the patriarchal heterosexist nuclear family and the spartan barracks of War Communism, there is surely a copious range of sexual and caretaking possibilities.

Third, the historical conditions in which women might anticipate sharing reproductive responsibility with men, or with the "community as a whole," would need to be ones in which democratic principles and processes were built into reproductive (and all) decision making. That is, we would need a radical social democracy in which domination by bureaucrats and medical professionals would not be allowed to repress those whose lives are most immediately affected.

Given such a context, we might imagine a number of concrete situations in which collectively organized social intervention into reproductive, or even "population" matters in a narrower sense, would be not only legitimate but necessary. Society would have to deal with economic and social questions concerning the allocation of resources to communal child care facilities, the mobilization of men on a systematic basis into child care activity, and, most difficult of all, the relationship between the responsibilities of collective organizations and those of parents or other related adults for children. Indeed, unless we adopt a crude anti-Malthusian position that refuses to acknowledge any such thing as population problems, we would have to deal with certain real "quantitative" concerns—for example, the ways that the age structure of the population affects its capacity to provide collective child care and educational resources.[15] The view of reproduction and parenting as essentially social relationships implies not only a commitment to the legitimacy, in principle, of social regulation of those areas of human activity, but also a rejection of the idea that there is a "natural right" to procreate indefinitely or to procreate at all. That idea must be distinguished sharply from the idea of a socially determined need (of both men and women) to participate in the care and rearing of children, as a very distinct and special part of human existence. The latter, it seems to me, is absolutely essential to a feminist and socialist vision of the future. The former is a remnant

15. See Steven Polgar, "Birth Planning: Between Neglect and Coercion," in *Population and Social Organization*, ed. Moni Nag (The Hague: Mouton Publishers, 1975), p. 197.

of biological determinist thinking (akin to "mother-right") that should have no place in feminist thought.

And yet, even in a society where the collective responsibility for reproduction and child rearing is taken seriously at all levels of public and interpersonal life, would there not still be aspects of reproductive and sexual relations that remain a "personal affair"? In particular, would women not still retain a preemptive claim to reproductive autonomy, especially around questions of abortion and childbearing, based on the principle of "control over one's body"? Even in the context of new, revolutionary social relations of reproduction, it would never be legitimate to compel a person to have sex or to bear a child, to have an abortion or be sterilized, to express or to repress sexuality in some prescribed way, or to undergo surgical or chemical or other bodily intervention for reproductive or contraceptive purposes. A sense of being a person, with personal and bodily integrity, would remain essential to the definition of social participation and responsibility, under any historical conditions I can imagine.

To deny that there will always be a residual conflict or tension between this principle—which is the idea of concrete individuality, or subjective reality—and that of a social and socially imposed morality of reproduction seems to me not only naive but dismissive of an important value. In any society, there will remain a *level of individual desire that can never be totally reconciled with social need*,[16] without destroying the individual personalities whose "self-realization," as Heller and Marcuse stress, is the ultimate object of social life. How would an individual woman's desire to have a child, or not to have a child, be harmonized in every case with a social policy that determines, on the basis of social need, the circumstances in which people should or should not have and raise children? Even if reproduction and pregnancy were technologically relegated to the laboratory, in the vision of Firestone, there would no doubt remain women who resisted the "technological revolution" as usurping a process that belonged to them individually, personally, to their bodies. The provision of adequate, universal child care services or male sharing in child rearing will eliminate neither the tension between the principles of individual control and collective responsibility over reproduction, nor the need to make reproductive choices that are hard. On the other hand, this very tension can be for feminism—and through feminism, socialism—a source of political vitality.

16. Agnes Heller, *The Theory of Need in Marx* (New York: St. Martin's Press, 1976), p. 45.

PART III

The Sexual Economy:

Resistance and Struggle

Women have rebelled throughout history against the controlling ideas and structures of their lives as they have been moved capriciously into and out of public roles. Although most such protest has been that of an individual woman with a specific grievance, isolated protest movements have surfaced from time to time as women, denied access to formerly held sources of prestige and authority, have attempted to reclaim lost public functions (Boulding 1976:21–22). The peasant uprisings that provoked the widespread persecution throughout Europe of the woman healer in the sixteenth and seventeenth centuries may have represented, in part, such an attempt. Our history books, placing emphasis upon privileged and deviant women

CHAPTER 6

The Ideas and Origins of Feminism

as shapers of female consciousness, have denied us accounts of the lives and thought of most women who have chafed under the bonds of patriarchal structures. In recent years, however, feminist scholars have begun to search such nontraditional sources as letters and diaries, generally ignored by classical approaches to history, for indications of individual and collective protest. Whether in such "protest" movements as that of the woman healer or in the writings of a Charlotte Brontë, whose *Jane Eyre* was an indictment of limitations on women's lives created by economic discrimination, women have not been so silent nor so accommodating of their oppression as traditional history books would have us believe.

In this chapter we examine the origins and ideas of a specific form of feminist protest that developed in the nineteenth century. For the ideological origins of feminism, we must look to the natural rights theory of the eighteenth-century Enlightenment and to the advent of liberal Protestantism. For an explanation of why feminism emerged when it did, we must examine the changes in class structure that accompanied the industrial revolution. It was the enormous growth of the middle class and the increasing importance of property and wealth as sources of power that created the conditions for the emergence of feminism. Social structures growing out of those economic transformations were discussed in the preceding chapter in relation to the evolution of women's roles. The decline of domestic production, as well as the doctrine of separate spheres and corresponding changes in the family, are essential to an understanding of feminism as it developed over the course of the nineteenth century.

In the following analysis of the ideas and origins of nineteenth-century feminism, we have drawn primarily on studies of American feminism. Unfortunately, a comparative analysis is beyond the scope of this book.[1] According to Richard J. Evans, however, the American experience provides us with a "classic" model from which we may draw generalizations about the development of feminism in other major Western nations (1977). While there are certain differences between the American experience and that of other countries, the aims and objectives of feminism throughout the Western world were remarkably uniform in its movement from a "women's rights" position, which demanded economic, educational, and legal rights for women, to an emphasis on suffrage. The feminist movement developed earlier and on a much wider scale in the United States than elsewhere, and it was to the American example that European feminists looked for precedents. Every other feminist movement, "howev-

---

1. Recent comparative studies have helped to correct the imbalance created by the emphasis of most studies on England and America. See, for example, Richard J. Evans, *The Feminists: Women's Emancipation Movements in Europe, America and Australasia, 1840–1920* (New York: Barnes and Noble, 1977); and Ross Evans Paulson, *Women's Suffrage and Prohibition: A Comparative Study of Equality and Social Control* (Glenview, Ill.: Scott Foresman, 1973).

er deep its roots in its own national politics was to a degree an imitation of the American one" (Evans 1977:44).

One more set of explanations is necessary before we move into our discussion of nineteenth-century feminism. A wide-ranging, loose, historical application of certain key terms such as "women's rights" and "feminism" necessitates our use here of precise definitions.[2] An advocate of women's rights, for example, as we shall see, is not necessarily a feminist, nor does a feminist necessarily advocate equity for women. *Women's rights* refers to the advocacy of legal, educational, economic, political, or social changes in order to enhance the position of women vis-à-vis others in the community. Women's rights advocacy has ranged from demands for (1) certain rights superior to those of men with retention of other inferior rights, to (2) rights superior to those currently held by women yet inferior to those held by men, to (3) rights different from but "equal" to those of men, to (4) rights identical to those held by men (see especially Kraditor 1968:7–8). "Behind every proposal for women's rights," Ross Evans Paulson writes,

... there stands an image of what woman's position in society ought to be. These images sum up ideas about sexual roles and identities, social relations, and concepts of self. Historically, these images have ranged along a continuum between two points: orthodoxy and feminism. The orthodox image at any point in time is the socially accepted definition of woman's "place," "sphere," or "destiny." The feminist image is that projected by writers, artists, or activists to delineate an autonomous selfhood. (1973:6)

Suffragism is the advocacy of the extension of the right to vote to a specific group of people (in this case, women). Suffrage may or may

2. In defining these terms, we have drawn from Paulson, *Women's Suffrage and Prohibition;* and Aileen Kraditor, *Up from the Pedestal: Selected Writings in the History of American Feminism* (Chicago: Quadrangle Books, 1968).

not be one of the rights included in a women's rights program. On the other hand, the demand for the suffrage ordinarily occurs in conjunction with the recognition of the need for other rights. A current debate among historians as to the relative importance in the nineteenth century of the securing of the vote compared to the achievement of other fundamental human rights is addressed later. While some historians consider the earlier broad-ranging social critique by women's rights advocates the most radical aspect of the feminist movement, others see the demand for the suffrage as the most serious challenge to male authority over women and therefore nineteenth-century feminism's most radical demand.[3] *Feminism*, a "self-defining process that usually operates in negation or extension of the current orthodoxy" (Paulson 1973:6) may be defined as the insistence upon self-determination or autonomy. Whatever her claim to specific rights, a feminist demands her freedom to discover her own "sphere" or "destiny."

The insistence on self-determination fundamental to feminism has its origins in the eighteenth-century intellectual Enlightenment, particularly in its belief in the power of reason as it is exercised by a properly educated electorate to build a new social order free of ignorance and oppression. Alice Rossi notes in the writings of the "heirs to the happy Enlightenment . . . an expectation that 'free enquiry' is the simple path to truth which, once arrived at, must absolutely persuade and easily translate into social reality" (1974:3). The Enlightenment theorists challenged traditional institutions that restricted free thought and anticipated a new social order predicated on the notion that all human beings were capable of reason. "In the face of reason," claims Evans, "no received wisdom was sacrosanct"

3. Among the former is Aileen Kraditor and among the latter are Ellen Du Bois and Richard J. Evans.

(1977:13). The leading philosophers of the eighteenth century engaged in broad-ranging debates on a variety of subjects including the position of women in society, marriage, and the family. But women, as we observed in an earlier chapter, were not necessarily assumed to be heirs of the fruits of the Enlightenment. Rousseau, whose *Emile* we considered, deemed woman by nature incapable of the reason that would liberate mankind. While other Enlightenment thinkers—including Montesquieu, Diderot, Voltaire, and Condorcet—were sympathetic if not committed to women's claim to natural rights on an equal footing with men, most shared Rousseau's view of women.

A feminist movement of sorts emerged briefly during the French Revolution, whose leading figures, swept among the currents of revolutionary thought, demanded equality for women in education, law, and employment. Best known of early French feminists is Olympe de Gouges (Marie Gouze) whose *Declaration of the Rights of Women* was modeled on the key document of the revolution, the *Declaration of the Rights of Man and Citizen*. But feminism during the French Revolution was a decidedly marginal and ill-organized movement ending in the execution or consignment to asylum of its leading figures. Feminism in France, as elsewhere in Europe, became primarily a literary phenomenon, whose major exponents were more interested in educational opportunity than in redressing the grievances of poor and working women (Evans 1977:16). As Enlightenment theoreticians generally excluded women from consideration as its heirs, so the French Revolution, argued its strongest critics, ignored women in its analysis of social ills and in its legislation.

The Enlightenment views of woman's nature were as heatedly debated in America as in Europe. In America, in particular, a tradition of strong, independent pioneer women tended to make acceptable more progressive views about women's intellectual worth than those held by Europeans. Women in the colonies were in a much better legal and economic position than their sisters in many European countries, women's status in the New World having been enhanced by their scarcity, the harsh exigencies of frontier life, and their important role in the building of a nation. In the years before the American Revolution, the position of women was widely discussed. Praised by many for their activities and achievements and considered capable of reason, women's potential political involvement was a focal point of that discussion. Letters from Abigail Smith Adams and John Adams with which we open this chapter indicate the scope of the debate. Abigail Adams has been praised by contemporary feminists for her letter to John Adams of March 31, 1776, in which she warned that the "ladies . . . are determined to foment a Rebellion" if those attending the first Continental Congress in Philadelphia did not remember and be generous to them. John Adams' bantering response insists that women need have no fears about men who have but "the Name of Masters." As John Adams was no doubt aware, the new republic, rejecting the tyranny of monarchy, might have drawn upon the Enlightenment belief in natural law to justify the extension of rights to women as well as men. However, as feminists were later to discover, the Declaration of Independence, in its interpretation if not its original conception, excluded women from citizenship in the new republic, deeming personhood to be synonomous with "man." The real position of women in America, as we have already observed, would decline rapidly from the end of the colonial period to the beginning of the nineteenth century.

Mary Wollstonecraft, whose *A Vindication of the Rights of Woman* was inspired by the egalitarian rhetoric of the French Revolution, shared the conviction of the writers of her age that reason would be the key to the development of a just, new social order. Education, she believed, would free women from age-old patterns of male domination and female submission. In *A Vindication*, Wollstonecraft notes systematic degradation of women in a long line of scholarship from the Genesis accounts of creation through Milton's *Paradise Lost* and Pope's *Moral Essays* and insists that women's faults so lovingly catalogued in those works are the products not of inferior intelligence but of deprivation. Full personhood for women, she claims in the selection included here, will come as the result of their independence and education. Wollstonecraft echoes a central tenet of her century when she argues that reason, the quality that differentiates humans from animals, is a gift from God to women as well as to men. It is an argument that we shall see developed later by the first American suffragists as the key to woman's full personhood. If women be denied reason, Wollstonecraft argues, they must also be denied personhood and therefore can be said to exist only for men. If, however, women are granted reason, "they must be permitted to turn to the fountain of light and not forced to shape their course by the twinkling of a mere satellite."

A Vindication was widely read and stimulated much controversy after its initial publication in England in 1792; but, interpreted as an indictment of marriage and an argument in support of free love, it was much neglected after Wollstonecraft's death. Only a few American feminists knew of her work by the middle of the nineteenth century, and these did not regard her as an appropriate champion of women's rights (Rossi 1974:39). It was not to Mary Wollstonecraft's tract, but rather to John Stuart Mill's essay *The Subjection of Women*, that nineteenth-century feminism looked for the articulation of the Enlightenment belief in the shaping force of rational thought and of woman's share in natural rights. Published in America, Australia, and New Zealand within a few months of its original publication in England in 1869, Mill's essay was soon translated in France, Germany, Austria, Sweden, Denmark, Poland, and Italy, its publication coinciding with the development of feminist movements in a number of European countries (Evans 1977:19). Its appearance in America, some twenty years after the official birth of the feminist movement at Seneca Falls, New York, lent force to the cause of women's suffrage at a time when early male supporters of women's rights were withdrawing their support in order to establish more firmly the right of the black man to the vote. Mill's work, excerpted in Chapter 1, was considered by educated women throughout the world the definitive analysis of women's position in society.

If the Enlightenment assembled "a whole battery of intellectual weapons to be wielded in the feminist cause" (Evans 1977:19), it was the reformed theology of Protestantism, with its proclamation of "the priesthood of all believers," that offered the possibility of a wider public role for women. Protestantism, occurring in sixteenth- and seventeenth-century Europe simultaneously with the strengthening of the middle class through early capitalism, originated in the dissatisfaction of early modern urban society with the restrictions of Catholicism. Feminism found congenial soil in Protestantism, with its emphasis on individual responsibility, and flourished in America and England, which had strong Protestant traditions. In predominantly Catholic countries such as Italy and France, feminism developed late and was short-lived (Evans 1977:30). As earlier chapters of this book indicate, the effect of the Protestant Reformation on the lives of women is largely a matter of speculation. While women under Protestantism "shared exalted status as saintly Christians, loving spouses, and responsible child rearers," their roles became more circumscribed as patriarchal dominance within the family was strengthened (Bloch 1978:243). But Protestantism, reducing the barrier between clergy and parishioner and placing responsibility for salvation on the individual, offered women a direct and unmediated relationship with God and a wider public role within the religious community. In the rebellious early years following the Protestant Reformation, women who joined the new religious communities in great numbers were even permitted to preach and debate theology with their pastors in public (Bloch 1978:239).

The opportunity to participate in public life was grasped widely by women in America, where Protestant religious doctrine was rendered more flexible than in Europe by the demands of frontier life as well as by rapidly changing demographic patterns created by industrial capitalism. Alice Rossi identifies as one of the social roots of the women's movement in America the religious revivalism that occurred as the "Second Great Awakening" (from about 1795 to 1835), during which American Protestantism was pushed even farther away from the "arid rationalism of the English church" (1974:253). From the Protestant belief in the responsibility of every man and woman for his or her own salvation was developed an acceptance of women's performance of "good works" or participation in reform movements. Women played a prominent role in the religious revivals that swept through New England, participating in prayer and personal witness, speaking in public before mixed groups for the first time—a prerogative formerly accorded only to Quaker women. American women were able to establish a new public role in part because such activities were not inconsistent with the premium placed on female piety.

More important, women continued to develop their interests beyond the confines of home in the rapidly proliferating benevolence and reform societies that followed the Second Great Awakening. In *The Remembered Gate: Origins of American Feminism*, Barbara Berg suggests that we look to the early decades of the nineteenth century for clues to the development of feminism, which would emerge as a political force after mid-century. Female benevolent societies with fairly innocuous beginnings "blossomed forth, cross-fertilizing one another as they sowed the seeds of American feminism" (Berg 1978:158). Such activities represented woman's first tentative steps outside the "private sphere" and exposed not only the plight of poor women whose destitution was underscored by the effects of urbanization but also made the middle-class reformer more aware of her own oppression:

No longer could they accept the isolating myths. No longer could they believe that their unhappiness, their anxieties, their "unwomanly interests" emanated from some individual failure. . . . These perceptions, scattered and incipient, subtly suggested a unity of all women emerging from the common bonds of oppression. (Berg 1978:174)

The active assumption by women of their Christian duties met with some resistance from New England clergymen, who reserved their highest praise for those women who exercised their feminine virtues within the home. Ministers, aware perhaps of women's potential power within the church, "bitterly feared and fought feminine assumption of conspicuously Christian tasks" (Douglas 1977:131). Despite such clergymen, who argued that when woman "assumes the place and tone of man as a public reformer . . . she yields the power which God has given her for her protection, and her character becomes unnatural" (quoted in *HWS* I, 1881:81),[4] women who participated in benevolence work were able to use that century's notion of proper feminine behavior as justification for channeling their discontent into public activities.

4. Throughout this chapter *HWS* will be used in references to the *History of Woman Suffrage*.

The ultimate source of that discontent must be sought in the transformations that were wrought in the fabric of society by the industrial revolution, transformations that were to be repeated throughout the Western world. The timing differed from country to country, changes occurring earlier in the United States and England than elsewhere. We noted in the preceding chapter the massive reorganization of society in the decline of domestic production and the radical restructuring of the family as feudal paternalism was replaced by industrial paternalism. The changes thus wrought were no doubt enormous for men, who were required to relinquish formerly held sources of power. But for a rapidly expanding group of women whose services were no longer "counted" in the wages of production, these changes would indeed prove revolutionary. It is ironic, as we have observed elsewhere, that nineteenth-century technological developments and the concept of specialization, both of which held the potential for minimizing physical distinctions and promoting economic equality of the sexes, appear instead to have contributed to the fiction of women's expendability in production, to the constriction of work roles for women, and to the further refinement of that century's doctrine of feminine domesticity.

That construction was fostered by an expanding middle class. In fact, the most fundamental development leading to the rise of feminism, as Evans points out, was the emergence and expansion of the middle class. No longer were sources of power determined by blood lines as

... virtue came to be redefined in terms of ability and achievement rather than in terms of heredity and office. The ethic of work and self-sacrifice came to replace the values of leisure and noblesse oblige. Feudal paternalism was abandoned as the dominant social mentality. Its substitute was the harsh creed of individualistic meritocracy. (Evans 1977:29)

And as a more vocal and powerful middle class began to fight its way to positions of authority, it closed ranks, excluding women almost entirely from the public sector. The period was characterized by enormous expansion of trade and industry, as well as the professionalization of such occupations as medicine, education, and law. Women were not to be admitted to commerce and industry on an equal footing with men; nor were they able to pursue even that work which earlier generations of women had deemed their proper domain. Provision of health care, for example, was closed to them by the introduction of educational and certification standards.

The growth and expansion of the middle class had special implications for American women. In perhaps no other country in the world in the nineteenth century were the possibilities for economic and political self-determination so great. But, as Alice Rossi points out,

... the transformation of the egalitarian ethos from a political ideal in the revolution into the fabric of society meant an expansion of many opportunities for an increasing number of men but a shrinking sphere of participation for women in education, work, and political affairs. (1974:253)

Rossi examines the position of American women in the early nineteenth century in the context of a colonial heritage in which women shared with men in the building of a nation:

From the perspective of man, American society in 1820 was an open vista of opportunity: by dint of hard work he could hope to improve his position in society; if he did not succeed in one locality, he could move on to another, carrying his skills with him. (1974:251).

American women, however, with the final separation of the home from the workplace, were cut off from their colonial heritage as men continued in the building of a nation. The contrast between the American man, who at least in theory possessed unlimited possibilities, and the American woman, denied access to education, economic success, and participation in the political process, would become increasingly greater during the first half of the nineteenth century. As women under industrialization became less valued for their contributions to production, they became more valued for their "womanly" qualities.

The effects of that separate and shrinking sphere were felt by a rapidly proliferating number of women. Early efforts to retrieve a measure of women's lost prestige and recognition were made by those whom Ellen Du Bois calls "domestic reformers" (1978:16). Such women as Emma Willard and Catherine Beecher, for example, who established the first seminaries for women in the United States, argued that woman's education would allow her to extend her "proper sphere" to include the classroom as well as the home. They did not challenge woman's relegation to the domestic sphere but argued instead for a broadening of woman's experience within that sphere. The difference between these early domestic reformers and later feminists who would articulate a politics of women's rights is subtle but essential to an understanding of the almost complete infusion of the doctrine of separate spheres into nineteenth-century life. Woman's rights advocates and suffragists, while not necessarily challenging the notion of woman's dominance within the private realm, "recognized that the locus of community life had shifted away from the family" and that participation in community affairs required that they move into the public realm (Du Bois 1978:16–17). If Willard and Beecher were perhaps more interested in softening the effects of women's subordination than in working toward its elimination, such reform, as a practical matter, nonetheless proved a decisive first step toward the articulation of other essential needs.

The aims of early feminism under industrial capitalism throughout the Western world were initially economic and middle class in derivation. The demands of feminists for education, for admission to the professions, control over property and person, equity in marriage contracts and in divorce and child custody agreements were prompted by the middle-class realities of their lives. As women's capacity to fend for themselves decreased, as their dependence on one man—in the flesh or in the hoped-for future—deepened, the quality and reliability of that male support assumed increased importance, as did alternatives for survival should that support fail. Thus, for example, property rights—particularly in regard to property that might be settled on a daughter before her marriage and end up at the disposal of a profligate husband—and protection against abusive or neglectful husbands became issues around which early feminists, with their middle-class orientation, rallied.

A speech delivered by Lucy Stone and reprinted here is representative of this phase of the women's rights movement. "In education, in marriage, in religion, in everything," claims Stone, "disappointment is the lot of woman." Her objectives are above all practical: education to equip women for a "profession worthy an immortal being," access to the marketplace on an equal footing with her brother, equitable salary scales, improved status in the marriage relationship, and dress reform. Stone, unlike earlier domestic reformers who accepted woman's relegation to the private sphere, insisted that women as a class should no more than men be confined to a proscribed sphere. What is needed, she continues, is a restructuring of the notion of spheres to take into account individual capabilities. Leave woman to find her own sphere, Stone advises, whether it be within the private or the public realm. In the conclusion to her speech, Stone frames an argument that will be taken up by feminists throughout the course of their battle for women's rights. Woman, after long centuries of subjection to man, *is* inferior, "dwarfed by her own weakness and imbecility." What is required, then, is compensatory education to enable woman to achieve equality and to find her own sphere in accordance with her abilities. Nor did Lucy Stone's concern exclude poor and working women, as this speech and her frequent contributions to the *Woman's Journal* illustrate. It is clear nonetheless that Lucy Stone's primary orientation was to the class of which she was a member; the degradation of woman that she most abhorred was that which turned middle-class women into "walking showcases."

Although the primary orientation of nineteenth-century feminists would remain with the middle class, the experiences of women in the early benevolence and reform societies enabled many of them to identify the shared bonds of womanhood between the middle-class "beneficiary" of industrial capitalism and its less fortunate victim. But it was in their association with the abolition movement that women were able to turn that growing awareness of shared oppression into feminist politics. The most important reform movement growing out of evangelical Protestantism was abolitionism, whose forces were beginning to materialize in the mid-1830s. As in benevolence work, women in the early stages of the abolition movement played a role not inconsistent with accepted notions of woman's "proper sphere," organizing separate women's auxiliaries in order to provide support services for antislavery organizations, whose membership was limited to men. As women's "public" skills matured, however, their work became central to the cause; a resulting tendency of women to overstep prescribed boundaries of appropriate feminine behavior met with frequent denunciations even within abolitionist ranks.

The American Anti-Slavery Society, established in 1834, among whose members were Theodore Weld and Henry Stanton, was one of the most influential of the national abolition societies. The only women trained by Weld for lecture tours under its sponsorship were Sarah and Angelina Grimké, themselves defectors from a southern slaveholding family. As the Grimké sisters investigated the condition of the slave, they were led to a better understanding of their own oppression. Borrowing from Enlightenment natural rights ideology, Angelina Grimké argued that all men and women have the same moral nature and therefore the same rights. If rights are founded on the principle of shared moral being, Grimké continued,

... then the *mere circumstance of sex* does not give to man higher rights and responsibilities, than to woman.... My doctrine then is, that whatever it is morally right for man to do, it is morally right for woman to do. Our duties originate, not from difference of sex, but from the diversity of our relations in life, the various gifts and talents committed to our care, and the different eras in which we live. (1969:115)

Both sisters were among the earliest American women to write and speak on the subject of sex equality, but as their arguments became more political they incurred the wrath of the clergy as well as of many within the movement itself, who resisted what they felt was the untimely linking of the "woman question" with the cause of the black man.

In her *Letters on the Equality of the Sexes and the Condition of Woman*, Sarah Grimké engaged in what was to be a heated theological debate during the first half of the century, surfacing frequently long after the suffrage movement was launched: God, according to the orthodox view, ordained man and woman to perform different functions; but far from implying her inferiority, the argument insisted on her supremacy within her assigned sphere (Kraditor 1971:14). In one letter, Grimké argues that the notion of preordained spheres was a fiction conceived by men to wrest from women their God-given and natural rights. "But I ask no favors for my sex," Grimké continues. "I surrender not our claim to equality. All I ask of our brethren is, that they will take their feet from off our necks, and permit us to stand upright on that ground which God designed us to occupy" (1970:10). Still, Sarah Grimké's analysis of woman's condition did not rest simply upon biblical exegesis. Her comprehensive analysis, based upon firsthand experience and shrewd observation, demanded a rethinking of the economic basis of marriage as well as the structures that maintained slavery. In a letter from her printed collection, included here, Sarah Grimké claims that the notion that marriage is a "kind of preferment" is not only absurd but dangerous. Moreover, like Stone, Grimké's concern is not simply for the women of her class. The American woman cannot, Grimké insists, "fold her hands in apathy" in the face of the degradation forced upon the female slave and be guiltless.

Although the Grimké sisters, in recognizing the relationship between the slavery of the black woman and the oppression of her white middle-class sister, were expressing a basic tenet of feminist ideology, feminism as a political force would not emerge until women in greater numbers became aware of each other and articulated their shared oppression. In her introduction to *Up from the Pedestal*, Aileen Kraditor discusses the events contributing to the emergence of the American feminist movement. Why, Kraditor asks, did the feminist movement appear in the United States when it did, and what were its immediate and ultimate causes? Feminism, obviously, did not emerge with a fully articulated and consistent set of goals. As American feminism developed, it drew from existing women's rights theory to shape its conception of what woman's place ought to be. While early claims of feminism to equality were grounded solidly in natural rights theory, most feminists accepted the doctrine of inherent sexual differences. Feminists, assuming full responsibility for the domestic sphere, insisted nonetheless on their right to develop their talents outside that sphere. Feminism would remain primarily a middle-class movement whose demands—for a university education, admission to the professions, and property rights—were significantly less important to underclass women than the need for a living wage. Kraditor identifies the source of the nineteenth-century feminists' ambiguity vis-à-vis women as a class in their economic and social dependency on the men with whom they lived. Kraditor's identification of two major forms of the suffrage argument, the "justice argument," based on principles derived from the Enlightenment and the Declaration of Independence, and the "expediency argument," which justified the claim to the vote because of the benefits to society that would result, will be helpful to keep in mind as we examine specific arguments posed by the suffragists. As we shall see, suffragists, as the century progressed, would make fewer claims to the franchise based on principles of justice; rather, they would present themselves as political allies of middle-class men in the effort to enact reform measures and counteract the immigrant, the black, and the underclass vote (1968:10–17).

Throughout the first half of the century, women's discontent would surface from time to time, but it was not until a relative handful of women came together at Seneca Falls, New York, in July 1848 that this discontent would be forged into a political movement. Plans for that first women's rights convention to be held anywhere in the world had been laid, according to the *History of Woman Suffrage*, eight years before at a World's Anti-Slavery Convention in London when American women delegates, among them Lucretia Mott, were denied their credentials and forced to sit in the visitors' gallery. At that time, Lucretia Mott and Elizabeth Cady Stanton "agreed to hold a woman's rights convention on their return to America, as the men to whom they had just listened had manifested their great need of some education on that question" (*HWS* I, 1881:61). Many of those in attendance at the Seneca Falls convention had been active in other reform movements or had grown up in families where such movements were discussed and supported. The early temperance meetings and the revivalist and missionary societies had provided American women with acceptable channels into which they could pour their energies without directly challenging the notion of "separate spheres." But it was in association with the abolition movement that women found the strength to question the structures that formed the basis of their oppression. Moreover, the earlier involvement of America's first feminists in the abolition movement had enabled them to acquire critical organizational and political skills which they applied to their own cause after 1848. Finally, the abolition movement provided feminists with a constituency from which the new movement could draw its members, as well as essential resources and continued support. In their *History of Woman Suffrage*, Stanton, Anthony, and Gage look to abolition as "above all other causes" of the suffrage movement (*HWS* I, 1881:52).

Seneca Falls was to be the first of a long series of conventions that would keep the question of women's rights before the public and would enable women to gain the organizational and oratorical skills critical to the achievement of their goals. Those in attendance at the first convention were presented with a document that had been drawn up a few days earlier by Elizabeth Cady Stanton, Lucretia Mott, and several other women who, like Mott, were members of the

Friends community. Borrowing from the American Declaration of Independence, a document that had not been intended for their benefit, and from an egalitarian ideology that, at least in practice, had generally excluded them, they had framed a document that articulated clearly women's grievances and enunciated a comprehensive list of feminist demands. The Declaration of Sentiments and Resolutions, reprinted here in full, challenged the most fundamental and deeply felt notions about woman's place. Although even these early feminists, as we shall see, accepted the doctrine of inherent sexual differences and the necessity of woman's central position in the home, the Declaration was a direct attack on the notion that her sphere was defined by her domesticity. As Stanton would write some thirty years later, the Declaration

... demanded all the most radical friends of the movement have since claimed—such as equal rights in the universities, in the trades and professions; the right to vote; to share in all political offices, honors, and emoluments; to complete equality in marriage, to personal freedom, property, wages, children; to make contracts; to sue and be sued; and to testify in courts of justice. (*HWS* I, 1881: 73)

Of the twelve resolutions included in the Declaration, all were adopted unanimously, with the exception of a resolution introduced by Stanton—"That it is the duty of the women of this country to secure to themselves their sacred right to the elective franchise"— which passed by a small majority. Suffrage was from the beginning of the women's rights movement an essential demand, though there was considerable disagreement even among feminists as to why women should secure the vote and what they would accomplish with it.

Among the issues of great importance to the first feminists was the right of a woman to control both the disposition of her person and of her property. Feminists fought for a woman's right to inherit and control her property, to make wills, and to choose her residence. A "protest" by Lucy Stone and Henry Blackwell against the suspension during marriage of a wife's legal existence was read as part of their marriage ceremony in 1855. In it, Stone and Blackwell wrote,

> . . . in justice to ourselves and a great principle, we deem it a duty to declare that this act on our part implies no sanction of, nor promise of voluntary obedience to such of the present laws of marriage, as refuse to recognize the wife as an independent, rational being, while they confer upon the husband an injurious and unnatural superiority, investing him with legal powers which no honorable man would exercise, and which no man should possess. (*HWS* I, 1881:260)

Although many issues of importance to the early feminists were clouded by the question of class, these feminists participated extensively in the struggles of working women for better working conditions, equal pay, and the right to retain their wages, as well as for the right of all women to divorce an abusive husband and retain custody of their children. Heated debates on the subject of divorce transcended class divisions. In 1860, Elizabeth Cady Stanton argued that marriage, a human institution, should be viewed as a contract with annulment as a legal remedy against deception or fraud. "If a man sell a horse," she argued, "and the purchaser find in him great incompatibility of temper—a disposition to stand still when the owner is in haste to go—the sale is null and void, and the man and his horse part company." No matter how cruelly a wife is treated, Stanton claimed, she has no such recourse (*HWS* I, 1881:717). Such feminist analysis did not enjoy widespread support, even within the women's movement; although significant economic, legal, and political gains were achieved, the century would remain resistant to such radical analyses of marriage and the family.

Feminist ideology, thoroughly grounded in Enlightenment natural rights theory, included the needs and interests of all women, across class and race lines. But on a practical level, as we have pointed out, the founders of the nineteenth-century women's movement were never able to separate their interests from those of the men with whom they lived. In an important article on "Class Roots of Feminism," Karen Sacks argues that the American women's movement was not one but three separate movements: an industrial-working-class women's movement, which traced its origins to the New England textile mills of the 1830s; a black women's movement with roots in the black conventions of the 1830s; and finally, the white middle-class movement we have been describing. Although they remained largely separate, the three movements enjoyed their greatest period of solidarity during the struggle for abolition. Their reasons for supporting abolition differed, Sacks points out, and are revealing: "The mill women argued that a labor force in slavery degraded free labor as well as slave labor, and that all labor had a two-faced enemy: 'the lord of the loom and the lord of the lash'" (1980:492). Those class and race differences, as we saw in earlier chapters, were never successfully transcended and would intensify as the nineteenth century progressed.

After 1848, as Kraditor points out, the most frequent feminist demand was the right to vote. Most historians of nineteenth-century feminism view the single-minded emphasis on winning the vote during the last few decades of the suffrage fight as a turning away from the radical and broad-ranging analyses of the feminist movement's founders. Nevertheless, some feminist historians claim that suffrage was the most radical of all the women's rights demands. Ellen Du Bois, for example, in an article on "The Radicalism of the Woman Suffrage Movement: Notes Toward the Reconstruction of

Nineteenth-Century Feminism," claims that suffrage was the corner-
stone of the feminist movement, going beyond the cataloguing of
women's wrongs to reveal the possibility of a changed sexual order.
Suffrage raised the prospect of female autonomy by postulating a
direct relationship between women and government, thus challenging the assumption of male authority over women. Du Bois' article
develops the thesis that

> ... the significance of the woman suffrage movement rested precisely on the
> fact that it bypassed women's oppression within the family, or private
> sphere, and demanded instead her admission to citizenship, and through it
> admission to the public arena. By focusing on the public sphere, and partic-
> ularly on citizenship, suffragists demanded for women a kind of power and
> a connection with the social order not based on the institution of the family
> and their subordination within it. (1975:63–64)

Although, as Du Bois admits, nineteenth-century feminists accepted
the predominance of women in the domestic sphere, their demand
for the vote was, nonetheless, a challenge to the entire sexual structure. In their expectation that the vote would bring about immediate,
measurable change, the suffragists were perhaps politically naive.
But as their writings indicate, the feminists saw the ballot not simply
as a political tool but as a means of reanchoring woman's self-image,
"not in the subordination of her familial role, but in the individuality
and self-determination that they saw in citizenship" (1975:67).

Early arguments for women's suffrage stressed the common
humanity of men and women and posed woman as the direct beneficiary of the fruits of Enlightenment ideology and republican principles
upon which the American government was based. Elizabeth Cady
Stanton's address "The Solitude of Self," though written late in the
nineteenth century, expresses well the argument typical of the early

period in the suffrage movement and as such is "the epitome of the natural right argument for woman suffrage" (Kraditor 1971:40). Woman's claim to specific rights, Stanton insisted, is grounded firmly in universal human rights. Woman was responsible for her own destiny, and the responsibility that she bore for her own life required that she be given "complete emancipation from all the crippling influences" that her upbringing had placed on her. Like other early suffragists, Stanton claimed that woman, though equal under the doctrine of natural rights, was unequal in her condition. The recognition of woman's self-sovereignty in the granting of the suffrage, Stanton predicted, would be cause as well as effect of her emancipation.

The alliance with abolitionism had provided feminists with a vision of a social and political order based on egalitarian principles, as well as an organizational structure on which to draw. But, as Du Bois points out, the availability of a constituency from abolitionist ranks meant that feminist leaders would not make a systematic effort to attract women who were not reformers. During the years of its close alliance with abolitionism, the feminist movement made few attempts to reach women living under conditions of poverty and employment discrimination. Then, during the Civil War, women's rights activities were discontinued as women poured all their energies into the war effort. After the war, the feminist movement regrouped, but it was reshaped significantly by Reconstruction politics. Former abolition societies began to concentrate their attention on obtaining the franchise for the black man, now free but not yet a citizen. Following the lead of the abolitionists, as Du Bois suggests, the feminist movement adopted suffrage as its primary concern, feminists now referring to themselves as the "woman suffrage movement" rather than the "women's rights movement" (Du Bois, 1978:54). In a critical way, the defeat of slavery contributed to the emergence of an independent women's movement. Abolitionists, who now found themselves in the center of Reconstruction politics, were reluctant to support their former allies in the women's movement. "This hour belongs to the Negro" insisted one long-time supporter of feminist demands, reflecting the view that the cause of women's enfranchisement would only strengthen the opposition to that of the black man.

Feminists, still hoping for a united effort for universal suffrage, pleaded the cause of the black woman, arguing that she needed the ballot more than anyone. Although few black women participated directly in the women's suffrage movement, a notable exception was Sojourner Truth, a frequent speaker for women's rights. Sojourner Truth was not in favor of black suffrage without women's suffrage because, "if colored men get their rights, and not colored women theirs, you see the colored men will be masters over the women, and it will be just as bad as it was before." Slavery is only partly destroyed, Truth declared in a famous speech reprinted here, and for it to be destroyed "root and branch," women must be included in the demand for suffrage.

But the feminists' attempts to build a united coalition were rebuffed by their former allies. Disillusionment of one wing of the women's movement with that rejection as well as ideological and tactical differences within the feminist camp led to the establishment after 1869 of two separate suffrage organizations. The American Woman Suffrage Association, led by Lucy Stone and her husband, Henry Blackwell, agreed with the Republican leaders and the former abolitionists that the issue of woman suffrage jeopardized the possibility of Negro enfranchisement and preferred, in Kraditor's words, "half a loaf" to none (1971:187). The AWSA committed itself to the single demand for women's suffrage but remained uncritical of Reconstruction politics. The National Woman Suffrage Association, however, under the leadership of Stanton and Anthony, was deeply aggrieved by their former allies' concurrence with the Republican party's refusal to include the enfranchisement of women with that of black men under the Fourteenth Amendment. The NWSA, which viewed suffrage as a right to be conferred by the federal government, was responsible for the introduction of what was popularly known as the "Susan B. Anthony Amendment" into Congress in 1878. It read, "The Right of Citizens of the United States to vote shall not be denied or abridged by the United States or by any state on account of sex." AWSA, believing that suffrage should be conferred by the voters of each state, concentrated its efforts on the laborious process of petitioning state legislatures. NWSA remained committed to the earlier women's rights program as enunciated in the Declaration of Sentiments and Resolutions and began to build alliances with working women. AWSA, however, became anti-labor, drawing its support primarily from professional and leisure-class women, and concentrated its efforts narrowly on the suffrage. The two groups would work separately until merging as the National American Woman Suffrage Association (NAWSA) twenty years later, during which time the earlier radical analysis of the Stanton-Anthony force had been modified by younger feminists, and the aims of the two suffrage organizations had become practically indistinguishable.

Reconstruction politics, then, contributed to an open break between feminists and their former allies and forced women to build the first autonomous and independent American women's movement. In their *History of Woman Suffrage*, the architects of that movement review the events prompting feminism to move beyond its abolitionist antecedents:

The fact of [the abolitionists'] silence deeply grieved us, but the philosophy of their indifference we thoroughly comprehended for the first time and saw as never before, that only from the woman's standpoint could the battle be successfully fought, and victory secured. . . Our liberal men counseled us to silence during the war, and we were silent on our own wrongs; they counseled us again to silence in Kansas and New York, lest we should defeat "negro suffrage," and threatened if we were not, we might fight the battle alone. We chose the latter, and were defeated. But standing alone we learned our power; we repudiated man's counsels forevermore; and solemnly vowed that there should never be another season of silence until woman had the same rights everywhere on this green earth, as man. (*HWS* II, 1881:267–68)

That break led feminists to explore alternate political alliances and develop new constituencies. *The Revolution*, a newspaper founded by Anthony and Stanton at this time, became the means by which one wing of the new, independent women's movement attempted to broaden its political base. *The Revolution* adopted as its motto "Principle, Not Policy—Justice, Not Favors—Men Their Rights and Nothing More—Women Their Rights and Nothing Less." Eleanor Flexner writes that *The Revolution* contained

. . . news not to be found elsewhere—of the organization of women typesetters, tailoresses, and laundry workers, of the first women's clubs, of pioneers in the professions, of women abroad. . . . *The Revolution* . . . gave their movement a forum, a focus, and direction. It pointed, it led, and it fought, with vigor and vehemence. (1974:151)

In one of her favorite speeches characteristic of the articles appearing in *The Revolution*, Anthony makes a plea to working women to join in the effort to secure the vote. She raises the basic issues, common to all women, of independence and influence versus paternalism and protection. As she points out, 3 million women are supporting themselves without the "protection of a man," and those women "must be clothed with equal power to protect" themselves. That power, she argued, was the ballot.

Yet, in spite of analyses such as that of Anthony, the alliance with labor was an uneasy one. The ironic title of Anthony's speech, "Woman Wants Bread, Not the Ballot!" was symbolic of the ideological differences that would continue to plague the labor and suffrage movements into the next century. Most feminists, labor leaders claimed, failed to adopt a genuine class analysis. "Organized labor," argued "Mother" Mary Jones, "should organize its women along industrial lines. . . . The plutocrats have organized their women. They keep them busy with suffrage and prohibition and charity." In an excerpt from a speech included here, which Mother Jones delivered before feminists eager to enlist her in the fight for suffrage, she succinctly measures the class differences that have never ceased to trouble the various women's movements.

Despite the insistence of a handful of feminists, among them Stanton and Anthony, on the importance of retaining a broad feminist platform with an appeal to diverse groups of women, arguments for women's suffrage after 1880 make fewer claims based upon natural rights principles and appeal more and more to middle-class and white interests. The break with abolitionism had done much to weaken the egalitarian philosophy of the women's movement. NAWSA, the organization that fused the two branches of the women's movement in 1890, pursued public respectability vigorously. NAWSA's new leaders, among whom was the young and energetic Carrie Chapman Catt, successfully built an efficient, tightly run organization emphasizing unity of purpose, and in so doing, moved feminism squarely into the mainstream. Stanton and Anthony, joined by a few young women such as Harriot Stanton Blatch, unsuccessfully fought the drift toward conservatism. When Stanton, maintaining her egalitarian vision, published in 1895 a *Woman's Bible*, which sought to correct generations of patriarchal bias, the new leadership, fearful of offending those who held more traditional beliefs, repudiated Stanton's unorthodox views.

The selection that follows from the *History of Woman Suffrage*, edited by Stanton, Anthony, and Matilda Joslyn Gage, illustrates the continuing allegiance of the earlier suffragists to the principle of justice, but demonstrates as well its willingness to incorporate into its battery of weapons what Kraditor calls the "expediency argument." In this selection, the writers present and counter the key arguments leveled against the movement for women's suffrage. The editors insist on woman's political equality as "the legitimate outgrowth of the fundamental principles of our Government." They claim that woman's present degraded position is a result not of inevitable sexual differences but of inconsistencies between principle and practice. The writers then move from the "justice argument" to several varieties of the "expediency argument." Woman needs the ballot, first, for self-protection; ranked as she is throughout the nation with "idiots, lunatics, criminals, and minors," she needs the franchise in order to participate in passing just and equal laws for her own benefit. Second, she needs the ballot in order better to carry out her duties within her traditional sphere; her equality will destroy her unnatural parasitic relationship to her husband and therefore work to the benefit of both. Third, her inclinations and upbringing equip her to "far more effectively guard the morals of society" than men are able to do. "The new era," Kraditor tells us, "saw a change from the emphasis by suffragists on the ways in which women were the same as men and therefore had the *right* to vote, to a stress on the ways in which they differed from men, and therefore had the *duty* to contribute their special skills and experience to government" (1971:52).

Some feminists felt that women were degraded by arguments

that emphasized the good that women would do with the vote, contending that women, like men, deserved a share of political power no matter how they would use it. But as the century progressed, suffragists felt pressed to justify their claim to the suffrage by citing the benefits that would accrue to society by their wise and prudent use of the vote. During the long period after its break with abolitionism, feminists, faced with building a "respectable" and independent political base, found themselves in the defensive position of justifying their middle-class orientation. They discovered increasingly, Kraditor claims, that their most effective argument as "native-born, white, middle-class women was one which would prove their own capacity but not that of men or women of other sections of the population." The claim would be heard more frequently that the enfranchisement of women from the "better" class would counteract the votes of the undesirable part of the electorate (1971:43). The acceptance of innate differences in moral constitution between women and men was crucial for feminists. By the 1890s suffrage rhetoric had incorporated nativist and racist arguments that assumed differences in both character and intellect not only between men and women in general but also between middle and working classes, whites and blacks, native-born and immigrant groups. The extension of the franchise to black, immigrant, and working-class men, it was claimed more and more frequently, was not only an insult to white femininity but a clear danger to American political traditions. An argument typical of this period is contained in Olympia Brown's speech "On Foreign Rule," reprinted here. Brown's contention that "the votes of women will eventually be the only means of overcoming this foreign influence and maintaining our free institutions," anticipates the intense class struggle that would develop after 1890 with the influx of millions of immigrants to America's shores.

Those views toward underclass men and women were modified

considerably in the closing years of the century with the advent of the Progressive era. Mary Ryan identifies in the proliferating women's reform movements of this period the "enlargement of the promise of motherly power" (1978:226). The notion of inherent sexual differences had been amplified by social Darwinism. Most feminists of this period, embracing the Darwinist idea that intellect and character were biologically determined, claimed moral superiority for women, who, according to the argument, had been formed to nurture and to serve humanity. The new notion of social motherhood, then, provided a rationale for women's flight from the home to civic and social clubs, settlement houses, and temperance and reform organizations. The suffrage movement experienced enormous growth during the Progressive period, drawing new members from reform-minded women. Through organizations such as the Women's Christian Temperance Union, women gained important organizational and leadership skills denied them by the larger society. Black women, generally rebuffed by middle-class reformers, formed their own clubs and organizations such as the National Association of Colored Women to combat racist attitudes and to perform important social services. The emphasis of generations of historians and journalists on caricatures of daughters of Victorian repression wielding their hatchets against the immorality of drink has done much to discredit this phase of the women's movement. Women did indeed enter saloons and destroy property, but they were also methodically investigating urban squalor, forming corporations to sanitize slums, scrutinizing the effects of the judicial system on women and children, and lobbying for factory inspection and child labor legislation.

By the beginning of the twentieth century, then, the feminist movement had become increasingly sympathetic to the special problems of working-class people and immigrants, although arguments such as that posed by Olympia Brown did not entirely disappear. In her article "The Women's Trade Union League and American Feminism," Robin Miller Jacoby examines an alliance that embroiled middle-class reformers and working women alike in legislative lobbying, trade union organizing and strikes. The Women's Trade Union League (WTUL) was founded in 1903 by a reform and labor coalition to assist in moving women into the trade unions. In time, the emphasis of the WTUL shifted to education and legislation, a change that reflected the interests of the leisure-class allies of working women. The leaders of the WTUL were committed to the principle of women's suffrage and worked actively both within the organization to convince working women of their need for the vote and in coalition with NAWSA to educate their feminist allies as to the working woman's special problems and needs (1975:132). The alliance between the WTUL and the feminist movement, however, remained troubled, Jacoby claims, because of the basic incompatibility between the ideology of feminism and that of class identity. "Feminism simultaneously complements and conflicts with the ideology of the primacy of class identity," Jacoby writes. "It is complementary in that it implies equal rights and opportunities for women within sexually mixed, class-based settings such as labor unions; it is conflicting in that it also implies that gender identification creates solidarities transcending class divisions (1975:128). For the middle-class allies of working women, Jacoby shows, class biases remained a barrier to the achievement of sisterhood.

As the struggle for women's rights merged more and more with such proliferating reform movements, middle-class women who had accepted the "cult of true womanhood" and had never before felt keenly about the suffrage issue agreed that they needed the vote to secure a political forum for their reform activities (Kraditor 1971:

48–52). Although membership in clubs and reform organizations far exceeded that of the National American Woman Suffrage Association, many women were both reformers and suffragists. By the end of the century suffragist speeches and convention resolutions emphasized the importance of child labor legislation and pure food laws as well as more equitable labor policies and wage scales. That shift coincided with national policy changes attendant upon the removal of production from the home and the widespread establishment of public education. Increasingly, the exercise of women's traditional duties fell more and more within the public sector. Government was now engaged in what the suffragists called "enlarged housekeeping," having assumed the responsibility of passing laws regulating the production of food, the purification of water, the sanitation of the tenement, and the education of children. Suffragists now began to argue that women needed to participate in the public sector in order more effectively to perform their traditional duties within the "private sphere." In an argument typical of this later period in the suffrage movement, "Why Women Should Vote" (1910), Jane Addams pointed out that "if woman would keep on with her old business of caring for her home and rearing her children she will have to have some conscience in regard to public affairs lying quite outside of her immediate household" (1960:105).

Critics of the feminist movement have raised questions about feminism's success. In their introduction to *The Concise History of Woman Suffrage*, Mari Jo and Paul Buhle ask,

But how were the historic goals of woman's rights to be realized in Progressive-styled movements that aimed at adjustments more than transformation of the existing order? Suffragists followed the mainstream and demanded the political inclusion of women into American society as one great estate among plural powers. Their moral strength remained in the nature of their goal, a democratic participation that suggested at least remnants of natural rights ideology however stripped of its once-revolutionary implications. (1978:37)

As feminism had matured, then, it had moved from a fringe position into the political center. The ultimate success of the suffrage movement was no doubt enhanced by the legions of middle-class and sometimes conservative women reformers who came to recognize the vote as a necessary tool. The Progressive party, acknowledging such women as probable allies in accomplishing reform, became in 1912 the first major party to endorse women's suffrage.

That endorsement was awarded further legitimacy by an appeal in 1918 by Woodrow Wilson to the U.S. Senate that the enactment of woman's suffrage was essential to the implementation of democracy. The Nineteenth Amendment was sent to the states for ratification in 1919 and became law in 1920. The passage of the "woman's suffrage amendment" was secured, we believe, as a result of the reorientation of feminist ideology from its early emphasis on the doctrine of individual equality to the acceptance of the notion of innate differences between men and women. And in that reorientation, we observe the seeds of the decline of what has been called the first wave of feminism.

Yet, as we shall see in the final chapter of this book, that decline was never complete. And if the suffragists were unduly optimistic in expecting the ballot to sweep away all inequalities, the nineteenth-century feminist movement did help millions of women enter public life, gain a political education, and respond creatively to rapidly changing political, economic, and social conditions. "In however limited a way," Richard J. Evans concludes in his study of the suffrage movement, "the feminists helped women to enter the modern world" (1977:240).

A survey of the American feminist movement would not be complete without Abigail Adams' famous "remember the ladies" letter to her husband, John Adams, as well as his response. If Abigail Adams' threat to "foment a Rebelion" was laced with humor, her sense of women's position was nonetheless real. Soon after the letters reprinted below were written, John Adams would join with other fathers of our country to write the American Declaration of Independence, one of history's most searing indictments of tyranny and man's inhumanity to man.

REMEMBER THE LADIES

Abigail Smith Adams (1744–1818)
John Adams (1735–1826)

Abigail Adams to John Adams

Braintree, March 31, 1776

I long to hear that you have declared an independancy—and by the way in the new Code of Laws which I suppose it will be necessary for you to make I desire you would Remember the Ladies, and be more generous and favourable to them than your ancestors. Do not put such unlimited power into the hands of the Husbands. Remember all Men would be tyrants if they could. If perticuliar care and attention is not paid to the Laidies we are determined to foment a Rebelion, and will not hold ourselves bound by any Laws in which we have no voice, or Representation.

That your Sex are Naturally Tyrannical is a Truth so thoroughly established as to admit of no dispute, but such of you as wish to be happy willingly give up the harsh title of Master for the more tender and endearing one of Friend. Why then, not put it out of the power of the vicious and the Lawless to use us with cruelty and indignity with impunity. Men of Sense in all Ages abhor those customs which treat us only as the vassals of your Sex. Regard us then as Beings placed by providence under your protection and in immitation of the Supreem Being make use of that power only for our happiness.

John Adams to Abigail Adams

Ap. 14. 1776

As to Declarations of Independency, be patient. Read our Privateering Laws, and our Commercial Laws. What signifies a Word.

As to your extraordinary Code of Laws, I cannot but laugh. We have been told that our Struggle has loosened the bands of Government every where. That Children and Apprentices were disobedient—that schools and Colledges were grown turbulent—that Indians slighted their Guardians and Negroes grew insolent to their Masters. But your Letter was the first Intimation that another Tribe more numerous and powerfull than all the rest were grown discontented.—This is rather too coarse a Compliment but you are so saucy, I wont blot it out.

Depend upon it, We know better than to repeal our Masculine systems. Altho they are in full Force, you know they are little more than Theory. We dare not exert our Power in its full Latitude. We are obliged to go fair, and softly, and in Practice you know We are the subjects. We have only the Name of Masters, and rather than give up this, which would compleatly subject Us to the Despotism of the Peticoat, I hope General Washington, and all our brave Heroes would fight. I am sure every good Politician would plot, as long as he would against Despotism, Empire, Monarchy, Aristocracy, Oligarchy, or Ochlocracy.

Mary Wollstonecraft's major work, A Vindication of the Rights of Woman, *was informed by the circumstances of her personal life and deeply imbued with the egalitarian ideas of her day. Having witnessed the effects of patriarchal marriage on the women in her own family, Wollstonecraft had been in revolt all her life against conventional morality and legal injustice. A vindication, in which she stresses the importance of education, was influenced by eighteenth-century thinkers, most notably John Locke. Yet her work is in no way derivative; her arguments bear her original stamp and reveal her passionate commitment to the cause of social justice. Wollstonecraft is important to feminists today as one of the first serious writers to insist upon women's ability to reason. In excerpts from Chapter 4 of* A Vindication, *included here, she laments the trivial attentions accorded women and argues that women should be educated to use their intelligence rather than inspire love and "intoxicate the senses."*

THE EXERCISE OF REASON

Mary Wollstonecraft (1759–1797)

FROM *A Vindication of the Rights of Woman*

That woman is naturally weak, or degraded by a concurrence of circumstances, is, I think, clear. But this position I shall simply contrast with a conclusion, which I have frequently heard fall from sensible men in favour of an aristocracy: that the mass of mankind cannot be anything, or the obsequious slaves, who patiently allow themselves to be driven forward, would feel their own consequence, and spurn their chains. Men, they further observe, submit everywhere to oppression, when they have only to lift up their heads to throw off the yoke; yet, instead of asserting their birthright, they quietly lick the dust, and say, Let us eat and drink, for to-morrow we die. Women, I argue from analogy, are degraded by the same propensity to enjoy the present moment; and, at last, despise the freedom which they have not sufficient virtue to struggle to attain. But I must be more explicit. . . .

The stamen of immortality, if I may be allowed the phrase, is the perfectibility of human reason; for, were man created perfect, or did a flood of knowledge break in upon him, when he arrived at maturity, that precluded error, I should doubt whether his existence would be continued after the dissolution of the body. But, in the present state of things, every difficulty in morals that escapes from human discussion, and equally baffles the investigation of profound thinking, and the lightning glance of genius, is an argument on which I build my belief of the immortality of the soul. Reason is, consequentially, the simple power of improvement; or, more properly speaking, of discerning truth. Every individual is in this respect a world in itself. More or less may be conspicuous in one being than another; but the nature of reason must be the same in all, if it be an emanation of divinity, the tie that connects the creature with the Creator; for, can that soul be stamped with the heavenly image, that is not perfected by the exercise of its own reason?[1] Yet outwardly ornamented with elaborate care, and so adorned to delight man, "that with honour he may love,"[2] the soul of woman is not allowed to have this distinction, and man, ever placed between her and reason, she is always represented as only created to see through a gross medium, and to take things on trust. But dismissing these fanciful theories, and considering woman as a whole, let it be what it will, instead of a part of man, the inquiry is whether she have reason or not. If she have, which, for a moment, I will take for granted, she was not created merely to be the solace of man, and the sexual should not destroy the human character.

Into this error men have, probably, been led by viewing education in a false light; not considering it as the first step to form a being advancing gradually towards perfection,[3] but only as a preparation for life. On this sensual error, for I must call it so, has the false system of female manners been reared, which robs the whole sex of its dignity, and classes the brown and fair with the smiling flowers that only adorn the land. . . .

The power of generalizing ideas, of drawing comprehensive conclusions from individual observations, is the only acquirement, for an immortal being, that really deserves the name of knowledge. Merely to observe, without endeavouring to account for anything, may (in a very incomplete manner) serve as the common sense of life; but where is the store laid up that is to clothe the soul when it leaves the body?

This power has not only been denied to women; but writers have insisted that it is inconsistent, with a few exceptions, with their sexual character. Let men prove this, and I shall grant that woman only

---

1. "The brutes," says Lord Monboddo, "remain in the state in which nature has placed them, except in so far as their natural instinct is improved by the culture *we* bestow upon them."

2. *Vide* Milton.

3. This word is not strictly just, but I cannot find a better.

exists for man. I must, however, previously remark, that the power of generalizing ideas, to any great extent, is not very common amongst men or women. But this exercise is the true cultivation of the understanding; and everything conspires to render the cultivation of the understanding more difficult in the female than the male world.

I am naturally led by this assertion to the main subject of the present chapter, and shall now attempt to point out some of the causes that degrade the sex, and prevent women from generalizing their observations.

I shall not go back to the remote annals of antiquity to trace the history of woman; it is sufficient to allow that she has always been either a slave, or a despot, and to remark, that each of these situations equally retards the progress of reason. The grand source of female folly and vice has ever appeared to me to arise from narrowness of mind; and the very constitution of civil governments has put almost insuperable obstacles in the way to prevent the cultivation of the female understanding:—yet virtue can be built on no other foundation! The same obstacles are thrown in the way of the rich, and the same consequences ensue.

Necessity has been proverbially termed the mother of invention—the aphorism may be extended to virtue. It is an acquirement, and an acquirement to which pleasure must be sacrificed—and who sacrifices pleasure when it is within the grasp, whose mind has not been opened and strengthened by adversity, or the pursuit of knowledge goaded on by necessity? Happy is it when people have the cares of life to struggle with; for these struggles prevent their becoming a prey to enervating vices, merely from idleness! But, if from their birth men and women be placed in a torrid zone, with the meridian sun of pleasure darting directly upon them, how can they sufficiently brace their minds to discharge the duties of life, or even to relish the affections that carry them out of themselves?

Pleasure is the business of woman's life, according to the present modification of society, and while it continues to be so, little can be expected from such weak beings. Inheriting, in a lineal descent from the first fair defect in nature, the sovereignty of beauty, they have, to maintain their power, resigned the natural rights, which the exercise of reason might have procured them, and chosen rather to be short-lived queens than labour to obtain the sober pleasures that arise from equality. Exalted by their inferiority (this sounds like a contradiction), they constantly demand homage as women, though experience should teach them that the men who pride themselves upon paying this arbitrary insolent respect to the sex, with the most scrupulous exactness, are most inclined to tyrannize over, and despise, the very weakness they cherish. . . .

I lament that women are systematically degraded by receiving the trivial attentions, which men think it manly to pay to the sex, when, in fact, they are insultingly supporting their own superiority. It is not condescension to bow to an inferior. So ludicrous, in fact, do these ceremonies appear to me, that I scarcely am able to govern my muscles, when I see a man start with eager and serious solicitude to lift a handkerchief, or shut a door, when the *lady* could have done it herself, had she only moved a pace or two.

A wild wish has just flown from my heart to my head, and I will not stifle it though it may excite a horse-laugh. I do earnestly wish to see the distinction of sex confounded in society, unless where love animates the behaviour. For this distinction is, I am firmly persuaded, the foundation of the weakness of character ascribed to woman; is the cause why the understanding is neglected, whilst accomplishments are acquired with sedulous care: and the same cause accounts for their preferring the graceful before the heroic virtues. . . .

It would be an endless task to trace the variety of meannesses, cares, and sorrows, into which women are plunged by the prevailing opinion, that they were created rather to feel than reason, and that all the power they obtain, must be obtained by their charms and weakness:

> *"Fine by defect, and amiably weak!"*

And, made by this amiable weakness entirely dependent, excepting what they gain by illicit sway, on man, not only for protection, but advice, is it surprising that, neglecting the duties that reason alone points out, and shrinking from trials calculated to strengthen their minds, they only exert themselves to give their defects a graceful covering, which may serve to heighten their charms in the eye of the voluptuary, though it sink them below the scale of moral excellence? . . .

I am fully persuaded that we should hear of none of these infantine airs, if girls were allowed to take sufficient exercise, and not confined in close rooms till their muscles are relaxed, and their powers of digestion destroyed. To carry the remark still further, if fear in girls, instead of being cherished, perhaps created, were treated in the same manner as cowardice in boys, we should quickly see women with more dignified aspects. It is true, they could not then with equal propriety be termed the sweet flowers that smile in the walk of man; but they would be more respectable members of society, and discharge the important duties of life by the light of their own reason. "Educate women like men," says Rousseau, "and the more they resemble our sex the less power will they have over us." This is the very point I aim at. I do not wish them to have power over men; but over themselves.

In the same strain have I heard men argue against instructing the poor; for many are the forms that aristocracy assumes. "Teach them to read and write," say they, "and you take them out of the station assigned them by nature." An eloquent Frenchman has answered them, I will borrow his sentiments. But they know not, when they make man a brute, that they may expect every instant to see him transformed into a ferocious beast. Without knowledge there can be no morality!

Ignorance is a frail base for virtue! Yet, that it is the condition for which woman was organized, has been insisted upon by the writers who have most vehemently argued in favour of the superiority of man; a superiority not in degree, but essence; though, to soften the argument, they have laboured to prove, with chivalrous generosity, that the sexes ought not to be compared; man was made to reason, woman to feel: and that together, flesh and spirit, they make the most perfect whole, by blending happily reason and sensibility into one character. . . .

. . . Gracious Creator of the whole human race! hast thou created such a being as woman, who can trace thy wisdom in thy works, and feel that thou alone art by thy nature exalted above her,— for no better purpose? Can she believe that she was only made to submit to man, her equal, a being, who, like her, was sent into the world to acquire virtue? Can she consent to be occupied merely to please him; merely to adorn the earth, when her soul is capable of rising to thee? And can she rest supinely dependent on man for reason, when she ought to mount with him the arduous steeps of knowledge?

Yet, if love be the supreme good, let women be only educated to inspire it, and let every charm be polished to intoxicate the senses; but, if they be moral beings, let them have a chance to become intelligent; and let love to man be only a part of that glowing flame of universal love, which, after encircling humanity, mounts in grateful incense to God.

*In 1855 when Lucy Stone delivered the following
extemporaneous speech before a national women's rights
convention, the doors to most educational institutions and
professions were closed to women. Oberlin College had
become the first coeducational college in the United States
when it opened its doors to women in 1837. But Lucy Stone
was not among those first women graduates. Because her
father did not approve of a college education for women,
Stone, unlike her more fortunate brothers, had to earn her
own way, and it was not until she was twenty-five that she
was able to launch her lifelong dream—to "secure a
profession worthy an immortal being." These experiences
impelled Stone to seek a career as public speaker. "I expect
to plead not only for the slave only," she wrote, "but for
suffering humanity everywhere. Especially do I mean to
labor for the elevation of my sex."*

DISAPPOINTMENT IS THE LOT OF WOMEN

Lucy Stone (1818–1893)

The last speaker alluded to this movement as being that of a few disappointed women. From the first years to which my memory stretches, I have been a disappointed woman. When, with my brothers, I reached forth after the sources of knowledge, I was reproved with "It isn't fit for you; it doesn't belong to women." Then there was but one college in the world where women were admitted, and that was in Brazil. I would have found my way there, but by the time I was prepared to go, one was opened in the young State of Ohio—the first in the United States where women and negroes could enjoy opportunities with white men. I was disappointed when I came to seek a profession worthy an immortal being—every employment was closed to me, except those of the teacher, the seamstress, and the housekeeper. In education, in marriage, in religion, in everything, disappointment is the lot of woman. It shall be the business of my life to deepen this disappointment in every woman's heart until she bows down to it no longer. I wish that women, instead of being walking show-cases, instead of begging of their fathers and brothers the latest and gayest new bonnet, would ask of them their rights.

The question of Woman's Rights is a practical one. The notion has prevailed that it was only an ephemeral idea; that it was but women claiming the right to smoke cigars in the streets, and to frequent bar-rooms. Others have supposed it a question of comparative intellect; others still, of sphere. Too much has already been said and written about woman's sphere. Trace all the doctrines to their source and they will be found to have no basis except in the usages and prejudices of the age. This is seen in the fact that what is tolerated in woman in one country is not tolerated in another. In this country women may hold prayer-meetings, etc., but in Mohammedan countries it is written upon their mosques, "Women and dogs, and other impure animals, are not permitted to enter." Wendell Phillips says, "The best and greatest thing one is capable of doing, that is his sphere." I have confidence in the Father to believe that when He gives us the capacity to do anything He does not make a blunder. Leave women, then, to find their sphere. And do not tell us before we are born even, that our province is to cook dinners, darn stockings, and sew on buttons. We are told woman has all the rights she wants; and even women, I am ashamed to say, tell us so. They mistake the politeness of men for rights—seats while men stand in this hall to-night, and their adulations; but these are mere courtesies. We want rights. The flour-merchant, the housebuilder, and the postman charge us no less on account of our sex; but when we endeavor to earn money to pay all these, then, indeed we find the difference. Man, if he have energy, may hew out for himself a path where no mortal has ever trod, held back by nothing but what is in himself; the world is all before him, where to choose; and we are glad for you, brothers, men, that it is so. But the same society that drives forth the young man, keeps woman at home—a dependent—working little cats on worsted, and little dogs on punctured paper; but if she goes heartily and bravely to give herself to some worthy purpose, she is out of her sphere and she loses caste. Women working in tailor-shops are paid one-third as much as men. Some one in Philadelphia has stated that women make fine shirts for twelve and a half cents apiece; that no woman can make more than nine a week, and the sum thus earned, after deducting rent, fuel, etc., leaves her just three and a half cents a day for bread. Is it a wonder that women are driven to prostitution? Female teachers in New York are paid fifty dollars a year, and for every such situation there are five hundred applicants. I know not what you believe of God, but I believe He gave yearnings and longings to be filled, and that He did not mean all our time should be devoted to feeding and clothing the body. The present condition of woman causes a horrible perversion of the marriage relation. It is asked of a lady, "Has she married well?" "Oh yes, her husband is rich." Woman must marry for a home, and you men are the sufferers by this; for a woman who loathes you may marry you because you have the means to get money which she can not have. But when woman can enter the lists with you and make money for herself, she will marry you only for deep and earnest affection.

Sarah Grimké and her younger sister, Angelina, were born into a prosperous South Carolina slave-owning family. First Sarah and then Angelina left the South to become the first women abolitionists trained for lecture tours under the sponsorship of the American Anti-Slavery Society. It was Sarah who wrote and lectured more frequently on the issue of women's rights, while Angelina attacked the institution of slavery and the oppression of women, and both wrote slavery and the oppression of women and both wrote extensively on equality of the sexes. In the following letter from her collection printed in 1838, Sarah Grimké measures the costs of the enslavement of women—both black and white—and concludes that woman as an equal is "unspeakably more valuable" than woman as an inferior.

THE BONDS OF WOMANHOOD

Sarah Grimké (1792–1873)

FROM *Letters on the Equality of the Sexes and the Condition of Woman*

During the early part of my life, my lot was cast among the butterflies of the *fashionable* world; and of this class of women, I am constrained to say, both from experience and observation, that their education is miserably deficient; that they are taught to regard marriage as the one thing needful, the only avenue to distinction; hence to attract the notice and win the attentions of men, by their external charms, is the chief business of fashionable girls. They seldom think that men will be allured by intellectual acquirements, because they find, that where any mental superiority exists, a woman is generally shunned and regarded as stepping out of her "appropriate sphere," which, in their view, is to dress, to dance, to set out to the best possible advantage her person, to read the novels which inundate the press, and which do more to destroy her character as a rational creature, than any thing else. . . .

There is another and much more numerous class in this country, who are withdrawn by education or circumstances from the circle of fashionable amusements, but who are brought up with the dangerous and absurd idea, that *marriage* is a kind of preferment; and that to be able to keep their husband's house, and render his situation comfortable, is the end of her being. Much that she does and says and thinks is done in reference to this situation; and to be married is too often held up to the view of girls as the sine qua non of human happiness and human existence. For this purpose more than for any other, I verily believe the majority of girls are trained. This is demonstrated by the imperfect education which is bestowed upon them, and the little pains taken to cultivate their minds, after they leave school, by the little time allowed them for reading, and by the idea being constantly inculcated, that although all household concerns should be attended to with scrupulous punctuality at particular seasons, the improvement of their intellectual capacities is only a secondary consideration, and may serve as an occupation to fill up the odds and ends of time. . . .

There is another class of women in this country, to whom I cannot refer, without feelings of the deepest shame and sorrow. I allude to our female slaves. Our southern cities are whelmed beneath a tide of pollution; the virtue of female slaves is wholly at the mercy of irresponsible tyrants, and woman are bought and sold in our slave markets, to gratify the brutal lust of those who bear the name of Christians. In our slave States, if amid all her degradation and ignorance, a woman desires to preserve her virtue unsullied, she is either bribed or whipped into compliance, or if she dares resist her seducer, her life by the laws of some of the slave States may be, and has actually been sacrificed to the fury of disappointed passion. . . .

"To the female character among our black population, we cannot allude but with feelings of the bitterest shame. A similar condition of moral pollution and utter disregard of a pure and virtuous reputation, is to be found *only without the pale of Christendom*. That such a state of society should exist in a Christian nation, claiming to be the most enlightened upon earth, without calling forth any *particular attention* to its existence, though ever before our eyes and *in our families*, is a moral phenomenon at once unaccountable and disgraceful."[1] Nor does the colored woman suffer alone: the moral purity of the white woman is deeply contaminated. In the daily habit of seeing the virtue of her enslaved sister sacrificed without hesitancy or remorse, she looks upon the crimes of seduction and illicit intercourse without horror, and although not personally involved in the guilt, she loses that value for innocence in her own, as well as the other sex, which is one of the strongest safeguards to virtue. She lives in habitual intercourse with men, whom she knows to be polluted by licentiousness, and often is she compelled to witness in her own domestic circle, those disgusting and heart-sickening jealousies and strifes which disgraced and distracted the family of Abraham. In addition to all this, the female slaves suffer every species of degra-

1. From the Circular of the Kentucky Union.

dation and cruelty, which the most wanton barbarity can inflict; they are indecently divested of their clothing, sometimes tied up and severely whipped, sometimes prostrated on the earth, while their naked bodies are torn by the scorpion lash.

> *"The whip on WOMAN'S shrinking flesh!*
> *Our soil yet reddening with the stains*
> *Caught from her scourging warm and fresh."*

Can any American woman look at these scenes of shocking licentiousness and cruelty, and fold her hands in apathy and say, "I have nothing to do with slavery"? *She cannot and be guiltless.*

I cannot close this letter, without saying a few words on the benefits to be derived by men, as well as women, from the opinions I advocate relative to the equality of the sexes. Many women are now supported, in idleness and extravagance, by the industry of their husbands, fathers, or brothers, who are compelled to toil out their existence, at the counting house, or in the printing office, or some other laborious occupation, while the wife and daughters and sisters take no part in the support of the family, and appear to think that their sole business is to spend the hard bought earnings of their male friends. I deeply regret such a state of things, because I believe that if women felt their responsibility, for the support of themselves, or their families it would add strength and dignity to their characters, and teach them more true sympathy for their husbands, than is now generally manifested,—a sympathy which would be exhibited by actions as well as words. Our brethren may reject my doctrine, because it runs counter to common opinions, and because it wounds their pride; but I believe they would be "partakers of the benefit" resulting from the Equality of the Sexes, and would find that woman, as their equal, was unspeakably more valuable than woman as their inferior, both as a moral and an intellectual being.

Thine in the bonds of womanhood.

One of the most important documents in the history of nineteenth-century feminism is the "Declaration of Sentiments and Resolutions" adopted on July 20, 1848, at Seneca Falls, New York, by the first women's rights convention. The response of the press was swift and unequivocal. The document was denounced, Stanton writes, in the parlor, the press, and the pulpit. Many of the one hundred brave signers of the "Declaration" withdrew their names in response to the torrent of ridicule heaped upon it. But the newly launched woman's rights movement would not be deterred. A long series of women's rights conventions held in New York, Ohio, Indiana, Massachusetts, and Pennsylvania would attest to the movement's staying power.

DECLARATION OF SENTIMENTS AND RESOLUTIONS

Seneca Falls Woman's Rights Convention

When, in the course of human events, it becomes necessary for one portion of the family of man to assume among the people of the earth a position different from that which they have hitherto occupied, but one to which the laws of nature and of nature's God entitle them, a decent respect to the opinions of mankind requires that they should declare the causes that impel them to such a course.

We hold these truths to be self-evident: that all men and women are created equal; that they are endowed by their Creator with certain inalienable rights; that among these are life, liberty, and the pursuit of happiness; that to secure these rights governments are instituted, deriving their just powers from the consent of the governed. Whenever any form of government becomes destructive of these ends, it is the right of those who suffer from it to refuse allegiance to it, and to insist upon the institution of a new government, laying its foundation on such principles, and organizing its powers in such form, as to them shall seem most likely to effect their safety and happiness. Prudence, indeed, will dictate that governments long established should not be changed for light and transient causes; and accordingly all experience hath shown that mankind are more disposed to suffer, while evils are sufferable, than to right themselves by abolishing the forms to which they were accustomed. But when a long train of abuses and usurpations, pursuing invariably the same object evinces a design to reduce them under absolute despotism, it is their duty to throw off such government, and to provide new guards for their future security. Such has been the patient sufferance of the women under this government, and such is now the necessity which constrains them to demand the equal station to which they are entitled.

The history of mankind is a history of repeated injuries and usurpations on the part of man toward woman, having in direct object the establishment of an absolute tyranny over her. To prove this, let facts be submitted to a candid world.

He has never permitted her to exercise her inalienable right to the elective franchise.

He has compelled her to submit to laws, in the formation of which she had no voice.

He has withheld from her rights which are given to the most ignorant and degraded men—both natives and foreigners.

Having deprived her of this first right of a citizen, the elective franchise, thereby leaving her without representation in the halls of legislation, he has oppressed her on all sides.

He has made her, if married, in the eye of the law, civilly dead.

He has taken from her all right in property, even to the wages she earns.

He has made her, morally, an irresponsible being, as she can commit many crimes with impunity, provided they be done in the presence of her husband. In the covenant of marriage, she is compelled to promise obedience to her husband, he becoming, to all intents and purposes, her master—the law giving him power to deprive her of her liberty, and to administer chastisement.

He has so framed the laws of divorce, as to what shall be the proper causes, and in case of separation, to whom the guardianship of the children shall be given, as to be wholly regardless of the happiness of women—the law, in all cases, going upon a false supposition of the supremacy of man, and giving all power into his hands.

After depriving her of all rights as a married woman, if single, and the owner of property, he has taxed her to support a government which recognizes her only when her property can be made profitable to it.

He has monopolized nearly all the profitable employments, and from those she is permitted to follow, she receives but a scanty remuneration. He closes against her all the avenues to wealth and distinction which he considers most honorable to himself. As a teacher of theology, medicine, or law, she is not known.

He has denied her the facilities for obtaining a thorough education, all colleges being closed against her.

He allows her in Church, as well as State, but a subordinate position, claiming Apostolic authority for her exclusion from the ministry, and with some exceptions, from any public participation in the affairs of the Church.

He has created a false public sentiment by giving to the world a different code of morals for men and women, by which moral delinquencies which exclude women from society, are not only tolerated, but deemed of little account in man.

He has usurped the prerogative of Jehovah himself, claiming it as his right to assign for her a sphere of action, when that belongs to her conscience and to her God.

He has endeavored, in every way that he could, to destroy her confidence in her own powers, to lessen her self-respect, and to make her willing to lead a dependent and abject life.

Now, in view of this entire disfranchisement of one-half the people of this country, their social and religious degradation—in view of the unjust laws above mentioned, and because women do feel themselves aggrieved, oppressed, and fraudulently deprived of their most sacred rights, we insist that they have immediate admission to all the rights and privileges which belong to them as citizens of the United States.

In entering upon the great work before us, we anticipate no small amount of misconception, misrepresentation, and ridicule; but we shall use every instrumentality within our power to effect our object. We shall employ agents, circulate tracts, petition the State and National legislatures, and endeavor to enlist the pulpit and the press in our behalf. We hope this Convention will be followed by a series of Conventions embracing every part of the country.

The following resolutions were discussed by Lucretia Mott, Thomas and Mary Ann McClintock, Amy Post, Catharine A. F. Stebbins, and others, and were adopted:

WHEREAS, The great precept of nature is conceded to be, that "man shall pursue his own true and substantial happiness." Blackstone in his Commentaries remarks, that this law of Nature being coeval with mankind, and dictated by God himself, is of course superior in obligation to any other. It is binding over all the globe, in all countries and at all times; no human laws are of any validity if contrary to this, and such of them as are valid, derive all their force, and all their validity, and all their authority, mediately and immediately, from this original; therefore,

Resolved, That such laws as conflict, in any way, with the true and substantial happiness of woman, are contrary to the great precept of nature and of no validity, for this is "superior in obligation to any other."

Resolved, That all laws which prevent woman from occupying such a station in society as her conscience shall dictate, or which place her in a position inferior to that of man, are contrary to the great precept of nature, and therefore of no force or authority.

Resolved, That woman is man's equal—was intended to be so by the Creator, and the highest good of the race demands that she should be recognized as such.

Resolved, That the women of this country ought to be enlightened in regard to the laws under which they live, that they may no longer publish their degradation by declaring themselves satisfied with their present position, nor their ignorance, by asserting that they have all the rights they want.

Resolved, That inasmuch as man, while claiming for himself intellectual superiority, does accord to woman moral superiority, it is pre-eminently his duty to encourage her to speak and teach, as she has an opportunity, in all religious assemblies.

Resolved, That the same amount of virtue, delicacy, and refinement of behavior that is required of woman in the social state, should also be required of man and the same transgressions should be visited with equal severity on both man and woman.

Resolved, That the objection of indelicacy and impropriety, which is so often brought against woman when she addresses a public audience, comes with a very ill-grace from those who encourage, by their attendance, her appearance on the stage, in the concert, or in feats of the circus.

Resolved, That woman has too long rested satisfied in the circumscribed limits which corrupt customs and a perverted application of the Scriptures have marked out for her, and that it is time she should move in the enlarged sphere which her great Creator has assigned her.

Resolved, That it is the duty of the women of this country to secure to themselves their sacred right to the elective franchise.

Resolved, That the equality of human rights results necessarily from the fact of the identity of the race in capabilities and responsibilities.

Resolved, therefore, That, being invested by the Creator with the same capabilities, and the same consciousness of responsibility for their exercise, it is demonstrably the right and duty of woman, equally with man, to promote every righteous cause by every righteous means; and especially in regard to the great subjects of morals and religion, it is self-evidently her right to participate with her brother in teaching them, both in private and in public, by writing and by speaking, by any instrumentalities proper to be used, and in any assemblies proper to be held; and this being a self-evident truth growing out of the divinely implanted principles of human nature, any custom or authority adverse to it, whether modern or wearing the hoary sanction of antiquity, is to be regarded as a self-evident falsehood, and at war with mankind.

At the last session Lucretia Mott offered and spoke to the following resolution:

Resolved, That the speedy success of our cause depends upon the zealous and untiring efforts of both men and women, for the overthrow of the monopoly of the pulpit, and for the securing to woman an equal participation with men in the various trades, professions, and commerce. . . .

The immediate postwar period brought an end to the many years of close cooperation between the feminist and abolitionist movements as those in the center of Reconstruction politics disengaged themselves from the feminist platform, proclaiming "the hour of the Negro." The Fourteenth Amendment to the Constitution, proposed to Congress in 1865, sought the enfranchisement of black men but not of women. Moreover, the amendment introduced the word "male" to the Constitution for the first time, making explicit a distinction that had before only been implied. Feminists felt justifiably outraged by their former allies' betrayal and insisted upon the reinstatement of their claim to citizenship. But in the ensuing clash between the abolitionists and the feminists, little real concern was shown for the black woman. In a speech delivered in 1867, Sojourner Truth demonstrates her commitment to the cause of suffering humanity, whether black or white.

KEEPING THE THING GOING WHILE THINGS ARE STIRRING

Sojourner Truth (1797?–1883)

I come from another field—the country of the slave. They have got their liberty—so much good luck to have slavery partly destroyed; not entirely. I want it root and branch destroyed. Then we will all be free indeed. I feel that if I have to answer for the deeds done in my body just as much as a man, I have a right to have just as much as a man. There is a great stir about colored men getting their rights, but not a word about the colored women; and if colored men get their rights, and not colored women theirs, you see the colored men will be masters over the women, and it will be just as bad as it was before. So I am for keeping the thing going while things are stirring; because if we wait till it is still, it will take a great while to get it going again. White women are a great deal smarter, and know more than colored women, while colored women do not know scarcely anything. They go out washing, which is about as high as a colored woman gets, and their men go about idle, strutting up and down; and when the women come home, they ask for their money and take it all, and then scold because there is no food. I want you to consider on that, chil'n. I call you chil'n; you are somebody's chil'n, and I am old enough to be mother of all that is here. I want women to have their rights. In the courts women have no right, no voice; nobody speaks for them. I wish woman to have her voice there among the pettifoggers. If it is not a fit place for women, it is unfit for men to be there.

I am above eighty years old; it is about time for me to be going. I have been forty years a slave and forty years free, and would be here forty years more to have equal rights for all. I suppose I am kept here because something remains for me to do; I suppose I am yet to help to break the chain. I have done a great deal of work; as much as a man, but did not get so much pay. I used to work in the field and bind grain, keeping up with the cradler; but men doing no more, got twice as much pay; so with the German women. They work in the field and do as much work, but do not get the pay. We do as much, we eat as much, we want as much. I suppose I am about the only colored woman that goes about to speak for the rights of the colored women. I want to keep the thing stirring, now that the ice is cracked. What we want is a little money. You men know that you get as much again as women when you write, or for what you do. When we get our rights we shall not have to come to you for money, for then we shall have money enough in our own pockets; and may be you will ask us for money. But help us now until we get it. It is a good consolation to know that when we have got this battle once fought we shall not be coming to you any more. You have been having our rights so long, that you think, like a slave-holder, that you own us. I know that it is hard for one who has held the reins for so long to give up; it cuts like a knife. It will feel all the better when it closes up again. I have been in Washington about three years, seeing about these colored people. Now colored men have the right to vote. There ought to be equal rights now more than ever, since colored people have got their freedom. I am going to talk several times while I am here; so now I will do a little singing. I have not heard any singing since I came here.

Susan B. Anthony, an indefatigable organizer and lecturer, was deeply concerned about the lack of interest shown toward the suffrage movement by American working women. A favorite speech, "Woman Wants Bread, Not the Ballot!" delivered frequently between 1880 and 1890, was never committed whole to paper but has been reconstructed from scattered notes and newspaper reports. Printed in part below, the speech is a testament to the understanding of leaders of the women's movement of the profound economic and political causes and effects of women's disenfranchisement and their poverty. Justice for women as well as men, Anthony finds, can be secured only when women are granted power over their own labor, for a degraded class will always be used by capitalists to oppress all.

WOMAN WANTS BREAD, NOT THE BALLOT!

Susan B. Anthony (1820–1906)

Wherever, on the face of the globe or on the page of history, you show me a disfranchised class, I will show you a degraded class of labor. Disfranchisement means inability to make, shape or control one's own circumstances. The disfranchised must always do the work, accept the wages, occupy the position the enfranchised assign to them. The disfranchised are in the position of the pauper. You remember the old adage, "Beggars must not be choosers"; they must take what they can get or nothing! That is exactly the position of women in the world of work today; they can not choose. If they could, do you for a moment believe they would take the subordinate places and the inferior pay? Nor is it a "new thing under the sun" for the disfranchised, the inferior classes weighed down with wrongs, to declare they "do not want to vote." The rank and file are not philosophers, they are not educated to think for themselves, but simply to accept unquestioned, whatever comes. . . .

It is said women do not need the ballot for their protection because they are supported by men. Statistics show that there are 3,000,000 women in this nation supporting themselves. In the crowded cities of the East they are compelled to work in shops, stores and factories for the merest pittance. In New York alone, there are over 50,000 of these women receiving less than fifty cents a day. Women wage-earners in different occupations have organized themselves into trades unions, from time to time, and made their strikes to get justice at the hands of their employers just as men have done, but I have yet to learn of a successful strike of any body of women. The best organized one I ever knew was that of the collar laundry women of the city of Troy, New York, the great emporium for the manufacture of shirts, collars and cuffs. They formed a trades union of several hundred members and demanded an increase of wages. It was refused. So one May morning in 1867, each woman threw down her scissors and her needle, her starch-pan and flat-iron, and for three long months not one returned to the factories. At the end of that time they were literally starved out, and the majority of them were compelled to go back, but not at their old wages, for their employers cut them down to even a lower figure.

In the winter following I met the president of this union, a bright young Irish girl, and asked her, "Do you not think if you had been 500 carpenters or 500 masons, you would have succeeded?" "Certainly," she said, and then she told me of 200 bricklayers who had the year before been on strike and gained every point with their employers. "What could have made the difference? Their 200 were but a fraction of that trade, while your 500 absolutely controlled yours." Finally she said, "It was because the editors ridiculed and denounced us." "Did they ridicule and denounce the bricklayers?" "No." "What did they say about you?" "Why, that our wages were good enough now, better than those of any other working-women except teachers; and if we weren't satisfied, we had better go and get married." "What then do you think made this difference?" After studying over the question awhile she concluded, "It must have been because our employers bribed the editors." "Couldn't the employers of the bricklayers have bribed the editors." She had never thought of that. Most people never do think; they see one thing totally unlike another, but the person who stops to inquire into the cause that produces the one or the other is the exception. So this young Irish girl was simply not an exception, but followed the general rule of people, whether men or women; she hadn't thought. In the case of the bricklayers, no editor, either Democrat or Republican, would have accepted the proffer of a bribe, because he would have known that if he denounced or ridiculed those men, not only they but all the trades union men of the city at the next election would vote solidly against the nominees advocated by that editor. If those collar laundry women had been voters, they would have held, in that little city of Troy, the "balance of political power" and the editor or the politician who ignored or insulted them would have turned that balance over to the opposing party. . . .

Governments can not afford to ignore the rights of those holding the ballot, who make and unmake every law and law-maker. It is not because the members of Congress are tyrants that women receive only half pay and are admitted only to inferior positions in the departments. It is simply in obedience to a law of political economy which makes it impossible for a government to do as much for the disfranchised as for the enfranchised. Women are no exception to the general rule. As disfranchisement always has degraded men, socially, morally and industrially, so today it is disfranchisement that degrades women in the same spheres.

Again men say it is not votes, but the law of supply and demand which regulates wages. The law of gravity is that water shall run down hill, but when men build a dam across the stream, the force of gravity is stopped and the water held back. The law of supply and demand regulates free and enfranchised labor, but disfranchisement estops its operation. What we ask is the removal of the dam, that women, like men, may reap the benefit of the law. Did the law of supply and demand regulate work and wages in the olden days of slavery? This law can no more reach the disfranchised than it did the enslaved. There is scarcely a place where a woman can earn a single dollar without a man's consent. . . .

Now that as a result of the agitation for equality of chances, and through the invention of machinery, there has come a great revolution in the world of economics, so that wherever a man may go to earn an honest dollar a woman may go also, there is no escape from the conclusion that she must be clothed with equal power to protect herself. That power is the ballot, the symbol of freedom and equality, without which no citizen is sure of keeping even that which he hath, much less of getting that which he hath not. Women are today the peers of men in education, in the arts and sciences, in the industries and professions, and there is no escape from the conclusion that the next step must be to make them the peers of men in the government—city, State, and national—to give them an equal voice in the framing, interpreting and administering of the codes and constitutions. . . .

*"Mother" Mary Harris Jones was an Irish-born daughter
of American immigrants. In her autobiography she describes
the tragedy that struck her in the loss of her husband and
four young children during a yellow fever epidemic. Her
response to that staggering loss was to obtain a permit to
nurse the remaining victims of the disease. That response to
pain of others while banishing on her own part both self-pity
and illusion characterized the long years of life that
remained to her. Her struggle took place within the
American labor movement and on behalf of a working class
whom she saw as those who "must bear the cross for others'
sins." Her insistence upon an economic and class analysis
caused her to disappoint suffragists who hoped for her
support of the women's movement. In the selection from her
autobiography that follows, Jones upbraids a group of
suffragists for failing to see the context of human rights
within which women's rights must rest.*

YOU DON'T NEED A VOTE
TO RAISE HELL!

Mary Harris Jones

Five hundred women got up a dinner and asked me to speak. Most of
the women were crazy about women suffrage. They thought that
Kingdom-come would follow the enfranchisement of women.

"You must stand for free speech in the streets," I told them.

"How can we," piped a woman, "when we haven't a vote!"

"I have never had a vote," said I, "and I have raised hell all
over this country! You don't need a vote to raise hell! You need convictions and a voice!"

Some one meowed, "You're an anti!"

"I am not an anti to anything which will bring freedom to my
class," said I. "But I am going to be honest with you sincere women
who are working for votes for women. The women of Colorado have
had the vote for two generations and the working men and women
are in slavery. The state is in slavery, vassal to the Colorado Iron and
Fuel Company and its subsidiary interests. A man who was present
at a meeting of mine owners told me that when the trouble started in
the mines, one operator proposed that women be disfranchised because here and there some woman had raised her voice in behalf of
the miners. Another operator jumped to his feet and shouted, 'For

355

God's sake! What are you talking about! If it had not been for the women's vote the miners would have beaten us long ago!'"

Some of the women gasped with horror. One or two left the room. I told the women I did not believe in women's rights nor in men's rights but in human rights. "No matter what your fight," I said, "don't be ladylike! God Almighty made women and the Rockefeller gang of thieves made the ladies. I have just fought through sixteen months of bitter warfare in Colorado. I have been up against armed mercenaries but this old woman, without a vote, and with nothing but a hatpin has scared them.

"Organized labor should organize its women along industrial lines. Politics is only the servant of industry. The plutocrats have organized their women. They keep them busy with suffrage and prohibition and charity."

In 1876, well before women had won the vote, the leaders of the feminist movement began writing their History of Woman Suffrage. *The collection of papers, speeches, documents, and records, ultimately comprising six volumes and containing nearly 4000 pages, would serve not only as a record for future generations but as a practical sourcebook for a women's movement already, by the 1880s, split into factions over questions of ideology and tactics. The following introduction to that ambitious work, which provides a summation of and response to the most frequently voiced arguments against the suffrage for women, might have been written for use of the suffragists who, for the next forty years, would engage in a relentless campaign to earn the vote.*

WOMAN'S NEED OF THE BALLOT

Elizabeth Cady Stanton (1815–1902)
Susan B. Anthony (1820–1906)
Matilda Joselyn Gage (1826–1898)

FROM *History of Woman Suffrage*

It requires philosophy and heroism to rise above the opinion of the wise men of all nations and races, that to be *unknown*, is the highest testimonial woman can have to her virtue, delicacy and refinement.

A certain odium has ever rested on those who have risen above the conventional level and sought new spheres for thought and action, and especially on the few who demand complete equality in political rights. The leaders in this movement have been women of superior mental and physical organization, of good social standing and education, remarkable alike for their domestic virtues, knowledge of public affairs, and rare executive ability; good speakers and writers, inspiring and conducting the genuine reforms of the day; everywhere exerting themselves to promote the best interests of society; yet they have been uniformly ridiculed, misrepresented, and denounced in public and private by all classes of society. . . .

While the laws affecting woman's civil rights have been greatly improved during the past thirty years, the political demand has made but a questionable progress, though it must be counted as the chief influence in modifying the laws. The selfishness of man was readily enlisted in securing woman's civil rights, while the same element in his character antagonized her demand for political equality.

Fathers who had estates to bequeath to their daughters could see the advantage of securing to woman certain property rights that might limit the legal power of profligate husbands.

Husbands in extensive business operations could see the advantage of allowing the wife the right to hold separate property, settled on her in time of prosperity, that might not be seized for his debts. Hence in the several States able men championed these early measures. But political rights, involving in their last results equality everywhere, roused all the antagonism of a dominant power, against the self-assertion of a class hitherto subservient. Men saw that with political equality for woman, they could no longer keep her in social subordination, and "the majority of the male sex," says John Stuart Mill, "can not yet tolerate the idea of living with an equal." The fear of a social revolution thus complicated the discussion. The Church, too, took alarm, knowing that with the freedom and education acquired in becoming a component part of the Government, woman would not only outgrow the power of the priesthood, and religious superstitions, but would also invade the pulpit, interpret the Bible anew from her own stand-point, and claim an equal voice in all ecclesiastical councils. With fierce warnings and denunciations from the pulpit, and false interpretations of Scripture, women have been intimidated and misled, and their religious feelings have been played upon for their more complete subjugation. While the general principles of the Bible are in favor of the most enlarged freedom and equality of the race, isolated texts have been used to block the wheels of progress in all periods; thus bigots have defended capital punishment, intemperance, slavery, polygamy, and the subjection of woman. The creeds of all nations make obedience to man the corner stone of her religious character. Fortunately, however, more liberal minds are now giving us higher and purer expositions of the Scriptures.

As the social and religious objections appeared against the demand for political rights, the discussion became many-sided, contradictory, and as varied as the idiosyncracies of individual character. Some said, "Man is woman's natural protector, and she can safely trust him to make laws for her." She might with fairness reply, as he uniformly robbed her of all property rights to 1848, he can not safely be trusted with her personal rights in 1880, though the fact that he did make some restitution at last, might modify her distrust in the future. However, the calendars of our courts still show that fathers deal unjustly with daughters, husbands with wives, brothers with sisters, and sons with their own mothers. Though woman needs the protection of one man against his whole sex, in pioneer life, in threading her way through a lonely forest, on the highway, or in the streets of the metropolis on a dark night, she sometimes needs, too, the protection of all men against this one. But even if she could be sure, as she is not, of the ever-present, all-protecting power of one strong arm, that would be weak indeed compared with the subtle, all-pervading influence of just and equal laws for all women. Hence woman's need of the ballot, that she may hold in her own right hand the weapon of self-protection and self-defense.

Again it is said: "The women who make the demand are few in number, and their feelings and opinions are abnormal, and therefore of no weight in considering the aggregate judgment on the question." The number is larger than appears on the surface, for the fear of public ridicule, and the loss of private favors from those who shelter, feed, and clothe them, withhold many from declaring their opinions and demanding their rights. The ignorance and indifference of the majority of women, as to their status as citizens of a republic, is not remarkable, for history shows that the masses of all oppressed classes, in the most degraded conditions, have been stolid and apathetic until partial success had crowned the faith and enthusiasm of the few.

The insurrections on Southern plantations were always defeated by the doubt and duplicity of the slaves themselves. That little band of heroes who precipitated the American Revolution in 1776 were so ostracised that they walked the streets with bowed heads, from a sense of loneliness and apprehension. Woman's apathy to the wrongs of her sex, instead of being a plea for her remaining in her present condition, is the strongest argument against it. How completely demoralized by her subjection must she be, who does not feel her personal dignity assailed when all women are ranked in every State Constitution with idiots, lunatics, criminals, and minors; when in the name of Justice, man holds one scale for woman, another for himself; when by the spirit and letter of the laws she is made responsible for crimes committed against her, while the male criminal goes free; when from altars where she worships no woman may preach; when in the courts, where girls of tender age may be arraigned for the crime of infanticide, she may not plead for the most miserable of her sex; when colleges she is taxed to build and endow, deny her the right to share in their advantages; when she finds that which should be her glory—her possible motherhood—treated everywhere by man as a disability and a crime! A woman insensible to such indignities needs some transformation into nobler thought, some purer atmosphere to breathe, some higher stand-point from which to study human rights.

It is said, "the difference between the sexes indicates different spheres." It would be nearer the truth to say the difference indicates different duties in the same sphere, seeing that man and woman were evidently made for each other, and have shown equal capacity in the ordinary range of human duties. In governing nations, leading armies, piloting ships across the sea, rowing life-boats in terrific gales; in art, science, invention, literature, woman has proved herself the complement of man in the world of thought and action. This difference does not compel us to spread our tables with different food for man and woman, nor to provide in our common schools a different course of study for boys and girls. Sex pervades all nature, yet the male and female tree and vine and shrub rejoice in the same sunshine and shade. The earth and air are free to all the fruits and flowers, yet each absorbs what best ensures its growth. But whatever it is, it requires no special watchfulness on our part to see that it is maintained. This plea, when closely analyzed, is generally found to mean woman's inferiority.

The superiority of man, however, does not enter into the demand for suffrage, for in this country all men vote; and as the lower orders of men are not superior, either by nature or grace, to the higher orders of women, they must hold and exercise the right of self-government on some other ground than superiority to women.

Again it is said, "Woman when independent and self-asserting will lose her influence over man." In the happiest conditions in life, men and women will ever be mutually dependent on each other. The complete development of all woman's powers will not make her less capable of steadfast love and friendship, but give her new strength to meet the emergencies of life, to aid those who look to her for counsel and support. Men are uniformly more attentive to women of rank, family, and fortune, who least need their care, than to any other class. We do not see their protecting love generally extending to the helpless and unfortunate ones of earth. Wherever the skilled hands and cultured brain of woman have made the battle of life easier for man, he has readily pardoned her sound judgment and proper self-assertion. But the prejudices and preferences of man should be a secondary consideration, in presence of the individual happiness and freedom of woman. The formation of her character and its influence on the human race, is a larger question than man's personal liking. There is no fear, however, that when a superior order of women shall grace the earth, there will not be an order of men to match them, and influence over such minds will atone for the loss of it elsewhere.

An honest fear is sometimes expressed "that woman would degrade politics, and politics would degrade woman." As the influence of woman has been uniformly elevating in new civilizations, in missionary work in heathen nations, in schools, colleges, literature, and in general society, it is fair to suppose that politics would prove no exception. On the other hand, as the art of government is the most exalted of all sciences, and statesmanship requires the highest order of mind, the ennobling and refining influence of such pursuits must elevate rather than degrade woman. When politics degenerate into bitter persecutions and vulgar court-gossip, they are degrading to man, and his honor, virtue, dignity, and refinement are as valuable to woman as her virtues are to him.

Again, it is said, "Those who make laws must execute them; government needs force behind it,—a woman could not be sheriff or a policeman." She might not fill these offices in the way men do, but she might far more effectively guard the morals of society, and the sanitary conditions of our cities. It might with equal force be said that a woman of culture and artistic taste can not keep house, because she can not wash and iron with her own hands, and clean the range and furnace. At the head of the police, a woman could direct her forces and keep order without ever using a baton or a pistol in her own hands. "The elements of sovereignty," says Blackstone, "are three: wisdom, goodness, and power." Conceding to woman wisdom and goodness, as they are not strictly masculine virtues, and substituting moral power for physical force, we have the necessary elements of government for most of life's emergencies. Women manage families, mixed schools, charitable institutions, large boarding-houses and hotels, farms and steam-engines, drunken and disorderly men and women, and stop street fights, as well as men do. The queens in history compare favorably with the kings.

But, "in the settlement of national difficulties," it is said, "the last resort is war; shall we summon our wives and mothers to the battle-field?" Women have led armies in all ages, have held positions in the army and navy for years in disguise. Some fought, bled, and died on the battle-field in our late war. They performed severe labors in the hospitals and sanitary department. Wisdom would dictate a division of labor in war as well as in peace, assigning each their appropriate department.

Numerous classes of men who enjoy their political rights are exempt from military duty. All men over forty-five, all who suffer mental or physical disability, such as the loss of an eye or a forefinger; clergymen; physicians, Quakers, school-teachers, professors, and presidents of colleges, judges, legislators, congressmen, State prison officials, and all county, State and National officers; fathers, brothers, or sons having certain relatives dependent on them for support,—all of these summed up in every State in the Union make millions of voters thus exempted.

In view of this fact there is no force in the plea, that "if women vote they must fight." Moreover, war is not the normal state of the human family in its higher development, but merely a feature of barbarism lasting on through the transition of the race, from the savage to the scholar. When England and America settled the *Alabama* Claims by the Geneva Arbitration, they pointed the way for the future adjustment of all national difficulties.

Some fear, "If women assume all the duties political equality implies, that the time and attention necessary to the duties of home life will be absorbed in the affairs of State." The act of voting occupies but little time in itself, and the vast majority of women will attend to their family and social affairs to the neglect of the State, just as men do to their individual interests. The virtue of patriotism is subordinate in most souls to individual and family aggrandizement. As to offices, it is not to be supposed that the class of men now elected will resign to women their chances, and if they should to any extent, the necessary number of women to fill the offices would make no apparent change in our social circles. If, for example, the Senate of the United States should be entirely composed of women, but two in each State would be withdrawn from the pursuit of domestic happiness. For many reasons, under all circumstances, a comparatively smaller proportion of women than men would actively engage in politics.

As the power to extend or limit the suffrage rests now wholly in the hands of man, he can commence the experiment with as small a number as he sees fit, by requiring any lawful qualification. Men were admitted on property and educational qualifications in most of the States, at one time, and still are in some—so hard has it been for man to understand the theory of self-government. Three-fourths of the women would be thus disqualified, and the remaining fourth would be too small a minority to precipitate a social revolution or defeat masculine measures in the halls of legislation, even if women were a unit on all questions and invariably voted together, which they would not. In this view, the path of duty is plain for the prompt action of those gentlemen who fear universal suffrage for women, but are willing to grant it on property and educational qualifications. While those who are governed by the law of expediency should give the measure of justice they deem safe, let those who trust the absolute right proclaim the higher principle in government, "equal rights to all."

By the time Olympia Brown delivered the following speech before the 1889 convention of the National American Woman Suffrage Association, women had already obtained many of the rights that feminists had claimed for them at Seneca Falls. In ever increasing numbers, women were graduating from colleges and entering professions formerly closed to them. The feminist movement had no doubt smoothed the way for Brown herself to become a Universalist minister in 1862. The by now conservative suffrage movement, however, had lost its earlier egalitarian vision and had begun to incorporate both racist and nativist arguments into its arsenal of weapons wielded in the fight for the vote.

ON FOREIGN RULE

OLYMPIA BROWN (1835–1926)

In Wisconsin we have by the census of 1880 a population of 910,072 native-born, 405,425 foreign-born. Our last vote cast was 149,463 American, 189,469 foreign; thus you see nearly 1,000,000 native-born people are out-voted and out-governed by less than half their number of foreigners. Is that fair to Americans? Is it just to American men? Will they not, under this influence, in a little while be driven to the wall and obliged to step down and out? When the members of our Legislatures are the greater part foreigners, when they sit in the office of mayor and in all the offices of our city, and rule us with a rod of iron, it is time that American men should inquire if we have any rights that foreigners are bound to respect. . . .

The last census shows, I think, that there are in the United States three times as many American-born women as the whole foreign population, men and women together, so that the votes of women will eventually be the only means of overcoming this foreign influence and maintaining our free institutions. There is no possible safety for our free school, our free church or our republican government, unless women are given the suffrage and that right speedily. . . . The question in every political caucus, in every political convention, is not what great principles shall we announce, but what kind of a document can we draw up that will please the foreigners? . . .

When we remember that the first foot to touch Plymouth Rock was a woman's—that in the first settlement of this country women endured trials and privations and stood bravely at the post of duty, even fighting in the ranks that we might have a republic—and that in our great Western world women came at an early day to make the wilderness blossom as the rose, and rocked their babies' cradles in the log cabins when the Indians' war-whoop was heard on the prairies and the wolves howled around their doors—when we remember that in the last war thousands of women in the Northwest bravely took upon themselves the work of the households and the fields that their husbands and sons might fight the battles of liberty—when we recollect all this, and then are told that loyal women, pioneer women, the descendants of the Pilgrim Fathers, are not even to ask for the right of suffrage lest the Scandinavians should be offended, it is time to rise in indignation and ask, Whose country is this? Who made it? Who have periled their lives for it?

Our American women are property holders and pay large taxes; but the foreigner who has lived only one year in the State, and ten days in the precinct, who does not own a foot of land, may vote away their property in the form of taxes in the most reckless manner, regardless of their interests and their rights. Women are reading and thinking and writing; and yet they are the political inferiors of all the riff-raff of Europe that is poured upon our shores. It is unbearable. There is no language that can express the enormous injustice done to women. . . .

We can not separate subjects and say we will vote on temperance or on school matters, for all these questions are part of government. . . . When women as well as men are voters, the church will get some recognition. I marvel that all ministers are not in favor of woman suffrage, when I consider that their audiences are almost entirely composed of women and that the church to-day is brought into disrepute because it is made up of disfranchised members. The minister would stand a hundred-fold higher than he does now if women had the suffrage. Everybody would want to know what the minister was saying to those women voters.

We are in danger in this country of Catholic domination, not because the Catholics are more numerous than we are, but because the Catholic church is represented at the polls and the Protestant church is not. The foreigners are Catholic—the greater portion of them; the foreigners are men—the greater part of them, and members of the Catholic church, and they work for it and vote for it. The Protestant church is composed of women. Men for the most part do not belong to it; they do not care much for it except as something to interest the women of their household. The consequence is the Protestant church is comparatively unrepresented at the ballot-box.

I urge upon you, women, that you put suffrage first and foremost, before every other consideration upon earth. Make it a religious duty and work for the enfranchisement of your sex, which means the growth and development of noble characters in your children; for you can not educate your children well surrounded by men and women who hold false doctrines of society, of politics, of morals. Leave minor issues, leave your differences of opinion about the Trinity, or the Holy Ghost, or endless misery; about high license and low license; or Dorcas Societies and Chautauqua Circles. Let them all go; they are of no consequence compared with the enfranchisement of women.

The adoption of an ideologically defensive posture by nineteenth-century feminists that we traced in the preceding chapter undermined feminism's essential egalitarian rationale and led, some critics have claimed, to that movement's disintegration and collapse. Other historians of American feminism judge that the achievement of suffrage itself sounded feminism's death knell, the whole movement having been built upon a very "flimsy alliance of widely differing women" that shattered in the absence of a consistent plan to enact that newly won citizenship (Freeman 1975:18). One critic announces in the title of his study of this period "The Rise and Fall of Feminism in America" (O'Neill 1969); another refers to the years between

CHAPTER

7

Feminism: The Second Wave

1920 and 1960 as "forty years in the desert" (Deckard 1975:283); still another writes of "the hope deferred" (Sochen 1974:97). While there is no doubt much truth in such historical commentary, the period between 1920 and 1960 is deserving of yet another glance before final judgment is passed on the fate of feminism during those years.

One must first ask, what was the response to suffrage of those women who had fought with such vigor for the vote? The National American Woman Suffrage Association (NAWSA), reconstituted after 1920 as the League of Women Voters (LWV), with only one-tenth its former membership, claimed unqualified victory. Insisting that they were primarily citizens and not feminists, the League of Women Voters would in the years following pour their energies into such issues as disarmament, child labor, and equal pay and jury service for women. They identified as their central concern not the special interests of women but the general good of the nation. By the end of the 1930s, the LWV would announce that "nearly all discriminations have been removed" (quoted in Chafe 1972:115).

A small, militant wing of the former NAWSA, organized as the National Women's Party (NWP), disagreed with the apparent consensus and proclaimed that women "are still in every way subordinate to men before the law, in the professions, in the church, and in the home" (quoted in Chafe 1972:114). This small cadre of feminists, led by Alice Paul, introduced the Equal Rights Amendment before the U.S. Congress in 1923 in order to translate the freedom won in the suffrage fight into public policy. The ensuing battle over the proposed amendment during the 1920s furnishes an index to the profound differences between the two organizations. The much larger League of Women Voters refused to support the ERA, fearing that the protective legislation for which its members had so recently fought would become unconstitutional. The more radical National Women's Party, viewing protective legislation as the denial of women's economic rights, would remain devoted exclusively to the issue of the ERA during the long years when feminism had ceased to be a political force. The NWP would keep the ERA before the U.S. Congress every year after 1923 until its passage in 1972. The National Women's Party, though in Freeman's words, "keeping a small flame of feminist feeling burning dimly" (1975:64), made few attempts to recruit other women to the cause of the ERA and remained a decidedly fringe organization. Even as late as 1969, Freeman writes, few feminists had ever heard of Alice Paul or the National Women's Party (1975:64).

What, then, happened to the elaborate network of women's organizations that had, during the Progressive period, without benefit of the vote, persuaded state legislatures and the U.S. Congress to enact a wealth of pure food, sanitation, and child labor laws, as well as protective legislation for women? The presuffrage reformers had predicted that an American womanhood, armed with the ballot, would take up the important work of reform and would vote as a bloc to transform the entire political system. But most enfranchised women remained disappointingly indifferent to politics, and if they voted at all, they voted in accordance with the social and economic backgrounds and the wishes of their husbands. The most powerful allies of the former suffrage movement—the Women's Christian Temperance League, the General Federation of Women's Clubs, the Women's Trade Union League—found that suffrage did not increase their political power or their lobbying effectiveness. In fact, both major political parties, after demonstrating an initial willingness to incorporate women's concerns into their programs, simply ignored them, having found that women did not vote in a bloc or in significant numbers. In addition, the Progressive era was coming to a close, and as it ebbed, the political climate became less responsive to reform in general. The enormous influx of more than 30 million immigrants to America's shores had crested in about 1910; therefore, while the slums remained, the problems of the immigrants who had begun the process of assimilation seemed less immediate than in the preceding decades. Nor did the situation of working women seem so pressing. Although women remained clustered in low-paying positions in the work force, working conditions had improved considerably by the end of the Progressive period.

Perhaps the most important factor contributing to the waning of feminism after 1920 was the absence of a clear vision of equality and a consistent plan of action. As we saw in the preceding chapter, most feminists by the end of the century accepted fully the notion of woman's special sphere, having lost the earlier vision of mid-century feminists, who understood better the nature of woman's institutional and ideological oppression. Women's organizations had found that their most effective political tool in the business of reform was the old cult of motherhood. Embracing the notion of an "enlarged motherhood," they had been remarkably successful in claiming for women a legitimate corner in the marketplace. But it was that same notion of an enlarged motherhood that limited women's political effectiveness after 1920. That notion, according to Mary Ryan, would enable women to continue to serve as "social housekeepers" but would keep them firmly outside the sources of political power (1978:245–48). In addition, few women of the younger generation exhibited the spirit of Charlotte Perkins Gilman or the crusading zeal of Jane Addams. By the early 1920s, then, the woman's brigade was beginning to turn from political to private concerns.

The retreat from feminist issues that had begun well before the passage of the Nineteenth Amendment was hastened by the arrival of the "new woman," the sexually liberated flapper of the 1920s whose behavior shocked remaining nineteenth-century social purists. But despite her blatant disregard for social conventions, her advent did not herald real equality for women. The increase in sexual freedom that she advocated did not disturb conventional notions about sex roles; she could smoke, drink, raise her skirts, and even have extra-marital affairs and still remain committed to traditional marriage and motherhood. Self-absorbed and intent upon sexual gratification, she was more attractive to the new consumer culture that in part created her (as we saw in Chapter 5) than was the settlement house worker or the suffragist of the preceding decade. "The genius of the packagers of this image," June Sochen writes, "was their ability to combine it with that of the respectable young wife and mother. The flapper was naughty but not evil; she was a flirt but not a whore" (1974:103).

The flapper was but one image of womanhood in the 1920s.

While it is true that crusading zeal had waned with the demise of Progressivism and the achievement of the vote, work continued on a number of important fronts. Through such organizations as the National Council of Women and the Women's International League for Peace and Freedom, as well as the League of Women Voters and the National Women's Party, women continued to voice their concerns and to participate, in however limited a manner, in the political process. Moreover, it is unlikely that the daughters of the reformers and suffragists were fundamentally different from their mothers. As Alice Rossi points out, there is a remarkable consistency from generation to generation in values and motivations, in spite of differences of style. The "public heroines of one generation," Rossi speculates, may be "the private heroines of the next." The generation that followed the suffragists "may have been consolidating feminist ideas into the private stuff of their lives and seeking new outlets for the expression of the values that prompted their mothers' public behavior" (1974:615–16). Strong-minded descendants of the suffragists from 1920 to 1960 were quietly channeling their energies into education and employment, options that were not, after all, readily available to early feminists.

The promise of economic equality did, for a time, appear to be within women's grasp as they continued after 1920 to make inroads in the work force and the professions. Women workers increased their numbers by 26 percent during the 1920s and could be found in 437 different job classifications. They "plastered walls, climbed steeples, preached in churches, trapped furs, managed offices and hauled freight" (Chafe 1972:49–50). But it was the young woman who had reached college age during the last years of the suffrage movement on whom the feminists' real hopes for equality were pinned. Indeed, all the signs in the 1920s were hopeful. The enrollment of women in public colleges and universities increased 1000 percent and in private institutions 482 percent in this period. College graduates

... became editors in publishing houses, sold real estate, practiced pharmacology, and took up important positions in banks and department stores. They formed their own business and professional associations, and published national journals focusing on their collective advancement. (Chafe 1972:90)

Nonetheless, the goal of economic equality would remain elusive. As we observed, women continued to be clustered primarily in traditional female jobs. Although the number of women professionals was growing, available professional work consisted largely of teaching and nursing. Hope for change over time of this situation dimmed during the ensuing years as the economic crisis of the Great Depression came to "discredit, for many people, any 'special' group's demand for more rights" (Kraditor 1968:291). In fact, many women were forced out of the marketplace during the depression to make room for the growing numbers of unemployed men. College and university enrollments of women decreased. Quotas for admissions of women to professional schools were established. Those women who were able to complete professional degrees would be faced with the problem of what to do with those degrees. Women doctors, for example, could not easily secure internships. In response to such retrenchment policies, the leading women's colleges adjusted their curricula to prepare their graduates for the chief vocations open to them—marriage, maternity, and homemaking. As Ehrenreich and English observe, this period spawned a new cadre of professional homemaking experts who "would organize to elevate their area of expertise beyond the stage of recipes and household hints and onto the higher ground of scientific professionalism" (1979:151). Women entering the new field of home economics would be taught to view homemaking as an exact science requiring dedication and skill.

The movement of women out of the marketplace during the depression is but one example of the enormous flexibility required of women in times of crisis. Another example was women's unprecedented movement, described in an earlier chapter, back into the work force during World War II. Of all the changes that enhanced women's economic position, none were so far-reaching as those brought about by the war. A growing need to feed the vast war machine prompted a sudden shift in public policy as female employment became a patriotic necessity. Industries that had earlier refused to hire women because of rigid protective labor legislation now found that they could quickly adjust to a predominately female work force. Accommodations included separate restroom and lounge facilities, new sanitation and safety standards, and mandated rest breaks in the workday. Government subsidies for the establishment of day care centers on factory premises and even hot dinners at cost for their female employees to carry home to their families at the end of the day were provided as inducements to women to leave homes they had been taught to regard as their proper place.

Sadly missing from the rhetoric of the period praising women's contribution to the war effort were feminist arguments about women's equality. Although women were filling positions formerly held by men, they were not perceived as challenging the old myths about women's inferior skills or altering the basic distribution of sex roles. Rather, their work was seen as temporary and therefore of lesser importance than men's work. Nonetheless, the war represented a significant turning point for women, offering them new opportunities to expand their sphere. Underclass women who had always been in the work force were now able to move from low-paying service industries to munitions, aircraft, and auto industries. But the group of women most significantly affected were middle-class women who had been relegated to the home, in particular women over thirty-five, whose primary homemaking duties were completed. By the end of the war, the attitude of Americans toward the issue of working women would shift from outright condemnation to grudging acceptance. Yet, because women failed to perceive the need to establish their right to a place in the work force, it was not difficult to force them back into the home at the end of the national crisis. There was no feminist outcry when all federal support for child care centers was discontinued in 1946. Although the war experience was responsible for the increased acceptance of women in the work force, traditional attitudes about woman's place remained largely unchanged (Chafe 1972:188).

More important, the attitude of women who went to work for the first time during the war was changed significantly by that experience. Many women who, at the beginning of the war, viewed their work as temporary were, at war's end, unhappy about returning home. Within two years after the end of the war, large numbers of women were back at work and had begun to climb to unprecedented levels of employment. And women's return to the work force was eased by conditions of postwar America that conspired to keep them there, whether they wanted to be or not. Spiraling inflation coupled with increasing pressures put upon the family by the new consumer culture made the income of even the middle-class wife a necessity. What made the presence of these women in the work force acceptable, however, was the inviolable notion of woman's sphere. Women could work as long as the home remained their primary concern. Women were not insisting on careers and thereby challenging the existing distribution of sex roles as had the feminists during the nineteenth century. They were perceived as "contributing to home life, not detracting from it" (Chafe 1972:191) by helping husbands with shrinking real incomes provide a better life for their families. The "expansion of women's economic role," then, according to Chafe, "depended on circumstances which prevented female employment from being perceived as a feminist threat" (1972:193). The double bind thus placed on the working woman continues to plague women today. By making her work secondary and supplementary, men could deny its significance, pay her less, and develop the fiction of the male as sole breadwinner. The home would remain her special sphere, and Americans could deny that women were "really" working in the marketplace. Thus, little progress would be made to provide women with the community support they so desperately needed to perform their dual role. A society that denies the presence of women in the marketplace is reluctant to provide them, for example, with child care services.

The searing analyses of women's position in society provided earlier by such feminists as Elizabeth Cady Stanton and Charlotte Perkins Gilman were notably absent in this period. Such an analysis might have shown women that, while they were increasing their numbers in the marketplace, they were not loosening their bondage in the home. Indeed, the bonds were being tightened as cadres of self-styled and professional "experts," detecting an undercurrent of discontent in women, adopted the "woman problem" as their mission.[1] These professionals—medical practitioners, domestic scientists, educators, childrearing experts—drew from new sources and new authorities in an age characterized by fascination with technology and science. One of the most influential of these authorities was,

---

1. For an analysis of this period, see Ehrenreich and English (1979).

of course, Sigmund Freud, whose uncovering of the "unconscious" led to the development of the field of psychology. As we saw in an earlier chapter, Freud's speculations on the nature of femininity lent credence to the new notion of womanhood as pathology developed by professionals whose work was spawned by Freud's own. Women were warned that their dreams of independence threatened the love and security provided by their harassed husbands. The phenomenon of "momism," articulated by Philip Wylie in 1942, became part of the contemporary jargon. The suburban middle-class woman who, in the 1950s, was expected to devote her energies to making her home a refuge for her family was suspected at the same time of preying on her children by smothering them with unnecessary affection and attention.

Yet there had hardly been a time in American history when women were less deserving of such epithets. Most American women had been brought up to believe that marriage and motherhood were woman's chief vocation and her best hope for personal fulfillment. As Betty Friedan points out in a selection here from *The Feminine Mystique*, never had so many women pursued the culture-myth of womanly fulfillment with such determination. The average age of marriage of American women had dropped to twenty by the end of the 1950s. The feminist ideal of the single professional woman had all but ceased to exist. Birthrates soared, and college educated women were having as many children as underclass women. If women were failing to live up to the ideal, it was not for want of effort. As Betty Friedan discovered in her study, no one had used words like "emancipation" and "career" for years. Yet, beneath the surface of the lives of the women interviewed by Friedan lay a profound sense of dissatisfaction, a yearning for "something more" that they struggled to suppress. Friedan's study, first published in 1963, effectively dispelled the myth of the "happy housewife heroine" and sounded the cry for the second wave of feminism. The discontent that Friedan uncovered in one suburban household after another would be channeled into a new feminist politics by women in the 1960s who would not so willingly accept what Friedan described as the "feminine mystique."

The origins of that new feminist movement are described in exerpts from *The Politics of Women's Liberation* by Jo Freeman, included here. The movement was given life by women whose principal knowledge of its historical antecedents consisted of the caricatures of the temperance fanatics and "suffragettes" of their history books. In many ways, Freeman points out, there were two movements, each with its unique style, orientation, and form of organization, which only later began to merge. The first of these, which Freeman calls the "older" branch,[2] was developed by a group of politically active women who had been brought together initially as participants in federal and state commissions on the status of women in 1963. The publication the same year of Friedan's *The Feminine Mystique* furnished the impetus to this group of women to found the National Organization for Women (NOW), for the purpose of expanding women's opportunities in government, education, and employment. The older branch, consisting of NOW as well as such groups as the Women's Equity Action League (WEAL) and the National Women's Political Caucus (NWPC), has operated as a traditional political organization, working within existing institutions to enhance women's social, legal, and political status. The initially moderate older branch of

2. Freeman uses the term "older" to refer to one branch of the movement both because it was formed earlier and because its members are slightly older than those of the second branch. The usual terms for the two branches, "reformist" and "radical," Freeman explains, are inadequate to explain a movement with such ideological complexity.

the women's movement, interested primarily in achieving equity in education and employment, has moved steadily toward the acceptance of a widening circle of issues and concerns until today distinctions between the branches are significantly blurred.

The differences between what Freeman calls the "older branch" and the "younger branch" can be traced in part to their origins. While the earlier feminists had been trained in, and had achieved moderate success within, traditional political structures, members of the second branch had received their political education in the civil rights movement, the New Left, and social action projects of the 1960s. The rejection by younger feminists of traditional group structures was largely a response to their own political experience where they saw "dominance for its own sake, competition for positions in the leadership hierarchy, and 'male ego-tripping' rule the day" (Freeman 1975:105). They had learned that relationships within the radical political movements, for all the homage paid to principles of egalitarianism, simply mimicked relationships within the larger society. The much proclaimed sexual revolution of the 1960s only confirmed the second-class status of women. Not only were they required to assume "service roles," typing speeches and making coffee, just as had women in the early years of the abolition movement a century earlier, but they were expected to provide sexual favors for the male leaders of the New Left. The emergence of radical feminism was in large measure a response to the sexual exploitation they experienced within the movement they had helped to build.

An immediate and powerful tool for change was developed by radical feminists and grasped widely by great numbers of women who had never before participated in political movements. The process is defined by Vivian Gornick in a 1971 article, "Consciousness Raising," as "the feminist practice of examining one's personal experience in the light of sexism; i.e., that theory which explains women's subordinate position in society as a result of a cultural decision to confer direct power on men and only indirect power on women" (1971:22). As women met week after week in small, anonymous "rap" groups that formed during those early years of the movement, they learned to share their anger and discontent and found striking similarities between their experiences and those of their "sisters." Alix Kates Shulman, a participant in one early group, describes earlier in this volume the outpouring of feeling that resulted as women "began to see how interconnected were all (their) experiences and (their) seemingly disparate lives" (1980:594). Among the important discoveries made in those early CR sessions was that they were not alone in feeling sexually exploited. "In those days," Shulman writes, "few of the women had had the opportunity to talk honestly about sex with anyone; it had been a taboo subject in the fifties and was still suspect in the sixties. Certainly, women had not felt free to talk about the intimate physical details, for not only were sexual topics embarrassing, but sexual problems had long been taken as signs of personal failings or illness and as such were shameful, and talk about sexual secrets was considered a betrayal of your man and thus dangerous" (1980:593).

Several clinical studies of female sexuality had challenged established myths of women's inferior sexual response but had not brought about appreciable changes in attitudes about sexual behavior. In a provocative report on "The Evolution and Nature of Female Sexuality" published in 1966, Mary Jane Sherfey discusses her clinical study of multiple orgasms in women and concludes that "the *forceful* suppression of women's inordinate sexual demands was a prerequisite to the dawn of every modern civilization and almost every living culture" (1970:224). An essay published two years later by Susan Lydon on "The Politics of Orgasm," and discussed here by Shulman, became a key document in the literature of the women's liberation movement. Lydon's essay contributes to the uncovering of the patriarchal bias that informed Freudian psychology and that even today continues to shape attitudes about women's sexuality. The thesis of Lydon's essay is that woman's sexuality has been defined by men as one means of keeping her "sexually, as well as economically, socially, and politically subservient" (1970:201). Lydon discusses the findings of *Human Sexual Response*, the Masters and Johnson clinical study of the physiology of sex, which had not, in the two years since its publication in 1966, brought about appreciable changes in attitudes toward women's sexual response. If the material of the report is "allowed to filter into the public consciousness," Lydon predicted, "woman at long last will be allowed to take the first step toward her emancipation, to define and enjoy the forms of her own sexuality" (1970:205).

In their personal explorations within a "rap" group and in the emerging body of literature of women's liberation, women discovered that the source of their discontent was to be found not in the individual pathology of women preached throughout the 1950s but within the patriarchal structures that we have defined as the sexual economy. While "rap" groups enabled many women to readjust a beleaguered self-concept to a profoundly altered world view, however, consciousness raising stopped well short of providing women with the necessary tools to change that world. A woman with a raised consciousness often found herself unable to use her newly earned insights in a world whose structures remained unchanged. Moreover, the ideology of "structurelessness" that emerged from those early groups created enormous problems for the women's movement. The consciousness-raising approach, with its stress on equal participation, worked quite well in enabling women to share personal insights, but it did not contribute to the efficient carrying out of specific tasks. As Freeman points out, it was difficult for women to move from a "rap" group to a project because most groups were unwilling to change their structure when they changed their tasks. Still, although the ideology condemned leadership, it was inevitable that some women would influence group decisions more than others. In addition, although the movement refused to recognize leaders, the media did not. Any woman thus designated by the press as a movement spokesperson, particularly in the period from 1969 to 1972 when the movement had achieved great notoriety, was likely to be denounced by feminists as an "elitist." Because the movement had rejected overt structures, it adopted such name-calling and other covert means to discipline its members. Freeman describes the purging from the movement of some women who had real contributions to make:

As in any group or movement there were certainly power- and fame-hungry individuals who found the movement an excellent opportunity for personal advancement; but in their fear of manipulation, feminists often failed to make a distinction between those who were "using" the movement and those who were "strong" women or had valuable talents. Although the attacks were initially aimed at "media stars," their scope widened to the point that some felt that any individual who had "painfully managed any degree of achievement" was victimized. (1975:121)

In the absence of acknowledged leaders, informal "friendship networks" arose to fill leadership gaps, excluding, inevitably, those women who were not part of such networks. These networks came to be used much as the "old boy" networks had been used to exclude some men and all women from sources of prestige and power. Freeman points out the irony of the movement's inflicting on itself a problem women had been fighting for centuries. The problem of covert power structures was thus exacerbated. Because the movement did not recognize power structures (friendship networks), it had no efficient means of ensuring their responsible use of power (1975:122).

As long as its major emphasis was on personal change, the movement was able to avoid confronting problems created by the ideology of structurelessness. As feminist consciousness spread widely over a broad spectrum of American society, the movement was expected to provide directions for the future. But, as Freeman points out, consciousness raising as a major function of the movement was becoming obsolete as early as 1971. If the movement was to survive, it would need to establish a clear set of goals. As feminist consciousness spread widely over a broad spectrum of American society, the movement was expected to provide directions for the future. There was, however, little agreement among feminists as to how to formulate feminist objectives and achieve feminist goals.

Some feminist theorists set themselves the task of envisioning a feminist future with a map for reaching it. Shulamith Firestone, in her early feminist analysis, *The Dialectic of Sex: The Case for Feminist Revolution*, gave us one of the first and perhaps still one of the most radical visions. In agreement with other theorists and historians who see the family as the essential source of the oppression of women, Firestone proposed the creation of social structures that would replace the family and the constraining roles for women within it. In selections from her book included here, Firestone places feminism in the service of revolutionary ecology. For practical as well as moral reasons, Firestone finds, "it has become necessary to free humanity from the tyranny of its biology." Although many of the new scientific possibilities outlined by Firestone in 1970 have since become realities, Firestone's "cybernetic solution" has not met wide acceptance among American women.

As the women's movement continued to grow, intense press coverage inflamed emerging divisiveness. Perhaps the best publicized of those divisions, the "gay/straight split," continues to plague the women's movement. For many women, lesbianism came to mean more than sexual preference; it was seen as a total world view that insisted women's primary orientation should be toward other women and should exclude men. A paper written by Radicalesbians in 1970, "The Woman-Identified Woman," was widely circulated and was the subject of much controversy. Interpreted by some as outright condemnation of heterosexual relationships and by others as a call for more open, human relationships, it fed the growing controversy. Radicalesbians challenged women to acknowledge "the primacy of women relating to women" (1973:245). It is crucial, they argued, for women to disengage themselves from "male-defined response patterns."

In the privacy of our psyches, we must cut those cords to the core. For irrespective of where our love and sexual energies flow, if we are male-identified in our heads, we cannot realize our autonomy as human beings. (1973:243–44)

Some early feminists saw in lesbian feminism the key to the breaking of the interlocking structures of the sexual economy. The lesbian feminist theorist Charlotte Bunch argues that the task must begin with challenge of the "institutional and ideological domination of heterosexuality, as a fundamental part of male supremacy." In her essay on "Lesbian-Feminist Theory," included in this chapter, Bunch argues that women's liberation will not be achieved within existing institutions—the school, the workplace, the family, organized religion—all of which "are based on the assumption that every woman either is or wants to be bonded to a man both economically and emotionally." Such analyses as that of Bunch provided a blueprint for the examination of the validity of gender-defined roles, although few women were prepared to sever completely the accustomed bonds.

The intense period of press scrutiny that highlighted growing divisions within the movement also carried feminist issues out of movement groups and into the homes of Middle America. Women assumed some control over that press coverage with a new women's publication, which appeared in preview form in December 1971. With that first issue of *MS.*, offering women advice about how to write marriage contracts, telling them why they fear success, and allowing them to share one housewife's "moment of truth," was launched what would prove to be an enormously powerful instrument for popularizing the ideas of the women's movement. As "women's liberation" became a household word, its issues were disseminated widely, and discussion groups were formed among many people who were not "movement" women. The excerpts reprinted here from Susan Jacoby's 1973 article "The Flatbush Feminists" illustrate the profound impact on a group of women who, but for women's liberation, might never have come consciously to examine the circumstances of their lives. The women interviewed by Jacoby, middle-aged wives of working-class men, were led by an increasingly widespread dissemination of the feminist perspective to view their personal experiences in a new light, to consider possibilities for their lives that were unforeseen when they were young wives and mothers. While their feminism seems rather diluted, and it is unlikely that they would identify with the women's movement as such, their support of movement issues—the need for child care centers and equal pay for equal work, for example—demonstrates the pervasive change in attitudes regarding woman's place, if not social structures, that twentieth century feminism has achieved.

Nor have black women wholeheartedly identified with the women's movement. Sandra Flowers, a coordinator of the Atlanta chapter of the National Black Feminist Organization, claims that black women "inherently are feminists" because of their struggle; yet, she continues, feminism is "a risky business for black women because the options it inevitably generates tend to alienate black men as well as those black women who read feminism as anti-male, hence anti-black" (quoted in Walker 1980:51). Yet, as Diane K. Lewis reports in "A Response to Inequality: Black Women, Racism, and Sexism," black women, in increasing numbers, have become responsive to feminism as they become aware of their additional burden of sexism (1977:339–41). At first hostile to the women's movement, the most recent generation of black women has observed the positive effects, such as they are, of the civil rights movement and the black liberation movement of the 1960s to be enjoyed primarily by black men. They note that the economic progress of black men, although slow, outstrips that of both white and black women. In addition, many of the goals of the women's movement are being seen as central to all women across class and race lines—day care, abortion, and maternity leaves, for example. The formation in the 1970s of Black Women Organized for Action (BWOA) and the National Black Feminist Organization (NBFO), Lewis points out, "indicates that some contemporary black women have begun to perceive the way both sex inequality and race inequality affect their lives" (1977:347). In the early 1980s it is not certain, however, that black women will continue to develop strong alliances with the primarily white middle-class women's movement, except around issues of clear and immediate importance. Whether a universal women's movement may one day organize itself, as Diane Lewis' article, excerpted here, and Sandra Flowers' comments indicate, is by no means certain. It remains a challenge for feminists to forge ways of transcending the class and race differences on which nineteenth-century feminism was impaled.

Undeniably, there is promise for the future of feminism in the accomplishments of the 1960s and '70s. Both in collective attitude and in the practical business of life, we have moved far from the cult of the lady. An "ongoing transformation of woman's place" has been ensured by a "constellation of social and economic forces" (Chafe 1977:145) set in motion by the second wave of feminism. That process of transformation has banished most of the blatant denials of legal rights and exclusion from opportunities that we have traced in earlier chapters. Women vote, own property, are occasionally elected to public office, and are in law, if not entirely in fact, protected from discrimination on the basis of sex in employment, education, the granting of credit, and many other areas of life.

While, as we noted in Chapter 4, only minimal progress has occurred in the movement of women into full participation in the work force, it is heartening to observe the increase in the numbers of women of all ages and backgrounds pursuing higher education and professional training. Women now account for 50.7 percent of the 11.9 million students enrolled at postsecondary institutions in the United States, a figure that includes unprecedented numbers of women aged 25 to 34. That category of female students increased by 187 percent from 1970 to 1978, compared with an increase of 36 percent for females aged 18 to 24. For men, the increase was 48 percent and 9 percent respectively (*On Campus with Women* 1980:8–9). Similar increases have occurred at all academic levels. The number of women receiving doctorate degrees between 1971 and 1978 increased by 80.9 percent, compared to a decline of 5.5 percent of men awarded the Ph.D. from 1977 to 1978. In professional schools, the rise is equally noteworthy. In 1979, almost one of every five first professional degrees (medical, legal, or theological) was earned by a woman, and at this writing, female medical students constitute 25.3 percent, or one-fourth, the student body nationwide (*On Campus With Women* 1980:9). These figures are unprecedented in American history and engender great hope for the fuller participation and influence of women in the social and economic arenas in the future. As token numbers of women now trained and working in most occupations and professions swell to more nearly proportional representation, even legal protection against sex discrimination should prove more effective.

The climate for these changes was for the most part created during the most active stage of the twentieth-century women's movement—the years roughly from 1968 to 1972, although some changes have been rather quietly achieved during the quiescent period that has overtaken the movement in recent years. All together, the events of two decades have engendered an aura of receptivity to change that has become a familiar part of the landscape here and in varying degrees in other parts of the world.

The most crucial among changed attitudes and practices must include some of the most entrenched structures of social organization—language, education, and reproductive patterns, for example. Attempts to render language gender-free through widely used, if much debated, neologisms such as "chairperson" are occurring among writers and speakers in nearly all social strata. Theological students are being taught to replace "Father" with "Creator" or "Sustainer" in worship services. Young boys participate in cooking and sewing classes with female classmates with no more thought of inappropriateness than have the girls who participate in manual arts ("shop") classes with boys. But the most important change, and one that in fact encompasses the others, is a new consciousness among women of their achievements and possibilities. The final accounting of the legacy of feminism's second wave is

... an enormous release, a joyful overflowing, as the female energy once channeled toward domesticity pours out in all directions.... Women who had been "ugly" became radiant. A women's culture flourishes: women's studies courses, women's poetry and music, new approaches to language, art, relationships. (Ehrenreich and English 1979:317)

More than a decade after the rebirth of feminism in the 1960s, however, we must concede the continuing vigor of the sexual economy. While it is clearly foolish to claim, as have some discouraged feminists, that no progress has been made, that the plight of modern women is indistinguishable from that of women through the ages, the absence of permanently transforming structural change is sobering, as is the present state of feminism. The import of the constrained quality of the current movement is difficult to measure and evaluate. Perhaps it signals only a hiatus of the kind that occurred between 1920 and the second wave of feminism in the 1960s, resulting in part from achievement of immediate goals and changes in the larger political context. Or it may indicate that feminism has failed to develop in ways necessary to counter sexual oppression at its base. One does suspect that at least to some degree, this century's movement has been captured by that successful diversionary tactic traced in Chapter 5 of this volume, the "individual solution." One must, of course, credit the women's movement for creating a climate in which women have found the strength to demand an end to sex discrimination and sexual harassment in the marketplace. But one regrets the limited definition of sexual equality in common currency that claims for women merely the opportunity to assimilate fully into existing economic, social, legal, and educational structures.

According to Zillah Eisenstein, in *The Radical Future of Liberal Feminism*, "the issue left unresolved in this view (that the present social and political structure can accommodate women's equality) is which men women will be equal to." "One hardly believes," she continues, "women are fighting to be equal with the coal miners of society or the male industrial workers in the California plant who were sterilized by the chemicals they work with." There is in this liberal feminist view, Eisenstein argues, a misplaced belief in the possibilities for the individual under an abstract equality that really does not exist and will not enable women to "rise according to the amount of initiative, intelligence, and energy they have" any more than it has allowed the male coal miners or chemical plant workers to do so. "In the end," she concludes, "women will be less than equal to men in whatever place they occupy until the sexual-class structure is addressed" (1981:231). Instead of perceiving and taking action against the firm grounding of sexual oppression in the economic order, in culturally determined social structures, and in the cultural values that both mirror and shape those structures, women in the twentieth century have allowed themselves to be seduced by the same promise of personal fulfillment that was instrumental in the dispersal of the women's movement after the granting of suffrage in 1920.

In a provocative essay written at a more active moment in the movement (1972), and published as part of her collection *The White Album* in 1979, Joan Didion takes the movement to task for having been thus diverted a second time. Not that Didion sees the present state of the women's movement as deviating in its fate from that of other radical political movements. Rather, she complains, the current "tendency for popular discussion of the movement to center for so long around day-care centers is yet another instance of that studied resistance to political ideas which characterizes our national life" (1979:109). In its understandable concern with the inequities of women's personal lives—with dishwashing and the burden of child care—Didion nonetheless regrets the failure of the movement to grasp the larger point, "to make that inductive leap from the personal to the political" (1979:114). Certainly in its original incarnation that phrase "the personal is the political," seized upon by the movement, was meant to signify the understanding by feminists of the second wave of the deep penetration of the political into personal lives, of the absence of opportunity to make truly "personal" choices afforded to women in the sexual economy. But the strategy for attacking the relationship has been to start at the narrow end of the telescope, to try to make changes in the personal arrangements of women's lives in order to effect change in the political construct of the sexual economy. The result has been, as Didion points out, "not only to stall the movement in the personal but to seriously delude oneself" (1979:114).

Barbara Ehrenreich and Deirdre English reach a similar conclusion in *For Her Own Good*. Having posited "ideological poles which dominate sexual politics in the twentieth century—the 'romanticism' of the sun-belt suburbs or the 'rationalism of the paperback self-help shelf,' " they seek to establish the place of feminism in the struggle. And they conclude, as do we, that feminism at this point hedges. Feminists are in the defensive posture of maintaining and widening the possibilities of "choice" for women—"choice for its own sake, and are less and less prone to pass judgment on the alternatives, or to ask how these came to be choices in the first place" (1979:291).

There are even indications of a diminished effort to analyze, to iden- tify and define the political in the personal. Ehrenreich and English are critical of feminism for this stance, but clear about and sym- pathetic to the reasons for it. And, indeed, the reasons are manifest. Real liberation of women, as Zillah Eisenstein has cogently argued, is predicated upon the most radical of changes in our social organi- zation, in the transformation of capitalist patriarchy (1981). In the face of the long wait, or the long struggle, that will attend change in the social order, how are women to live?

For most women, the "individual solution" does not hold the promise of a better life, much less the promise of release from the sexual economy. The white middle-class woman who has successfully climbed the corporate ladder is neither a practical nor perhaps even an attractive role model for most women of all races, who, in the words of Ehrenreich and English, "join black men and youth in a weary army of subsistence wage-earners to make two to three dollars an hour typing, cleaning, fetching, soldering, stitching (1979:318). Indeed, the current movement toward conservatism in the United States, which appears to have surprising strength among members of the less privileged classes and more specifically, for our purposes, among women, represents not some arbitrary swing of a politically driven pendulum but a failure of the prophets of the new order to fulfill the promise of the twentieth-century movement's early vision. The current abortion controversy points up the continuing impedi- ment to feminism presented by class differences. Although much of the leadership of antiabortion forces is traditional, conservative, and privileged, the wide support this movement engenders among work- ing men and women and among the underclass should give us pause. While we will not recapitulate the feminist perspective on abortion presented in Chapter 5, it is revealing to recall in this context the complaint of the young black woman interviewed by Robert Coles that "they" want to take away from "you" the only "hope, the only chance that things will get better," that "a real, live growing baby" represents to the underclass (1967:368–69). If the admittedly mitigated joys of traditional roles within the family, of motherhood, are to be foregone or cast into unfamiliar form, other rewarding functions must take their place. For privileged women, new careers, and to a lesser extent, participation in a consumer culture have served that purpose, as they have for men of their class. For the underclass, or even for a reasonably prosperous blue-collar class, jobs rather than careers fall short as providers of meaning, and exclusion from full participation in the consumer culture mandates other demonstrations of achievement and hope.

A poignant example of the embracing of traditional roles in the face of limited options is provided by the recent increase of teen-age pregnancies. "Every year, more than a million girls from 15 to 19 years of age—plus another 30,000 from 10 to 14—become pregnant in this country and three-fifths carry through to birth" (Clines 1979:48). For the poor Puerto Rican adolescents who are the subject of an article on "Children of Desire" by Francis X. Clines, motherhood is a rite of passage, an assertion of function and meaning in lives that promise no other. One's own baby, moreover, is a means for qualifying for one's own welfare check, and therefore a vehicle for the establishment of the separate home and independence that often seem attainable in no other way. For those girls, or for women like "The Flatbush Feminists" who know what it is to grow older with very little money and education, to relinquish whatever meaning and respect accompany the performance of traditional roles is unrealistic. Little wonder, then, that many women have so energetically resisted change. And little wonder that other women have assumed that "studied resistance to political ideas" to which Didion refers. The needed changes depend finally on the destruction of a sexual economy that has assumed over the centuries every appearance of natural human reality. Survival, for most women, has required the assumption of a less radical vision.

The historian William H. Chafe does not disagree with critics of the contemporary women's movement who find that it is stalled in its inability to focus on the root causes of women's oppression. Yet he insists that the movement be credited with creating a climate receptive to wider roles for all women across barriers of race and class. In his book *Women and Equality: Changing Patterns in American Culture*, Chafe charts the changes that have brought about an "ongoing transformation of woman's 'place'" and measures the distance that remains toward achievement of full equality for women. Young college-age men and women, in particular, became, by the mid-1970s, "converts to the norm of egalitarian relationships," he observes. Yet, beyond the blush of that conviction, it was not at all clear by then, nor is it now, how to achieve equality or what equality means. Most Americans who by the mid-1970s supported the doctrine of equality believed that women should be allowed equal opportunity to compete within the free enterprise system. But, argued some critics, only if everyone in fact started from the same social and economic place could the idea of equal opportunity retain credibility. The libertarian ideal, Chafe argues,

... could become a reality only through significant substantive change involving employment practices, education, family life, the training of children for both nurturant and employment roles, and the development of new cultural values and priorities. In almost all cases such issues called for a political as well as a personal response, posing a fundamental challenge to traditional values of individualism and laissez-faire liberalism. (1977:151)

The goal of equality, whether it is to be won within the context of personal relationships or within the larger society, is in fundamental opposition to the achievement ethic paramount in American society. At the beginning of the 1980s, Chafe concludes, it is not certain that Americans are prepared to make the kinds of institutional adjustments—in employment, in education, in attitudes about and structure of the traditional nuclear family, in leisure and work priorities— necessary to ensure equality for women.

That "fundamental challenge to traditional values of individualism and laissez-faire liberalism" has not been made successfully by two centuries of feminism operating as it has within a sexual economy powerfully influenced by class and race distinctions. It remains the overriding task for the current women's movement to break the interlocking structures of that economy. At least one proponent of the Equal Rights Amendment sees in its ratification one of feminism's most effective weapons against the sexual economy. In an essay on "The ERA in Context: Its Impact on Society," Hazel Greenberg points out that equal rights laws legitimate the attack on what we have called the sexual economy, inviting conflict, a necessary condition for progress. Greenberg is critical of social analysts who view the ERA as little more than the culmination of the women's rights movement, a legal instrument stating only that both sexes will be given equal rights under the law. Such a viewpoint does not question traditional values, merely women's access to them, thereby contributing to the obscuring of the root causes of women's oppression. Greenberg suggests that the Equal Rights Amendment to the Constitution has the capacity to "affect social values, on the macrocosmic level, and psychological attitudes, on the individual level" (1977:5–6). Apart from its direct impact upon the law, the ERA will challenge traditional notions of sex roles. "Its extralegal impact is further expanded," Greenberg continues, "by the fact that changes in society are systemic, acting like concentric circles, causing at first minor changes here and there, effecting in their turn other changes, and so on. These formal and symbolic advantages in conjunction with its 'radical' ideology provide the potential for constructing a new social reality . . . these changes, as they nourish one another, will not simply incorporate women into the present social structure but can qualitatively change that social structure—for the greater good of humankind" (1977:12).

While much of this book has argued against the possibility for "individual solutions" to the oppression of women, and has conversely insisted upon economic, class, race, and other material bases of the sexual economy, we have sought to pay due tribute to the feminine experience as it is lived within a masculine world and to measure past and potential future contributions of individual women to the struggle against the sexual economy. The lives of successful, achieving, or protesting women, whose words and deeds are recorded on these pages, have helped sharpen our awareness of the institutional impediments to achievement. Still, the fundamental—and most resistant—questions remain only partially formulated and largely unanswered. Will women share in or accept an epistemology developed largely by men over centuries that excluded them from participation? Do women want merely to enter the fray of a marketplace economy grounded in patriarchal capitalism and to compete with men for places in it? Or do they want to take on more formidable challenges and seek the transformation of a masculinist world?

Perhaps greater impetus toward both ideological and structural change favorable to women will be provided in our increasingly uncertain future. While two centuries of plenty have contributed to the creation and maintenance of traditional gender roles and such concepts as "women's sphere," it is quite possible that solutions to problems of overpopulation and an economy of scarcity caused by diminishing energy resources will result in change in women's status thus far unachieved by appeal or political activism. At the center of the sexual economy that clouds the future of women is that central structure of modern life—the family. Carl Degler's recent historical analysis of the relationship between women and the family concludes accurately that the "central values of the modern family stand in opposition to those that underlie women's emancipation. . . . Where the women's movement has called for a recognition of individualism, the family has insisted upon subordination of individual interests to those of the group" (1980:471). And of course the subordination of women has been crucial to the survival of the family and the political, social, and economic structures it has been shaped to serve. From Frederich Engels to Eli Zaretsky, from Simone de Beauvoir to Juliet Mitchell, historians and theorists represented here have pointed out this fundamental conflict. Transformation of the sexual economy depends ultimately upon the future shape of the linchpin, the family.

We have traced in these pages the development of the culture, the politics, the deeply entrenched values, and the social structures and interrelationships we have called the sexual economy. And we have collected sobering reflections on the wrenching changes that will be required if that sexual economy is to be replaced by a culture and politics predicated on and capable of sustaining equality between the sexes. Still, we take heart in the progress we have made, and in the prospect of new relationships rendered more fully human by equality and by the integration of the feminine experience into a world that has so far given it short shrift.

Without illusions about the extent of the struggle or the distance to be covered, we end by "Stepping Westward" with Denise Levertov. We end in commitment to the journey and in celebration of the special gifts we bring as women to the effort.

The Feminine Mystique has been called the bomb that set off the twentieth-century women's movement. While younger women involved in the civil rights and student movements of the 1960s were being made aware of their own oppression by male members of those movements, older, middle-class, and largely suburban women were being jolted into an acknowledgment of "the problem that has no name"· by Friedan's book. Women now in their fifties and sixties talk of having passed the book among themselves in wordless comprehension.

THE PROBLEM THAT HAS NO NAME

Betty Friedan

FROM *The Feminine Mystique*

The problem lay buried, unspoken, for many years in the minds of American women. It was a strange stirring, a sense of dissatisfaction, a yearning that women suffered in the middle of the twentieth century in the United States. Each suburban wife struggled with it alone. As she made the beds, shopped for groceries, matched slipcover material, ate peanut butter sandwiches with her children, chauffeured Cub Scouts and Brownies, lay beside her husband at night—she was afraid to ask even of herself the silent question—"Is this all?"

For over fifteen years there was no word of this yearning in the millions of words written about women, for women, in all the columns, books and articles by experts telling women their role was to seek fulfillment as wives and mothers. Over and over women heard in voices of tradition and of Freudian sophistication that they could desire no greater destiny than to glory in their own femininity. Experts told them how to catch a man and keep him, how to breastfeed children and handle their toilet training, how to cope with sibling rivalry and adolescent rebellion; how to buy a dishwasher, bake bread, cook gourmet snails, and build a swimming pool with their own hands; how to dress, look, and act more feminine and make marriage more exciting; how to keep their husbands from dying young and their sons from growing into delinquents. They were taught to pity the neurotic, unfeminine, unhappy women who wanted to be poets or physicists or presidents. They learned that truly feminine women do not want careers, higher education, political rights—the independence and the opportunities that the old-fashioned feminists fought for. Some women, in their forties and fifties, still remembered painfully giving up those dreams, but most of the younger women no longer even thought about them. A thousand expert voices applauded their femininity, their adjustment, their new maturity. All they had to do was devote their lives from earliest girlhood to finding a husband and bearing children. . . .

The suburban housewife—she was the dream image of the young American women and the envy, it was said, of women all over the world. The American housewife—freed by science and labor-saving appliances from the drudgery, the dangers of childbirth and the illnesses of her grandmother. She was healthy, beautiful, educated, concerned only about her husband, her children, her home. She had found true feminine fulfillment. As a housewife and mother, she was respected as a full and equal partner to man in his world. She was free to choose automobiles, clothes, appliances, supermarkets; she had everything that women ever dreamed of. . . .

In the fifteen years after World War II, this mystique of feminine fulfillment became the cherished and self-perpetuating core of contemporary American culture. Millions of women lived their lives in the image of those pretty pictures of the American suburban housewife, kissing their husbands goodbye in front of the picture window, depositing their stationwagonsful of children at school, and smiling as they ran the new electric waxer over the spotless kitchen floor. They baked their own bread, sewed their own and their children's clothes, kept their new washing machines and dryers running all day. They changed the sheets on the beds twice a week instead of once, took the rug-hooking class in adult education, and pitied their poor frustrated mothers, who had dreamed of having a career. Their only dream was to be perfect wives and mothers; their highest ambition to have five children and a beautiful house, their only fight to get and keep their husbands. They had no thought for the unfeminine problems of the world outside the home; they wanted the men to make the major decisions. They gloried in their role as women, and wrote proudly on the census blank: "Occupation: housewife."

For over fifteen years, the words written for women, and the words women used when they talked to each other, while their husbands sat on the other side of the room and talked shop or politics or septic tanks, were about problems with their children, or how to keep their husbands happy, or improve their children's school, or cook chicken, or make slipcovers. Nobody argued whether women were inferior or superior to men; they were simply different. Words like "emancipation" and "career" sounded strange and embarrassing; no one had used them for years. When a Frenchwoman named Simone de Beauvoir wrote a book called *The Second Sex*, an American critic commented that she obviously "didn't know what life was all about," and besides, she was talking about French women. The "woman problem" in America no longer existed.

If a woman had a problem in the 1950's and 1960's, she knew that something must be wrong with her marriage, or with herself. Other women were satisfied with their lives, she thought. What kind of a woman was she if she did not feel this mysterious fulfillment waxing the kitchen floor? She was so ashamed to admit her dissatisfaction that she never knew how many other women shared it. If she tried to tell her husband, he didn't understand what she was talking about. She did not really understand it herself. For over fifteen years women in America found it harder to talk about this problem than about sex. Even the psychoanalysts had no name for it. When a woman went to a psychiatrist for help, as many women did, she would say, "I'm so ashamed," or "I must be hopelessly neurotic." "I don't know what's wrong with women today," a suburban psychiatrist said uneasily. "I only know something is wrong because most of my patients happen to be women. And their problem isn't sexual." Most women with this problem did not go to see a psychoanalyst, however. "There's nothing wrong really," they kept telling themselves. "There isn't any problem."

But on an April morning in 1959, I heard a mother of four, having coffee with four other mothers in a suburban development fifteen miles from New York, say in a tone of quiet desperation, "the problem." And the others knew, without words, that she was not talking about a problem with her husband, or her children, or her home. Suddenly they realized they all shared the same problem, the problem that has no name. They began, hesitantly, to talk about it. Later, after they had picked up their children at nursery school and taken them home to nap, two of the women cried, in sheer relief, just to know they were not alone. . . .

If the secret of feminine fulfillment is having children, never have so many women, with the freedom to choose, had so many children, in so few years, so willingly. If the answer is love, never have women searched for love with such determination. And yet there is a growing suspicion that the problem may not be sexual, though it must somehow be related to sex. I have heard from many doctors evidence of new sexual problems between man and wife—sexual hunger in wives so great their husbands cannot satisfy it. "We have made woman a sex creature," said a psychiatrist at the Margaret Sanger marriage counseling clinic. "She has no identity except as a wife and mother. She does not know who she is herself. She waits all day for her husband to come home at night to make her feel alive. And now it is the husband who is not interested. It is terrible for the woman, to lie there, night after night, waiting for her husband to make her feel alive." Why is there such a market for books and articles offering sexual advice? The kind of sexual orgasm which Kinsey found in statistical plenitude in the recent generations of American women does not seem to make this problem go away. . . .

Can the problem that has no name be somehow related to the domestic routine of the housewife? When a woman tries to put the problem into words, she often merely describes the daily life she leads. What is there in this recital of comfortable domestic detail that could possibly cause such a feeling of desperation? Is she trapped simply by the enormous demands of her role as modern housewife: wife, mistress, mother, nurse, consumer, cook, chauffeur; expert on interior decoration, child care, appliance repair, furniture, refinishing, nutrition, and education? Her day is fragmented as she rushes from dishwasher to washing machine to telephone to dryer to station wagon to supermarket, and delivers Johnny to the Little League field, takes Janey to dancing class, gets the lawnmower fixed and meets the 6:45. She can never spend more than 15 minutes on any one thing; she has no time to read books, only magazines; even if she had time, she has lost the power to concentrate. At the end of the day, she is so terriby tired that sometimes her husband has to take over and put the children to bed. . . .

It is easy to see the concrete details that trap the suburban housewife, the continual demands on her time. But the chains that bind her in her trap are chains in her own mind and spirit. They are chains made up of mistaken ideas and misinterpreted facts, of incomplete truths and unreal choices. They are not easily seen and not easily shaken off.

How can any woman see the whole truth within the bounds of her own life? How can she believe that voice inside herself, when it denies the conventional, accepted truths by which she has been living? And yet the women I have talked to, who are finally listening to that inner voice, seem in some incredible way to be groping through to a truth that has defied the experts.

I think the experts in a great many fields have been holding pieces of that truth under their microscopes for a long time without realizing it. I found pieces of it in certain new research and theoretical developments in psychological, social and biological science whose implications for women seem never to have been examined. I found many clues by talking to suburban doctors, gynecologists, obstetricians, child-guidance clinicians, pediatricians, high-school guidance counselors, college professors, marriage counselors, psychiatrists and ministers—questioning them not on their theories, but on their actual experience in treating American women. I became aware of a growing body of evidence, much of which has not been reported publicly because it does not fit current modes of thought about women—evidence which throws into question the standards of feminine normality, feminine adjustment, feminine fulfillment, and feminine maturity by which most women are still trying to live.

I began to see in a strange new light the American return to early marriage and the large families that are causing the population explosion; the recent movement to natural childbirth and breastfeeding; suburban conformity, and the new neuroses, character pathologies and sexual problems being reported by the doctors. I began to see new dimensions to old problems that have long been taken for granted among women: menstrual difficulties, sexual frigidity, promiscuity, pregnancy fears, childbirth depression, the high incidence of emotional breakdown and suicide among women in their twenties and thirties, the menopause crises, the so-called passivity and immaturity of American men, the discrepancy between women's tested intellectual abilities in childhood and their adult achievement, the changing incidence of adult sexual orgasm in American women, and persistent problems in psychotherapy and in women's education.

If I am right, the problem that has no name stirring in the minds of so many American women today is not a matter of loss of femininity or too much education, or the demands of domesticity. It is far more important than anyone recognizes. It is the key to these other new and old problems which have been torturing women and their husbands and children, and puzzling their doctors and educators for years. It may well be the key to our future as a nation and a culture. We can no longer ignore that voice within women that says: "I want something more than my husband and my children and my home."

How did the women's movement emerge from the preceding decades of feminist inactivity to become a political force in the late 1960s? Jo Freeman, rejecting the "spontaneous generation" theory of movement formation, argues that women drew upon a well-established communication network that was adaptable to the purposes of the new movement. The Commissions on the Status of Women and a feminist cadre of the Equal Employment Opportunity Commission on the one hand and the student and radical community on the other created that communication network and became the training ground for the leaders and organizers of the women's liberation movement.

THE ORIGINS OF THE MOVEMENT

Jo Freeman

FROM *The Politics of Women's Liberation*

The movement manifests itself in an almost infinite variety of groups, styles, and organizations. Yet this diversity has sprung from only two distinct origins, representing two different strata of society, with two different styles, orientations, values, and forms of organization. In many ways there were two different movements which only in the last two years have begun to merge.

The first of these I call the older branch of the movement, partially because the median age of its original activists was older and partially because it began first. Its most prominent organization is the National Organization for Women (NOW) but it also contains such groups as the National Women's Political Caucus (NWPC), Federally Employed Women (FEW), and the self-defined "right-wing" of the movement, the Women's Equity Action League (WEAL). While the programs and aims of the older branch span a wide spectrum, their activities have tended to be concentrated on legal and economic problems. These groups are primarily made up of women—and men—who work, and they are substantially concerned with the problems of working women. The style of organization of the older branch groups tends to be traditionally formal, with elected officers, boards of directors, bylaws, and the other trappings of democratic structure and procedure. All started as top-down national organizations lacking a mass base. Some have subsequently developed that base, some have not yet done so, and others do not want to.

The younger branch of the movement is all mass base and no national organization. It consists of innumerable small groups engaged in a variety of activities, whose contact with one another is at best tenuous. Its composition, like that of the older branch, tends to be predominantly white, middle class, and college educated, but much more homogeneously so.[1]

It is common mistake to try to place the various feminist organizations on the traditional left/right spectrum and, concomitantly, to describe the two branches as "women's rights" and "women's liberation."[2] The terms "reformist" and "radical" by which the two branches are so often designated are convenient and fit into our preconceived notions about the nature of political activity, but they tell us little of relevance. In fact, if an ideological typography were possible it would show minimal consistency with any organizational characteristic.[3] Some groups often called "reformist" have a platform that would so completely change our society it would be unrecognizable. Other groups called "radical" concentrate on the traditional female concerns of love, sex, children, and interpersonal relationships (although with nontraditional views). The ideological complexity of the movement is too great to be categorized so simply.

The activities of the two branches are similarly incongruous. Ironically, the most typical division of labor is that those groups labeled "radical" engage primarily in educational work and service projects, while the so-called reformist groups are the political activists. Structure and style rather than ideology more accurately differentiate the two branches, and even here there has been much borrowing on both sides. In general the older branch has used the traditional forms of political action while the younger branch has been experimental.

As will be seen, the different style and organization of the two branches was largely derived from the different kind of political education and experiences of each originating group of women.

---

1. This observation was confirmed by Patricia Bayer Richard's 1972 questionnaire study in Syracuse, N.Y., of "The Feminist Movement: Parameters of Participation" (Paper given at the March 1974 convention of the Ohio Association of Economists and Political Scientists).

2. Judith Hole and Ellen Levine, *Rebirth of Feminism* (New York: Quadrangle, 1971); Maren Carden Lockwood, *The New Feminist Movement* (New York: Russell Sage Foundation, 1974). Both make this mistake.

3. I am using ideology in the narrow sense to refer to a specifically feminist belief system rather than a general world view on the nature of politics and society. Participants in younger branch groups would be more likely to call themselves socialists or use revolutionary rhetoric than those in older branch groups. However, if one questions individuals in each branch on their views of the major feminist issues (e.g., abolition of marriage, continuation of the nuclear family, payment for housewives, abolition of the housewife role, child care, abortion, access of women to predominantly male occupations, abolition of sex roles, building a female culture, welfare, lesbianism, etc.), the answers will not correspond with branch membership. See the *Psychology Today* survey showing that respondents claiming membership in NOW compared with those participating in small groups showed no differences in their positions on various women's issues. Carol Tavris, "Woman and Man," *Psychology Today*, March 1972, p. 57.

Women of the older branch were trained in and had used the traditional forms of political action; while the younger branch inherited the loose, flexible, person-oriented attitude of the youth and student movements. The different structures that have evolved from these two distinctly different kinds of experience have, in turn, largely determined the strategy of the two branches, irrespective of any conscious intentions of their participants. These different structures and strategies have each posed different problems and possibilities. Intramovement differences are often perceived by the participants as conflicting, but it is their essential complementarity that has been one of the strengths of the movement.

Despite the multitude of differences, there are very strong similarities in the way the two branches came into being. These similarities serve to illuminate some of the microsociological factors involved in movement formation. NOW was the first older branch organization to be formed and is the parent of many of them. The forces that led to its formation were set in motion in 1961 when President Kennedy established the President's Commission on the Status of Women, at the behest of Esther Petersen, then director of the Women's Bureau.[4] Operating under a broad mandate, its 1963 report, *American Women,* and subsequent committee publications documented just how thoroughly women are still denied many rights and opportunities. The most concrete response to the activity of the President's Commission was the eventual establishment of fifty state commissions to do similar research on a state level. These commissions were often urged by politically active women and were composed primarily of women. While many governors saw them as an easy opportunity to pay off political favors, many women saw them as opportunities to turn attention to their concerns. These commissions in turn researched and wrote their own reports, which varied widely in quality and depth.

The activity of the federal and state commissions laid the groundwork for the future movement in three significant ways: (1) it brought together many knowledgeable, politically active women who otherwise would not have worked together around matters of direct concern to women; (2) the investigations unearthed ample evidence

4. The Women's Bureau was created in 1920. Although its main concern has been with women workers it has done an excellent job of producing reports and pamphlets on many aspects of women's situation. Its *Handbook on Women Workers* is the movement's main source book on legal and economic discrimination. The existence of an agency such as the Women's Bureau with its cooperative attitude and freely available publications facilitated the development and spread of the movement by, in effect, having done much of the basic fact-gathering and primary research necessary to support the feminist interpretation of women's status. However, it once had a conservative influence by directing (nonfeminist) women's groups away from support of such issues as the Equal Rights Amendment. Nonetheless, it was a latent resource for the spread of feminism, once groups developed that could make use of its material.

of women's unequal status, especially their legal and economic difficulties, in the process convincing many previously uninterested women that something should be done; (3) the reports created a climate of expectations that something would be done. The women of the federal and state commissions who were exposed to these influences exchanged visits, correspondence, and staff and met with each other at an annual commission convention. Thus they were in a position to share and mutually reinforce their growing awareness and concern over women's issues. These commissions created an embryonic communications network among people with similar concerns.

During this time two other events of significance occurred. The first was the publication of Betty Friedan's book *The Feminine Mystique* in 1963. An immediate best seller, it eventually stimulated many women to question the status quo and some to suggest to Friedan that a new organization should be formed to attack their problems. The second was the addition of "sex" to Title VII of the 1964 Civil Rights Act, prohibiting discrimination in employment.

Many men thought the "sex" provision was a joke—that its initiator, Representative Howard W. Smith of Virginia, only wanted to make the employment section of the bill look silly and sufficiently divide the liberals to prevent its passage.[5] However, the provision was taken very seriously by most of the female members of the House, regardless of party or politics. Representative Martha Griffiths of Michigan, the leading feminist of the House, claims she intended to sponsor the amendment but held off when she learned of Smith's intentions as she knew he could bring another 100 votes with him. Most of the House liberals opposed the provisions, arguing that it would weaken the bill, and Representative Griffiths knew it needed every vote it could get. Despite their many disagreements, both Smith and the liberal opponents played the provision for all the laughs it was worth and the ensuing uproar went down in congressional history as "Ladies Day in the House."[6]

Thanks to determined leadership by the congresswomen and concerted lobbying by the provision's supporters, "sex" joined the bill, only to be aborted by the very agency set up to administer it. The first executive director of the Equal Employment Opportunity

5. Caruthers Gholson Berger, "Equal Pay, Equal Employment Opportunity and Equal Enforcement of the Law for Women" *Valparaiso Law Review* 5 (Spring 1971):326–73, maintains that hearings the previous year on the Equal Pay Act and pressure by the National Women's Party (infra, p. 63) were primarily responsible for the addition of the sex provision to Title VII. However, Berger has been a member of the National Council of the National Women's Party since 1960, and Rep. Martha Griffiths (D.–Mich. until 1974) told me in 1969 that the NWP did not have a great influence on congress.

6. For a thorough documentation of this event, see Caroline Bird, *Born Female: The High Cost of Keeping Women Down* (New York: David McKay, 1968), chap. 1. For a blow-by-blow account of the floor happenings, see *Congressional Record*, House, 8 February 1964.

Commission (EEOC), Herman Edelsberg, publicly stated that the provision was a "fluke" that was "conceived out of wedlock." He felt "men were entitled to female secretaries."[7] This attitude caused Griffiths to blast the agency in a June 20, 1966, speech on the House floor. She declared that the EEOC had "started out by casting disrespect and ridicule on the law" but that their "wholly negative attitude had changed—for the worse."[8]

Not everyone within the EEOC was opposed to the "sex" provision. There was a "pro-woman" coterie which argued that "sex" would be taken more seriously if there were "some sort of NAACP for women" to put pressure on the government. As government employees they could not organize such a group, but they spoke privately with those whom they thought could do so.

On June 30, 1966, these three strands of incipient feminism were knotted together to form NOW. The occasion was the last day of the Third National Conference of Commissions on the Status of Women, ironically titled "Targets for Action." The participants had all received copies of Representative Griffiths' remarks. The opportunity came with a refusal by conference officials to bring to the floor a proposed resolution that urged the EEOC to treat sex discrimination as seriously as race discrimination. Despite the fact that these state commissions were not federal agencies, officials of the Interdepartmental Committee on the Status of Women and the Citizen's Advisory Committee on the Status of Women who were running the conference replied that those attending were not elected delegates and thus that resolutions would be inappropriate. The small group of women who had desired the resolution had met the night before in Friedan's hotel room to discuss the possibility of a civil rights organization for women. Not convinced of its need, they chose instead to propose the resolution. When the resolution was vetoed, the women held a whispered conversation over lunch and agreed to form an action organization "to bring women into full participation in the mainstream of American society now, assuming all the privileges and responsibilities thereof in truly equal partnership with men." The time for conferences was over, they felt. Now was the time to fight. The name NOW was coined by Friedan, in town researching her second book. Before the day was over, 28 women paid $5 each to join.[9]

By the time the organizing conference was held the following October 29–30, over 300 men and women had become charter mem-

7. Herman Edelsberg, at the New York University 18th Conference on Labor, cited in *Labor Relations Reporter* 61 (25 August 1966):253–55.
8. U.S. Congress, House, speech of Martha Griffiths, 89th Cong., 2nd sess., 20 June 1966, *Congressional Record.*
9. Betty Friedan, "NOW: How It Began," *Women Speaking*, April 1967.

bers. It is impossible to do a breakdown on the composition of the charter membership, but one of the first officers and board is possible. Such a breakdown accurately reflected NOW's origins. Friedan was president, two former EEOC commissioners were vice-presidents, a representative of the United Auto Workers Women's Committee was secretary-treasurer, and there were seven past and present members of the State Commissions on the Status of Women on the twenty-member board. Of the charter members, 126 were Wisconsin residents—and Wisconsin had the most active state commission. Occupationally, the board and officers were primarily from the professions, labor, government, and the communications industry.[10] Of these, only those from labor had any experience in organizing, and they resigned a year later in a dispute over support of the Equal Rights Amendment. Instead of organizational expertise, what the early NOW members had was media experience, and it was here that their early efforts were aimed. They could create an appearance of activity but did not know how to organize the substance of it. As a result, NOW often gave the impression of being larger than it was. It was highly successful in getting publicity, much less so in bringing about concrete changes or organizing itself. It suffered from constant administrative chaos during the first years of its life and was frequently unable to answer the mail from potential members let alone coordinate the activities of current ones. NOW's initiators were very high-powered women who lacked the time or patience for the slow, unglamorous, and tedious work of putting together a mass organization. Chapter development had to wait for the national media to attract women to the organization or the considerable geographical mobility of contemporary women to bring proponents into new territory.

In the meantime, unaware of and unknown to NOW, EEOC, and the state commissions, younger women began forming their own movement. Contrary to popular myth, it did not begin on the campus, nor was it started by Students for a Democratic Society (SDS). However, its activators were, to be trite, on the other side of the generation gap. While few were students, all were "under 30" and had obtained their political education as participants or concerned observers of the social-action projects of the 1960s. These projects, parti-

10. The employment background of the national board and officers was as follows: Board—labor, 3; academe, 7; church-related, 1; government, 2; law, 2; communications, 2; miscellaneous, 3. Officers—labor, academe, church, and communications, 1 each; government, 2. Most recent occupation as of the 1966 conference was used as the criterion for classification, and potential cross-filing was arbitrarily eliminated. For example, two academic nuns were counted under "academe" rather than "church." According to observers present at the conference, the participants tended to reflect the occupational background of the board, but to have a lower median age. Participants were primarily between the ages of 25 and 45, while officers tended to be at least 35.

cularly the civil rights movement, attracted a large number of women. Many were to say later that one of the major appeals of this movement was that the social role if not the economic condition of blacks was similar to that of women. But this observation was a retrospective one. At the time most women would not have expressed these thoughts even if they could have articulated them. The few who did were quickly put down.

Whether as participants in civil rights groups, the New Left, peace groups, or in the free universities, women found themselves quickly shunted into traditional roles. One early pamphlet described these roles as those of the "workers" and the "wives"; the former serviced the radical organizations with their typing and clerical skills and the latter serviced the radical men with their homemaking and sexual ones. Those few women who refused these roles and insisted on being accepted in the "realm of the mind" found themselves de-sexed and often isolated by their comrades.[11]

The situation in which these women found themselves unavoidably conflicted with the ideologies of "participatory democracy," "freedom," and "justice" that they were expressing. They were faced with the self-evident contradiction of working in a "freedom movement" but not being very free. Nor did their male colleagues brook any dissent. The men followed the example of Stokeley Carmichael who cut off all debate on the issue at a 1964 Student Non-violent Coordinating Committee conference by saying "the only position for women in SNCC is prone."

The problems for women in the radical movement were raised again and again over the next three years. In Seattle, members of the Socialist Workers Party (SWP) defected and formed the independent Freedom Socialist Club in 1964. The refusal of the SWP to consider "the woman question" was a major cause. Civil rights workers, housewives, and students in New Orleans formed a summer free-school discussion group in 1965. Women on the 1966 Meredith Mississippi march held secret nightly meetings after they were ordered to walk on the inside of the march line and be accompanied by a man at all times.

The idea of women's "liberation" was first raised at an SDS convention in December 1965. It was laughed off the floor by the male radicals. Undaunted, some New Left women circulated papers on the issue[12] and tried to interest SDS women in organizing them-

11. Judi Bernstein, Peggy Morton, Linda Seese, Myrna Woods, "Sisters, Brothers, Lovers... Listen...," originally distributed by the Student Union for Peace Action, Toronto, Canada, 1966.

12. "A Kind of Memo" by Casey Hayden and Mary King was circulated in mimeograph form for many months prior to the 1965 SDS convention and largely stimulated the discussion there. The essay was later published in *Liberation* 11, no. 2 (April 1966): 35 entitled "Sex and Caste: A Kind of Memo."

selves. Although they largely failed, the workshops on women in SDS regional conferences attracted many women who were later to be instrumental in the formation of feminist groups. At the summer 1967 national conference, SDS women finally succeeded in passing a resolution calling for the full participation of women in SDS. Generalizing from their experiences (and unknowingly paralleling the developing NOW program), they also suggested that SDS work on behalf of all women for communal child care, wide dissemination of contraceptives, easily available abortions, and equal sharing of housework. More specifically, they requested that SDS print relevant literature and that the SDS paper solicit articles on women. These requests were largely ignored. Instead, the SDS organ, *New Left Notes*, decorated the page on which the women's resolution appeared with a freehand drawing of a girl in a baby-doll dress holding a picket sign and petulantly declaring "We want our rights and we want them now!"[13]

No single group of organization among these protest movements directly stimulated the formation of independent women's liberation groups. But together they created a "radical community" in which like-minded women continually interacted or were made aware of each other. This community consisted largely of those who had participated in one or more of the many protest activities of the 1960s and had established its own ethos and its own institutions. Thus the women in it thought of themselves as "movement people" and had incorporated the adjective "radical" into their personal identities. The values of their radical identity and the style to which they had been trained by their movement participation directed them to approach most problems as political ones that could be solved by organizing. What remained was to translate their individual feelings of "unfreedom" into a collective consciousness. Thus the radical community provided not only the necessary network of communication; its radical ideas formed the framework of analysis that "explained" the dismal situation in which radical women found themselves.

In this fertile field the younger branch of the women's movement took root in 1967 and 1968. At least five groups in five different cities (Chicago, Toronto, Seattle, Detroit, and Gainsville, Florida) formed spontaneously, independently of each other. They came at a very auspicious moment. 1967 was the year in which the blacks kicked the whites out of the civil rights movement, student power had been discredited by SDS, and the organized New Left was on the wane. Only draft-resistance activities were on the increase, and this

13. *New Left Notes*, 10 July 1967.

movement more than any other exemplified the social inequities of the sexes. Men could resist the draft. Women could only counsel resistance.[14] What was significant about this point in time was that there was a lack of available opportunities for political work. Some women fit well into the "secondary role" of draft counseling. Many did not. For years, their complaints of unfair treatment had been ignored by movement men with the dictum that those things could wait until after the revolution. Now these movement women found time on their hands, but the men would still not listen.

For months, women met quietly to analyze their perpetual secondary roles in the radical movement, to assimilate the lessons learned in free university study groups, or to reflect on their treatment in the civil rights movement. They were constantly ridiculed by the men they worked with and told that their meetings with other women were "counterrevolutionary" because they would further splinter an already badly factioned movement. In many ways this very ridicule served to increase their growing rage.

A typical example was the August 1967 National Conference on New Politics convention held in Chicago. Although a women's caucus met for days, it was told its resolution was not significant enough to merit a floor discussion. By threatening to tie up the convention with procedural motions, the women succeeded in having their statement tacked to the end of the agenda. It was never discussed. The chair refused to recognize any of the women standing by the microphones, their hands straining upward. When instead he called on someone to speak on "the forgotten American, the American Indian," five women rushed the podium to demand an explanation. But the chairman just patted one of the women on the head and told her, "Cool down, little girl, we have more important things to talk about than women's problems."

The "little girl" was Shulamith Firestone, future author of *The Dialectic of Sex* (1971), and she did not cool down. Instead, she joined with another Chicago woman, at the NCNP who had been trying to organize a women's group that summer, to call a meeting of those women who had halfheartedly attended the summer meetings. Telling their stories to those women, they stimulated sufficient rage to carry the group for three months; and by that time it was a permanent institution. . . .

Initially the new movement found it hard to organize on the campus, but, as a major congregating area of women and, in particular, of women with political awareness, campus women's liberation

14. Barrie Thorne, "Girls Who Say Yes to Guys Who Say No: Women in the Draft Resistance Movement" (Paper given at the 1972 convention of the American Sociological Association).

groups eventually became ubiquitous. While the younger branch of the movement never formed any organization larger or more extensive than a city-wide coordinating committee, it would be fair to say that, at least in the first years, it had a larger "participationship" than NOW and the other older branch organizations. While the members of the older branch knew how to use the media and how to form national structures, the women of the younger branch were skilled in local community organizing.

Radical feminist theorist Shulamith Firestone conceives of the feminist revolution as inseparable from modern technological advances. Her vision of the future is of a society driven by what she calls "cybernetic socialism." In the following selection, Firestone describes the benefits to be derived from the establishment of a "new ecological balance."

FEMINISM AND ECOLOGY

Shulamith Firestone

FROM *The Dialectic of Sex*

The best new currents in ecology and social planning agree with feminist aims. The way that these two social phenomena, feminism and revolutionary ecology, have emerged with such seeming coincidence illustrates a historical truth: new theories and new movements do not develop in a vacuum, they arise to spearhead the necessary social solutions to new problems resulting from contradictions in the environment. In this case, both movements have arisen in response to the same contradiction: animal life within a technology. In the case of feminism the problem is a moral one: the biological family unit has always oppressed women and children, but now, for the first time in history, technology has created real preconditions for overthrowing these oppressive "natural" conditions, along with their cultural reinforcements. In the case of the new ecology, we find that *independent of any moral stance*, for pragmatic—survival—reasons alone, it has become necessary to free humanity from the tyranny of its biology. Humanity can no longer afford to remain in the transitional stage between simple animal existence and full control of nature. And we are much closer to a major evolutionary jump, indeed, to direction of our own evolution, than we are to a return to the animal kingdom from which we came.

Thus in terms of modern technology, a revolutionary ecological movement would have the same aim as the feminist movement: control of the new technology for humane purposes, the establishment of a beneficial "human" equilibrium between man and the new artificial environment he is creating, to replace the destroyed "natural" balance.

What are some of the concerns of ecology that are of direct interest to the feminist movement? I shall discuss briefly two issues of the new ecology that particularly pertain to the new feminism: reproduction and its control, including the seriousness of the population explosion and new methods of fertility control, and cybernation, the future takeover by machines of increasingly complex functions, altering man's age-old relation to work and wages. . . .

What are the new scientific developments in the control of this dangerously prolific reproduction? Already we have more and better contraception than ever before in history.* The old spanner-in-the-works intervention of conception (diaphragms, condoms, foams, and jellies) was only the beginning. Soon we shall have a complete understanding of the entire reproductive process in all its complexity, including the subtle dynamics of hormones and their full effects on the nervous system. Present oral contraception is at only a primitive (faulty) stage, only one of many types of fertility control now under experiment. Artificial insemination and artificial inovulation are already a reality. Choice of sex of the fetus, test-tube fertilization (when capacitation of sperm within the vagina is fully understood) are just around the corner. Several teams of scientists are working on the development of an artificial placenta. Even parthenogenesis—virgin birth—could be developed very soon.

Are people, even scientists themselves, culturally prepared for any of this? Decidedly not. A recent Harris poll, quoted in *Life* magazine, representing a broad sampling of Americans—including, for example, Iowa farmers—found a surprising number willing to consider the new methods. The hitch was that they would consider them only where they reinforced and furthered present values of family life and reproduction, e.g., to help a barren woman have her husband's child. Any question that could be interpreted as a furthering of "sexual revolution" alone was rejected flatly as unnatural. But note that it was not the "test tube" baby itself that was thought unnatural (25 percent agreed off the bat that they themselves would use this method, usually given the preconditions we have described), but the new value system, based on the elimination of male supremacy and the family. . . .

Fears of new methods of reproduction are so widespread that as of the time of this writing, 1969, the subject, outside of scientific circles, is still taboo. Even many women in the women's liberation movement—perhaps especially in the women's liberation movement—are afraid to express any interest in it for fear of confirming everyone's suspicions that they are "unnatural," spending a great deal of energy denying that they are anti-motherhood, pro-artificial reproduction, and so on . . .

* I must ask the reader to forgive me here—this chapter was written before the "Pill Hearings," indeed, before the mushrooming of the ecology movement itself. Such is the speed of modern communications—a book is outdated before it even makes it into galleys.

Artificial reproduction is not inherently dehumanizing. At very least, development of an option should make possible an honest re-examination of the ancient value of motherhood. At the present time, for a woman to come out openly against motherhood on principle is physically dangerous. She can get away with it only if she adds that she is neurotic, abnormal, childhating and therefore "unfit." ("Perhaps later . . . when I'm better prepared.") This is hardly a free atmosphere of inquiry. Until the taboo is lifted, until the decision not to have children or not to have them "naturally" is at least as legitimate as traditional childbearing, women are as good as forced into their female roles.

Another scientific development that we find difficult to absorb into our traditional value system is the dawn of cybernation, the takeover of work functions by increasingly complex machines— machines that may soon equal or surpass man in original thinking and problem-solving. While it may be argued, as with artificial re-production, that such machines are barely past the speculative stage, remember that it was only five to ten years ago that experts in the field were predicting that five or six computers would satisfy per-manently the needs of the whole country.

Cybernation, like birth control, can be a double-edged sword. Like artificial reproduction, to envision it in the hands of the present powers is to envision a nightmare. We need not elaborate. Everyone is familiar with Technocracy, 1984: the increased alienation of the masses, the intensified rule of the elite (perhaps cyberneticians), baby factories, increased government efficiency (Big Brother), and so on. In the hands of the present society there is no doubt that the machine could be used—is being used—to intensify the apparatus of repression and to increase established power.

But again, as with the population explosion, and birth control, the distinction between *misuse* of science and the value of science it-self is not often kept clear. In this case, though perhaps the response may not be quite so hysterical and evasive, we still often have the same unimaginative concentration on the evils of the machine itself, rather than a recognition of its revolutionary significance. Books and research abound on how to avoid Technocracy, 1984 (e.g., Alan Weston's *Privacy and Freedom*), but there is little thought about how to deal effectively with the qualitative changes in life style that cybernation will bring.

The two issues, population control and cybernation, produce the same nervous superficial response because in both cases the underlying problem is one for which there is no precedent: qualita-tive change in humanity's basic relationships to both its production and its reproduction. We will need almost overnight, in order to deal with the profound effects of fertility control and cybernation, a new culture based on a radical redefinition of human relationships and leisure for the masses. To so radically redefine our relationship to production and reproduction requires the destruction at once of the class system as well as the family. We will be beyond arguments about who is "bringing home the bacon"—no one will be bringing it home, because no one will be "working." Job discrimination would no longer have any basis in a society where machines do the work better than human beings of any size or skill could. Machines thus could act as the perfect equalizer, obliterating the class system based on exploitation of labor.

What might the immediate impact of cybernation be on the position of women? Briefly, we can predict the following: (1) While at first automation will continue to provide new service jobs for women, e.g., keypunch operator, computer programmer, etc., these positions are not likely to last long (precisely why women, the transient labor force *par excellence*, are sought for them). Eventually, such simple specialized control of machines will give way to a more widespread common knowledge of their control and, at the same time, at top levels, increased specialized knowledge of their more complex functions by a new elite of engineers, cyberneticians. The kinds of jobs into which women have been welcomed, the lower rung of white-collar service jobs, will be cybernated out. At the same time, housework will become more fully automated, reducing women's legitimate work functions even further. (2) Erosion of the status of the "head of the household," particularly in the working class, may shake up family life and traditional sex roles even more profoundly. (3) Massive unrest of the young, the poor, the unemployed will increase: as jobs become more difficult to obtain, and there is no cushioning of the cultural shock by education for leisure, revolutionary ferment is likely to become a staple. Thus, all in all, cybernation may aggravate the frustration that women already feel in their roles, pushing them into revolution.

A feminist revolution could be the decisive factor in establishing a new ecological balance: attention drawn to the population explosion, a shifting of emphasis from reproduction to contraception, and demands for the full development of artificial reproduction would provide an alternative to the oppressions of the biological family; cybernation, by changing man's relationship to work and wages, by transforming activity from "work" to "play" (activity done for its own sake), would allow for a total redefinition of the economy, including the family unit in its economic capacity. The double curse that man should till the soil by the sweat of his brow and that woman should bear in pain and travail would be lifted through technology to make humane living for the first time a possibility. The feminist movement has the essential mission of creating cultural acceptance of the new ecological balance necessary for the survival of the human race in the twentieth century.

The conflict between lesbian and heterosexual feminists in the women's movement has periodically reached rather serious proportions. Often, the conflict emerges clearly as one between those feminists anxious to achieve parity within the existing economic, social, and legal structures and those who argue that prevailing structures are predicated on unacceptable patriarchal attitudes and therefore must be fundamentally changed if there is to be equality between the sexes. In the following essay, leading lesbian feminist theoretician Charlotte Bunch maintains the latter and offers her "Lesbian-Feminist Theory" as a challenge to "heterosexism—the institutional and ideological domination of heterosexuality, as a fundamental part of male supremacy."

LESBIAN-FEMINIST THEORY

Charlotte Bunch

Lesbianism and feminism are both about women loving and supporting women and women revolting against the so-called supremacy of men and the patriarchal institutions that control us. Politically, understanding the connection between lesbianism and feminism is essential to ending the oppression of all women and of all homosexuals, both female and male. The political theory that embodies and defines that connection is called lesbian feminism. It is a theory that has grown out of the experiences of lesbians in both the feminist and the gay movements; out of both our participation in those movements and our separation from them at various times and places. It is the theory that holds the key to the relationship between homosexual oppression and female oppression—a connection linked in the lives of lesbians. And it is a theory that is unknown or misunderstood by many feminists, lesbians, and gay men.

In this article, I hope to erase that last sentence by clarifying the principles of lesbian feminism: to illustrate to the homosexual that *no queers* will ever be free as long as sexism persists because male supremacy is at the root of both gay oppression and homophobia. To demonstrate to the woman that *no females* will ever be free to choose to be anything until we are also free to choose to be lesbians, because the domination of heterosexuality is a mainstay of male supremacy. And above all, to show the lesbian (the homosexual and woman) that these two parts of our oppression are linked and not only need not but also should not be separated in our struggles for liberation.

416

The development of lesbian-feminist theory began for most of us with the recognition on some level that in a male supremacist culture, heterosexuality is a political institution as well as a sexual preference, and, therefore, lesbianism is political as well as personal. "The Woman-Identified Woman" statement,[1] one of the earlier lesbian-feminist documents issued by Radicalesbians in 1970, pointed to the political implications of lesbianism when it stated: "On some level, she [the lesbian] has not been able to accept the limitations and oppressions laid on her by the most basic role of her society—the female role." That paper and subsequent discussion and writings went on to analyze the nascent political power and consciousness in the personal act of being a lesbian in a male supremacist society; it is the act, whether consciously or not, of putting women first in defiance of a culture that has structured the female life around the male. Based on this recognition, the concept of woman-identification came to describe the life stance of self-affirmation and love for women; of primary identification with women that gives energy through a positive sense of self, developed with reference to ourselves, and not in relation to men.

In this context, lesbian feminism takes on its political significance. It is not just a personal choice about life-style, although it involves one in a highly personal and intimate way. It is not limited to civil rights for queers, although equal rights and job protection are absolutely essential. It is more than the dynamic female culture and community that has emerged recently, although that is crucial to our survival and power as a people. Lesbian feminism as it has developed over the past decade involves all of these, but as a political theory, it is primarily a critique of heterosexism—the institutional and ideological domination of heterosexuality, as a fundamental part of male supremacy. This theory extends the feminist analysis of sexual politics to an analysis of sexuality itself, as it is structured into our society today. Its practical application involves an orientation of one's life around women (woman-identification) and a commitment to women as a political force capable of changing society as well as our lifestyle.

Before discussing lesbian-feminist analysis further, let me clarify my use of terms that have often caused confusion. *Lesbian-feminist theory*, as a critique of male supremacy and heterosexism, is a perspective, analysis, and commitment that can be embraced by anyone, gay or straight, female or male—just as socialism or Pan-Africanism are theories that can be adopted by anyone regardless of race, sex, or

---

1. "The Woman-Identified Woman," by Radicalesbians, is included in *Radical Feminism*, edited by Anne Koedt, Ellen Levine and Anita Rapone, Quadrangle, 1973.

class. A *lesbian* is a woman whose sexual/affectional preference is for women, and who has thereby rejected the female role on some level, but she may or may not embrace a lesbian-feminist political analysis. A *Woman-Identified-Woman* is a feminist who adopts a lesbian-feminist ideology and enacts that understanding in her life, whether she is a lesbian sexually or not. All lesbians are not woman-identified; all feminists are not woman-identified; but a clearer understanding of lesbian feminism should enable more of both to unite around this common identification.

As more lesbians recognized the political significance of lesbianism, we began to see that heterosexism functions in every institution that feminists have shown to be oppressive to women: the work place, schools, the family, the media, organized religion, etc. All of society's institutions are based on the assumption that every woman either is or wants to be bonded to a man both economically and emotionally and they depend on the idea that heterosexuality is both the only natural and the superior form of human sexuality. These assumptions—the ideology of heterosexism—help to maintain the institutional oppression of all women and of those men who openly deviate from the heterosexist masculine norm.

The family and women's oppression within it are obviously based on heterosexism, as are forms of discrimination against single women or any who live outside the nuclear family. Less obvious, but equally important, discrimination against women in the work place is also supported by the ideology of heterosexism. Women are defined and exploited as secondary or marginal workers on the assumption that work is not our primary vocation: even if we work outside of the home all of our lives, we are assumed to be primarily committed to family and to have another (major) breadwinner (male) supporting us. This assumption has been proved false repeatedly, not only for lesbians but also for many others, especially Third World and lower-class women. Nevertheless, the myth prevails—the ideology of heterosexism linked with the institution of the nuclear family continues to justify job discrimination and the refusal to regard work as a serious goal for women.

One could similarly describe how heterosexist attitudes permeate all the other institutions of our society. Perhaps most important is how heterosexism has been used to deny woman's strength, to tie her self-concept and survival to men. According to society, if you are not with a man, you are not fully a woman; whether celibate or lesbian, you are seen as "queer." If you are independent and aggressive about your life, you are called a "dyke," regardless of sexual preference. Such labels have been used to terrify women—to keep straight women in their place and to keep lesbians in the closet.

Labels are not just name-calling. Behind each label is the implicit threat of social, economic, or physical reprisal—the denial of life-supporting systems or even life itself if you step too far out of line. Thus, the most pervasive and insidious thing that keeps heterosexual domination going is the control over granting or denying women heterosexual privileges: social and family acceptance, economic security, male legitimacy, legal and physical protection. The degree to which you receive these benefits depends on race, sex, and class, and on how much you play by the patriarchy's rules. Through heterosexual privilege, a woman is given a stake in behaving properly (or, in the case of a lesbian, of pretending to behave properly) and thus in maintaining the system that perpetuates her own oppression. Women, no matter what their sexual orientation or personal ties to men, must realize that our ultimate survival is more connected to that of all women than to one man. Heterosexual privileges are not lasting benefits or power but small, short-term bribes in return for giving up lasting self-discovery and collective power.

If we examine the labels and the language that have been used against us from another angle, they reveal the potential power of lesbianism and woman-identification. Why does society equate female assertiveness, independence, and wholeness (ability to live without a man) with the terms "lesbian," "man-hating dyke," "butch" (male imitator or potent one), "ball-breaker," etc.? The language used against us is the language of power and battle. Men sense in the presence of lesbians the power to revolt, to threaten their "supremacy." They perceived this potential power before we ourselves understood it, and they sought to repress our sexuality as one aspect of our potential for independence of them and for changing society.

Lesbian-feminist theory did not spring up in a vacuum; it developed out of our experiences in coming out, from the reaction against us, and particularly from our efforts to understand and analyze that reaction. Most of us who enthusiastically came out and asserted our right to be "lesbian, woman, and proud" in the late sixties and early seventies did not understand fully the threat to patriarchal society of our statements and actions. We had been warned by "older" lesbians about the dangers, but we only learned what a threat lesbianism is by the reactions we experienced both in society and in the movements that we knew—civil rights, feminist, leftist, and even gay male. Then we learned that we are outlaws. We realized that it was not okay to be lesbian in America. And we learned that it is not okay for a reason that goes far beyond individual attitudes and bigotry. It is not okay because self-loving and independent women are a challenge to the idea that men are superior, an idea that patriarchy's institutions strengthen and depend upon.

The lesbian is most clearly the antithesis of patriarchy—an offense to its basic tenets: It is woman-hating; we are woman-loving. It demands female obedience and docility; we seek strength, assertiveness and dignity for women. It bases power and defined roles on one's gender and other physical attributes; we operate outside gender defined roles and seek a new basis for defining power and relationships. Our very existence is an attack on what men have defined as "their" territory. The lesbian's future lies not in surrendering our position as outlaws for token acceptance but in seizing and using it to bring change in patriarchal society. It is our very situation as outlaws that gives us much of the strength and imagination to challenge male definitions of us and of the social order. Some of the early lesbian slogans and titles caught the essense of that power: The Lavendar Menace; The Furies; Spectre; We Are the Women Your Mother Warned You About.

While working for our civil rights and the space to develop our own life-styles and institutions, we must not think that we can be absorbed into patriarchy as it is. We must be cautious about using the "we are just like you" strategy. We are different. And society needs our differences: our ability to love women in a woman-hating world; our strength and self-sufficiency in a society that says you must have a man; our powers of imagining and discovering new possibilities that come from having to create our lives without models or the support of existing institutions. While all lesbians are obviously not the same, we are also not the same as straights. To deny our differences is to deny both our particular oppression and our particular strength. Rather we must bring our experiences and differences to all who are seeking to develop a new reality for women and thus for men as well. Some of these differences will be shared by others who do not fit society's norms of color, age, physical appearance, marital status, class, etc. In fact, the more any woman is already or steps outside of society's assumptions of who she should be, the more "queer" she is and the more she can usually see how sexist and heterosexist assumptions confine her individually and women as a group.

Since lesbian-feminist theory is also based on our experiences of female oppression, we have come to see that homophobia and gay oppression, even for men, are based in sexism and the institutional power of male supremacy. Gay men have some male privileges in society, particularly if they remain closeted or out-woman-hate heterosexual men. But they will remain scorned as less than men and more like women, as long as women are scorned and as long as real men must fuck and fuck over real women in patriarchy. Their long-term interests therefore lie not in identifying with and attempting to gain more male privilege but in challenging male supremacy along with heterosexual domination. Gay men face a choice similar to that of straight women: They can accept society's offers of short-term benefits (male privilege for one and heterosexual privilege for the other) or they can challenge the patriarchal basis of those very privileges and work for a long-term elimination of the entire system of sexual oppression.

Lesbians as both homosexuals and women have no real stake in maintaining either aspect of sex-based oppression and should be the quickest to see the importance of lesbian feminism and to enact it politically and personally. It is, then, the lesbian's ignorance about or indifference toward lesbian feminism that I find most perplexing and disturbing. To embrace and transform our status as outlaws and challenge the dual problems of sexism and heterosexism may not always be the most comfortable option; it is, however, the most powerful and fulfilling one. No matter what one's particular sphere of activity, it is a perspective that provides the basis for both individual and group strength in the struggle to gain control over our lives and to bring fundamental change in society. It sometimes appears easier to seek acceptance on patriarchy's turf and terms, but ultimately our freedom depends less on society's acceptance than on changing its basic tenets.

In discussing the lesbian-feminist theory and the lesbian as outlaw to patriarchy, I am not speaking about what specific tactics to use when (e.g., legislation versus demonstrations). Rather I am referring to the underlying analysis and approach that we bring to any political action and the view that we have of how heterosexism and male supremacy reinforce one another in maintaining our oppression. Tactics will vary widely according to circumstances, but lesbians must ground ourselves in lesbian-feminist theory. From this point, we can decide which issues to pursue in what manner and we can make alliances with other individuals and groups who also understand that patriarchy does not serve their individual interests or the interests of a more just and humane world order.

When Susan Jacoby began her career as a newspaper reporter in 1963, she promised herself that she would never write about women's subjects, for "to write about women was to write about trivia." The Possible She, Jacoby's collection of articles on women, however, attests to the profound influence of feminism on her life and work. "The Flatbush Feminists," from that collection, is an eloquent tribute to the feminist movement.

THE FLATBUSH FEMINISTS

Susan Jacoby

FROM *The Possible She*

I'm short, fat and forty-five."

Rose Danielli digs her fork into a large piece of Sara Lee cherry cheesecake as she begins to describe herself at the first meeting of a women's consciousness-raising group. Twelve women are crowded into the living room of a small red-brick house in the East Flatbush section of Brooklyn; many are old friends who have shared senior proms, weddings, births, miscarriages, family deaths, and all of the other minor and major events of life in a close-knit working-class community where neighbors still care about one another. Now they are supporting one another in a new experience: an effort to expand their middle-aged lives beyond the comfortable roles of wife, mother, and grandmother. No group of women seems further removed from the worlds of Gloria Steinem and Betty Friedan, *Ms.* magazine, marriage contracts, "alternative life styles," and all of the upper-middle-class paraphernalia frequently associated with the feminist movement. Nevertheless, the very existence of this group proves that the worlds are not as far apart as they seem.

"My mother-in-law asked me the other day if I was one of those 'women's libbers,'" continues Mrs. Danielli, "and I told her I had always been something of a 'libber' even though I like being called 'Mrs.' She said she guessed I was telling the truth, because she remembered how hard I fought for my girls to go to college. My husband and I never went to college, and everyone in the family thought our three girls would go to work to help put my son, Johnny, through. Way back when the kids were in grade school, I told my husband, 'Joe, if one of our kids is going to college, all of them are going. Your girls aren't gonna have ten children like your mama—they've gotta do something with their lives just like our boy.'

"Both of our families were shocked when our oldest girl went off to college—Joe's papa kept asking if we didn't need the extra money she could bring in working as a typist. We needed money, all right, but I never gave in—even when times were toughest and we were eating spaghetti without meat sauce three nights a week."

There is a note of solid satisfaction in Rose Danielli's voice as she finishes both her story and the cheesecake. The women have agreed to begin their first session by describing the most significant failures and successes of their lives; they will start to talk about the future after evaluating the past. The old friendship and neighborly bonds give their discussion a more comfortable aura than the one that usually prevails in Manhattan consciousness-raising sessions, which frequently reflect the fragmented and transient nature of affluent high-rise apartment living. . . .

The life stories outlined by the women have many common elements. The women are all in their forties; most grew up in first- and second-generation Italian or Jewish immigrant homes. A few have lived in East Flatbush since they were children, and the rest came from nearby blue-collar neighborhoods. Most of the women graduated from high school, went to work for a year or two at poorly paid jobs, married by age twenty, and quickly started having children. Only two of the twelve had any education beyond high school. Rose Danielli's background is typical; she worked as a telephone operator for a year before marrying Joe, a telephone installer, when they were both nineteen.

The husbands are blue-collar union men or white-collar workers employed by the city government; their income range is between $9,000 and $14,000 a year. Most of the families have at least three children. Homemade soups and clothes are a necessary economy for them rather than an expression of the "traditional female role." Their houses represent the only important financial investment of their lives and are maintained with appropriate care—postage-stamp lawns raked free of leaves, living-room sofas glazed with plastic slip-covers and reserved for company, starched kitchen curtains, home freezers stocked with the specials the women unearth in numerous grocery stores on Saturday mornings. . . .

Whatever their problems, the women love their husbands and are not about to leave them. They do not expect to liberate themselves by living alone although they understand why some younger women find marriage an unsatisfactory state. They have neither the education nor the work experience to be tapped as token women for high-powered jobs in high-powered companies. One woman in the group says she is waiting breathlessly for the day when the local six o'clock news will feature a broadcaster who is not only black and female but over forty, thereby providing on-screen representation for three oppressed groups instead of two.

Nevertheless, the women are convinced that they can build a future different from the traditional path laid out by their mothers and grandmothers. The feminist movement is responsible in large measure for their belief that they can change the course of their middle-aged lives.

The movement was gaining strength and national publicity at a time when the women who make up the East Flatbush group began to face the void most full-time mothers experience after their children grow up and leave home. Their comments in the group sessions indicate that two main concerns spurred their interest in feminism: the feeling that society in general, and their husbands in particular, no longer viewed them as sexually interesting or even sexually functioning women, and the realization that they were "out of a job" in the same sense as a middle-aged man who is fired by his employer of twenty years. . . .

Ruth Levine, who had never worked outside her home, surprised the rest of the group by becoming the first to take the plunge into the job market. She applied for a job as a file clerk in a large advertising agency and was hired with a warning from the personnel department that "most of the girls on your floor will be twenty-five years younger than you are."

Feminist opponents of job discrimination are correct in their assertion that file clerking is a thankless, dead-end task reserved by large companies for women. However, the upper-middle-class, college-educated feminists often fail to realize that a woman with no training may look upon a mundane job as an opportunity rather than an insult. For Ruth Levine, who had rarely left her neighborhood for twenty-five years, the file clerk's job was an important step into a wider world. . . .

Ruth is taking a shorthand course so that she can move into a better-paying secretarial job next fall. After she took the first step, four other women in the group found jobs. Two returned to the secretarial work they had done before they were married, one found an opening as a teacher aide in the Head Start program for preschool children, and another put her fluent Italian to work as an interpreter for older immigrants in their dealing with city agencies. Two women in the group decided they would go to college and were accepted in adult-education programs leading toward a bachelor's degree. . . .

Not all the women have had as much success in changing their own lives or the attitudes of their husbands. Judith Katz, who worked as a secretary before her marriage twenty years ago, encountered stiff opposition when she went back to work in the counseling office of a Brooklyn junior high school. Her husband especially resents the fact that she wanted a job enough to take an opening in a ghetto school with a tough reputation. As an expression of his disapproval, he refuses to ride the subway with his wife in the morning. Another of the women, an accountant's wife who is already attending classes at Brooklyn College, did not speak to her husband for several weeks after he told her, "You're too featherbrained to finish cleaning the house, much less four years of college."

In general, the East Flatbush men who disapprove of feminism express their reactions more openly than the professional husbands of upper-middle-class women who are the most vocal and visible participants in the movement. College-educated men are often reluctant to attack women's liberation in principle, but their practical behavior is another matter. Judging from the wide variety of male reactions described by the Flatbush wives, blue-collar men are no more or no less disturbed than other American men when the women in their lives try to break out of the traditional female pattern.

The East Flatbush women have considerable difficulty identifying with the widely publicized leaders of the movement. Said one: "I confess I don't feel much of a sense of sisterhood when I see pictures of Gloria Steinem with her streaked hair and slinky figure. I feel somehow that these people don't know how it is to be getting older with very little money and educaton. They have it a lot better than we do—it's not true that we're all in the same boat."

Another woman disagreed: "Well, there's one thing we all have in common—we're all afraid of muggers and rapists when we walk down a dark street at night. And that's something we have in common with the colored women who live right here in East Flatbush, even though most of us are better off financially than they are."

The women do identify with the movement on a variety of specific issues—day-care centers, equal pay for equal work, the right to abortion and contraceptive information, the need to educate young girls to think of themselves as individuals in their own right instead of viewing themselves only as future wives and mothers. Several of the women now spend considerable time trying to introduce these ideas into the conservative social environment of East Flatbush. . . .

Next fall, the East Flatbush group will take in five new women because several of the founding members will be too busy with jobs and college courses. All of the women call that progress.

The emergence of a feminist movement among black women as a result of a growing awareness of the barrier of sexism is documented in the following selection by Diane K. Lewis. Initially resistant to the feminist movement, black women viewed racism as a more powerful cause than sexism of their oppression. Lewis notes, however, in the emergence of such organizations as Black Women Organized for Action (BWOA) and the National Black Feminist Organization (NBFO), a growing responsiveness to feminist issues.

A RESPONSE TO INEQUALITY: BLACK WOMEN, RACISM, AND SEXISM

Diane K. Lewis

If, as an aftermath of the 1960s, a number of black men were recruited into higher-paying, more authoritative, and prestigious positions, black women generally moved into the lower-status and lower-paying jobs traditionally reserved for women in the dominant society. During this process they made significant strides relative to white women. Although the difference in earnings between black men and women has widened, the income gap between black women and white women has tended to narrow (see table 1). Black women earned 62 percent of the median income of white women in 1963; this increased to 90 percent in 1974.[1] Similarly, recent census data indicate that the overall occupational distribution of black women has improved relative to white women. Since 1963 black women have moved out of domestic work and into clerical positions in greater numbers. Thus, in 1963, 34 percent of black women were domestics,

Table 1

Wage Differential between Black Women, Black Men and White Women

	1963	1970	1974
Between black women and black men	$1,739	$1,899	$2,334
Between black women and white women	1,407	1,000	650

[Signs: Journal of Women in Culture and Society, 1977, vol. 3, no 2] © 1977 by The University of Chicago. All rights reserved.

1. For a comparison of increases in the ratio of black to white median income from 1967 to 1973 for men and women, see U.S. Bureau of the Census, *Money Income in 1973 of Families and Persons in the United States,* Current Population Reports, Series P-60, No. 97 (Washington, D.C.: Government Printing Office, 1975), table F, p. 12.

426

and only 10 percent were clerical workers; in 1974, 11 percent were domestics and 25 percent were clerical workers. Since the percentages for white women clerical workers have remained relatively stable between 1963 and 1974 (34 percent and 36 percent, respectively), black women appear to be moving toward parity with white women in that occupation. Although the position of black women has improved in relationship to white women, the data show that for women as a whole sexism continues to constitute a major barrier in the wider society. In fact, the ratio of white female to white male earnings has *decreased* slightly between 1963 and 1974, women earning 59 percent of the male's median income in 1963 and only 56 percent in 1975. The existence of sex bias in the wider society explains the observation that the civil rights movement elicited active efforts to provide career opportunities for black men, while little attention was paid to the employment needs of black women.[2]

Class and Sexism

The black liberation movement began to generate important structural changes in the relationship between blacks and whites in American society. For black women, these changes serve to heighten their perception of sexism, since they experience deep-seated sex discrimination as they engage in increased participation in the public sphere. Middle-class black women, in particular, are becoming more sensitive to the obstacle of sexism as racial barriers begin to fall and as the bulk of the higher-status, authoritative positions reserved for blacks have gone to black men. Nevertheless, if the leadership of black organizations recently formed to combat both racism and sexism appears to be middle class, the membership in these black women's groups seems to crosscut class lines. Thus the BWOA notes that its members include welfare recipients, maids, and the unemployed as well as high-income earners. In recognition of this diversity, the organization has adopted a flexible membership policy.[3] Similarly, the NBFO conference attracted domestic workers, welfare mothers, and other poor black women as well as students, housewives, and professionals. As one participant put it, "We were able to do what white feminists have failed to do: transcend class lines and eradicate labels."[4]

2. See Pauli Murray, "Jim Crow and Jane Crow," in Gerda Lerner, ed., *Black Women in White America: A Documentary History* (New York: Pantheon Books, 1972), p. 596.

3. Dues are computed on a sliding scale from $5 to $25 a year, but members pay when and what they can. Moreover, a woman can become a member *either* by paying dues *or* attending meetings *or* working on a committee. (See Patsy G. Fulcher, Aileen C. Hernandez, and Eleanor R. Spikes, "Sharing the Power and the Glory," *Contact* 4 (Fall, 1974): 52, 63.

4. Ashaki Habiba Taha, letter *MS.* 3 (August, 1974):12. See also Bernette Golden, "Black Women's Liberation," *Essence* 4 (February 1974): 35–36, 75–76, 86.

A further examination of the structural position of black women suggests why not only upwardly mobile black women but also poor black women will become more responsive to feminist issues. They, along with middle-class black women, are seriously affected by sex discrimination on the job. For example, Dietrich and Greiser in a study of black blue-collar workers found sexism to be an important factor in black poverty.[5] Furthermore, demographic and occupational trends, which affect all black women, should also elicit among them a sense of common interest which crosscuts class lines. There has been a steadily declining sex ratio from 95.0 in 1940 to 90.8 in 1970.[6] This probably contributes to the fact that black women are more often single than white women, more often work, and are more often heads of household. Thus, in 1974 about one half of minority women worked compared with 44 percent of white women.[7] In 1973, while 77 percent of white women who were fourteen years old and over and ever married were married and living with their husbands, only 54 percent of black women in the same category were married and residing with their spouses.[8] In 1975, while only 11 percent of white families were female headed, 35 percent of black families were supported by women.[9] Black women with preschool-aged children were also more likely to work than white mothers; in 1973, 49 percent of black women as compared with 32 percent of white women with small children were in the labor force.[10]

Black women, then, are more often self-supporting than white women and far more likely to carry single-handedly responsibilities for dependent children. These factors, together with their continued greater concentration in lower-paying service-related jobs than either white women or black men, cause poor black women, particularly, to be vitally affected by matters of inadequate income and child-care facilities, both major issues in the women's movement. For poor women, as a black welfare mother notes, women's liberation is "a matter of survival," a perception increasingly held by such groups

5. Kathryn Dietrich and Lee Greiser, "The Influence of Sex on Wage-Income of Black, Blue-Collar Workers in Selected Non-metropolitan and Metropolitan Areas of Texas" (paper presented at the annual meeting of the Southern Association of Agricultural Scientists, Memphis, Tennessee, February 1974).

6. Jackson, "But Where Are the Men?" table 3, p. 39. The sex ratio among whites has also declined steadily but in 1970 was, at 95.3, far more favorable for whites.

7. U.S. Bureau of the Census, *The Social and Economic Status of the Black Population in the United States, 1973*, p. 93.

8. Ibid., table 64, p. 90.

9. U.S. Bureau of the Census, *The Social and Economic Status of the Black Population in the United States, 1974*, table 72, p. 107.

10. U.S. Bureau of the Census, *The Social and Economic Status of the Black Population in the United States, 1973*, table 68, p. 95.

devoted to removing obstacles to the legitimate interests of poor black women as the National Welfare Rights Organization.[11]

Since both poor and middle-class black women participate in and have been aware of some of the successes of the black liberation movement, their expectations of greater access to resources have been raised. As these expectations have been frustrated, a sense of common interest is beginning to emerge which may increasingly include all classes of black women. A study of race and class factors affecting women's attitudes toward the women's liberation movement in Cleveland found that white working-class women were far less likely than white middle-class women to be interested in women's rights, while black working-class women were somewhat *more* receptive than black middle-class women to efforts to change women's status (see table 2).[12]

Table 2

Percentage of Black and White Women Manifesting a High or Low Degree of Interest in Women's Rights

Degree of Interest	Black Women		White Women	
	Middle Class	Working Class	Middle Class	Working Class
High	44	48	54	27
Low	56	52	46	73

Source: From Willa Mae Hemmons. "Toward an Understanding of Attitudes Held by Black Women on the Women's Liberation Movement" (Ph.D. diss., Case Western Reserve University, 1973), tables 7 and 8, p. 101.

The shared experience of racism has also tended to blur class lines among blacks. This, too, probably will contribute to a greater tendency for both poor and middle-class black women to agree regarding women's rights. For example, middle-class black families are in a more precarious position than middle-class white families because of racism. Especially in times of economic recession and high

11. Johnnie Tillmon, "Welfare Is a Woman's Issue," in *Marriage and the Family: A Critical Analysis and Proposals for Change*, ed. Carolyn C. Perrucci and Dena B. Targ (New York: David McKay, 1974), pp. 108, 109, 111.

12. Willa Mae Hemmons, "Toward an Understanding of Attitudes Held by Black Women on the Women's Liberation Movement" (Ph.D. diss., Case Western Reserve University, 1973). Her sample for this exploratory study was a purposive one, including eighty-three women, forty-five black and thirty-seven white. She notes that she sought women from different classes and residential and occupational areas; however the size of her sample makes her results more suggestive than conclusive (see her discussion of the sample, pp. 80–86).

unemployment, they may find themselves in economic straits similar to lower-class blacks.[13]

Whether black women develop a sense of common interests that is manifested more in opposition to sexism or to racism will depend upon the structural relationship between the sexes and between the races. With growing black participation in the wider society some black women, experiencing frustration of their interests primarily as women, now probably share the viewpoint a member of NBFO expressed. "White women are our natural allies; we can't take on the system alone."[14] Middle-class black women will increasingly feel their interests as women illegitimately frustrated if a combination of factors continues: (1) the income gap between themselves and white women narrows even more, (2) the overall position of women remains low, and (3) the white male hierarchy persists in admitting minority males but excluding minority females from equitable participation in the wider society. Middle-class black women, even more than middle-class white women, occupy a structural position likely to generate a pervasive sense of relative deprivation and an ideology of discontent.

However, on the other hand, black women may see that racism still affects a considerable number of blacks, including black men. Jessie Bernard, analyzing occupations and earnings for black and white men and women for the period 1939–70, concluded: ". . . racism tends to be more serious for black men than black women . . . (and) sexism tends to be more serious for black women than racism.[15] While some middle-class black men have made significant advances, a careful inspection of the trends of the ratio of black to white earnings shows that black men, as a whole, are making much slower headway in closing the income gap between them and white men than are black women relative to white women. Black men earned 64 percent of the median income of white men in 1967; 67 percent of the income of white men in 1973.[16] This would appear to matter to black women. For example, if they marry, there will probably be more pressure on them to work in order to supplement the family income than on married white women. Indeed, now black married women are more likely to work outside the home than their white counterparts.[17]

13. Andrew Billingsley, *Black Families in White America* (Englewood Cliffs, N.J.: Prentice-Hall, 1968), pp. 10–15.

15. Jessie Bernard, "The Impact of Sexism and Racism on Employment Status and Earnings, with Addendum," Module 25 (New York: MSS Modular Publications, Inc., 1974), p. 5.

16. U.S. Bureau of the Census, *Money Income in 1973 of Families and Persons in the United States*, table F, p. 12. This was similar to the rate of growth of black female income to the black male's, i.e., black women earned 67 percent of the income of black men in 1967 and 70 percent of the income of black men in 1973.

17. U.S. Bureau of the Census, *The Social and Economic Status of the Black Population in the United States, 1973*, table 67, p. 95.

Perpetuation of a situation in which all black men, irrespective of their socioeconomic status, are subject to racism, might well propel increasing numbers of black women, irrespective of their class backgrounds into overt opposition to both sexism and racism. Their way of doing so, however, might involve organizations concerned with women's rights, but limited to blacks and strongly racially oriented.[18] The concern with racism would preclude too exclusive a concern with sexism.

18. For an alternate thesis on the possible direction of change in the relationship between blacks and whites, males and females, see Clyde W. Franklin, Jr. and Laurel R. Walum, "Toward a Paradigm of Substructural Relations: An Application to Sex and Race in the United States," *Phylon* 33 (Fall 1972): 247–52. See also Geraldine Richman, "A Natural Alliance: The New Role for Black Women," *Civil Rights Digest* 6 (Spring 1974): 57–65, for an interesting discussion of the black professional woman's structural position which enables her to act as catalyst for change in the position of both women and blacks.

*In a spirit of celebration, Denise Levertov invokes the
strength of woman in her refusal to allow the sexual
economy to dim the satisfactions and pleasures of
womanhood.*

STEPPING WESTWARD

Denise Levertov

*What is green in me
darkens, muscadine.*

*If woman is inconstant,
good, I am faithful to*

*ebb and flow, I fall
in season and now*

*is a time of ripening.
If her part*

*is to be true,
a north star,*

*good, I hold steady
in the black sky*

*and vanish by day
yet burn there*

*in blue or above
quilts of cloud.*

*There is no savor
more sweet, more salt*

*than to be glad to be
what, woman,*

*and who, myself,
I am, a shadow*

*that grows longer as the sun
moves, drawn out*

*on a thread of wonder.
If I bear burdens*

*they begin to be remembered
as gifts, goods, a basket*

*of bread that hurts
my shoulders but closes me*

*in fragrance. I can
eat as I go.*

BIBLIOGRAPHY

Chapter 1. The Origins of the Patriarchy

Aristotle. *Politics*. Translated by Benjamin Jowett. New York: Random House, 1943.

Bachofen, Johann Jakob. *Myth, Religions and Mother Right*. Translated by Ralph Manheim. Princeton: Princeton University Press, 1967.

Briffault, Robert. *The Mothers: A Study of the Origin of Sentiments and Institutions*. 3 vols. New York: Macmillan, 1927.

Brownmiller, Susan. *Against Our Will: Men, Women and Rape*. New York: Simon and Schuster, 1976.

Campbell, Joseph. *The Masks of God: Occidental Mythology*. New York: Viking Press, 1964.

Daly, Mary. *The Church and the Second Sex*. New York: Harper & Row, 1968.

Davis, Elizabeth Gould. *The First Sex*. Baltimore: Penguin, 1972.

De Beauvoir, Simone. *The Second Sex*. New York: Knopf, 1952.

Diner, Helen. *Mothers and Amazons: The First Feminine History of Culture*. Garden City, New York: Anchor, 1973.

Engels, Frederick. *The Origin of the Family, Private Property, and the State*. New York: International Publishers, 1942.

Gilbert, Sandra M. "Patriarchal Poetry and Women Readers: Reflections on Milton's Bogey." PMLA 93:368–82.

Harris, Marvin. *Cannibals and Kings: The Origins of Culture*. New York: Vintage, 1978.

The Interpreter's Bible. Vol. 1. New York: Abingdon Press, 1952.

Mill, John Stuart. *The Subjection of Women*. New York: Dutton, 1970.

Milton, John. *Paradise Lost* and *Paradise Regained*. New York: New American Library, 1968.

Montagu, Ashley. *The Natural Superiority of Women*. New York: Macmillan, 1972.

Morgan, Lewis Henry. *Ancient Society: Researches in the Lines of Human Progress from Savagery Through Barbarism to Civilization*. Chicago: Kerr, 1907.

Reed, Evelyn. *Woman's Evolution from Matriarchal Clan to Patriarchal Family*. New York: Pathfinder Press, 1975.

Ruether, Rosemary Radford. *New Woman/New Earth: Sexist Ideologies and Human Liberation*. New York: Seaburg Press, 1975.

Watson, Barbara Bellow. *Women's Studies: The Social Realities*. New York: Harper & Row, 1976.

Woolf, Virginia. *A Writer's Diary*. New York: Harcourt, 1954.

Zihlman, Adrienne. "Women in Evolution, Part II: Subsistence and Social Organization among Early Hominids." *Signs* 4, no. 1 (1978): 4–20.

Chapter 2. The Origins of Sex Differences

Baker, Susan W. "Biological Influences on Human Sex and Gender." *Signs* 6, no. 1 (1980): 80–96.

Chodorow, Nancy. "Family Structure and Feminine Personality." In *Women, Culture and Society*, edited by Michele Zimbalist Rosaldo and Louise Lamphere. Stanford: Stanford University Press, 1974, pp. 43–66.

———. *The Reproduction of Mothering: Psychoanalysis and the Sociology of Gender*. Berkeley: University of California Press, 1978.

de Beauvoir, Simone. *The Second Sex*. New York: Knopf, 1952.

Firestone, Shulamith. *The Dialectic of Sex: The Case for Feminist Revolution*. New York: Bantam, 1970.

Freud, Sigmund. *New Introductory Lectures on Psychoanalysis*. Translated by James Strachey. New York: Norton, 1965; orig. pub. 1933.

Harris, Marvin. *Cannibals and Kings: The Origins of Culture*. New York: Vintage, 1978.

Lessing, Doris. *The Golden Notebook*. New York: Bantam, 1973; orig. pub. 1962.

Maccoby, Eleanor Emmons, and Carol Nagy Jacklin. *The Psychology of Sex Differences*. Stanford: Stanford University Press, 1974.

Mitchell, Juliet. *Psychoanalysis and Feminism*. New York: Vintage, 1975.

Ortner, Sherry B. "Is Female to Male as Nature Is to Culture?" In *Woman, Culture and Society*, edited by Michele Zimbalist Rosaldo and Louise Lamphere. Stanford: Stanford University Press, 1975, pp. 67–87.

Rossi, Alice. "A Biosocial Perspective on Parenting." *Daedalus* 106, no. 2 (1977): 1–31.

Stoller, Robert J., M. D. *Sex and Gender*. New York: Aronson, 1974.

Tavris, Carol, and Carole Offir. *The Longest War: Sex Differences in Perspective*. New York: Harcourt Brace Jovanovich, 1977.

Woolf, Virginia. *To the Lighthouse*. New York: Harcourt, Brace and World, 1927.

Chapter 3. From Pit to Pedestal

Bloch, Ruth H. "Untangling the Roots of Modern Sex Roles: A Survey of Four Centuries of Change." *Signs* 4, no. 2 (1978): 237–52.

Brownmiller, Susan. *Against Our Will: Men, Women and Rape*. New York: Simon and Schuster, 1976.

Bullough, Vern L. *The Subordinate Sex: A History of Attitudes Toward Women*. New York: Penguin, 1974.

Cash, W. J. *The Mind of the South*. New York: Vintage, n.d.; orig. pub. Knopf, 1941.

Dworkin, Andrea. *Woman Hating*. New York: Dutton, 1974.

Fox, Greer Litton. "'Nice Girl': Social Control of Women Through a Value Construct." *Signs* 2, no. 4 (1977): 805–17.

Genovese, Eugene. *Roll, Jordan, Roll*. New York: Pantheon, 1972.

Gilman, Charlotte Perkins. "Parasitism and Civilized Vice." In *Woman's Coming of Age*, edited by Samuel Schmalhausen and V. F. Calverton. New York: Liveright, 1931, pp. 110–26.

———. *The Yellow Wallpaper*. Old Westbury, New York: Feminist Press, 1973.

Gordon, Linda. *Woman's Body, Woman's Right: A Social History of Birth Control in America*. New York: Penguin, 1977.

Gutman, Herbert G. *The Black Family in Slavery and Freedom, 1750–1925*. New York: Pantheon, 1976.

Himmelfarb, Gertrude. "A History of the New History." *New York Times Book Review*, 10 January 1982, pp. 9, 24–25.

Hughes, Pennethorne. *Witchcraft*. Middlesex: Penguin, 1965.

Johnson, Allan Griswold. "On the Prevalence of Rape in the United States." *Signs* 6, no. 1 (1980).

Kramer, Heinrich, and Jacob Sprenger. *Malleus Maleficarum*. Translated and edited by Montague Summers. London: Rodker, 1928.

Lerner, Gerda. *The Majority Finds Its Past: Placing Women in History*. New York: Oxford University Press, 1979.

Luther, Martin. *What Luther Says*. 3 vols. Compiled by Ewald M. Plass. St. Louis: Concordia, 1959.

Metzker, Isaac, ed. *A Bintel Brief*. New York: Ballantine, 1972.

Millett, Kate. *Sexual Politics*. New York: Doubleday, 1970.

Morrison, Toni. *The Bluest Eye*. New York: Simon and Schuster, 1972.

Pomeroy, Sara B. *Goddesses, Whores, Wives and Slaves: Women in Classical Antiquity*. New York: Schocken, 1975.

Power, Eileen. *Medieval Women*, edited by M. M. Postan. Cambridge: Cambridge University Press, 1975.

Rigney, Barbara. *Madness and Sexual Politics in the Feminist Novel*. Madison: University of Wisconsin Press, 1978.

Rousseau, Jean Jacques. *Emile*. Translated by Barbara Foxley. London: Dent, 1974; orig. pub. 1762.

Ruether, Rosemary Radford. *Religion and Sexism: Images of Women in the Jewish and Christian Traditions*. New York: Simon and Schuster, 1974.

Scott, Anne Firor. *The Southern Lady: From Pedestal to Politics, 1830–1930*. Chicago: University of Chicago Press, 1970.

Smith-Rosenberg, Carroll. "The New Woman and the New History." *Feminist Studies* 3, no. 1/2 (1975).

Thomas, Keith. *Religion and the Decline of Magic*. New York: Scribners, 1971.

Tillyard, E. M. W. *The Elizabethan World Picture*. New York: Vintage, n.d.

Trevor-Roper, H. R. *Religion, the Reformation and Social Change*. London: Macmillan, 1967.

Truth, Sojourner, "Ain't I a Woman?" In *History of Woman Suffrage*, vol. 1, edited by Elizabeth Cady Stanton, Susan B. Anthony, and Matilda Joslyn Gage. Rochester, N.Y.: Charles Mann, 1881, pp. 116–17.

Tuchman, Barbara. *A Distant Mirror: The Calamitous 14th Century*. New York: Knopf, 1978.

Vicinus, Martha. *Suffer and Be Still: Women in the Victorian Age*. Bloomington: University of Indiana Press, 1973.

Welter, Barbara, "The Cult of True Womanhood, 1966." In *The American Sisterhood*, edited by Wendy Martin. New York: Harper & Row, 1972, pp. 243–56.

Chapter 4. Women and the Marketplace

Almquist, Elizabeth M. "Black Women and the Pursuit of Equality." In *Women: A Feminist Perspective*, edited by Jo Freeman. Palo Alto: Mayfield, 1979.

Baum, Charlotte, Paula Hyman, and Sonya Michel. *The Jewish Woman in America*. New York: New American Library, 1977.

Baxandall, Rosalyn, Linda Gordon, and Susan Reverby. *America's Working Women*. New York: Random House, 1976.

Boulding, Elise. "Familial Constraints on Women's Work Roles." *Signs* 1, no. 3, part 2 (1976): 95–117.

———. *The Underside of History: A View of Women Through Time*. Boulder: Westview Press, 1976.

Chesler, Phyllis. *Women, Money and Power*. New York: Morrow, 1976.

Degler, Carl. *At Odds: Women and the Family in America from the Revolution to the Present*. New York: Oxford University Press, 1980.

Eisenstein, Zillah. *The Radical Future of Liberal Feminism*. New York: Longman, 1981.

Friedan, Betty. *The Feminine Mystique*. New York: Dell, 1970; orig. pub. 1963.

Goldman, Emma. "The Traffic in Women." In *Red Emma Speaks: Selected Writings and Speeches by Emma Goldman*. Compiled and edited by Alix Kates Shulman. New York: Random House, 1972.

Gutman, Herbert G. *The Black Family in Slavery and Freedom, 1750–1925*. New York: Vintage, 1977.

Ibsen, Henrick. *A Doll's House*. Available in many collections of plays.

Kanowitz, Leo. *Women and the Law: The Unfinished Revolution*. Albuquerque: University of New Mexico Press, 1969.

Mitchell, Juliet. *Woman's Estate*. New York: Vintage, 1973.

Oakley, Ann. *Woman's Work: The Housewife, Past and Present*. New York: Vintage, 1976.

Olsen, Tillie. "One Out of Twelve: Writers Who Are Women in Our Century." In *Silences*. New York: Delacorte Press, 1978.

Rossi, Alice. *The Feminist Papers: From Adams to de Beauvoir*. New York: Bantam, 1974.

Rothman, Sheila. *Woman's Proper Place: A History of Changing Ideals and Practices, 1870 to the Present*. New York: Basic, 1978.

Ryan, Mary. Womanhood in America: From Colonial Times to the Present. New York: Basic, 1978.

Seifer, Nancy. *Absent from the Majority: Working Class Women in America*. New York: National Project on Ethnic America of the American Jewish Committee, 1973.

Sinclair, Upton. *The Jungle*. New York: Signet, 1960; orig. pub. 1905.

Tobias, Sheila, and Lisa Anderson. *What Really Happened to Rosie the Riveter? Demobilization and the Female Labor Force, 1944–47*. New York: MSS Modular Publications, 1973.

Trieman, Donald J., and Heidi L. Hartmann, eds. *Women, Work and Wages: Equal Pay for Jobs of Equal Value*. Washington, D.C.: National Academy Press, 1981.

Veblen, Thorstein. *The Theory of the Leisure Class*. New York: Macmillan, 1953.

Wertheimer, Barbara. *We Were There: The Story of Working Women in America*. New York: Pantheon, 1977.

Woolf, Virginia. *A Room of One's Own*. New York: Harcourt, Brace and World, 1957; orig. pub. 1929.

Chapter 5. The Personal as Political

Ariès Philippe. *Centuries of Childhood: A Social History of Family Life*. Translated by Robert Baldick. New York: Vintage, 1962.

Arms, Suzanne. *Immaculate Deception*. Boston: Houghton Mifflin, 1975.

Barker-Benfield, G. J. *The Horrors of the Half-Known Life: Male Attitudes Towards Women and Sexuality in Nineteenth Century America*. New York: Harper & Row, 1976.

Bart, Pauline. "Depression in Middle-Aged Women." In *Woman in Sexist Society*, edited by Vivian Gornick and Barbara K. Moran. New York: Basic, 1971.

Bernard, Jessie. *The Future of Motherhood*. New York: Dial Press, 1974.

Brooks, Gwendolyn. "The Mother." In *The World of Gwendolyn Brooks*. New York: Harper & Row, 1971.

Coles, Robert. *Children of Crisis: A Study of Courage and Fear.* Vol. 1. Boston: Atlantic Monthly Press/Little, Brown, 1967.

de Beauvoir, Simone. *The Second Sex.* New York: Knopf, 1952.

Douglas, Ann. *The Feminization of American Culture.* New York: Borzoi, 1977.

Dye, Nancy Schrom. "History of Childbirth in America." *Signs* 6, no. 1 (1980): 97–108.

Ehrenreich, Barbara, and Deirdre English. *For Her Own Good: 150 Years of the Experts' Advice to Women.* New York: Anchor, 1979.

Eisenstein, Zillah. *The Radical Future of Liberal Feminism.* New York: Longman, 1981.

Ewen, Stuart. *Captains of Consciousness.* New York: McGraw-Hill, 1976.

Friedan, Betty. *The Feminine Mystique.* New York: Dell, 1970; orig. pub. 1963.

Larned, Deborah. "The Epidemic in Unnecessary Hysterectomy." In Claudia Dreifus, *Seizing Our Bodies: The Politics of Women's Health.* New York: Vintage, 1978, pp. 195–208.

Lasch, Christopher. "Life in the Therapeutic State." *New York Review of Books*, 12 June 1980, pp. 24–32.

Leavitt, Judith Walzer. "Birthing and Anesthesia: The Debate over Twilight Sleep." *Signs* 6, no. 1 (1980): 147–64.

Mitchell, Juliet. *Woman's Estate.* New York: Vintage, 1973.

Olsen, Tillie. *Tell Me a Riddle.* New York: Dell, 1961.

Person, Ethel Spector. "Sexuality as a Mainstay of Identity: Psychoanalytic Perspectives." *Signs* 5, no. 4 (1980): 605–30.

Petchesky, Rosalind Pollack. "Reproductive Freedom: Beyond 'A Woman's Right to Choose.'" *Signs* 5, no. 4 (1980): 661–85.

Rich, Adrienne. *Of Woman Born: Motherhood as Experience and Institution.* New York: Norton, 1976.

Rossi, Alice. "Life-Span Theories and Women's Lives." *Signs* 6, no. 1 (1980): 4–32.

Shulman, Alix Kates. "Sex and Power: Sexual Bases of Radical Feminism." *Signs* 5, no. 4 (1980): 590–604.

Stimpson, Catherine. "The Fallacy of Body Reductionism." Paper presented at Interdisciplinary Research Conference on Menopause, April 1979.

Weideger, Paula. *Menstruation and Menopause.* New York: Delta/Dell, 1975.

Zaretsky, Eli. *Capitalism, the Family and Personal Life.* New York: Harper Colophon, 1976.

Chapter 6. The Ideas and Origins of Feminism

Adams, Abigail Smith, and John Adams. *The Book of Abigail and John: Selected Letters of the Adams Family, 1762–1784*, edited by L. H. Butterfield, Marc Friedlaender and Mary-Jo Kline, Cambridge, Mass.: Harvard University Press, 1975.

Addams, Jane. *Jane Addams: A Centennial Reader.* New York: Macmillan, 1960.

Anthony, Susan B. "Woman Wants Bread, Not the Ballot!" In *Life and Work of Susan B. Anthony*, vol. 3, edited by Ida H. Harper. Indianapolis: Hollenbeck Press, 1898, pp. 996–1003.

Berg Barbara. *The Remembered Gate: Origins of American Feminism.* New York: Oxford University Press, 1978.

Bloch, Ruth H. "Untangling the Roots of Modern Sex Roles: A Survey of Four Centuries of Change." *Signs* 4, no. 2 (1978): 237–52.

Boulding, Elise. *The Underside of History: A View of Women Through Time.* Boulder, Colo.: Westview Press, 1976.

Brown, Olympia. "On Foreign Rule." In *History of Woman Suffrage*, vol. 4, edited by Susan B. Anthony and Ida H. Harper. Rochester, N.Y.: Hollenbeck Press, 1902, pp. 148–49.

Buhle, Mary Jo, and Paul Buhle. *The Concise History of Woman Suffrage: Selections from the Classic Work of Stanton, Anthony, Gage, and Harper*. Champaign: University of Illinois Press, 1978.

Douglas, Ann. *The Feminization of American Culture*. New York: Borzoi, 1977.

Du Bois, Ellen. *Feminism and Suffrage: The Emergence of an Independent Women's Movement in America, 1848–1869*. Ithaca: Cornell University Press, 1978.

Du Bois, Ellen. "The Radicalism of the Woman Suffrage Movement: Notes Toward the Reconstruction of Nineteenth-Century Feminism." *Feminist Studies* 3 (Fall 1975): 63–71.

Evans, Richard J. *The Feminists: Women's Emancipation Movements in Europe, America and Australasia 1840–1920*. New York: Barnes and Noble, 1977.

Flexnor, Eleanor. *Century of Struggle: The Woman's Rights Movement in the United States*. New York: Atheneum, 1974.

Grimké, Angelina Emily. *Letters to Catherine Beecher*. New York: Arno Press, 1969; reprint of 1836 ed.

Grimké, Sarah Moore. *Letters on the Equality of the Sexes and the Condition of Woman*. New York: Source Book Press, 1970; reprint of 1838 ed.

History of Woman Suffrage. 6 vols. Vols. 1–3 edited by Elizabeth Cady Stanton, Susan B. Anthony, and Matilda Joslyn Gage. Rochester, New York: Charles Mann, 1881, 1877. Vol. 4 edited by Susan B. Anthony and Ida Husted Harper. Indianapolis: Hollenbeck Press, 1902. Vols. 5 and 6 edited by Ida Husted Harper. New York: Little and Ives, 1922.

Jacoby, Robin Miller. "The Women's Trade Union League." *Feminist Studies* 3 (Fall 1975): 126–40.

Jones, Mary Harris. *The Autobiography of Mother Jones*, edited by Mary Field Parton. Chicago: Kerr, 1925.

Kraditor, Aileen. *The Ideas of the Woman Suffrage Movement, 1890–1920*. Garden City, New York: Doubleday, 1971.

Kraditor, Aileen. *Up from the Pedestal: Selected Writings in the History of American Feminism*. Chicago: Quadrangle, 1968.

Paulson, Ross Evans. *Women's Suffrage and Prohibition: A Comparative Study of Equality and Social Control*. Glenview, Ill.: Scott Foresman, 1973.

Rossi, Alice. *The Feminist Papers: From Adams to de Beauvoir*. New York: Bantam, 1974.

Ryan, Mary. *Womanhood in America: From Colonial Times to the Present*. New York: Basic, 1973.

Sacks, Karen. "Class Roots of Feminism." In Sheila Ruth, *Issues in Feminism: A First Course in Women's Studies*. Boston: Houghton Mifflin, 1980, pp. 489–501.

Seneca Falls Women's Rights Convention. "Declaration of Sentiments and Resolutions." In *History of Woman Suffrage*, vol. 1, edited by Elizabeth Cady Stanton, Susan B. Anthony, and Matilda Joslyn Gage. Rochester, N.Y.: Charles Mann, 1881, pp. 70–73.

Stanton, Elizabeth Cady, Susan B. Anthony, and Matilda Joselyn Gage, *History of Woman Suffrage*, vol. 1. Rochester, New York: Charles Mann, 1881.

Stone, Lucy. "Disappointment Is the Lot of Woman." In *History of Woman Suffrage*, vol. 1. Rochester, New York: Charles Mann, 1881, pp. 165–66.

Truth, Sojourner. "Keeping the Thing Going While Things are Stirring." In *History of Woman Suffrage*, vol. 2. Rochester, N.Y.: Charles Mann, 1881, pp. 193–94.

Wollstonecraft, Mary. *A Vindication of the Rights of Woman*. New York: Norton, 1975.

Chapter 7. Feminism: The Second Wave

Bunch, Charlotte. "Lesbian-Feminist Theory." In *Our Right to Love*, edited by Virginia Vida. Englewood Cliffs, N.J.: Prentice-Hall, 1978, pp. 180–82.

Chafe, William H. *The American Woman: Her Changing Social, Economic, and Political Roles, 1920–1970*. New York: Oxford University Press, 1972.

———. *Women and Equality: Changing Patterns in American Culture*. New York: Oxford University Press, 1977.

Clines, Francis X. "Children of Desire." *New York Times Magazine*, 30 September 1979, pp. 36–48.

Coles, Robert. *Children of Crisis: A Study of Courage and Fear*. vol. 1. Boston: Atlantic Monthly Press/Little, Brown, 1967.

Deckard, Barbara Sinclair. *The Women's Movement: Political, Socioeconomic, and Psychological Issues*. New York: Harper & Row, 1975.

Degler, Carl. *At Odds: Women and the Family in America from the Revolution to the Present*. New York: Oxford University Press, 1980.

Didion, Joan. *The White Album*. New York: Simon and Schuster, 1979.

Ehrenreich, Barbara, and Deirdre English. *For Her Own Good: 150 Years of the Experts' Advice to Women*. Garden City, New York: Anchor, 1979.

Eisenstein, Zillah. *The Radical Future of Liberal Feminism*. New York: Longman, 1981.

Firestone, Shulamith. *The Dialectic of Sex: The Case for Feminist Revolution*. New York: Bantam, 1970.

Freeman, Jo. *The Politics of Women's Liberation*. New York: Longman, 1975.

Friedan, Betty. *The Feminine Mystique*. New York: Dell, 1970; orig. pub. 1963.

Gornick, Vivian. "Consciousness Raising." *New York Times Magazine*, 10 January 1971, pp. 22–23, 77–84.

Greenberg, Hazel. "The ERA in Context: Its Impact on Society." In *Women's Rights and the Law: The Impact of the ERA on State Laws*. New York: Praeger, 1977, pp. 1–12.

Jacoby, Susan. *The Possible She*. New York: Farrar, Straus and Giroux, 1979.

Kraditor, Aileen. *Up from the Pedestal: Selected Writings in the History of American Feminism*. Chicago: Quadrangle, 1968.

Levertov, Denise. *The Sorrow Dance*. New York: New Directions, 1966.

Lewis, Diane K. "A Response to Inequality: Black Women, Racism, and Sexism." *Signs* 3, no. 2 (1977): 339–61.

Lydon, Susan. "The Politics of Orgasm." In *Sisterhood Is Powerful*, edited by Robin Morgan. New York: Random House, 1970, pp. 197–205.

On Campus with Women. Washington, D.C.: American Association of Colleges and Universities, 1980.

O'Neill, William. *Everyone Was Brave: The Rise and Fall of Feminism in America*. Chicago: Quadrangle, 1969.

Radicalesbians. "The Woman-Identified Woman." In *Radical Feminism*, edited by Anne Koedt, Ellen Levine, and Anita Rapone. New York: Quadrangle, 1973.

Rossi, Alice. *The Feminist Papers: From Adams to de Beauvoir*. New York: Bantam, 1974.

Ryan, Mary. *Womanhood in America: From Colonial Times to the Present*. New York: Basic, 1978.

Sherfey, Mary Jane. "The Evolution and Nature of Female Sexuality." In *Sisterhood Is Powerful*, edited by Robin Morgan. New York: Random House, 1970, pp. 220–30.

Shulman, Alix Kates. "Sex and Power: Sexual Bases of Radical Feminism." *Signs* 5, no. 4 (1980): 590–604.

Sochen, June. *Movers and Shakers: American Women Thinkers and Activists, 1900–1970*. New York: Quadrangle, 1974.

Walker, Alice. "Other Voices, Other Moods." *MS.*, February 1978, pp. 50–52, 70.

Suggested Further Readings

Chapter 1. The Origins of the Patriarchy

Bourguignon, Erika, ed. *A World of Women: Anthropological Studies of Women in the Societies of the World*. New York: Praeger, 1979.

Clark, Elizabeth and Herbert Richardson, eds. *Women and Religion: A Feminist Sourcebook of Christian Thought*. New York: Harper & Row, 1977.

Clark, Lorenne M. and Lynda Lange, eds. *The Sexism of Social and Political Theory: Women and Reproduction from Plato to Nietzsche*. Toronto: University of Toronto Press, 1979.

Figes, Eva. *Patriarchal Attitudes*. New York: Stein and Day, 1970.

Fisher, Elizabeth. *Woman's Creation*. Garden City, N.Y.: Anchor Press, 1979.

Frazer, James G. *The Golden Bough*. 12 vols. London and New York: Macmillan, 1907–15.

Freund, Philip. *Myths of Creation*. New York: Washington Square Press, 1965.

Gilman, Charlotte Perkins. *The Manmade World: Our Androcentric Culture*. New York: Source Book Press, 1970.

Herschberger, Ruth. *Adam's Rib*. New York: Harper & Row, 1948.

Janeway, Elizabeth. *Man's World—Woman's Place: A Study in Social Mythology*. New York: Morrow, 1971.

Malinowski, Bronislaw. *Sex, Culture and Myth*. New York: Harcourt Brace, 1962.

Newmann, Erich. *The Great Mother: An Analysis of the Archetype*. Translated by Ralph Manheim Princeton: Princeton University Press, 1963.

Otwell, John H. *And Sarah Laughed: The Status of Women in the Old Testament*. Philadelphia: Westminster Press, 1977.

Reiter, Rayna R., ed. *Toward an Anthropology of Women*. New York: Monthly Review Press, 1975.

Rosaldo, Michelle Zimbalist and Louise Lamphere, eds. *Woman, Culture and Society*. Stanford: Stanford University Press, 1974.

Sanday, Peggy Reeves. *Female Power and Male Dominance*. New York: Cambridge University Press, 1981.

Tanner, Nancy M. *On Becoming Human*. New York: Cambridge University Press, 1981.

Weisstein, Naomi. *The Godfathers: Freudians, Marxists and the Scientific and Political Protection Societies*. New Haven: Belladonna Publishing, 1975.

Chapter 2. The Origins of Sex Differences

Bardwick, Judith. *Psychology of Women: A Study of Bio-Cultural Conflicts*. New York: Harper & Row, 1971.

Bardwick, Judith M., Elizabeth Douvan, Matina S. Horner and David Gutman. *Feminine Personality and Conflict*. Westport, Conn.: Greenwood Press, 1980.

Chetwynd, Jane and Oonagh Hartnett. *The Sex Role System: Psychological and Sociological Perspectives.* Boston: Routledge & Kegan Paul, 1978.

Deutsch, Helene. *The Psychology of Women: A Psychoanalytic Interpretation.* New York: Grune & Stratton, 1944–45.

Ellman, Mary. *Thinking about Women.* New York: Harcourt Brace, 1968.

Friedl, Ernestine. *Women and Men: An Anthropologist's View.* New York: Holt, Rinehart & Winston, 1975.

Friedman, Richard C., M. D., Ralph M. Richart, M.D., and Raymond L. Vande Wiele, M. D. *Sex Differences in Behavior.* New York: John Wiley, 1975.

Gilman, Charlotte Perkins. *Herland.* New York: Pantheon Books, 1979.

Horney, Karen. *Feminine Psychology*, edited by Harold Kelman. New York: Norton, 1967.

Kaplan, Alexandra G. and Joan P. Bean. *Beyond Sex Role Stereotypes: Readings in the Psychology of Androgyny.* Boston: Little, Brown, 1976.

Klein, Viola. *The Feminine Character: History of an Ideology.* Urbana: University of Illinois Press, 1972 (reprint of 1946 edition).

Mead, Margaret. *Male and Female: A Study of the Sexes in a Changing World.* New York: Dell Publishing Co., 1970 (first published 1949).

Rivers, Caryl, Rosalind Barnett, and Grace Baruch. *Beyond Sugar and Spice: How Women Grow, Learn and Thrive.* New York: Putnam, 1978.

Romer, Nancy. *The Sex-Role Cycle: Socialization from Infancy to Old Age.* Old Westbury, N.Y.: Feminist Press, 1981.

Singer, Jane. *Androgyny: Toward a New Theory of Sexuality.* Garden City, N.Y.: Doubleday, 1976.

Chapter 3. From Pit to Pedestal

Angelou, Maya. *I Know Why the Caged Bird Sings.* New York: Random House, 1970.

Arnow, Hariette. *The Dollmaker.* New York: Avon Books, 1972.

Bernikow, Louise, ed. *The World Split Open: Four Centuries of Women Poets in England and America, 1552–1950.* New York: Vintage, 1974.

Brighton Women and Science Group. *Alice Through the Microscope: The Power of Science over Women's Lives.* London: Virago, 1980.

Dean, Nancy and Myra Stark. *In the Looking Glass: Twenty-One Modern Short Stories by Women.* New York: G. P. Putnam, 1977.

Dworkin, Andrea. *Pornography: Men Possessing Women.* New York: Pedigree Books, 1981.

Ehrenreich, Barbara and Deirdre English. *Witches, Midwives and Nurses: A History of Women Healers.* Old Westbury, N.Y.: Feminist Press, 1973.

Greer, Germaine. *The Obstacle Race: The Fortune of Women Painters and Their Work.* New York: Farrar, Straus & Giroux, 1979.

Griffin, Susan. *Rape and the Power of Consciousness,* New York: Harper & Row, 1979.

Goulianos, Joan, ed. *By a Woman Writt: Literature from Six Centuries by and about Women.* Indianapolis: Bobbs-Merrill, 1973.

Hunt, David. *Parents and Children in History.* New York: Basic, 1970.

Lerner, Gerda. *Black Women in White America: A Documentary History.* New York: Pantheon, 1972.

Morrison, Toni. *Sula.* New York: Knopf, 1978.

O'Faolain, Julia and Laura Martines, eds. *Not in God's Image: A History of Women from the Greeks to the Nineteenth Century.* New York: Harper & Row, 1973.

Rabb, Theodore K. and Rotberg, Robert I. *The Family in History: Interdisciplinary Essays*. New York: Harper & Row, 1974.

Rogers, Katherine. *The Troublesome Helpmate: A History of Misogyny in Literature*. Seattle, Washington: University of Washington Press, 1966.

Rougemont, Denis de. *Love in the Western World*. Revised edition, translated by M. Belgion. New York: Pantheon, 1956.

Reuther, Rosemary Radford and Eleanor McLaughlin, eds. *Women of Spirit*. New York: Simon & Schuster, 1979.

Smart, Carol. *Women, Crime and Criminology: A Feminist Critique*. Boston: Routledge & Kegan Paul, 1978.

Chapter 4. Women and the Marketplace

Almquist, Elizabeth M. *Minorities, Gender, and Work*. Lexington, Mass.: Lexington Books, 1979.

Andre, Rae. *Homemakers: The Forgotten Workers*. Chicago: University of Chicago Press, 1981.

Bird, Caroline. *The Two-Paycheck Marriage: How Women at Work Are Changing Life in America*. New York: Rawson, Wade, Inc., 1979.

Blaxall, Martha and Barbara B. Reagan, eds., *Women and the Workplace: The Implications of Occupational Segregation*. Chicago: University of Chicago Press, 1976.

Brownlee, W. Elliot and Mary M. Brownlee. *Women in the American Economy: A Documentary History, 1675 to 1929*. New Haven: Yale University Press, 1976.

Bullough, Vern L. *The History of Prostitution*. New Hyde Park, New York: University Books, 1964.

Davis, Rebecca Harding. *Life in the Iron Mills*, with a biographical interpretation by Tillie Olsen. Old Westbury, N.Y.: Feminist Press, 1977.

Dexter, Elisabeth A. *Colonial Women of Affairs: Women in Business and Professions in America Before 1776*. Boston: Houghton Mifflin, 1931.

Foner, Philip S. ed. *The Factory Girls*. Urbana: University of Illinois Press, 1977.

Gilbert, Sandra M. and Susan Gubar. *Shakespeare's Sisters: Feminist Essays on Women Poets*. Bloomington: Indiana University Press, 1979.

Gilman, Charlotte Perkins. *Women and Economics*. Boston: Small, Maynard, 1898; reprint ed., New York: Harper & Row, 1966.

Greenwald, Maurine Weiner. *Women, War, and Work: The Impact of World War I on Women Workers in the United States*. Westport, Conn.: Greenwood Press, 1980.

Kahn, Kathy. *Hillbilly Women*. New York: Avon Books, 1972.

Harris, Barbara J. *Beyond Her Sphere: Women and the Professions in American History*. Westport, Conn.: Greenwood Press, 1978.

Hedges, Elaine and Ingrid Wendt. *In Her Own Image: Women Working in the Arts*. Old Westbury. N.Y.: Feminist Press, 1980.

Kreps, Juanita. *Women and the American Economy: A Look to the Future*. Prentice-Hall, 1976.

Leghorn, Lisa and Katherine Parker. *Women's Worth: Sexual Economics and the World of Women*. Boston: Routledge & Kegan Paul, 1981.

Lerner, Gerda, ed. *The Female Experience: An American Documentary*. Indianapolis: Bobbs-Merrill, 1977.

Pinchbeck, Ivy. *Women Workers in the Industrial Revolution 1850–1950*. London: G. Routledge, 1930.

Seller, Maxine Schwartz, ed. *Immigrant Women*. Philadelphia: Temple University Press, 1980.

Smedley, Agnes. *Daughter of Earth*. Old Westbury, N.Y.: Feminist Press, 1977.

Smith, Ralph E., ed. *The Subtle Revolution: Women at Work.* Washington: The Urban Institute, 1979.

Spruill, Julia. *Women's Life and Work in the Southern Colonies.* New York: W. W. Norton, 1972.

Chapter 5. The Personal as Political

Brehm, Henry P. and Helena Z. Lopata. *Widowhood.* New York: Praeger, 1979.

Cade, Toni. *The Black Woman: An Anthology.* New York: Signet, 1979.

Davidson, Cathy N. and E. M. Broner, eds. *The Lost Tradition: Mothers and Daughters in Literature.* New York: Ungar, 1980.

de Beauvoir, Simone. *The Coming of Age,* trans., Patrick O'Brien. New York: G. P. Putnam, 1972.

Demeter, Anna. *Legal Kidnaping: What Happens to a Family When the Father Kidnaps Two Children.* Boston: Beacon Press, 1977.

Ehrenreich, Barbara and Deirdre English. *Complaints and Disorders: The Sexual Politics of Sickness.* Old Westbury, N.Y.: Feminist Press, 1973.

Ferguson, Mary Anne. *Images of Women in Literature.* Boston: Houghton Mifflin, 1973.

Hurston, Zora Neale. *Their Eyes Were Watching God.* Urbana: University of Illinois Press, 1978.

Konek, Carol and Dorothy Walters, eds. *I Hear My Sisters Saying: Poems by Twentieth Century Women.* New York: Thomas Y. Crowell, 1976.

Kuhn, Annette and Annmarie Wolpe. *Feminism and Materialism: Women and Modes of Production.* Boston: Routledge & Kegan Paul, 1978.

McConnell-Ginet, Sally, Ruth Borker and Nelly Furman, eds. *Women and Language in Literature and Society.* New York: Praeger, 1980.

O'Brien, Mary. *The Politics of Reproduction.* Boston: Routledge & Kegan Paul, 1981.

Olsen, Tillie. *Tell Me a Riddle.* New York: Dell, 1976.

Peck, Ellen and Judith Senderowitz, eds. *Pronatalism: The Myth of Mom & Apple Pie.* New York: Thomas Y. Crowell, 1974.

Ponse, Barbara. *Identities in the Lesbian World: The Social Construction of Self.* Westport, Conn.: Greenwood Press, 1978.

Sacks, Karen. *Sisters and Wives: The Past and Future of Sexual Equality.* Westport, Conn.: Greenwood Press, 1978.

Shuttle, Penelope and Peter Redgrove. *The Wise Wound: Menstruation and Everywoman.* London: Victor Gollancz Ltd., 1978.

Smart, Carol and Barry Smart, eds. *Women, Sexuality and Social Control.* Boston: Routledge & Kegan Paul, 1978.

Spinner, Stephanie, ed. *Motherlove: Stories by Women about Motherhood.* New York: Laurel, 1978.

Stimpson, Catherine and Ethel Person, M. D., eds. *Women, Sex and Sexuality.* Chicago: University of Chicago Press, 1981.

Voda, Ann M., Myra Dinnerstein and Sheryl R. O'Donnell, eds. *Changing Perspectives on Menopause.* Austin: University of Texas Press, 1982.

Wertz, Richard W. and Dorothy C. Wertz. *Lying-in: A History of Childbirth in America.* New York: Macmillan (Free Press), 1977.

Zimmerman, Mary K. *Passage Through Abortion: The Personal and Social Reality of Women's Experiences.* New York: Praeger, 1978.

Chapter 6. The Ideas and Origins of Feminism

Allen, Robert L. and Pamela Allen. *Reluctant Reformers: Racism and Social Reform Movements in the United States*. New York: Doubleday, 1975.

Cott, Nancy F. *The Bonds of Womanhood: "Woman's Sphere" in New England, 1780–1835*. New Haven: Yale University Press, 1977.

Cott, Nancy F. and Elizabeth H. Pleck, eds. *A Heritage of Her Own: Toward a New Social History of Women*. New York: Simon & Schuster, 1979.

Douglass, Frederick. *Frederick Douglass on Women's Rights*, ed. Philip S. Foner. Westport, Conn.: Greenwood Press, 1976.

Eliot, George. *Adam Bede*. New York: Rinehart, 1948.

Fuller, Margaret. *Woman in the Nineteenth Century*. New York: Norton, 1971 (orig. pub. 1855).

James, Henry. *The Bostonians*. New York: Random House, 1956.

La Follette, Suzanne. *Concerning Women*. New York: Arno Press, 1972 (orig. pub. 1926).

Nicolas, Susan Cary, Alice Price and Rachel Rubin. *Rights and Wrongs: Women's Struggle for Legal Equality*. Old Westbury, N.Y.: Feminist Press, 1979.

Norton, Mary Beth. *Liberty's Daughters: The Revolutionary Experience of American Women, 1750–1800*. Boston: Little, Brown, 1980.

O'Neill, William L. *Everyone Was Brave: The Rise and Fall of Feminism in America*. Chicago: Quadrangle Press, 1969.

Parker, Gail, ed. *The Oven Birds: American Women on Womanhood, 1820–1920*. Garden City, N.Y.: Doubleday, 1972.

Spencer, Anna Garlin. *Woman's Share in Social Culture*. New York: Arno Press, 1972 (orig. pub. 1913).

Welter, Barbara. *Dimity Convictions: The American Woman in the Nineteenth Century*. Athens: Ohio University Press, 1976.

Chapter 7. Feminism: The Second Wave

Baxter, Sandra and Marjorie Lansing. *Women and Politics: The Invisible Majority*. Ann Arbor: University of Michigan Press, 1981.

Becker, Susan D. *The Origins of the Equal Rights Amendment: American Feminism Between the Wars*. Westport, Conn.: Greenwood Press, 1981.

Boyle, Kay. *The Underground Woman*. New York: Doubleday, 1975.

Building Feminist Theory: Essays from Quest. New York: Longman, 1981.

Carroll, Berenice, ed. *Liberating Women's History: Theoretical and Critical Essays*. Urbana: University of Illinois Press, 1975.

Daly Mary. *Gyn/Ecology: The Metaethics of Radical Feminism*. Boston: Beacon Press, 1978.

Dinnerstein, Dorothy. *The Mermaid and the Minotaur: Sexual Arrangements and Human Malaise*. New York: Harper & Row, 1976.

Evans, Sara. *Personal Politics: The Roots of Women's Liberation in the Civil Rights Movement and the New Left*. New York: Alfred A. Knopf, 1979.

Ferguson, Kathy E. *Self, Society and Womankind: The Dialectic of Liberation*. Westport, Conn.: Greenwood Press, 1980.

Godwin, Gail, *The Odd Woman*. New York: Alfred A. Knopf, 1978.

Gould, Carol C. and Marx W. Wartofsky, eds. *Women and Philosophy: Toward a Theory of Liberation*. New York: G. P. Putnam, 1976.

Howe, Florence and Ellen Bass. *No More Masks! An Anthology of Poems by Women.* Garden City, New York: Anchor Press/Doubleday, 1973.

Jaggar, Alison and Paula Rothenberg Shruhl. *Feminist Frameworks: Alternative Theoretical Accounts of the Relations Between Women and Men.* New York: McGraw-Hill, 1978.

Lessing, Doris. *The Golden Notebook.* New York: McGraw-Hill, 1963.

Murray, Michele, ed. *A House of Good Proportion: Images of Women in Literature.* New York: Simon & Schuster, 1973.

Piercy, Marge. *Small Changes.* New York: Fawcett Crest, 1973.

Showalter, Elaine, ed. *Women's Liberation and Literature: A Thematic Sourcebook on Feminism in Literature.* New York: Harcourt, Brace, 1971.

Index

447